PRICING AND MANAGING EXOTIC AND HYBRID OPTIONS

Other Books in The Irwin Library of Investment & Finance

Convertible Securities: Instruments, Portfolio Strategies and Valuation Analysis, Second Edition, by John P. Calamos

Risk Management and Financial Derivatives: A Guide to the Mathematics, Edited by Satyajit Das

PRICING AND MANAGING EXOTIC AND HYBRID OPTIONS

VINEER BHANSALI

McGraw-Hill

New York   San Francisco   Washington, D.C.   Auckland   Bogotá
Caracas   Lisbon   London   Madrid   Mexico City   Milan
Montreal   New Delhi   San Juan   Singapore
Sydney   Tokyo   Toronto

Library of Congress Cataloging-in-Publication Data
Bhansali, Vineer.
   Pricing and managing exotic and hybrid options /
Vineer Bhansali.
       p.   cm.
     ISBN 0-07-006669-8
     1. Derivative securities.   2. Exotic options (Finance)   I. Title.

HG6024.A3B52   1998
332.63′228—dc21

97-32770
CIP

McGraw-Hill

A Division of The McGraw-Hill Companies

1 2 3 4 5 6 7 8 9 0 DOC/DOC 9 0 2 1 0 9 8

ISBN 0-07-006669-8

The sponsoring editor for this book was Stephen Isaacs, the editing supervisor John M.
Morriss and the production supervisor was Suzanne W. B. Rapcavage. It was set in
11/13 Palatino through the services of Keyword Publishing Services.

Printed and bound by R. R. Donnelley & Sons Company.

McGraw-Hill books are available at special quantity discounts to use as premiums
and sale promotions, or for use in corporate training programs. For more
information, please write to the Director of Special Sales, McGraw-Hill, 11 West
19th Street, New York, NY 10011. Or contact your local bookstore.

The views and opinions expressed in this book are solely those of the author.
Neither the author's current nor past employers are responsible for any material
contained herein. This work contains no proprietary information. All material
referenced in this book is available from publicly available archives.

This book is printed on recycled, acid-free paper containing a
minimum of 50% recycled de-inked fiber.

*To my family for their support and pride in my
frequent detours in unexplainable directions.
Above all, to my father and to my son.*

CONTENTS

Chapter 4

Correlation   120

Chapter 5

Numerical Methods   172

Chapter 6

Strategic Risk Management   218

Appendix J

PDE Methods   349

INTRODUCTION

The purpose of this book is to introduce methods for pricing, trading, and managing modern derivative products that derive a significant proportion of their value from *correlation* and *volatility*. We will embrace practical and tested techniques that not only provide a launch pad for the development of a future generation of tools, but also efficiently unify the approaches used in the derivative markets of the past and the present.

Contrary to common belief, hybrid options in particular, and exotic options in general, are not a new development of the 1990s. They have existed in one form or another for over 300 years. From the options written in Japan on the rice harvest, to the call options on tulips in eighteenth-century Holland, speculators and hedgers have managed to find a way to transact in risk. Perhaps the most impressive transaction in this field, the so-called "Cotton Bond," was executed in the middle 1800s. On June 1, 1863, the Confederate States of America, hard up for credit and desperate for money, issued a "7 Per Cent Cotton Loan" [9,19,199]. The principal amount was not repayable in Confederate dollars, nor was it repayable at the Confederate Capitol in Richmond, Virginia. Instead, it was set at "3 Millions Sterling or 75 Millions Francs," with additional protection embedded in the repayment that would protect the holder against a change in the sterling/pound exchange rate. The loan was repayable in 40 semiannual installments in Paris, London,

Amsterdam, or Frankfurt, at the option of the bondholder. In addition, the bondholder could take payment in cotton rather than in money, at the rate of sixpence per pound, "at any time not later than six months after the ratification of a Treaty of Peace between the belligerents." From the point of view of the Confederate government, the temptation for English and French investors to enter this deal would provide them with urgently needed foreign exchange reserves for the purchase of armaments abroad. The risk of devaluation of the Confederate dollar was hedged by the payment in a currency other than the dollar. The risk of inflation was hedged by the allowance to collect the debt in cotton (in today's language, the option was "deeply in the money" to begin with, since the prevailing price of cotton in Europe was 24 pence). By selling these "embedded options" in the bond, the Confederate states were able to finance their war loan for a rate much lower than their credit quality was worth. The spread was only a percentage point higher than the rate at which the U.S. government was borrowing long-term money! The bonds were first offered in March 1863, but the proceeds were not received till September of that year. The bonds traded above their offering price for a brief period after March. The Confederates met the payments due in September 1863 and the two payments in 1864, but that was the end of the repayments. About 370,000 sterling worth of par value was redeemed in cotton.

In today's parlance, this bond captured quanto risk, hybrid risk as well as credit risk. Thus, while the idea of managing risk across asset classes, or *integrated hedging*, is not new, perhaps the last few centuries have taught us some new techniques so that we can value and manage, at least in theory, portfolios of exotic transactions in so-called "bias-free" ways.

With new developments in mathematical technology, and with the evolution of the "risk-neutral" approach, valuation and risk-management methods have come a long way. The purpose of this book is to reintroduce this new paradigm in a larger setting and to explore its practical applications. As pricing and hedging methodologies become more sophisticated, the effects of correlation in the options markets, for both intramarket and intermarket products, will play a role that is conceptually as important as the notion of "volatility" that every option trader understands. How does one capture the consequences of correlation as a practitioner in a trading environment, knowing that the hedging algorithm is only as good as one's assumptions about the nature of the fundamental variables?

We will not try to be exhaustive in the consideration of all types of exotics that are traded in the market. The emphasis is on general principles and enabling the user to have the technology to price and manage a number of different exotic contracts within the same framework—especially products that derive a significant portion of their value from correlation effects. A good source that contains numerous examples of single-factor exotics is Reference [179]. We will rederive a number of results of these pricing formulas from a very different approach that has been studied recently by numerous authors. Recall that the endeavor of option pricing can be stated in terms of the construction of a riskless hedge. By definition, if continuous hedging is possible, the classic results of Black-Scholes and Merton state that the value of any option is exactly equal to the cost of hedging a dynamical portfolio that replicates the payoff of the option. The difference between the new approach and the old approach is that the portfolios that are used to replicate the exotic options will largely be static-option portfolios, i.e., the exotics will be constructed from options themselves. In most cases of interest, it is possible to show that the exotic-option position is equivalent to a portfolio of simple calls and puts (plus risk-free lending and borrowing), so that once the value of the individual options is known, the exotics can easily be priced. Thus, the basic building blocks themselves are more complicated. An added advantage of this methodology is that "relative pricing" is automatic. All the assumptions that one makes about the options market, i.e., liquidity adjustments, smiles, skews, and frowns, etc., are incorporated in a consistent manner for the exotics that are being priced. Also, the hedges themselves capture, from the beginning, all the effects that make option trading interesting, i.e., shocks and jumps. The whole approach for managing a portfolio is, for lack of a better word, "holistic."

A little bit of philosophy on the financial markets might not be out of place at this stage. Financial markets develop rapidly around concepts and quantities that have potential to be tradable. For instance, one can create option positions, such as straddles to trade volatility, without reference to the directional movements of the underlying assets. Since volatility is simply a representation of uncertainty, by trading options then one is trading uncertainty. However, as more complexity is introduced in the movement of assets, e.g., asset comovement, we are forced into quantifying the correlation of different assets (functions of the same asset with distinct time horizons may be considered to be distinct related assets). Correlation then becomes the variable around which trades can be structured. As we will see, this is a relative volatility in a very direct way, and trades can be structured to transact correlation in isolation. Whether one likes it or not, coming to grips with correlation is crucial, even for trading products in the financial markets of the day that depend only on one asset class. In this respect, correlation, along with its lesser cousin volatility, forms the backbone of most exotics that are traded in the market today. The approach we take here is to build new concepts on top of old concepts, and new exotics on top of old exotics. A useful lesson of this book is to understand that many exotic and hybrid options can be priced (or bounded tightly) as combinations of other exotic and simple options.

Chapter 1 presents a discussion of a number of exotic and hybrid transactions with various payoff and contingency structures to emphasize the economics that motivates such structures. The objective of this discussion is to emphasize that the purpose of innovation in the market is not simply to design products motivated by the ability to put mathematical results to work, but quite the opposite. Customized products that draw from different market classes have, as their first and foremost motivation, the desire to enhance an increase in the overall utility of the end-user. We will discuss in much detail the example of a Nikkei-linked interest-rate cap, which illustrates a number of qualitative features that we will quantify in the chapters that follow.

Chapter 2 gives a rapid and informal review of the four major market classes in which most of the exotic and hybrid products find applications. The purpose is to present a summary of market facts that play a key role in pricing and hedging. Also surveyed in this chapter are the various names under which single-market and multimarket exotic and hybrid options trade in the marketplace. For readers who have experience of trading a significant number of these markets, and/or the products in one form or another, this chapter may be skipped.

In Chapter 3 we dive into pricing in earnest. The purpose of this chapter is to lay down our assumptions about the stochastic process for pricing, and then to introduce mathematical techniques for analytic solutions of pricing problems, with a number of illustrations worked out in explicit detail. We will also discuss at length the symmetry properties of the underlying processes, and the equations derived from them. These symmetry properties end up having a phenomenal impact, not only in the speed and efficiency of pricing, but also in finding optimal hedge algorithms at the portfolio level.

Chapter 4 discusses the statistical estimation of correlation, which plays a crucial role in the pricing of hybrids. Also discussed, in some detail, are methods for the construction of a reasonable term structure of correlation from empirical data. The important concept of transmutability between correlation and volatility is explored, along with applications and consequences. We will work out some examples of correlation computations using the representation of time series as random vectors. Finally, we measure the deviations from joint multinormality exhibited by real underlying data series.

Chapter 5 details the major numerical techniques to value multifactor and exotic options. This chapter introduces the essential features of numerical integration, Monte-Carlo simulation, binomial trees and pyramids, and direct solution of the PDE with finite differences in one and many dimensions. Numerous "codelets" in Mathematica, which the interested reader may use for real-time pricing, are also provided.

Chapter 6 discusses aspects of risk management of a portfolio of exotics and hybrids. Again, the emphasis is on general methods. We discuss the optimal selection of trades and the marginal gain from modifying the portfolio composition. We also explore the added complexity of the cross risks that arise when dealing with hybrids. Static hedging techniques are discussed. We also show the explicit construction of an aggregation or indexation scheme to simplify the complexity of a large portfolio. Finally, some measures of risk vs reward for specific trades and a systematic approach to trading correlation options, based on specification of beliefs and preferences, are presented.

In Chapter 7 an attempt is made to tie up some loose ends that are more metafinancial in nature. The important issues here are the use of a utility-based approach to transacting options, in general, and exotics, in particular. Also, we discuss the peculiar problem of revenue deferral for an exotic desk that is entering a new territory. I also take the liberty of expressing optimism on why the complex products being traded in the marketplace are eventually going to simplify risk management for the end-user.

The appendixes are crucial to the book. They contain numerous details and techniques that should be considered central to the purpose of this text, i.e., "methods." The only reason that they are not part of the main text is because they would impede the flow. Practitioners should hopefully find in the appendixes the tools that they can refer to readily in the process of pricing, and trading, and managing their own option portfolios.

Finally, let me emphasize again that, although I have tried to make the book accessible to the widest audience, to get maximal benefit from it the reader is expected to have a fairly good *working* knowledge of plain vanilla options, and some experience with exotic options.[1] In general, someone who has spent 2 or 3 years in finance should have no difficulty with most of the topics in the book. A good ability in upper-level mathematics, e.g., Reference [216], especially probability theory and statistics, is also essential. In addition, since the approach to the wide field of time series analysis will be driven by utilitarian considerations for methods that have found practical use on trading desks, matters have sometimes been simplified to an extent that might annoy purists. These holes may be plugged with a supplementary reading of Reference [99]. My apologies in advance for assuming all this prior preparation. The emphasis is on lucidity and clarity, and a general attempt not to lose view of the "big picture" has been made. All omission of detail should be largely irrelevant to the understanding of general principles. Approximations are readily made that lead to a better understanding of the problem. Using the words of an old collea-

---

1. At least at the level of Reference [113].

gue—"models are but blotters on which to put trades for accounting purposes"—the trading world is imperfect, and it is better to
have an approximate model with lots of imperfections but sound,
quantifiable, and intuitively appealing inputs, rather than to have a
perfect model that only a few understand and which allows no
extensions and breaks easily. With this in mind, I have tried to
spend more time in the estimation of the input parameters for
simple models and the economics motivating them. Simple limits
or complex models are great aids for building intuition, and, wherever I could, I have tried to use them. For instance, in Chapter 3 we
discuss long-dated forex options using the equivalent volatility for
a single-factor Black-Scholes model at the same time as we discuss
the more rigorous no-arbitrage pricing.

My hope is that by the end of the last chapter, the curious
reader should be able to go back in time and check whether the
Cotton-Bond was priced fairly or not. Was it really such a good
deal? Would you want to do it again in the environment today?
Unfortunately, the techniques of risk management evolve too
swiftly to capture with a single snapshot; the best that an author
can expect to do is to ask questions which require thought processes whose appearance in print is not a guarantee of obsoles-
cence. I would consider this book a success if I am able to
communicate the fundamental dependence and consequences of
correlation effects for the new generation of financial products.

Innumerable people have contributed to this book in their
own way and I thank them all for my continuing education. In
particular, thanks are due to Kent Freeman for his friendship and
useful comments on the manuscript. Above all, it would have been
impossible to complete this book without the considerable sacri-
fices of Kate and Zane, and I am grateful to them for all their
support.

Vineer Bhansali
New York, Spring 1997

CHAPTER 1

Transactions

The purpose of this chapter is to introduce, by way of real examples, hybrid and exotic transactions that were carried out recently in the market, highlighting, in particular, the advantages that these structures have over simple, plain vanilla structures (namely, drastic cost savings without a significant loss of protection). The aim is to focus in qualitative terms on the economics motivating the trades and the various aspects of risk that a trader managing these structures has to focus on.

Correlation considerations have become an important part of risk-management and asset-liability management decisions for various reasons [228,230]:

- Correlation effectively allows the buyer of the correlation-based option to *trade upside windfall for downside protection*. As the need for the protection offered by structured options disappears with a favorable move in the underlying, they can be used to monetize *intrinsic* option-type positions that the end-user holds. In terms of utility theory, even though the absolute wealth value of what is given up (premium) may exactly equal the wealth value of what is gained (protection), there might be an overall increase in expected utility due to hedging (this is because the utility can be a complicated function of the wealth).

1

- Correlation provides *automatic diversification,* hence reduced volatility. For example, a basket of negatively correlated assets is significantly less volatile than the individual components. So an option on a basket is cheaper than a basket of options on the individual assets.

- Correlation considerations may be *unavoidable.* For instance, implementation of asymmetric risk–reward positions in spreads, or pricing long-dated options on foreign exchange, force one to take stock of intra- and intermarket correlations. Also, frequently legal restrictions, such as capital controls, might force corporates to enter into structures, such as nondeliverable swaps, which have embedded correlation risk.

- The term structure of correlation can help a user *modify and extend the shape of the forward curve* of one asset class using another asset class. Below we will see how the foreign exchange forward curve can be modified by making it contingent on a commodity price level. Using correlated assets, more *customized cash-flows* for one or both assets can be invented.

EQUITY INDEX-LINKED INTEREST-RATE OPTIONS

Towards the end of 1994, it was clear that the Japanese economy was going to be in its recessionary phase for at least a couple of years more. The fall of yen short-term rates was swift (see Figure 1–1), and anyone who was paying fixed yen rates on swaps in exchange for receiving floating rates was severely under water in a mark-to-market sense.

To match the fixed liabilities from the float side in the swap, i.e., to compensate for loss due to falling rates, one simple strategy was to sell interest-rate caps and embed the premium received into the swap mark to market. This strategy would benefit from the fact that the yield curve in Japan was quite steep (the spread between the 2-year treasury and the 10-year treasury being roughly 250 basis points), so the distant caplets were quite valuable. In addition, the implied volatility for options was in relative terms at the higher end of recent trading ranges. The cost of a 5-year, 3.25 percent

F I G U R E 1–1

Yen Libor Short-Term Rates vs Nikkei 225 Stock Index, 1986–1997

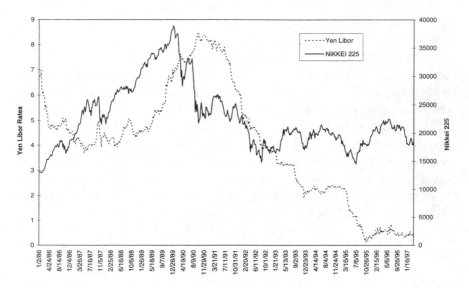

(deeply out of the money) plain vanilla cap setting semiannually was quoted at this time to be around 160 basis points.

This strategy of selling interest-rate options, while quite nice, had an enormous shortcoming: namely, it left the client, as a seller of the cap, exposed to a large run-up in rates. Whereas the initial swap had been set up so that it would benefit in the high-rate environment, the short cap position, if put on the books of the client, would essentially neutralize any gains, and, in addition, make dynamic rehedging necessary. Not being in the business of financial speculation, this strategy was not something that the seller of the cap was interested in pursuing. What the seller of the cap desired, in effect, was to get the premium from selling a cap, but with limited downside for him if rates were to run up. Sounds like a world where you could get something for nothing? Enter correlation. Suppose the client is a growth company who is likely to do very well in stock terms as the overall stock market in Japan rallies. Now consider the following structure: the client sells a 3.25 percent interest-rate cap for 5 years, but all remaining caplets are knocked out if the value of the Nikkei 225 index touches some trigger above the current level at any time before expiration of the contract (a *one-touch* barrier).

Let us investigate in detail the economics of the trade. In the prevailing state of the Japanese economy, the overall stock market was quite depressed. Rates had to move lower to provide the economy with the necessary stimulus to grow. As the economy picks up, rates are expected to go up slowly; however, the Nikkei index, which has traditionally acted as a leading indicator of the health of the economy, would move higher in advance anticipation, similar to the situation in the mid 1980s (see Figure 1–1). By the time rates are high enough for any of the short position caplets to be in the money, they will already have been knocked out (assuming the correlation was really borne out—the scatterplot in Figure 1–2 seems to suggest it is!). Here is a systematic scenario analysis from the point of view of the correlation cap seller:

F I G U R E 1–2

Yen Libor vs Nikkei 225 Index Scatterplot, 1986–1997

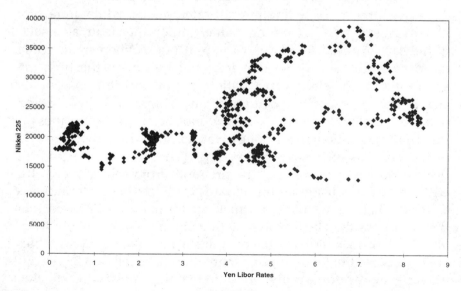

1. Nikkei up, rates up: high-probability scenario, but the cap is worthless as it is knocked out—the seller gets to keep the premium.
2. Nikkei up, rates low: medium-probability scenario since the Nikkei leads the overall economy as reflected in the rates—the cap is knocked out of the money—the seller gets to keep the premium.
3. Nikkei down, rates up: low-probability scenario since inflation is low in Japan, so there is no reason for the Bank of Japan (BOJ) not to keep rates low to stimulate the economy. But, if this happens, the client loses money. However, the float side of the swap becomes valuable.
4. Nikkei down, rates down: high-probability scenario; though the cap survives being knocked out for longer, it is out of the money, so there is no payoff. In addition, the seller collects time decay on the short cap position.

With these assumptions about the relative probabilities of the occurrence of an interest rate and related Nikkei performance scenario, in concurrence with the specific exposure of the client, it is easy to see that the correlation cap is a good structure for the seller. As we have mentioned before and will discuss in much detail, the real utility of correlation structures is for clients who have a natural reason to be in such a trade. Put in other words, there is some sacrifice of upside to protect the downside. However, the sacrifice of upside has, for the particular structure, a relatively lower value than the protection of downside. In a sense, what correlation does is to add another dimension to the pricing, so that the transaction can be carried out with a probability distribution that is more favorable for the deal in question (and can frequently be different from the market-implied distribution for a single variable). As it turns out, rates remained low and the Nikkei spiked up—so the buyer of the cap, who would have essentially been short the one-touch binary option on the Nikkei, would have lost his (worthless) interest-rate options.

The advance scenario analysis described above, however, begs the question of *how* we ascribe the relative probabilities to the occurrence of correlated events, and how we quantify them into pricing tools and risk-management principles. The first part of this question is exactly equivalent to the question: What is the multivariate distribution of the correlated variables? How does it evolve with time? A full chapter has been dedicated to estimating this distribution—in short, one can either use historical data along with statistical techniques (historical correlation distribution), or one can "back-out" the correlation information from the prices of traded options (implied correlation distribution). This is similar to what is practiced for simple options for volatility estimates. In analogy to volatility, estimation of the implied correlation information requires that one have a model already at hand in which correlation is a free parameter. There is a simple generalization of the Black-Scholes model, which is widely used for single-variable options to multivariable options, that provides a launching pad for simple cross-option pricing. This, as well as the time evolution of the dis-

FIGURE 1–3

Yen Libor vs Nikkei 225 Index Moving Correlation Time Chart, 1986–1997

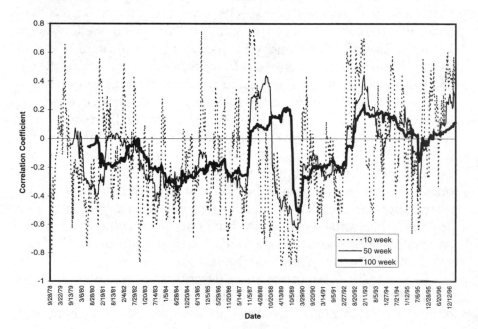

FIGURE 1-4

Yen Libor vs Nikkei 225 Index Moving Correlation Histogram, 1986-1997

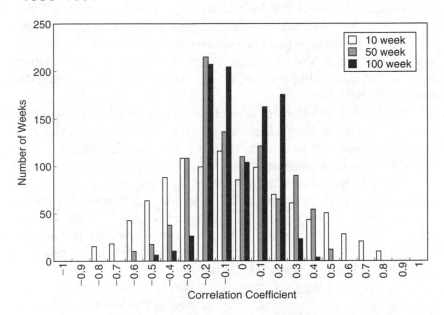

tribution and the implied risk-management principles, will be described in the chapters to follow. For now, a quick glance at Figure 1-3 shows that if we take correlation over long periods, it is much more stable than the short-period correlation, even though it shows significant variation. The same information is presented in a time-independent form as a histogram in Figure 1-4 and shows the relatively narrow dispersion of the longer term correlation, and the corresponding high peakedness ("kurtosis") compared with the short-term correlation.

Looking forward to Figure 4-5, we also see another useful depiction in terms of the statistics of the correlation parameter displayed as a function of the time period used. Both the high and the low values converge toward zero correlation as the time window gets larger. The shorter term correlation shows higher deviation from its average than the longer term correlation, and, quite interestingly, the median correlation and the mean correlation are somewhat negative for small time horizons (assuming history will repeat on the average) and somewhat positive for an interval of 2 years or so. We will study the term structure of correlation in much more detail later. For now, the inference that one can draw from all these figures is that the correlation, though not very positive, is expected not to be too negative, i.e., both economic reasoning and the multi-faceted analysis of time series seem to suggest that a positive correlation bet has a higher probability of success than a negative correlation bet.

Before we move on to a description of some other correlation transactions, let us take a look at the risks involved from the point of view of the client in this trade. We have already listed the effect of the directional movements in yen rates and Nikkei. Since there is optionality in two correlated variables, we also need to consider the effects of movements of the volatilities and the correlation.

As Nikkei volatility rises, one expects to see a decrease in the price of the cap, even though there is no movement in the rates themselves. This is because a higher Nikkei volatility implies that the probability of knockout is higher.

As yen interest-rate volatility rises, the caps become more valuable, given no corresponding change in the level or volatilities of Nikkei.

If both volatilities are positively correlated, then there is an increase in the value of the caps, but that is compensated to some degree by the increased probability of knockout. A model is needed to quantify by how much exactly. In general, the effects due to correlations between volatilities are higher order effects, though we must mention that specific products have been designed (in the forex market) where multifactor options are written on the out-performance of one currency volatility versus another.

As the correlation between the rate movements and Nikkei movements becomes more positive, it is also more likely that as the cap becomes more valuable due to a favorable move up in rates, it is going to get knocked out by a corresponding move up in the Nikkei. On the other side, as rates fall, the Nikkei is more likely to fall also, but the proportional increase in the value of the caplets due to a fall in the Nikkei is overcome by the fall in the value of rates (of course, this depends on the level of actual correlation).

Recall that for single-factor options, the risk of the jumpiness of an option can be quantified in terms of the option gamma, which is simply the change of the delta as the underlying variable changes a little bit. For multifactor structures, in addition to the notion of gammas with respect to each individual variable, there is also the notion of a "cross-gamma." Cross-gamma is, in simple terms, the change in the delta with respect to one variable, caused by small movements in another variable. Let us explain this in somewhat more detail. Assume that our Nikkei-linked interest-rate cap is perfectly delta-hedged at a given instant in time. From the point of view of the cap seller, this entails selling Euroyen futures and options to hedge the risk of rates moving higher, or interest-rate cap volatility rising in the market. Also, at the same time, the seller of the cap has to go short the Nikkei index in some form (i.e., by buying puts on the index), so that if the mark-to-market value of the cap rises due to a fall in the Nikkei, he can regain it in the form of an increase in the value of his Nikkei puts. Now let us assume that in a very short period of time, the interest rates do not move, but the Nikkei moves a little bit. What cross-gamma does, in effect, is to force the cap seller to readjust his *interest-rate hedge*! The explanation is simple—as the Nikkei moves, the likelihood of the cap being knocked out changes, and since the interest-rate hedge is essentially the present value of the probability-weighted value of the cap payout, the interest-rate hedge has to be readjusted. This change of delta-hedge with respect to one variable, caused by a move in the other variable, is the manifestation of cross-gamma.

While cross-gamma poses the most significant problem of hedging for a market maker in cross-market options, it is not unique. Cross-theta, cross-rho, etc., are higher order generalizations of one-dimensional risk parameters that pose problems which require new hedging technology. For single-factor options, it is normally taken on faith that being short gamma, i.e., taking the jump risk, is paid for by earning time decay on the option position. For multifactor options, one can be simultaneously short an option and long an option. For example, the writer of the Nikkei cap described above is short the interest-rate option, but long the Nikkei option. At a given stage in time, depending on how close to at-the-money the level of rates and the Nikkei index is, he could be earning or losing time decay on the premium for the whole structure, and this profile can change quite rapidly for large moves in one or more of the underlying assets. In fact, what this entails is that for a completely hedged position, it is essential that the hedge be dynamical in options, not just the underlying assets. Due to the relative illiquidity of options vis-à-vis the underlying variables and the need for continuous readjustment, it is rather expensive to do the most simple-minded option hedges for cross-market options. Chapter 6 is dedicated to discussing optimal hedging from the point of view of managing a full correlation book. For now, suffice it to say that static hedging techniques, intraportfolio cancellations, and judicious trade selection play a central role in the management of an exotic hybrid option book.

One other aspect of the deal just described needs to be pointed out. Since the deal was done in Japan, but the value realized for us in the United States in dollars, we had an implicit

F I G U R E 1–5

Rolling Correlation of Yen Libor vs Dollar/Yen Exchange Rate, 1986–1997

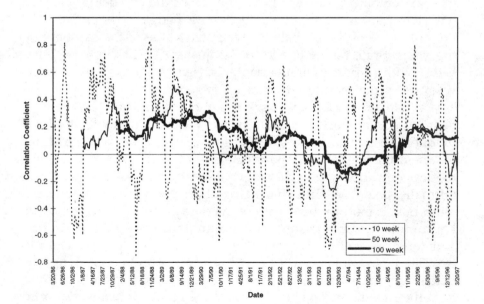

foreign exchange risk. As the dollar gets stronger against the yen, the value of the cap diminishes (see Figures 1–5 and 4–6). In fact, what this means is that currency hedging also has to be carried out. Since, recently, there is extremely strong positive correlation between the movements of the dollar/yen exchange rate and the level of the Nikkei, i.e., as the dollar gets stronger the Nikkei gets stronger, the currency exposure has to be managed with this correlation in mind.

FOREIGN-EXCHANGE-LINKED CAPS

Staying in Japan for the moment, consider the typical risk of an exporter. The exporter manufactures goods in Japan by borrowing money at short-term yen interest rates, so he (or she) is adversely affected if rates rise. To protect this, he might buy an interest-rate cap. At the same time, he exports the manufactured goods to the United States and other Western nations (e.g., automobiles, cameras, etc.). Let us assume that the revenue received from the sale of these items is in dollars. When the dollars are converted back to yen, the yen inflow amount may or may not be enough to match the liabilities on the yen borrowing. There is thus an explicit cash-flow risk due to foreign exchange risk. If the dollar is stronger than the forwards at the time of receipt of the cash, more yen is repatriated; if the dollar is weaker, less inflow cash in yen is generated. In one case, there is a windfall; in the other case, a possible disaster. If the dollar is too strong vis-à-vis the yen, there is money left over after the payment on the interest-rate borrowing. So one strategy to trade the windfall is to enter into a contract where the interest-rate protection cap knocks out if the dollar reaches some level higher than a prespecified strike. Clearly, when the dollar is that strong, the extra yen generated can be used to pay some of the interest-rate borrowing costs. The advantage is that due to the knockout feature, the price of the cap is much less than the price of a plain vanilla cap. Thus, instead of having separate asset and liability management of cash flows on different asset classes, significant cost savings can be realized by linking them.

MULTIFACTOR RANGE ACCRUAL NOTES

Commodity producers naturally tend to sell their products forward to hedge sharp drops in prices of commodities. At the same time, because of flexibility in production, they have an intrinsic long position in the commodity market, i.e., if the markets move sharply higher, they can temporarily increase production to generate higher profits. In other words, they are intrinsically long an option "strangle" position. This kind of position is volatility loving. To monetize this intrinsic long-volatility position, the following strategy may be devised: in a given time period, count the number of days that the price of the commodity stays within a prescribed range. On the days that this is true, the producer receives a higher-than-market coupon payment. On the other hand, on the days that the commodity price is outside the band, the producer receives lower-than-market or zero coupon accruals. The dominant correlation effect here is from the correlation between commodity price volatility and interest-rate volatility. While commodity price shocks usually are reflected very quickly in the interest-rate market, the decay of the response is very quick, so the long-term correlation between commodities and interest rates is not too large (at least for the major currency interest rates). In later chapters we will see why this fact is very important in the consideration of correlation-type trades that are put on a book. Since correlation is a statistical concept and, in general, mean-reverting in the long run, it thus depends on a large number of experiments (events) for its validation. Thus, writing short-dated options with large correlation exposure is a very dangerous activity, similar to writing short-dated options that are highly vulnerable to sharp price moves and gapping. While there have been a number of trades that use the correlation between the commodity markets and the interest rate, forex, or equity markets, the separation of the financial groups from the commodity hedging groups at most large commodity producers has made it hard for such trades to become common.

SELF-ADJUSTING FORWARDS

Consider, for example, an Australian producer of a base metal like nickel. Much of the production is exported to the United States, so the revenue is in U.S. dollars (USD). When the USD is converted back to Aussie dollars (AUD), it is favorable for the producer to receive an exchange rate that generates more Aussie dollars, i.e., a weaker Aussie dollar and a stronger U.S. dollar (just as in the case of the yen example above). From the viewpoint of the producer, it is preferable if the exchange-rate risk is fine-tuned to the net revenues, i.e., if the price of the commodity rises, the producer would be willing to receive a worse exchange rate than if the price of the commodity drops, on a proportionately larger notional amount. So the following cash-flow formula is devised:

$$\text{AUD rec'd at time } t = P(t)N\left[\frac{1}{a + bP(t)}\right] \qquad (1.1)$$

where $P(t)$ is the price of the commodity at time t in USD per units of the commodity, N is some fixed number of units of commodity, and a and b are numbers with b having units of commodity per Aussie dollar and a having units of U.S. dollars per Aussie dollar. Here, both the notional amount in the contract and the exchange rate (in the square brackets) scale so the holder of the contract (not necessarily the producer) gets a better exchange rate on a large notional and a worse exchange rate on a worse notional. Thus, the forward exchange-rate curve is modified using a second asset.

YIELD CURVE BASKET OPTIONS

In later sections of the book, we will study the interesting technical aspects of pricing and managing yield curve options. Here, we present some general features of yield curve basket options that have made them products of choice for fixed-income portfolio managers and hedgers [21]. By using basket options, risk on a portfolio of assets can be managed more efficiently and cheaply than with separate options on a number of different underlying components. A basket option allows a risk manager to specify a weighted combination of interest-rate tenors, and to control the sensitivity of the portfolio to the changing gradient of the yield curve, to the yield differential between different currencies, or even to combinations of interest-rate-sensitive indices. The reason that basket options are cheaper than distinct options on the underlying components is that there might be negative correlations, or less-than-complete positive correlations, among the component assets. This can dampen the volatility of the basket vis-à-vis the volatility of an individual asset. The greater the positive correlation between any pair of assets, the higher the likelihood that a large change in one asset will result in a large change in the same direction in the other part of the pair. Thus, highly positively correlated assets behave like each other and a basket composed of them will behave in a manner very close to any one of them. In this case, the price of the basket option will be very close to the price of the sum of the component options.

Consider, for instance, a basket option that hedges the user against the short part of the yield curve, i.e., a cap on a basket consisting of the 2-year CMT (constant maturity treasury) yield and the 5-year CMT. The high correlation between these rates means that the price of the cap will be similar to the net price of the cap on the two separate yields. However, if we replace the 5-year yield with the 30-year yield, the correlation is much lower since the short rates and the long rates can move in opposite directions frequently. Thus, the price of a 2-year/30-year basket cap is much cheaper than the prices of two separate caps on each of these yields.

Clearly, the key input from a pricing viewpoint is the volatility of the basket. Given the individual volatilities and the correlation between the yields, this is the equivalent volatility of the basket, thought of as an asset in itself, such that the price of the basket option equals its price if the dynamics of the basket are reconstructed from the dynamics of the underlying components.

Consider, as an application, the following basket that offers a portfolio manager the opportunity to take advantage of a hypothetical low-rate currency with a flattening environment (as in the United States in 1993).

$$B = (0.75 * 30\text{-Year CMT})$$
$$+ (0.25 * 10\text{-Year CMT})$$
$$- (0.25 * 5\text{-Year CMT})$$
$$- (0.75 * 2\text{-Year CMT})$$

Using spot levels of these, for instance, 5.93 percent, 5.32 percent, 4.76 percent, and 3.86 percent for the 30-year, 10-year, 5-year, and 2-year yields, respectively, the at-the-money basket option strike is about 1.7 percent with the payout for a 3-month option:

$$\max[0, 1.7 - B_t] * \text{Notional} * 0.25 * 0.01 \qquad (1.2)$$

The price of this option according to one model, which directly estimates the volatility of the basket, turns out to be about 6.5 basis points of the notional amount. This is significantly cheaper than being long a 3-month option on the 30-year yield and short a 3-month option on the 10-year yield in a 3:1 ratio, and simultaneously being short a 3-month option on the 5-year CMT and long a 3-month option on the 2-year CMT in a 1:3 ratio. Note that as the basket weights are varied, any yield curve profile can be constructed. In fact, as we will discuss later, it is easy to show that if the set of such basket options is valued and traded for a sufficiently large number of weighting choices, then the full joint distribution function of the components can be reconstructed. The recent development of yield curve futures and options in the exchange traded markets, such as the Chicago Board of Trade (CBOT), has thus made it possible to trade yield curve correlations directly.

OUTPERFORMANCE OPTIONS

Assume that a portfolio manager has a collection of bonds of different countries, but, because of the fluctuation of the currencies, his cash flows in his own currency may change, even though the local currency cash flows remain fixed. He can buy an option such that the payoff is linked to the best-performing bond on a currency-adjusted basis. Another example of such outperformance is some outstanding long-term "rainbow debt," where the holder of the bond has the period-to-period option of being paid a fixed coupon on one of many different currencies. As another example, from within one asset class, consider the delivery option on most futures contracts, such as the bond futures contracts, which entitle the parties holding the short position to deliver from one of many eligible treasury bonds [174].

PORTFOLIO INSURANCE

Assume that a fund manager has a portfolio with asset allocation amongst different individual equities, bonds, and cash with performance benchmarked to appropriate equity, bond, and money market indices, and he wants to insure the portfolio against sharp drops in the net value. He can buy a put on the value of the portfolio. This is the simplest example of an option on a basket. Due to the intercorrelations between the various asset classes, the value of the basket option is generally cheaper than a basket of individual options. Hence, correlations actually provide an extremely efficient way of maintaining the risk profile while reducing the cost of the hedge.

CONVERTIBLE ISSUANCE HEDGES

Another active arena in which cross-market correlation has been actively exploited is in the hedging of convertible bonds. Corporation A decides to issue a floating-rate bond at some future date, and wants to hedge itself against adverse interest-rate movements in the period to the issuance. However, if in that period the price of its equity rises, it has the extra operating capital to bear easily any additional interest-rate costs. So it uses its equity price as a knockout trigger for an interest-rate option. By purchasing a knockout cap cheaply, it reduces its risk at a much cheaper cost.

"DIFFS" AND CROSS-CURRENCY SWAPS

Differential swaps are used to hedge and take views on interest-rate differentials without incurring explicit foreign exchange exposure [224,233]. They are sensitive to the covariance between the interest rates and the foreign exchange rate. Liability managers can use diff swaps to assume short-term interest-rate positions to reduce the interest-rate risk on borrowings. For instance, if Canadian rates are much lower than U.S. rates, then a U.S. corporate could borrow in Canadian dollars, short-term, to pay off U.S. floating-rate debt. Diff swaps are especially attractive when yield curves in two different currencies have drastically different shapes. Suppose curve A is steep and upward sloping, while curve B is inverted. Then, borrowing in the low-interest-rate currency and lending in the high-interest-rate currency can frequently prove to be beneficial.

A simplified yet highly profitable (and risky) version of cross-currency bond swaps was used in 1995. The trade, known as the yen repo trade, consists of borrowing yen cheaply, because of low yen interest rates, to finance the purchase of U.S. treasury bills, notes, and bonds of all maturities. The economic scenario was perfect for the trade on three counts—the Japanese economy was weak, so yen rates were expected to remain low; the dollar was on a strengthening trend, so the liabilities, when they became due, were expected to be at favorable exchange rates; and the U.S. economy had low inflation, so U.S. treasuries were expected to perform well. The spread between the United States and Japanese 10-year notes was higher than 300 basis points. The execution of the trade was carried out by borrowing yen for a specific period of time (by buying Japanese government bonds (JGBs) and repoing them out to get short-term yen), exchanging the yen for dollars, and then lending the dollars in the higher yielding market in the United States. For instance, purchase 10-year JGBs yielding 2.558 percent, and lend them at 0.55 percent in the Japanese repo market for 1 month for a positive spread of 211.2 basis points for 1 month. Then exchange the yen for dollars at the spot exchange rate of 116.47 and buy 10-year U.S. treasuries yielding 6.6125 percent, which is a positive 590.2 basis point spread over the repo in Japan. Finally, adding the 211.2 basis points from the JGB repo, the net gain is 801.4 basis points. A U.S.$100 million position for 1 month would generate a total profit, if nothing changes, of U.S.$700,000. The reality was even better: the Japanese government bond market rallied, the U.S. treasury market rallied from the decline of 1994, and the dollar got stronger—so excess gains were realized in all sectors. The long position in JGBs, U.S. treasuries, and the dollar were all positively correlated. The flip side of the excess leverage due to high positive correlation was increased risk if the markets moved the other way. For instance, in early 1996, the U.S. bond market and the dollar started to decline, and rapid losses were realized on the trade, leading to a vicious cycle of liquidation of positions in JGBs, U.S. treasuries, and the dollar. While no one was brave enough to sell options on such a highly leveraged trade, in principle all the ingredients for pricing and hedging options

were present—developed options markets, liquidity of the underlying assets, and solid long-term comovements in the underlying
markets dictated by rational economic principles. The buyer of the
option could have protected the upside from the triple whammy of
outperforming U.S. treasuries, appreciating dollar, and falling yen
rates by purchasing an option on any change in the covariance.

INTERMARKET SPREAD OPTION

Consider the quandary of a utility company whose utility production cost is fixed and financed by short-term borrowing. At the
same time, the price it can charge its customers is pegged to how
well the customers perform (i.e., their use of the utility is proportional to the price they can charge for the end-product). The utility
company suffers if either the price of the end-product falls or the
interest rates rise. To protect themselves, they can buy a put option
on the total dollar amounts, i.e.,

$$\text{Payoff} = \max[K - P_{\text{Commodity}}N_{\text{Commodity}} + rN_{\text{Borrowing}}, 0] \qquad (1.3)$$

Hence, the put option is on a dollar amount, with possibly different
notional amounts for the interest-rate part and the commodity part.
This highlights the fact that if we are structuring a product that
combines different market classes, it is crucial to decide what the
"numeraire" is, i.e., what the currency is—or, in coarser terms,
what the working units of the equations are. Many fancy-looking
exotic structures quickly end up in structured-product graveyards
because someone has overlooked the fact that they are combining
apples with oranges.

LONG-DATED FOREIGN EXCHANGE OPTIONS

Options on foreign exchange are intricately related to the options
market in interest-rate instruments. This is not a surprise because,
even for simple European options on foreign exchange, the probability distribution of the foreign exchange forward depends (nonlinearly) on the probability distributions of the spot foreign
exchange rate, as well as the probability distribution of the two
interest rates from which the forwards are derived.

While this is true for both short- and long-dated foreign exchange options, as the option tenor increases, the effect of interest-rate volatility becomes more and more pronounced, and can easily equal or exceed the effect of spot foreign-exchange-rate volatility.

We will describe later the mechanisms by which we can estimate the parameters that are relevant for pricing long-dated foreign exchange options. As usual, the most important input is the volatility parameter. A cursory look at the over-the-counter (OTC) forex option market shows that for most major currency pairs, foreign exchange options are fairly liquid out to 2 years, and broker screens even exist which list two-sided Black-Scholes volatilities. However, traditionally, foreign exchange options beyond 2 years have been treated on a similar footing to exotics—this is natural since the interest-rate differential volatility can overwhelm the effects of the spot rate volatility. Most foreign exchange options desks are flow oriented and are extremely competitive with tight bid-ask spreads; these desks are not too comfortable taking on the interest-rate risk that requires management of volatile long-term bonds or swaps. Hence, the development of the exotic foreign exchange option market has been characterized in terms of adding more depth to the variations in the payoff structures, i.e., various kinds of barriers, ranges, and choosers, etc., have been priced and dealt. In sharp contrast, most interest-rate options desks are fairly comfortable doing long-dated options on interest rates, i.e., swaptions, caps, and the plethora of other mortgage-based indexed structures, and have evolved in a culture where the direction of flow between dealers and end-users is mostly one-directional for a given type of structure.

In addition to a knowledge of the individual foreign exchange and bond markets, management of long-dated foreign exchange options requires a good understanding of the correlations between spot exchange-rate movements and the individual bonds, as well as the correlation between the bonds themselves. For these reasons, a hybrid exotic options desk with expertise in managing risks both in spot foreign exchange and in bonds of different currencies, as well as exposure in volatilities, is perfectly suited to doing vanilla and exotic *long-dated* foreign exchange options. In fact, the very origins of the volatility term structure for foreign exchange options may be attributed partially to changes in zero coupon bond volatilities. We will reserve a detailed investigation of these issues for Chapter 4, once we have introduced some mathematical technology.

MULTIASSET BARRIER SWAPS

Consider the following swap. Counterparties A and B enter into a transaction where A receives some fixed rate while paying some floating rate, e.g., 3-month libor. This trade is supplemented with the contingency that if the dollar/yen exchange rate exceeds a barrier, let us say 120, then the swap terminates. While we will show the detailed pricing of this trade in later chapters, we would like to make some quick qualitative statements here. Since there is a contingency in the trade, at first glance it seems that if the correlation between the exchange-rate movements and interest rates is positive, it is to the benefit of the floating-rate payer to enter this swap. This is because exactly when the likelihood of him paying a higher interest rate increases, the likelihood of the swap being knocked out is higher also. This will command a lower fixed-rate coupon (since for positive correlation between interest rates and the exchange rate, the receiver of the fixed rate is essentially long a call option on the exchange rate). On the other hand, if the correlation between the exchange rate and the interest rate is negative, it is less likely that the swap will knock out when interest rates are higher, so the receiver of the fixed rate will require a higher fixed rate so as to be compensated for the additional risk. In this case, counterparty A, the receiver of the fixed rate, is essentially short an equivalent put option on the exchange rate (again, whose payoff depends on what is happening to interest rates). Now consider the situation in which the correlation is expected to be close to zero, but, due to the statistical nature of the estimate, the "bid" correlation is somewhat positive and the "offer" correlation is somewhat negative. Then, as market makers, it is entirely possible that the fixed rate at which counterparty A is willing to receive is higher then the non-knockout or plain vanilla case, and the fixed rate at which it is willing to pay is less than the plain vanilla swap rate.

As we will see in much detail in later chapters, at the microscopic level of risk, there is another way to understand transactions of this type. The risks that one finds in simple single-factor options have to be modified drastically when one considers complex, multi-factor option products. In particular, the change in the "delta" risk of the swap, which can be translated into terms of expected duration of the swap, has to be modified by new convexity effects caused by the interaction between the different asset classes. If the correlation changes sign, the contribution of these new convexity effects, also called cross-gamma effects, can switch from extending expected maturity to reducing expected maturity. In such a case, it is crucial to know what the exact assumptions about correlation are. In the present example, we have assumed that the yield curve is upward sloping and that the correlation between the two variables is constant. For more complex shapes of the yield curve of expected rates, and/or more complex term structures of correlation, it is possible to get even more counterintuitive behavior for the pricing. In this respect, multifactor options show all the complexities that one has traditionally found with mortgage-backed securities, and hence the recourse to good models is an absolute necessity.

MULTIASSET AMERICAN PUTS

Suppose a portfolio manager does not believe that it is possible for him or anyone else to forecast the future direction of prices of individual stocks. Also, he does not believe that anyone can intelligently pick stocks, bonds, or even asset classes, in general, that are more likely to outperform others. However, he thinks that there is widespread belief that the stock market is overvalued and that there is a big "bear" camp which believes that the Dow Jones is going to fall. The portfolio manager can show even better returns than all other portfolio managers if he can generate some extra premium income by selling puts to the bears. He would like to sell to your desk an American put on the Dow stocks, such that you get paid, either at exercise or at expiry, the difference between the strike and the highest price stock in the Dow Jones index.

Put in payoff language, he wants to sell an American put option on the maximum of n assets. So the payoff for the buyer is

$$\max(K - \max(S_1, S_2, \ldots, S_n), 0) \tag{1.4}$$

at any time that he chooses to exercise the option. Clearly, this is not a simple option to price. Even for single assets, American puts are exotic enough to require the apparatus of dynamic programming techniques. How much is the price different from a European multi-dimensional put? How does the price depend on the correlation?

Let us make a simplification to begin with. Assume that all the stocks are trading at the same price to begin with and that they also have the same volatility. Also assume that all pairwise correlations are the same. As the correlation between the stocks increases, the price of the put option on the maximum increases. This can be understood heuristically from the fact that as the correlation increases, there is less likelihood that one of the stocks remains at a higher level than the others and this reduces the likelihood of payoff from the option. The situation is different for the call option on the maximum. Uncorrelated stocks are more likely to break away from the pack and go to high prices, so the call price increases as the correlation falls. Numerical verification of these results will be presented in Chapter 5 (numerical methods). Note though that we can write, for the two-asset case (see Appendix E for the algebra behind these manipulations):

$$\max(K - \max(S_1, S_2), 0) = \max(K - \max(S_1 - S_2, 0) - S_2, 0) \quad (1.5)$$

and for the call:

$$\max(\max(S_1, S_2) - K, 0) = \max(\max(S_1 - S_2, 0) + S_2 - K, 0) \quad (1.6)$$

Now it is easy to accept that the payoff function for the put in Equation (1.5) reaches its maximum when, in all stochastic states of prices, S_1 and S_2 are positively correlated (since then the spread of prices can be minimal). On the other hand, the maximum on the call in Equation (1.6) appears when the S_1 and S_2 are less positively correlated (since the spread can then get larger). Thus, depending on the payoffs, the effect of correlation can be very different. In some cases, symmetry relationships may be used to relate one set of payoffs to another set of payoffs, in which case the effects of correlation can be discerned without detailed computations. Such techniques, which will be discussed in Chapter 3, have to play a prominent role in the arsenal of the exotic options trader.

CHAPTER 2

Markets and Products

This chapter is intended to be a rapid survey of the marketplace in exotic and hybrid options and give the bibliography of the accompanying research literature. The number of books available on the market that contain detailed information on the discussion presented in this chapter has recently exploded; a couple of them should contain almost all of the pertinent material [2,156]. For readers not familiar with the markets and the products that are discussed here, and whose emphasis is on product development, these references may be used as complements to our discussion. The second part of this chapter and the extensive bibliographical references may also be used for details on specific exotic option products and pricing and hedging methods.

Exotic as a term applies to any nonstandard product. Not too long ago, American options were considered exotic, and in the not too distant future, even the fanciest payoff structure of the current market will probably be traded as a commodity (if it survives). Hybrids is a term applicable to both vanilla and exotic options that have more than one market class in the determination of their payoff. There really are no simple hybrids, because as soon as correlation is included in the pricing and hedging algorithm, the complexity of the problem equals that of the most bizarre exotic. We have chosen, in this book, to approach the discussion of the newest generation of derivatives, using hybrids, which have correlation as their key ingredient, as the working framework. Not only does this approach allow us to work in total generality, but also all the standard exotic and vanilla option results and intuition are obtained easily in the zero correlation limit.

Exotic and hybrid options make it possible to transform the nature of risk by using customization. However, the risk, once transformed, must be hedged in available markets. This chapter will first provide a rather informal survey of the markets in which the options discussed in this book can be priced, and the market-specific motivations for indulging in the use of exotics. While the list is not complete, it is expected to cover a significant subset of the underlying variables in which the options position may ultimately be hedged. With the increased interest in customized financial solutions in each of these markets, as well as a movement toward integration of risks that spans multiple market classes, it is crucial that we understand the basic dynamics and prices conventions for the contracts that trade in them.

The second part of this chapter will survey the spectrum of important exotic products and classify them. While there is simply not space in this book to discuss here the pricing and hedging of each of the products in any significant detail, we are confident that the methods presented in the chapters that follow will be general enough to price and hedge any of the products in this chapter.

In this book we spend a significant amount of time approaching the pricing of both European and American spread options from a number of different approaches, and we introduce them in this chapter for the first time. Spread options not only trade in almost every asset class, but also many complex option structures can be reduced to the pricing of spread options. Also, they highlight some important pricing aspects of multiasset options, i.e., should one think of the spreads and combinations as independent variables with their own volatility, or should one think of them as functions of two or more variables with a term structure of correlation? Fortunately, either method works as long as there is ample liquidity for recalibration purposes.

MARKETS

Debt and Interest-Rate Markets

The debt market is basically a market for borrowing and lending. Borrowing and lending may be carried out by institutions of different credit ratings, and the credit rating affects the interest rates that are applicable. The U.S. treasury market is one of the largest and most liquid debt markets in the world, and it has the highest credit rating since the likelihood of default by the U.S. government is expected to be minimal. Other developed nations, including Japan, Germany, Italy, France, Canada, and the United Kingdom have their own highly developed government bond markets. Moving vertically in the credit dimension, the bonds of major corporate issuers come next, and usually trade at some small interest rate premium to the government market. Moody's, Standard and Poor's, and others have elaborate classification schemes for the rating of bonds based on the fundamentals of each corporate bond issuer.

Borrowing may be carried out at both fixed and floating interest rates. Fixed rates usually allow the borrower and the lender to agree on a contract for the use of money for a term that can go from as short as a day (overnight) to as long as a hundred years (for instance, "Disney" bonds). Usually, however, the more liquid part of the borrowing is in the zero to 30-year sector in the case of U.S. bonds, and the zero to 10-year sector in the case of other major currencies. Fixed-rate bonds are issued to pay a coupon at fixed intervals—semiannually for U.S. treasuries—plus redemption of the principal amount at maturity. Floating-rate bonds are usually issued at a discount to their final value, with the discount determining the effective interest rate.

For most corporate hedging requirements, the important markets are not the treasuries themselves, but the interest-rate swap market, and most exotics and hybrids use the swap yield curve for indexation or contingencies. The swap market is much larger than the treasury market in general, since it is possible to express any credit premium as a spread off the treasuries. Whereas there are slight differences in contract specifications from country to country, basically the interest-rate swap market lets issuers exchange fixed-rate corporate liabilities and assets for floating-rate liabilities and assets. The floating-rate index of choice is LIBOR—the London Interbank Offer Rate, which is the market for borrowing short-term funds in Eurocurrency in London. Most money-market trades refer to this rate for their indexation. Interest-rate caps, floors, and swaptions of increasing complexity may be based on libor or other floating rates (e.g., the constant maturity swap rates) for determining their payoff. The swap-spread, i.e., the difference of the interest-rate swap coupon from the underlying constant maturity treasury of the same length, is the key variable that must be warehoused and traded by dealers with large swap portfolios.

For practical hedging purposes, the over-the-counter market in swaps and options on swaps is supplemented by products that trade on exchanges. Treasury futures and futures options trade on the Chicago Board of Trade, with the CBOT bond and note futures markets being amongst the deepest exchange traded markets in the world. Eurodollar futures, which are futures contracts on the future short-term Eurocurrency deposit rates, and options on them, trade at the Chicago Mercantile Exchange. When the U.S. Eurodollar futures closes, SIMEX (Singapore International Monetary Exchange) may be used to trade the first few (four or five) Euros, which mutually offset to IMM the next day. These are also very liquid markets and quotes can be found on Reuters, Telerate, or Bloomberg on a live basis. On Bloomberg, the keystrokes EDA <Commodity Key> CT <Go Key> will give the list of all futures active contracts on the Eurodollars. EDA <Commodity Key> OMON <Go> gives the option monitor, while EDA <Commodity Key> DES <Go> gives the specification of the contracts.[1] We highly recommend the use of the Bloomberg system because of the extremely logical and hierarchical organization of information, as well as state-of-the-art pricing models for nonexotic plain vanilla products.

European interest-rate instruments trade in the London International Financial Futures Exchange (LIFFE) for all maturities. There are also smaller exchanges for these instruments in Frankfurt, Milan, and Paris. Japanese financial futures trade in Tokyo and Osaka, and the Euroyen futures trade in SIMEX as well as IMM.

---

1. With appropriate variations for other Eurocurrency deposits.

Numerous vendors provide valuation and portfolio management systems for bonds of all currencies.[2]

New developments in the exchange traded markets are the yield curve futures and options that trade in the CBOT on the spread between treasury yields of different maturities, as well as futures contracts on the treasury inflation-protected securities (TIPS). The spread futures allow direct hedging in future yield spreads and hedging of roll-risks for new issuances. In addition, they enable direct calibration of yield correlations. The inflation-indexed securities enable the first extraction of a real, inflation-adjusted yield curve.

Spread Options: A First Look at Modeling

The problem inherent in using simple models for pricing options on interest-rate-dependent security are nowhere more apparent than in the pricing of long-term spread options on yields. Consider, for instance, an option that pays out the difference, if positive, between the 2-year constant maturity treasury (CMT) and the 10-year constant maturity treasury rates minus some constant, K, times some notional at expiration. In short, the payoff is

$$\mathcal{P} = \max[2y - 10y - K, 0] \tag{2.1}$$

This is a classic "inversion protection" trade, i.e., if the yield curve inverts, then an option holder who holds long-term paper financed short term does not have to suffer negative carry effects in which the short-maturity yields exceed the long-maturity yields. In economic environments such as the one in the United States, the yield curve has historically inverted, so consideration of such options is especially relevant.

As of late 1996, these options have actually started to trade in the Chicago Board of Trade, so a knowledge of the pricing and hedging methodology is no longer academic. In this chapter, we will simply consider the case of the European spread option, i.e., where the payoff can only happen at the terminal date, with no interim exercise possibilities. The options trading in the CBOT are actually more complex for two reasons. First, they are American

---

2. For instance, Barra's Cosmos system.

options, so early exercise is possible. Second, they are options on a futures contract, where the futures contract is an underlying contract on the future value of the spread. Hence, valuation has to be carried out by taking the effect of daily mark-to-market. After we have introduced more advanced numerical technology in later chapters, i.e., multifactor binomial pyramids for the American problem, and term-structure models, both these complications can be easily taken care of.

The effect of correlation comes from recognizing that if the two yield movements were perfectly correlated, the difference between them would only change because of the "yield beta" effect, i.e., because of the higher intrinsic volatility of the short end of the yield curve compared with the long end of the yield curve. This fact can also be restated in terms of the volatility of the spread variable. If the two yields always move in sync by the same amount, then if the correlation is unity, the spread is nonvolatile, i.e., there is no uncertainty in it, so any option price must be identically zero if it is not in the money. For non unit correlation, the volatility of the spread is increased simply because the two yields can move in opposite directions.

One can price this spread option along three separate lines. In the first method, the spread between the long yield and the short yield is considered to be a Gaussian or normal random variable. Note that assuming it to be a lognormal variable would prohibit negative values, i.e., the very phenomenon of inversion that we are interested in capturing. The option depends on the *forward Gaussian volatility curve.*[3] In the second method, the individual yields are evolved according to lognormal dynamics, and market-derived volatilities, but with a *forward correlation term structure* for the two yields. The final method is to value the options using a full, arbitrage-free, *term structure model* like the Heath-Jarrow-Morton model [102], which provides the most self-consistent results, but which is also computationally quite intensive and hides a number of key features that we want to highlight.

---

3. For pricing options on yield curve futures contracts in the CBOT, this method can be approximated by 100 + Spread as a lognormal variable [41].

Single-Factor Gaussian Model

With μ and σ, respectively, being the expected growth rate and the Gaussian volatility for the *spread*, and z being a standard normal random variate, the Gaussian stochastic process for the spread is

$$dS = \mu\,dt + \sigma\,dz \qquad (2.2)$$

Once the initial condition is given, the expected value of the payoff can be computed by carrying out a simple single-factor integral (see below).

While the expected forward spread can be easily inferred by computing the forward yields from the spot yield curve, estimating the correct spread volatility for all times in the future is somewhat tricky. First, under the assumption of Gaussian spread distribution, the volatility is simply the annualized standard deviation (s.d.) of the period-to-period changes. In practice:

1. Calculate the spread for each time period.
2. Calculate the period-to-period changes of the spread.
3. Calculate the standard deviation (s.d.) of the last time series for the interval of interest.
4. Annualize the s.d. by multiplying by $\sqrt{\text{Number of periods in 1 year}}$.

Figure 2–1 shows a graph of the Gaussian spread volatility computed in this way for different length of weekly data sets as a "correlation cone." Clearly, there is lot of variation in the volatility if short-term periods are compared, but for the long term, the average volatility is around 100 bp per annum and the distribution has very little dispersion.

If we assume one constant spread volatility calculated in this way, the dispersion of the final state distribution grows without bound, i.e., the model predicts that the yield curve can become very inverted and remain that way for extended periods of time along some of the simulation paths. If we average over all paths generated from the simulation, we find that the probability of inversion generated by the simulation is much higher than is actually observed. Thus, the call option on the inversion will be highly overvalued.

Clearly, the correct way to interpret this is that the constant volatility Gaussian model is not capturing economic constraints on

F I G U R E 2–1

Gaussian Spread Volatility Cone for 2-Year and 10-Year CMT Yields, 1987–1997

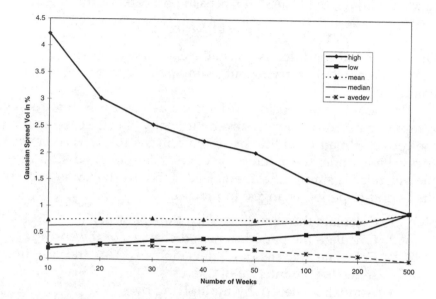

yield curve dynamics. In other words, once the real yield curve has inverted, it does not remain inverted for too long, since the economy usually slows down rather quickly after the inversion, and short rates fall more rapidly than longer rates to restore an upward-sloping yield curve.

One way to incorporate actual history into the yield curve dynamics is to insert a *mean-reversion* term for the spread in the first part of the right-hand side of Equation (2.2). Introducing a new parameter means that it has to be fitted to the data. What the fit achieves is to try to keep the spread of the univariate normal distribution of the spread at all future times constrained to what is historically observed. We will address how to achieve this practically later.

For a general stochastic process,

$$dx = a(x, t)\, dt + b(x, t)\, dz \tag{2.3}$$

Ito's formula states that (more detail in the next chapter)

$$dG = \left(\frac{\partial G}{\partial x} a + \frac{\partial G}{\partial t} + \frac{1}{2} \frac{\partial^2 G}{\partial x^2} b^2 \right) dt + \frac{\partial G}{\partial x} b \, dz \qquad (2.4)$$

Then, with the simple diffusion model for the spread option in Equation (2.2), where $a = \mu$ is equal to the drift, $b = \sigma$ equal to the Gaussian spread volatility, and T represents the time to expiration, we obtain the solution that the terminal spread is normally distributed with terminal expected value $S_0 + \mu(T - t)$ and variance $\sigma^2(T - t)$:

$$S_T \equiv S_{2T} - S_{1T} = N[S_0 + \mu(T - t), \sigma\sqrt{T - t}] \qquad (2.5)$$

Writing

$$d(S_{2t} - S_{1t}) = \mu \, dt + \sigma \, dz \qquad (2.6)$$

the price of the spread call option $\max(S_{2T} - S_{1T} - K, 0)$ at time t can be obtained exactly by computing the discounted present value of the expected payoff:

$$C = e^{-r(T-t)} \frac{1}{\sqrt{2\pi}} \int_{-\infty}^{\infty} \max[S_0 + \mu(T - t) + \sigma\sqrt{T - t}z - K, 0] e^{-\frac{1}{2}z^2} dz$$

$$= e^{-r(T-t)} \int_{\frac{K - S_0 - \mu(T-t)}{\sigma\sqrt{T-t}}}^{\infty} [S_0 + \mu(T - t) + \sigma\sqrt{T - t}z - K] e^{-\frac{1}{2}z^2} dz$$

$$= e^{-r(T-t)} \left[(S_0 + \mu(T - t) - K) \left[1 - N\left(\frac{K - S_0 - \mu(T - t)}{\sigma\sqrt{T - t}} \right) \right] \right.$$

$$\left. + \frac{\sigma\sqrt{T - t}}{\sqrt{2\pi}} e^{-\frac{1}{2}\xi^2} \right]$$

$$= e^{-r(T-t)} \sigma\sqrt{T - t} \left[\xi N(\xi) + \frac{1}{\sqrt{2\pi}} e^{-\frac{1}{2}\xi^2} \right] \qquad (2.7)$$

where

$$\xi = \frac{(S_{2T} - S_{1T} + \mu(T - t) - K)}{\sigma\sqrt{T - t}} \qquad (2.8)$$

and we have used $1 - N(a) = N(-a)$.

Note that in the approach of Reference [41] for yield curve futures traded on the CBOT, the Black model is directly used for $100 + \text{Spread}$.

Two-Factor Lognormal Model with Correlation

The alternative to modeling the spread as a Gaussian variable is to assume that the individual rates follow standard lognormal processes with changes that are correlated for all time steps. Define

$$S_1 = f_1\, e^{-\frac{1}{2}\sigma_1^2 t + \alpha\sqrt{t}\sigma_1}$$

$$S_2 = f_2\, e^{-\frac{1}{2}\sigma_2^2 t + \beta\sqrt{t}\sigma_2} \tag{2.9}$$

where the f_i values are the forwards for the two separate variables in a jointly lognormal environment. The high, low, mean, and median correlations for each time length for the yield returns are shown as a correlation cone in Figure 2–2. Again, the short-term correlation is quite variable, with the long-term correlation being fairly stable around a median of about 75 percent.

F I G U R E 2–2

The 2-Year and 10-Year U.S. Yield Correlation Cone, 1987–1997

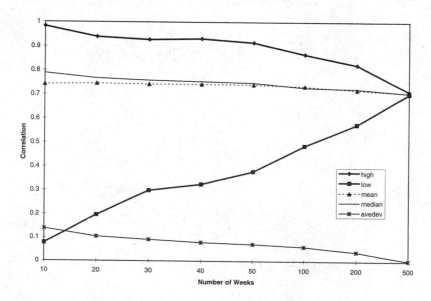

Using Equation (2.9), the value of the option is, with ρ the estimated correlation between the two return variables in the terminal joint distribution:

$$C = \frac{1}{2\pi\sqrt{1-\rho^2}} \int_{\alpha=-\infty}^{\infty} \int_{\beta=-\infty}^{\infty} \max(S_2 - S_1 - K, 0) e^{-\frac{1}{2}\frac{(\alpha^2 - 2\rho\alpha\beta + \beta^2)}{(1-\rho^2)}} \, d\alpha \, d\beta$$

(2.10)

This may be solved exactly[4] if $K = 0$, and numerically in the general case.

Locally, the single-factor Gaussian model given above and the two-factor joint lognormal model can be related by setting

$$d(S_{2t} - S_{1t}) = (rS_{2t} - rS_{1t}) \, dt + (\rho\sigma_2 S_{2t} - \sigma_1 S_{1t}) \, dz_{1t}$$
$$+ \sqrt{1 - \rho^2} \sigma_2 S_{2t} \, dz_{2t}$$

(2.11)

i.e., the drift is related to the drift of the two-factor model by

$$\mu = r(S_{2t} - S_{1t})$$

(2.12)

and the variance is related by

$$\sigma = \sqrt{(\rho\sigma_2 S_{2t} - \sigma_1 S_{1t})^2 + (1 - \rho^2)\sigma_2^2 S_{2t}^2}$$

(2.13)

So, one way of constraining the unbounded spread volatility in the Gaussian model is to make the correlation more positive in the two-factor lognormal model as a function of time.

Before we leave the topic of yield curve spread options, I would like to mention a correlation effect that has substantial effect on the hedging of these options. Suppose that the yield curve is flat at 6 percent and we price the option of Equation (2.1) for $K = 0$. Then, the delta, or hedge ratio, with respect to the 10-year yield is computed by moving the 10-year yield by one basis point and computing the change in the option price. Now suppose there is a shock and the 2-year rate moves to 7 percent, without a change in the 10-year yield. This completely changes the delta with respect to the 10-year yield because of *cross-gamma*, i.e., the nonvanishing of the mixed partial derivatives.

---

4. We will address this in detail in the next chapter.

Forex Markets: Currency Cross-Options

The foreign exchange markets are probably the largest and most liquid markets in the world. Since currency transactions happen without break throughout the day, access to the over-the-counter market in spot and forward currency, as well as options on them, proves to be a significant competitive edge for dealers who want to build a significant base in products for end-users. This market is largely dominated by large banks and financial institutions.

Key to the valuation of long-dated forwards and futures is the concept of interest-rate parity. This requires a liquid market in the underlying deposit or "depo" instruments. Thus, there is a natural relationship between the interest-rate markets and the foreign exchange markets. This relationship becomes pronounced as the term of contracts under consideration gets longer. In the absence of liquidity preference for one currency over another, the forward exchange rate can be computed from the spot exchange rate and the ratio of discount factors for the term for the two currencies. However, when one currency is preferred over another, there is a very finite "basis swap" that must be taken into consideration [84]. In fact, the forward foreign exchange rates incorporate by market consensus the value of this basis swap, and should be taken as fundamental inputs in the valuation of cross-currency contracts. This currency basis swap is widely quoted (e.g., the Reuter's page ICAY has broker (Intercapital) contributed rates vs U.S. libor flat).

The options market for foreign exchange is highly developed. However, the progression of option products in forex is fundamentally different than the options traded in the OTC debt market. Forex options markets have moved towards more and more complexity in their payoff structure, as well as in the contingencies on which the payoff may depend. Due to the complexities forced upon the valuation methodology from the volatility of the bonds used to obtain the forward exchange rates, forex option traders have been hesitant to write options for longer than 3–5 years. On the other hand, the forex option market has the most well-developed zoo of complex payoff options imaginable, as well as binaries, knockins, knockouts, and averages.

In the non-OTC market, the futures and options traded in the IMM on the yen (JY), deutschemark (DM), British pound, and

Canadian dollar are relatively liquid. However, due to nonstandard specification of the contracts, they are not used for the primary hedging requirements of larger transactions. At this stage of the market, anybody interested in getting involved in the more esoteric forex products is probably better off getting access to the much larger OTC market for their hedging requirements.

Just as there is a triangle relationship between the crosses constructed out of a triple of currencies, there is a triangle relationship between volatilities of three crosses. For instance, knowing the value of at-the-money options for a given tenor on \$/DM, \$/JY completely determines the price of at-the-money options on DM/yen. Then, taking appropriate positions in pure volatility instruments, e.g., straddles, in the three related option markets, an explicit view can be implemented on correlation vis-à-vis one currency as "numeraire." We will have a lot more on this in Chapters 4 and 6.

Commodity Markets

It is fair to say that, except for precious metals such as gold and silver, almost all hedging in commodities is carried out in the exchanges or in a relatively thin over-the-counter market. Commodity swaps can be created and are traded in the OTC market to exchange fixed and floating commodity assets and liabilities.

The futures market prices are used to construct the commodity term structure. The first contract is usually taken to be the "spot" price. Note that since the underlying commodity is not a liquid traded instrument in the same way as financial bonds or stocks, it is impossible to use a given cash commodity price as the "spot price."

It is important to realize some of the differences inherent in pricing contingent claims with commodity factors as compared with claims without them.

Note, first, the following property between futures prices and forward prices: forward prices are equal to futures prices when interest rates are constant or a known function of time. This is because on futures positions, the profits and losses are marked to market on a daily basis, so in the deterministic interest-rate case, the correlation between the futures price movement and interest rates is zero. Since, on an average, the futures returns are expected to be as negative as positive, there is no advantage to holding a futures over a forward and so the price of the futures contract cannot exceed the forward contract as long as interest rates are constant or deterministic. On the other hand, if interest rates cannot be assumed to be deterministic, or, in general, there is a nonzero correlation between interest rates and the futures prices, it is advantageous to be long the futures contract whenever the price of the contract is positively correlated with interest rates. This is because the long position posts a gain that can be invested at higher interest rates and posts a loss that has to be financed at a lower interest rate.

For commodities such as gold or oil, where there is a positive correlation of the futures price with interest rates, it is valuable to hold long positions in the futures contracts; hence, futures prices are pushed above forward prices. The study of futures prices as compared with forward prices is one way of ascertaining the implied correlation of the commodity and interest rates that we will explore later. The effect of the correlations increases as the time to maturity of the futures contract increases.

Investment Commodities

Suppose an investor invests in a commodity like gold. He has two costs: the first one is the cost of borrowing funds to finance the purchase (or equivalently the loss of interest if he uses cash for the purchase), r, and the second one is the cost of storing the commodity at some continuous annualized rate, s. So he would like to get compensated for these costs incurred, at maturity, via the cost of the future price of the commodity, i.e.,

$$F = Se^{(r+s)t} \tag{2.14}$$

where t is the time to expiration, S is the spot price of the commodity, and F is the futures price.

Convenience Yield

For an investor who is long a futures contract on a commodity like gold, and short the underlying commodity, the storage cost is saved and is included in the computation of his profit at expiration. On the other hand, for consumable commodities such as oil and gas, the holder of the commodity holds it not because of investment value, but because of the value of having it when it is needed for consumption. In that case, it can happen, and frequently does happen, that

$$F \leq S e^{(r+s)t} \tag{2.15}$$

since the users of the commodity feel that it is more beneficial to hold the commodity than to hold the futures contract, which cannot be consumed. The *convenience yield* is the correction to the futures such that this inequality becomes an equality, i.e., y is defined such that

$$F e^{yt} = S e^{(r+s)t} \tag{2.16}$$

so that

$$F = S e^{(r+s-y)t} \tag{2.17}$$

whenever the commodity price term structure is negative sloped or "backwardated," and the cost of holding the commodity (including financing or opportunity cost and storage costs) is below the convenience yield. In cases of shocks to the supply mechanism, such as in the case of wars, the convenience yield goes up.

Note that for most commodities, the delivery of the actual commodity underlying the futures contracts can be carried out by the shorts at any time during a few weeks. This gives the shorts a *delivery option* whose characteristics can be described here. If the price of the commodity is upward sloping, it is beneficial for the party with the short position to deliver at the beginning of the delivery period since the cost from holding the underlying variable is higher than the convenience. On the other hand, when the curve is backwardated, the party with the short position is better off delivering at the end of the delivery period.

The Commodity Exchange (COMEX) and New York Mercantile Exchange (NYMEX) are main exchanges for trading precious metals and energy futures. The CBOT and Chicago Mercantile Exchange (CME) have the oldest grain and livestock futures trading.

The London Metal Exchange (LME) is the dominant exchange for trading of base metal financial futures and options. For a trader more familiar with the exchanges in the United States, the way the LME functions is somewhat strange. The clearing firms act both as traders for their own account and as brokers for customers. Actual trades are done in short intervals of "ring" trading.

Options on the Crack Spread

The process of refining crude oil to produce heating oil or gasoline can be replicated in the financial "refinery" by selling contracts on one asset and buying contracts on another. If the end-user wants to implement the view that the price of refining will increase, he can go long on heating oil and go short on crude oil.

In a similar way, if one wants to implement a view on the uncertainty, or volatility of the refining costs, options can be bought or sold on the "crack" spreads. In fact, options on the crack spread provide a ready means for backing out the correlation between the crude product and the finished product.

Options on the Spark Spread

Since electricity futures and options have started to trade in the commodity exchanges, one can also construct options on the "spark" spread, i.e., the differential between the cost of electricity in \$/MWh off the grid or the cost of producing it from natural gas, after the inclusion of overheads such as transmission costs.

The pricing and hedging of these options is analogous to the pricing and hedging of interest-rate spread options, discussed earlier in this chapter [231].

Equity Market Baskets: Options on Stock Indices vs Options on Stocks

The equity markets provide many layers of complexity due to the enormous size of individual equity trading, as well as the trading of aggregate indices. Almost anyone is extremely well-educated in the basic functioning of the equity markets, so we will not dwell on it. Numerous books deal in detail with equity derivatives [82,83]; this has recently become an extremely active area in which structured hedging techniques have become quite sophisticated. Writing puts on its own equity, hedging of employee stock incentive plans, warrants, and hedging credit quality have been some intramarket equity trades that have been unusually popular.

Pricing forwards and futures in the equity markets requires a good idea of the dividend yields. The fair value of an equity index forward can be calculated from the difference of the forward contract and the dividend-adjusted risk-free rate of growth. In many ways, the discussion of exotics in the framework of foreign exchange can be translated to equity options by replacing the foreign currency yield by the dividend yield.

In the world of index option trading, it has been popular to trade or hedge index options against options on the components. This "covariance trading" is easy to understand. The volatility of an index can be decomposed in terms of the volatility of the components. Closed-form expressions are available if the components are assumed to be jointly normally distributed and contribute marginally to the index with weight a_i.[5] Then,

$$\sigma_{\text{index}}^2 = \sum_i a_i^2 \sigma_i^2 + \sum_i \sum_{i \neq j} a_i a_j \rho_{ij} \sigma_i \sigma_j \qquad (2.18)$$

In practice, if the number of components is large, estimating each pairwise correlation is impossible. However, useful results can be obtained by replacing all the pairwise correlations with an average correlation ρ:

$$\rho = \frac{\sigma_{\text{index}}^2 - \sum_i a_i^2 \sigma_i^2}{\sum_i \sum_{i \neq j} a_i a_j \sigma_i \sigma_j} \qquad (2.19)$$

so that if the average correlation is close to zero, the index volatility is extremely dampened compared with the component volatility (diversification).

If one believes that the systematic risk, as represented by the volatility of the market index (e.g., the Standard and Poor's 500) has, in general, gone down because of diversification, the extra volatility of the components can only arise because of nonsystematic risk of the individual stocks.

---

5. In practice, this is a good approximation even if the components are assumed to be lognormally distributed.

"Dispersion arbitrage" applies to the methods of extracting value from mismatched volatilities between index and component options. One can construct two separate portfolios: one of index options and another of options on individual equities, which, for a given value of average correlation, should be equally valuable. It is also a method for taking advantage of volatility skews [132]. As the market declines, one finds that the correlation between the components increases, i.e., the volatility of the index increases, even though the component volatility remains constant. The inverse of this strategy can be used to trade correlation. If the market is expected to enter a period of increased correlation between the components, one can buy index options and sell a weighted portfolio of options on the individual stocks.

PRODUCT VARIATIONS

Exotic options, in general, may be classified in terms of whether they are on a single asset or multiple assets, whether they have barrier risk or not, whether they are path dependent or path independent, and whether early exercise is allowed or forbidden. Of course, the list below is not intended to be complete, and combinations of one or more types can yield even more exotic structures [67]. Only imagination restricts the design. Frequently, customized structures are purchased by financing the premium through the sale of other exotics of the same kind at different strikes or barriers, or by the sale of plain vanilla options on smaller notionals.

The simplest exotic options are the simplest non-European options, i.e., American options. The early exercise feature makes them exotic. The only known way to price them is on lattices or trees, though some recent work on simulation-based approaches seems to be promising (see Chapter 5 on numerical methods). Somewhat less exotic are *Bermudan* options, which can be exercised early, but only on fixed dates before expiration. Interesting examples of these options are callable bonds, or cancellable or extendable swaps.

Digital or *binary* or *all-or-nothing* options are the simplest type of option products since their price is the discounted value of pure probability. Binary options may pay cash if the preset level is hit, or they may pay the underlying asset. Binaries can be European style, i.e., whether or not the level is hit is only checked at expiration. They may also be American style, where the contingency level can be hit before expiration. Binaries are notoriously difficult to hedge near the barrier since the change in hedge ratios is discontinuous [50,169,180,208,222].

Contingent premium options do not require the option buyer to pay the premium at inception. The holder usually has an option whose premium is paid only if the same or another underlying asset hits a preset level before expiration. To make up for the price, the contingent premium is higher than the premium paid up front. Contingent premium options can be easily priced and hedged as a combination of plain vanilla options and leveraged binary options [130,198,209].

Delayed or *deferred* or *forward-start* options are options that are struck at the money forward at some future date. These are most commonly found in employee stock options, and are sensitive to the forward volatility of the asset [24,27,143,144,184,204].

Chooser options allow the holder to choose whether he wants to exercise into a future vanilla call or a put on the expiration of the chooser option. This is a good substitute for a straddle where a portfolio of both the call and put is bought. Since the chooser can never be worth more than a straddle, and it is always more profitable than either a call or a put, it is more expensive than the call or the put, but cheaper than the sum [157,181].

Installment or *rental* options allow the user to buy a string of options where, on each reset date, he can choose to have the remaining sequence of options by paying a fixed premium determined in advance, or decline to have the remaining string of options.

"Maxi" options allow the user to choose a certain number of best options out of a package of options with time. This gives the users a sequence of choice dates on which they can either "use up" some of their options, or save them for later [146].

Cumulative options pay the excess of some cumulative sum from a predetermined strike. These have traditionally been useful for capping total liability when the timing of risk is not quantifiable.

Power options pay off some power of the underlying. Thus, they act as options where the number of options held continuously increases, so they are leveraging options. A notorious example was the libor squared note.

Decaying options are almost the inverse of the power option. For instance, the log option has the payoff scale as the log in the underlying.

Compound options are simply options on options. You can have calls on calls, or calls on puts, or puts on calls, or puts on puts. You can have European options on either European or American, or vice versa. Popular compound options are options on caps or floors [92,95,144,157,182,192,193].

Resettables are options that have their strikes set by the settlement of some index on a given date. Usually, they are transacted in packages with many resets [44].

Barrier options get activated (knocked in) or extinguished (knocked out) if one or more underlying assets cross a preset barrier. Calls and puts can have up or down barriers. When there is a barrier that is in the money, the barrier option is called a reverse barrier option. There have been some interesting trades recently where the option is on one index, such as a long-term treasury yield, and the barrier is on another interest-rate index, usually short-term libor. Barriers can be one-touch, i.e., the barrier condition is valid at any time during the life of the option, or end-touch, i.e., the barrier condition is valid only at expiration. Some recent variations have barriers that are monitored at discrete time intervals. Barriers have also been used for the modeling of default risk. *Double-barrier* options have barriers on either side. The most popular application has been in the form of *range accrual notes*, where there is effectively a separate barrier for each day on a fraction of the total notional for the life of the option, and the payoff accrues over the life as long as the barrier conditions are met. There is a large literature on barrier options [17,28,31,32,38,59,60, 94,100,104,105,108,112,115,123,126,129,137,152,153,166,169,173,187, 191,206,221].

Asian or *average* options are options on the average price. They are relatively inexpensive because the averaging reduces the volatility. Averages can be computed as geometric averages (i.e., multiply n asset prices and take the nth root), or arithmetic averages, and they can be computed with different discrete price intervals as inputs. Since the sum of lognormals is not lognormal, arithmetic averages are hard to price. However, the Edgeworth expansion method can be used for approximation (we describe this for baskets in the next chapter). A related class of options is the average strike option where the average determines the strike [18,27,30,47,51,53, 54,65,66,90,91,101,103,114,133,136,138,139,143,166,171,172,176,190, 194,207,210,211,219,220].

Lookback options or "options of least regret" are the most expensive options because they allow the holder to receive the maximal in the money value, if any [1,15,28,52,55,70,71,75, 87,96,97,106,114,131,137,155,166]. *Russian* options are infinite life options, which pay off, at any time chosen by the holder, the maximum realized asset price up to that date. Generalization of lookbacks are *shout* options, where, if the option is in the money, the buyer can set the minimum in the moneyness by "shouting" the contemporaneous asset price. *Cliquet* options set the minimum in-the-moneyness by taking the asset price at one time point or "click." *Ladder* options have their in-the-moneyness determined by some preset level of the spot price, if it is attained at any intermediate time, or the strike, if the preset level is not attained. *Perpetual* options have no expiration date [88].

Multiasset options can take their underlying variables from one market class or from different market classes [6,11–14,29,33, 39,40,43,49,81,89,93,103,104,107,108,114,117,118,119,120,122,126, 134,148,149,159,162,170,175,178,185,189,191,200,223]. Regardless of the underlying variables, *outperformance* or *better-off* options [34,61, 62,85,183] allow the holder to exchange one asset for another asset. *Rainbow* options allow the holder to have the best performing asset or cash [86]. Clearly, these two are related and can be priced together by a simple transformation. *Spread* options let the holder benefit from spreads between two different related assets [197]. We have mentioned yield curve spread options earlier. Also crack spreads that allow one to have a "virtual refinery" between the unrefined and the refined product are traded on the NYMEX [167]. *Basket* options are options on a weighted linear combination of underlying assets. *Quanto* options pay off in a numeraire different from the one that is native to the asset [111,168,186,212,213].

We can extend these to examples of products that incorporate, in their payoff profiles, interrelationships between more than one market class. We will, for simplicity, assume that we can break up the universe of markets into four classes, as above: i.e., debt, forex, commodity, and equity. This is an assumption within which most active transactions fit quite easily in the current state of the derivatives market.

Debt-Forex: long-dated foreign exchange options, cross-currency swaptions.

Debt-Equity: convertible bonds.

Debt-Commodity: utility-price bond options. Range notes with commodity triggers.

Forex-Equity: quanto index options, i.e., Nikkei options traded in SIMEX vs Nikkei options traded in IMM [68].

Forex-Commodity: foreign exchange forwards and options whose notional readjusts are based on the price of the underlying commodities. Gas and soft commodity options traded in the United States vs Tokyo.

Equity-Commodity: puts on the equity of a commodity producer whose notional readjusts are based on the price of the commodity.

Debt-Forex-Equity: convertible bonds whose payments are settled in a foreign currency. Caps, such as the Nikkei cap of Chapter 1, that knock out on a foreign equity index.

Debt-Forex-Commodity: the classic example of the "cotton-bond" mentioned in the introduction, and modern generalizations thereof.

Debt-Forex-Commodity-Equity: convertible bonds that can be settled in a number of currencies and whose coupon adjusts based on a commodity or equity index. Cross-market baskets of various kinds.

The reader will no doubt be able to extend this list indefinitely with more sophisticated examples. In the next chapter, we turn to the pricing machinery with direct reference to some of these examples.

CHAPTER 3

Pricing Analytics

This chapter focuses on the theoretical aspects of modeling, closed-form solutions of the partial differential equations obtained from the models, and the use of symmetries in the equations and the boundary conditions for finding analytic solutions and their properties. Behind any pricing and hedging methodology are significant assumptions about the future behavior of the underlying variables that affect the price of the options under consideration. In the framework of single-factor option pricing, the simplest assumption is that the prices are lognormally distributed about some expected value, i.e., the period-to-period returns are normally distributed about some mean return. These set of assumptions are key to the Black-Scholes pricing environment that we will explore in some detail here for multifactor options. In Appendix C, the reader is reminded how a simple application of these assumptions from the framework of probability theory leads to the classic formula for a stock option as given by Black and Scholes. In Appendix J, the Green function solution is obtained by a brute force integration of the partial differential equation (PDE) governing infinitesimal time evolution of prices using integral transform methods. The very fact that the final product of two apparently different approaches is the same is convincing evidence that there are a number of different ways of solving the same problem—and different methods work in different contexts. While this chapter focuses on elaborating some of these different analytic methods of solution, Chapter 5 focuses on numerical methods, which are the methods of last resort when all analytic trickery is of no use.

However, we insist that the reader should understand that this is an idealization. As highlighted in Appendix H, it might be more accurate, from the perspective of a risk manager, not to make these assumptions, but simply to imply the specific multivariate distributions to which his portfolio is exposed using actual data. This is even more important if one has a large number of illiquid exotics or hybrids, for the simple reason that the fine-level adjustments one can make in the case of single-factor options to enable a better reflection of reality are simply not possible for illiquid exotic contracts. So the process of marking hedges to market might be flawed if one assumes some idealized, yet incorrect, form for the joint distribution of many assets, e.g., lognormal. The relative illiquidity of these products simply makes it impossible to recalibrate or refit the parameters of the idealized model so that local price variations in time are small. As an example, consider options on the S&P 500 index valued according to a lognormal distribution and the Black-Scholes framework, which, in its traditional form, has constant, strike-independent volatility. The index options market captures the reality of sharp sell-offs by introducing a volatility skew in the return distribution by making out-of-the-money put options more expensive compared with out-of-the-money call options (struck equidistant from the forward price). The volatility skew not only affects relative pricing of options, but also the risk parameters that are used for dynamical hedging (see Appendix F on vol skews). While this skew information is easy to extract for single-factor options because of their liquidity, and we can construct full forward volatility surfaces with strike and time forming the two independent variables [63,72,188], it may be totally impractical to extract these corrections for one-of-a-kind exotic multifactor options.

However, the standard joint lognormal framework is sufficiently general and specific corrections for the market(s) under scrutiny can easily be made. In defense of the use of the multifactor normal environment for returns, we can provide an argument based on the method of maximum entropy. This is equivalent to the fundamental assumption of probabilistic valuation known as the *principle of insufficient reason*: "In the absence of any prior knowledge, we must assume that all events have equal probabilities." If p_i are probabilities corresponding to some events in a partition of probability space, then the entropy of that partition equals $-\sum_i p_i \ln p_i$. Then, the principle of maximum entropy is the analytic restatement of the principle of insufficient reason: The probabilities, if unknown, must be so chosen that the entropy is maximized. For a continuous density $f(x)$, we want to maximize $-\int_{-\infty}^{\infty} f(x) \ln f(x)\, dx$.

Now suppose $X: [x_1, \ldots, x_n]$ is a random vector in n dimensions subject to some constraints:

$$E[g_i(X)] = \int_{-\infty}^{\infty} \cdots \int_{-\infty}^{\infty} g_i(x) f(x_1, \ldots, x_n)\, dx_1 \ldots dx_n = \eta_i \qquad (3.1)$$

for $i = 1, \ldots, n$ for arbitrary well-behaved functions g_i. Then, the maximum entropy principle leads to the conclusion that the density $f(X) = f(x_1, \ldots, x_n)$ has to satisfy (for a proof see Reference [160])

$$f(X) = A\, e^{-\lambda_1 g_1(X) - \cdots - \lambda_n g_n(X)} \qquad (3.2)$$

where the λ_i values are constants determined from the constraints, and A is determined from normalization. Now, if we have a covariance matrix estimated from data $C = E[X^T X]$, then its matrix elements are by definition the expected value of $g_{jk}(X) = x_j x_k$, so substitution in Equation (3.1) using Equation (3.2), gives,

$$f(X) = A\, e^{-\sum_{j,k} \lambda_{jk} x_j x_k} \qquad (3.3)$$

where the covariance matrix determines that $\lambda_{jk} = \frac{1}{2} C_{jk}^{-1}$. Putting this into the expression for the density, we get

$$f(X) = A\, e^{-\frac{1}{2} x_j C_{jk}^{-1} x_k} \qquad (3.4)$$

which is exactly the density of n joint normal variables. Thus, the joint normal assumption is the maximally entropic density that we can write down for n assets in the absence of special reasons to the contrary. If prices of options from the market are taken as the true representation of the probability distribution of assets, the same technique may be used to infer the most general implied probability density consistent with option prices.

I recommend that the user learn the mathematical aspects of analytic multifactor option pricing with these concerns in mind. With some meditation, it is usually easy to figure out which part of the valuation methodology needs adjustment. Thus, we will unapologetically turn to the general theoretical, though admittedly gross, idealizations of multifactor option pricing.

Regardless of what assumptions are made about the stochastic processes underlying options, many powerful statements can be made simply by looking at relationships evident from symmetries that the fundamental equations governing the time evolution of nonlinear payoff structures have to follow. In mathematical terms, if the fundamental differential equations (along with their boundary conditions) of finance have "invariances" or equivalences under change or relabeling of variables, then the dynamics of the underlying option prices have to hold strong relationships amongst themselves. A classic example of this is the simple relationship between puts and calls even in single-factor options. One of the most important questions that a risk manager who is managing a book of exotic options can ask is:

What are the model-independent fundamental relationships between the different contracts dictated by symmetries?

An important purpose of this chapter is to illustrate the pricing of a number of different kinds of correlation options in relationship to each other. We will spend a lot of time motivating the existence of put–call parity-type relationships for multifactor options, in addition to showing how such relationships may be extracted to a large degree by simple mathematical manipulations. Note that relationships like the ones between puts and calls are manifestations of "discrete" symmetries, whereas continuous parametric generalizations of the symmetries are entirely possible. Note that the study of these symmetry relationships is central to the pricing and managing of complex securities because the relationships can be used to transform the original valuation and risk-management issues into other equivalent, but simpler, systems for which the underlying dynamics has no direct relevance. As we will see in Chapter 6 on risk management, if the effect of symmetries is ignored, positions that have exactly cancelling risks at the nonlinear level may nevertheless be hedged in the linear approximation, leading to additional transaction costs that could have been avoided.

ZERO-CORRELATION PRICING

Before we delve deep into the mathematics of correlated assets and the options based on them, I would like to give the reader some tools that are useful for sanity checks. The simplest one of them is to assume that even though a number of assets come into play in the pricing of the contingent claim with complex term structures of correlation, they are, as a first approximation, essentially uncorrelated. Then, the expectation of a conditional density can be factored into products of expectations over marginal densities. In other words, the full probability of a particular outcome is given by the product of partial probabilities from individual assets.

Consider an example: suppose I sell an option in which I am obliged to pay the holder the value of a call option on asset A if asset B exceeds some level L on time t. Clearly, to price this "option," all I need to know is (1) the probability that B will reach L, and multiply it with the probability that A will exceed the strike price (given that B exceeds the preset level); and (2) the difference between its terminal price and the strike price if it does do so. Including the discounting factor, this procedure is symbolically equivalent to

$$e^{-rt} \int_A \int_L^\infty C(A)P(A, B)\, dA\, dB \tag{3.5}$$

where $P(A, B)$ is the joint density of A and B, and $C(A)$ represents the call payoff. Now, depending on the assumption of the joint density, this integral is somewhat complicated to perform. But, if we assume that A and B are uncorrelated, then we can replace $P(A, B)$ by $P(A)P(B)$ where $P(A)$ and $P(B)$ are the marginal densities. Then, the integral factors into two integrals, the first one of which is the value of the call option on A and the second one of which is the probability that B exceeds L. This is clearly an easier problem and, in most cases, gives a very good starting point for situating the full pricing problem. In other words, once this zero-correlation valuation is completed, everything else is a "correlation adjustment." In many cases, one can even guess at the correct correlation adjustment from market intuition.

The mathematics behind the factorization is simple. Consider the value of two related variables, X_t and Y_t, which we assume to be jointly lognormally distributed (see the form of the density below). We assume that the mean of X_t is ξ and its variance is σ_X^2, and the mean of Y_t is η and its variance is σ_Y^2. Given a value of X_t, the conditional distribution of Y_t is normal, with mean $\eta + (\rho\sigma_Y/\sigma_X)(X_t - \xi)$ and variance $(1 - \rho^2)\sigma_Y^2$. If the correlation ρ vanishes, the mean and variance of the conditional distribution are exactly equal to those of the distribution of Y_t. As the reader may know (or can learn from Appendix H), the bivariate joint normal distribution is completely specified, i.e., all moments are known to all orders once the means, variances, and correlation are known, and the ordinary normal is known completely when its mean and standard deviation are known. Thus, we start with a completely defined correlation problem that decouples into a factor of two completely defined functions as the correlation goes to zero. So the pricing problem is a point estimate of a family of prices given by only the variation of the correlation parameter. In principle, then, once the infinitesimal rate of change of the price is known with respect to correlation, then the price for all correlations is known by solving a differential equation in the correlation.

THE MULTIFACTOR STOCHASTIC PROCESS

Within the joint lognormal framework, an n factor process is described by the n state variables following continuous time Ito diffusions.[1] For $1 \leq i \leq n$, the ith state variable follows

$$dS_i = (\mu_i - d_i)S_i\,dt + \sigma_i S_i\,dz_i \tag{3.6}$$

---

1. For readers not familiar with Ito calculus, References [128] and [158] are excellent.

where

S_i = the ith asset
μ_i = the expected growth rate of the ith asset
d_i = the dividend yield of the ith asset
σ_i = the volatility of the ith asset
dz_i = the ith stochastic process

We can also use the special riskless asset S:

$$\frac{dS_0}{S} = r\,dt \tag{3.7}$$

where r is the riskless interest rate.

Note that the i stochastic processes, z_i, are not necessarily independent. If the correlation between dz_i and dz_j is given by ρ_{ij}, this is the same as using a jointly normal probability distribution for the logarithms of S_i. To make this statement clear, consider two variables, S_1 and S_2, with correlation ρ. Then (with $d_i = 0$),

$$\frac{dS_1}{S_1} = \mu_1\,dt + \sigma_1\,dz_1$$

$$\frac{dS_2}{S_2} = \mu_2\,dt + \sigma_2\,dz_2 \tag{3.8}$$

Since S_1 and S_2 are assumed to be jointly lognormal, with cumulative distribution function

$$\frac{1}{2\pi\sigma_1\sigma_2 t\sqrt{1-\rho^2}} \int_{-\infty}^{a} \int_{-\infty}^{b} e^{-\frac{1}{2}\frac{1}{1-\rho^2}\left[\frac{(\ln S_1 - \mu_1 t)^2}{\sigma_1^2 t} - \frac{2\rho(\ln S_1 - \mu_1 t)(\ln S_2 - \mu_2 t)}{\sigma_1 \sigma_2 t} + \frac{(\ln S_2 - \mu_2 t)^2}{\sigma_2^2 t}\right]} \frac{dS_1}{S_1}\frac{dS_2}{S_2}$$

$$\tag{3.9}$$

it can be checked by integrating over any of the two variables, that the other variable is then also marginally lognormal, which is consistent in the limit where only a single-variable process is considered.

Note that in the single-variable case, we have the Markov representation

$$\frac{dS}{S} = \mu\,dt + \sigma\,dz = \mu\,dt + \sigma\epsilon\sqrt{dt} \tag{3.10}$$

where ϵ is drawn from the standard normal with mean zero and variance unity.

The expected values can be evaluated by performing the integral over the ϵ space:

$$E\left[\frac{dS}{S}\right] = \frac{1}{\sqrt{2\pi t}\sigma} \int_{-\infty}^{\infty} (\mu\, dt + \sigma\, dz) e^{-\epsilon^2/2}\, d\epsilon = \mu\, dt \qquad (3.11)$$

and

$$\begin{aligned}
\mathrm{var}\left[\frac{dS}{S}\right] &= \frac{1}{\sqrt{2\pi t}\sigma} \int_{-\infty}^{\infty} [(\mu\, dt + \sigma\, dz)^2 - (\mu\, dt)^2] e^{-\epsilon^2/2}\, d\epsilon \\
&= \frac{1}{\sqrt{2\pi t}\sigma} \int_{-\infty}^{\infty} [(\mu\, dt + \sigma\epsilon\sqrt{dt})^2 - (\mu\, dt)^2] e^{-\epsilon^2/2}\, d\epsilon \\
&= \sigma^2\, dt \qquad\qquad\qquad\qquad\qquad\qquad\qquad\qquad (3.12)
\end{aligned}$$

In the multivariable case, since dS_1/S_1 and dS_2/S_2 are jointly normal as well as marginally normal, the following are trivial to prove using the joint normal density (since the integral over the variable that does not appear in the integrand is unity by normalization):

$$E\left[\frac{dS_1}{S_1}\right] = \mu_1\, dt$$

$$\mathrm{var}\left[\frac{dS_1}{S_1}\right] = \sigma_1^2\, dt$$

$$E\left[\frac{dS_2}{S_2}\right] = \mu_2\, dt$$

$$\mathrm{var}\left[\frac{dS_2}{S_2}\right] = \sigma_2^2\, dt \qquad (3.13)$$

We can also check that, indeed,

$$\frac{E\left[\left(\dfrac{dS_1}{S_1} - \mu_1\, dt\right)\left(\dfrac{dS_2}{S_2} - \mu_2\, dt\right)\right]}{(\sigma_1\sqrt{dt})(\sigma_2\sqrt{dt})} = \rho \qquad (3.14)$$

To prove this, we can reduce the bivariate integration of the product over the bivariate lognormal density with nonzero mean and standard deviation to an integral over the joint standard normal density by two changes of variables: the first one replacing

$dS_1/S_1 = d \ln S_1$ by x_1, and $dS_2/S_2 = d \ln S_2$ by x_2; and the second one rescaling out the mean and standard deviation terms. This yields

$$E[xy] = \frac{1}{\sqrt{2\pi}} \frac{1}{\sqrt{1-\rho^2}} \int_{-\infty}^{\infty} xy\, e^{-\frac{1}{1-\rho^2}(x^2+y^2-2\rho xy)}\, dx\, dy \qquad (3.15)$$

With the Cholesky decomposition (see Appendix A),

$$x = w\sqrt{1-\rho^2} + \rho z$$
$$y = z \qquad (3.16)$$

and multiplying by the Jacobian $\sqrt{1-\rho^2}$ we get

$$\frac{1}{2\pi} \int_{-\infty}^{\infty} (wz\sqrt{1-\rho^2} + \rho z^2)\, e^{-\frac{1}{2}(w^2+z^2)}\, dw\, dz \qquad (3.17)$$

which, using the integration formulas in Appendix A, equals the correlation coefficient ρ.

For n variables, we can generalize the above results in terms of the n dimensional covariance matrix, $\mathbf{C}$ and the n dimensional joint normal density:

$$f(X) = f(x_1, x_2, \ldots, x_n) = \frac{1}{2\pi^{n/2} \det \mathbf{C}} e^{-\frac{1}{2}\mathbf{x}^T \mathbf{C}^{-1} \mathbf{x}}\, d\mathbf{x} \qquad (3.18)$$

The corresponding joint lognormal density consists of logarithms of the assets in the exponentials and corresponding products of the asset prices in the denominator.

The General Ito Lemma

Suppose the governing stochastic process is

$$dx_i = a_i\, dt + b_i\, dz_i \qquad (3.19)$$

with dz_i being the Weiner processes. The continuous limit in Equation (3.19) is really obtained by taking the limit of the discrete time Brownian motion,

$$\Delta x_i = a_i \Delta t + b_i \epsilon_i \sqrt{\Delta t} \qquad (3.20)$$

so that

$$\lim_{\Delta t \to 0} \Delta x_i^2 = b_i^2 \, dt$$

$$\lim_{\Delta t \to 0} \Delta x_i \, \Delta x_j = b_i b_j \rho_{ij} \, dt \tag{3.21}$$

where we have already identified, in the previous section, ρ_{ij} as the correlation between dz_i and dz_j.

Suppose a function f depends on time t and n variables $x_1, x_2, \ldots x_n$. We can do a simple Taylor expansion of f:

$$\Delta f = \sum_i \frac{\partial f}{\partial x_i} \Delta x_i + \frac{\partial f}{\partial t} \Delta t + \frac{1}{2} \sum_i \sum_j \frac{\partial^2 f}{\partial x_i \, \partial x_j} \Delta x_i \, \Delta x_j$$

$$+ \frac{1}{2} \sum_j \frac{\partial^2 f}{\partial x_i \, \partial t} \Delta x_i \, \Delta t + \cdots \tag{3.22}$$

The first three terms in Equation (3.22) are thus all of order Δt, whereas the third term is higher order. So, in the limit of infinitesimal time intervals, we can throw away the last term and use Equation (3.19) to obtain

$$df = \sum_i \frac{\partial f}{\partial x_i} dx_i + \frac{\partial f}{\partial t} dt + \frac{1}{2} \sum_i \sum_j \frac{\partial^2 f}{\partial x_i \, \partial x_j} b_i b_j \rho_{ij} \, dt$$

$$= \left(\sum_i \frac{\partial f}{\partial x_i} a_i + \frac{\partial f}{\partial t} + \frac{1}{2} \sum_i \sum_j \frac{\partial^2 f}{\partial x_i \, \partial x_j} b_i b_j \rho_{ij} \right) dt$$

$$+ \sum_i \frac{\partial f}{\partial x_i} b_i \, dz_i \tag{3.23}$$

In principle, once this form for the multifactor stochastic process is given, any security that depends on any function of these n variables can be valued numerically. The Monte-Carlo procedure, to be discussed in Chapter 5 (on numerical methods), takes the last equation and generates "paths" based on draws from correlated random variates with the specified joint distribution and covariance matrix.

Now, we want to value a general derivative asset $C(S_i, t)$, which depends on the n assets i and time t. From Ito's lemma, given above, applied for joint lognormal assets as in Equation (3.6):

$$dC = \left[\frac{\partial C}{\partial t} + \sum_i (\mu_i - d_i) S_i \frac{\partial C}{\partial S_i} + \frac{1}{2} \sum_{i,j} \rho_{ij} \sigma_i \sigma_j S_i S_j \frac{\partial^2 C}{\partial S_i \, \partial S_j} \right] dt$$

$$+ \sum_i \sigma_i S_i \frac{\partial C}{\partial S_i} \, dz_i \qquad\qquad (3.24)$$

We can construct a locally riskless portfolio $\mathcal{P}$ consisting of one unit of C and $-\Delta_i = \partial C / \partial S_i$ units of S_i:

$$dP = \left[\frac{\partial C}{\partial t} + \sum_i (\mu_i - d_i) S_i \frac{\partial C}{\partial S_i} + \frac{1}{2} \sum_{i,j} \rho_{ij} \sigma_i \sigma_j S_i S_j \frac{\partial^2 C}{\partial S_i \, \partial S_j} \right.$$

$$\left. - \sum_i \mu_i S_i \frac{\partial C}{\partial S_i} \right] dt + \sum_i \sigma_i S_i \frac{\partial C}{\partial S_i} \, dz_i - \sum_i \sigma_i S_i \frac{\partial C}{\partial S_i} \, dz_i \quad (3.25)$$

Then,

$$dP = \left[\frac{\partial C}{\partial t} - \sum_i d_i S_i \frac{\partial C}{\partial S_i} + \frac{1}{2} \sum_{i,j} \rho_{ij} \sigma_i \sigma_j S_i S_j \frac{\partial^2 C}{\partial S_i \partial S_j} \right] dt \qquad (3.26)$$

should simply equal the risk-free growth (otherwise there are arbitrage opportunities):

$$dP = rP \, dt = r \left(C - \sum_i S_i \frac{\partial C}{\partial S_i} \right) dt \qquad (3.27)$$

so that, finally, we get the multivariate Black-Scholes equation

$$\frac{\partial C}{\partial t} + \sum_i (r - d_i) S_i \frac{\partial C}{\partial S_i} + \frac{1}{2} \sum_{i,j} \rho_{ij} \sigma_i \sigma_j S_i S_j \frac{\partial^2 C}{\partial S_i \, \partial S_j} = rC \qquad (3.28)$$

Thus, the local change $\partial C / \partial t$ in the option price can be written as the sum of three terms:

$$r\left(C - \sum_i S_i \frac{\partial C}{\partial S_i}\right) = \text{interest earned on cash position}$$

$$\sum_i d_i S_i \frac{\partial C}{\partial S_i} = \text{gain from dividend yield}$$

$$-\frac{1}{2}\sum_{i,j} \rho_{ij}\sigma_i\sigma_j S_i S_j \frac{\partial^2 C}{\partial S_i \partial S_j} = \text{hedging costs or slippage} \qquad (3.29)$$

Note that the term identified as the "hedging cost" term has a general dependence on the covariance matrix. Since the covariance matrix is composed of variances and correlations, we see clearly that the cost of hedging will vary as the volatilities of the assets change, as well as when the *cross-correlations* change. In particular, as the cross terms relate one asset to another asset, hedges in one asset have, in general, to be readjusted as the other asset's levels and relationships change.

Deriving Densities

As shown in Appendix J, and as is well known, the Equation (3.28) we have obtained above is nothing but the diffusion equation, in a nonstandard form. In one dimension, it takes the form

$$\frac{\partial C}{\partial t} = rC - (r - d)S\frac{\partial C}{\partial S} - \frac{1}{2}\sigma^2 S^2 \frac{\partial^2 C}{\partial S^2} \qquad (3.30)$$

To make it more tractable, we can change variables to go to dimensionless form:

$$R = \frac{S}{K}$$

$$G = KC$$

$$\tau = \sigma^2(T - t)$$

$$\rho = \frac{r}{\sigma^2}$$

$$\mu = \frac{r - d}{\sigma^2} \qquad (3.31)$$

so that the equation becomes, for a single asset,

$$\frac{\partial G}{\partial \tau} = \frac{1}{2} R^2 \frac{\partial^2 G}{\partial R^2} + \mu R \frac{\partial G}{\partial R} - \rho G \qquad (3.32)$$

Now change variables again:

$$y = \ln R \qquad (3.33)$$

to get

$$\frac{\partial G}{\partial \tau} = \frac{1}{2} \frac{\partial^2 G}{\partial y^2} + \alpha \frac{\partial G}{\partial y} - \rho G \qquad (3.34)$$

where

$$\alpha \equiv \mu - \tfrac{1}{2} \qquad (3.35)$$

Now we can Fourier transform in y (see Appendix J[2]):

$$H(k) = \frac{1}{\sqrt{2\pi}} \int_{-\infty}^{\infty} dy \, e^{iky} G(y) \qquad (3.36)$$

to get the Fourier-transformed version of the PDE:

$$\frac{\partial H}{\partial \tau} = -\left(\frac{k^2}{2} + ik\alpha + \rho \right) H \qquad (3.37)$$

which has the solution

$$H(\tau) = H(0) \, e^{-\left(\frac{k^2}{2} + ik\alpha + \rho \right)\tau} \qquad (3.38)$$

Now if we assume that the initial condition at time $t = 0$ is simply a delta function payoff,[3] then, since its Fourier transform is simply a constant:

$$\frac{1}{\sqrt{2\pi}} \int_{-\infty}^{\infty} e^{-iky} \, \delta(y) \, dy = \frac{1}{\sqrt{2\pi}} \qquad (3.39)$$

---

2. We could have alternatively chosen to solve the PDE using a Laplace transform in time, or an eigenfunction expansion. Alternative techniques of solution are also described in Appendix J.

3. This is appropriate since we want to simply evaluate the probability density or Green function, which is the basic building block. Once the value for a delta function payoff is known, the solution of any other payoff can be obtained by appropriately weighting a number of delta function payoffs. This is the manipulation that lets option traders decompose any option payoff into combinations of so-called "microbinaries" or "digitals."

we have

$$H(\tau) = \frac{1}{\sqrt{2\pi}} \, e^{-(\frac{k^2}{2} + ik\alpha + \rho)\tau} \tag{3.40}$$

Now that we have the solution in k space, we can simply do an inverse Fourier transform:

$$
\begin{aligned}
G(y) &= \frac{1}{\sqrt{2\pi}} \int_{-\infty}^{\infty} dk \, e^{-iky} H(k) \\
&= \frac{e^{-\rho t}}{2\pi} \int_{-\infty}^{\infty} dk \, e^{-\frac{1}{2}\left(k\sqrt{\tau} + i\frac{y+\alpha\tau}{\sqrt{\tau}}\right)^2 - \frac{(y+\alpha\tau)^2}{2\tau}} \\
&= \frac{e^{-\rho\tau - \frac{(y+\alpha\tau)^2}{2\tau}}}{2\pi} \int_{-\infty + i\frac{(y+\alpha\tau)}{\tau}}^{\infty + i\frac{(y+\alpha\tau)}{\tau}} dk' \, e^{-\frac{1}{2}k'^2\tau} \\
&= \frac{1}{\sqrt{2\pi\tau}} e^{-\rho\tau - \frac{(y+\alpha\tau)^2}{2\tau}} \tag{3.41}
\end{aligned}
$$

and now, putting back the original definitions, we get back the familiar lognormal density for a single asset. Note that we could have chosen arbitrary initial conditions right from the very beginning, in which case the Equation (3.38) would have the value of the Fourier transform of that initial condition. In this method of solution, the initial condition gets incorporated directly.

Now we will generalize the Fourier transform method to the vector Fourier transform method for multiple assets. We start with

$$\frac{\partial C}{\partial t} + \sum_{i} (r - d_i) S_i \frac{\partial C}{\partial S_i} + \frac{1}{2} \sum_{i,j} \rho_{ij} \sigma_i \sigma_j S_i S_j \frac{\partial^2 C}{\partial S_i \, \partial S_j} = rC \tag{3.42}$$

and make the change of variables:

$$
\begin{aligned}
y_i &= \ln\left(\frac{S_i}{K_i}\right) \\
\tau &= T - t \\
G &= C K_1 \dots K_n \\
a_i &= r - d_i - \tfrac{1}{2}\sigma_i^2 \tag{3.43}
\end{aligned}
$$

so that we get the dimensionless form

$$\frac{\partial G}{\partial \tau} - \sum_i a_i \frac{\partial G}{\partial y_i} - \frac{1}{2} \sum_{i,j} \rho_{ij}\sigma_i\sigma_j \frac{\partial^2 G}{\partial y_i \, \partial y_j} = -rG \qquad (3.44)$$

Now we do an n dimensional Fourier transform:

$$H(\mathbf{y}) = \frac{1}{(2\pi)^{n/2}} \int_{-\infty}^{\infty} \cdots \int_{-\infty}^{\infty} e^{-i\mathbf{k}\cdot\mathbf{y}} G(y_1, \ldots, y_n) \, dy_1 \ldots dy_n \qquad (3.45)$$

Applying the Fourier transform to the PDE and using the initial condition that we have an n dimensional point source or delta function, i.e.,

$$G(0) = \delta(y_1, \ldots, y_n) \qquad (3.46)$$

which has the Fourier transform

$$H(0) = \frac{1}{(2\pi)^{n/2}} \qquad (3.47)$$

we get, in terms of the covariance matrix $\mathbf{C}$:

$$\frac{\partial H}{\partial \tau} = -(\tfrac{1}{2}\mathbf{k}^T\mathbf{C}\mathbf{k} + i\mathbf{a}\mathbf{k} + r)H \qquad (3.48)$$

Solving this, we get

$$H(\tau) = H(0)e^{(-\frac{1}{2}\mathbf{k}^T\mathbf{C}\mathbf{k} + i\mathbf{a}\mathbf{k} + r)\tau}$$

$$= \frac{1}{(2\pi)^{n/2}} e^{(-\frac{1}{2}\mathbf{k}^T\mathbf{C}\mathbf{k} + i\mathbf{a}\mathbf{k} + r)\tau} \qquad (3.49)$$

To invert this Fourier transform,

$$G(\mathbf{y}) = \frac{1}{(2\pi)^n} e^{-r\tau} \int_{-\infty}^{\infty} \cdots \int_{-\infty}^{\infty} e^{-(\frac{\tau}{2}\mathbf{k}^T\mathbf{C}\mathbf{k} + i(\mathbf{a}\tau + \mathbf{y})\mathbf{k})} \, d\mathbf{k} \qquad (3.50)$$

we change variables (using the Cholesky decomposition given in Appendix A):

$$d\mathbf{k} = \frac{d\mathbf{q}}{\sqrt{|\tau \mathrm{Det}\mathbf{C}|}} \qquad (3.51)$$

So

$$G(\mathbf{y}) = \frac{e^{-r\tau}}{(2\pi)^n\sqrt{|\tau \mathrm{Det}\mathbf{C}|}} \int_{-\infty}^{\infty} \cdots \int_{-\infty}^{\infty} d\mathbf{q}\, e^{-[\frac{1}{2}\mathbf{q}^T\mathbf{q} + i(\mathbf{a}\tau + \mathbf{y})(\tau\mathbf{C})^{-\frac{1}{2}}\mathbf{q}]} \qquad (3.52)$$

which gives

$$G(\mathbf{y}) = \frac{e^{-r\tau - \frac{1}{2}(\mathbf{a}\tau + \mathbf{y})\mathbf{C}^{-1}(\mathbf{a}\tau + \mathbf{y})}}{(2\pi)^n \sqrt{\tau |\mathrm{Det}(\mathbf{C})|}} \int_{-\infty}^{\infty} \cdots \int_{-\infty}^{\infty} d\mathbf{q}\, e^{-\frac{1}{2}[\mathbf{q} + i(\mathbf{a}\tau + \mathbf{y})(\tau\mathbf{C})^{-\frac{1}{2}}]^2}$$

$$= \frac{e^{-r\tau - \frac{1}{2\tau}(\mathbf{a}\tau + \mathbf{y})\mathbf{C}^{-1}(\mathbf{a}\tau + \mathbf{y})}}{(2\pi\tau)^{n/2}|\mathrm{Det}\mathbf{C}|^{\frac{1}{2}}} \qquad (3.53)$$

Now, replacing all the definitions with the original variables, we get

$$C(S_t, t) = \frac{e^{-r(T-t)}}{(2\pi(T-t))^{n/2}|\mathrm{Det}\mathbf{C}|^{\frac{1}{2}}S_{1,T}\cdots S_{n,T}}$$

$$\times e^{-\frac{1}{2(T-t)}[(\ln\frac{S_T}{S_t} - \mathbf{a}(T-t))^T\mathbf{C}^{-1}(\ln\frac{S_T}{S_t} - \mathbf{a}(T-t))]} \qquad (3.54)$$

which is the general form of the multivariate lognormal density with n lognormal variables, of which we have seen a special case above for two assets. Thus, we see that the joint lognormal density is the Green function or point source solution of the multidimensional Black-Scholes equation. From here on, this density will be used as the fundamental multivariate probability for valuing multi-asset options.

Barrier Densities

Now, we generalize the above densities to two simple cases where there are contingencies, i.e., the option only pays off as some function of the terminal asset price S_T if the asset price never crosses a barrier B at any time before the terminal time T. In Appendix J we show the details of the explicit solution of this problem using Laplace transforms in time for the partial differential equation. Here, note that if the drift $\alpha = 0$, then we can exactly cancel out the density at the barrier by subtracting off the density of a Brownian motion starting at $2b$ by using the reflection principle as displayed in Figure 3–1. We define the barrier in logarithmic or return space as

$$b = \ln(B/S_T) \qquad (3.55)$$

Then,

$$G_{\text{Single barrier, zero drift}} = \frac{1}{\sqrt{2\pi\tau}} \left(e^{\frac{-y^2}{2\tau}} - e^{\frac{-(y-2b)^2}{2\tau}} \right) \qquad (3.56)$$

We can correct for a nonzero drift using the Girsanov theorem (Appendix I) to get, finally,

$$G_{\text{Single barrier, nonzero drift}} = \frac{1}{\sqrt{2\pi\tau}} e^{\alpha\left(y - \frac{1}{2}\alpha\tau\right)} \left(e^{\frac{-y^2}{2\tau}} - e^{\frac{-(y-2b)^2}{2\tau}} \right) \qquad (3.57)$$

Now we can again derive the density for a double-barrier option, which has an upper barrier at u and a lower barrier at b in logarithmic space, using the method of images as shown in Figure 3–2. Appendix J shows the Laplace transform solution straight from the PDE. Correcting for the driftless case $\alpha = 0$ with the Girsanov factor, we obtain:

FIGURE 3–1

Single-Barrier Method of Images

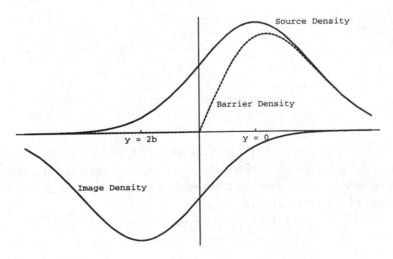

Double-Barrier Method of Images

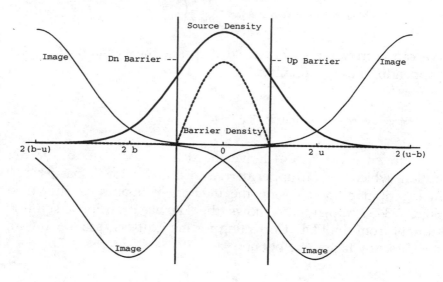

$$G_{\text{Double barrier}} = \frac{1}{\sqrt{2\pi\tau}} e^{\alpha(y - \frac{1}{2}\alpha\tau)}$$

$$\times \left[e^{-\frac{1}{2}\frac{y^2}{\tau}} \right.$$

$$+ \sum_{i=1}^{\infty} e^{-\frac{1}{2\tau}(y - 2iu + 2(i-1)b)^2} + e^{-\frac{1}{2\tau}(y - 2ib + 2(i-1)u)^2}$$

$$+ \left. \sum_{i=1}^{\infty} e^{-\frac{1}{2\tau}(y - 2i(u-b))^2} + e^{-\frac{1}{2\tau}(y - 2i(b-u))^2} \right] \qquad (3.58)$$

where the first term in the sum is the contribution from the non-barrier density, the second term is the contribution from the images for the upper and lower boundaries, and the last sum is the extra term required to cancel the "intersection."

Finally, we will derive an "outside" barrier density which will be used to price barrier options that have two assets. Assume that the two Brownian motions are

$$dX_t = \mu_1 \, dt + \sigma_1 \, dz_1, \qquad X_0 = 0$$
$$dY_t = \mu_2 \, dt + \sigma_2 \, dz_2, \qquad Y_0 = 0 \tag{3.59}$$

where μ_1 and μ_2 are known constant drifts, and σ_1 and σ_2 are known constant volatilities. Also,

$$dz_1 \, dz_2 = \rho \, dt \tag{3.60}$$

where ρ is assumed to be deterministic. We will take the Y process to be the contingent process, i.e., the one with the barrier. The X process could have a call option based on it as long as the Y process remains clear of the barrier. To be specific, we will first imagine that we are pricing an up-and-out call based on X which knocks out if Y reaches b. The call option pays off only if during the life of the option T the Y process does not cross b.[4] Since $Y_0 = 0$, we also assume that $b > 0$, so the barrier is being approached from below. Now let τ_b^Y be the first time before expiration that the Y process crosses the barrier b from below. To compute the value of the option, we will need the joint distribution of X and Y, given that Y is less than the barrier at expiration and at all times prior to expiration.

Thus, we need

$$\int_{-\infty}^{X} \int_{-\infty}^{b} f(X_T, Y_T | \tau_b^Y > T) \, dY_T \, dX_T \tag{3.61}$$

i.e., the cumulative joint conditional distribution at expiration given that the Y process does not cross b at any interim time.

We first make the change of variables:

$$Z_t = X_t - \rho Y_t$$
$$Y_t = Y_t \tag{3.62}$$

so that

$$Z_t \cdot Y_t = X_t \cdot Y_t - \rho Y_t^2 = \rho \sigma_1 \sigma_2 - \rho \sigma_2^2 \tag{3.63}$$

Now, if we assume that $\sigma_1 = \sigma_2 = 1$, then $Z_t \cdot Y_t = 0$, i.e., Z_t and Y_t are independent. Thus, we will first solve the problem with this

---

4. Note that b is the barrier in return space.

assumption and then rescale the variances back to get the final solution. In these units, the mean of Z_T equals $\mu_1 T - \rho\mu_2 T$.

With $\sigma_1 = \sigma_2 = 1$, the independence implies factorization of the joint density

$$f(X_T, Y_T | \tau_b^Y > T) = f(Z_T)f(Y_T | \tau_b^Y > T) \tag{3.64}$$

which implies that the cumulative distribution (with the + signifying crossing from below)

$$F_+(X_T < X, \tau_b^y > T)$$

$$= \frac{1}{\sqrt{2\pi(1-\rho^2)T}} \int_{-\infty}^{X} \int_{-\infty}^{b} e^{-\frac{1}{2(1-\rho^2)T}(X_T - \rho Y_T - \mu_1 T - \rho\mu_2 T)^2}$$

$$f(Y_T | \tau_b^Y > T) \, dX_T \, dY_T$$

But $f(Y_T | \tau_b^Y > T)$ is simply the one-sided first-passage time density for a Brownian motion with drift, which has the distribution

$$F(Y_T < Y | \tau_b^Y > T) = N\left(\frac{1}{\sqrt{T}}(Y - \mu_2 T)\right)$$

$$- e^{2\mu_2 b} N\left(\frac{1}{\sqrt{T}}(Y - 2b - \mu_2 T)\right) \tag{3.65}$$

in terms of the standard cumulative normal distribution.

Now we will revert back to our original variances by rescaling:

$$X_T \rightarrow \frac{X_T}{\sigma_1}$$

$$Y_T \rightarrow \frac{Y_T}{\sigma_2}$$

$$\mu_1 \rightarrow \frac{\mu_1}{\sigma_1}$$

$$\mu_2 \rightarrow \frac{\mu_2}{\sigma_2}$$

$$b \rightarrow \frac{b}{\sigma_2}$$

to obtain, finally, the distribution for X at terminal time T given that at any interim time the barrier b has not been breached *from below* by Y:

$$F_+(X_T < X, \tau_b^Y > T) = N\left(\frac{X - \mu_1 T}{\sigma_1\sqrt{T}}, \frac{b - \mu_2 T}{\sigma_2\sqrt{T}}; \rho\right) \qquad (3.66)$$

$$- e^{\frac{2b\mu_2}{\sigma_2^2}} N\left(\frac{X - \mu_1 T - 2\rho b}{\sigma_1\sqrt{T}}, \frac{-b - \mu_2 T}{\sigma_2\sqrt{T}}; \rho\right)$$

where $N(a, b; \rho)$ is the standard bivariate cumulative normal distribution with upper limits a and b and correlation ρ.

When $b < 0$, i.e., the barrier is approached from above, we get, by changing (this is a symmetry)

$$b \to -b$$

$$\mu_2 \to -\mu_2$$

$$\rho \to -\rho$$

the appropriate outside distribution

$$F_-(X_T < X, \tau_b^Y > T) = N\left(\frac{X - \mu_1 T}{\sigma_1\sqrt{T}}, \frac{-b + \mu_2 T}{\sigma_2\sqrt{T}}; -\rho\right) \qquad (3.67)$$

$$- e^{\frac{2b\mu_2}{\sigma_2^2}} N\left(\frac{X - \mu_1 T - 2\rho b}{\sigma_1\sqrt{T}}, \frac{b + \mu_2 T}{\sigma_2\sqrt{T}}; -\rho\right)$$

We can also derive a double-barrier outside density in the same way in terms of an infinite summation. This will be left as an exercise for the interested reader.

SYMMETRIES, INVARIANCES, AND EQUIVALENCES

The study of symmetry properties of the Black-Scholes equation with given boundary conditions for a single asset easily yields some key results, such as put–call parity.[5] In general, a multiasset Ito diffusion process possesses some invariances, i.e., transformations of variables and/or parameters under which it remains invariant. If the procedure by which we derive the local differential equation does not violate any of these invariances, the final partial differential equation that one obtains should also respect the sym-

---

5. Its generalization—put–call symmetry, for calls and puts with different strikes—is discussed later.

metries. Hence, the solutions of the partial differential equations will also respect the symmetries, *unless some extraneously imposed boundary conditions break the invariances*. If, after imposing the boundary conditions, the system of partial differential equations plus boundary conditions still respects some symmetries, then the final solutions with boundary conditions should certainly respect the residual symmetries. Once we know what the residual symmetries are, any solution of the PDE that respects these symmetries is a good solution. Any solution that does not respect the residual symmetries can be eliminated. In many cases, this is enough to determine uniquely the solution of fairly complicated problems.

Symmetries can come in two distinct varieties. Simple symmetries, such as the exchange of asset price with strike and dividend yield with interest rate, which leads to put–call parity, are discrete symmetries. Also, the symmetry given in Equation (3.67) that takes the up-barrier density to the down-barrier density is a discrete symmetry. This is analogous to the symmetry of a square on flipping it, or rotating it by a multiple of 90 degrees. In mathematical parlance, the discrete symmetry of parity defines a *discrete group* Z_2, in the same way as all the actions that keep the square a square (a finite number of them) are closed among themselves to form a group. Quite distinct from discrete symmetries are continuous symmetries. The hallmark of continuous symmetries is that the number of actions that leave the system invariant are, in general, infinite, and they can be parametrized in terms of some parameters and generators of the symmetry. Continuous groups go under the name of Lie Groups, and they have played an important role in the development of modern science. All group structures, whether discrete or continuous, possess a unique identity transformation which does nothing, a unique inverse transformation which undoes things, and a rule for composing a sequence of transformations (commutation laws and associative laws). Once additional structure, such as boundary conditions, is imposed, some of the original set of invariances may cease to be invariances, and the new subset of invariances, or subgroups, may restrict the possible form of the final solutions differently than the original set of symmetries.

The reason we have gone into such detail in describing the mathematics of symmetry is because it makes life much easier on the trading desk, where speed of calculation and hedging is critical.

For instance, calls on one currency are puts on the countercurrency; or spreads and ratios can be priced in terms of single-asset options. For single-factor options, it is easy to run the pricing algorithm and reprice a structure without recourse to external knowledge about the relationships between different exotic structures. However, when a multiasset exotic, path-dependent portfolio is considered, knowledge of simple symmetry-based relationships can not only make the pricing and hedging faster, but can also lead to better profits due to exact analytic solutions rather than numerical approximations. In addition to linear cancellations performed in the process of dynamical hedging, recognition of symmetry properties enables nonlinear cancellations to "all-orders," i.e., it provides a mechanism for discovering static hedges.

These are tools that have proved useful in practical life, and I advise that they be learnt. We turn thus to symmetries of general multifactor processes and a discussion of how are they broken and what remains, after the symmetry breaking, for special payoffs.

Single-Asset Symmetries

Recall that in the Black-Scholes model for one asset, the formula for a call option with strike K maturing at time T is given by

$$C = S e^{-dT} N(x_1) - K e^{-rT} N(x_2) \qquad (3.68)$$

where

$$x_1 = \frac{\ln(S/K) + (r - d)T}{\sigma\sqrt{T}} + \frac{1}{2}\sigma\sqrt{T}$$

$$x_2 = \frac{\ln(S/K) + (r - d)T}{\sigma\sqrt{T}} - \frac{1}{2}\sigma\sqrt{T}$$

Dividing Equation (3.68) throughout by K, we can write

$$\frac{C}{K} = \frac{S}{K}e^{-dT}N(x_1) - e^{-rT}N(x_2) \qquad (3.69)$$

which shows that if we multiply S and K by the same factor, we do not change the pricing problem—since the right-hand side is invariant, the left-hand side is invariant and picks up the same scaling. This is a special property of the Brownian motion for the return process since both the drift and stochastic terms there are proportional to the same power of S.[6]

For a put, we can also write down the price

$$P = K e^{-rT} N(y_1) - S e^{-dT} N(y_2) \tag{3.70}$$

where

$$y_1 = \frac{\ln(K/S) + (d - r)T}{\sigma\sqrt{T}} + \frac{1}{2}\sigma\sqrt{T}$$

$$y_2 = \frac{\ln(K/S) + (d - r)T}{\sigma\sqrt{T}} - \frac{1}{2}\sigma\sqrt{T}$$

which is identical to the formula for the call as in Equation (3.69) but with

$$S \leftrightarrow K$$
$$d \leftrightarrow r$$

For traders who trade currency options this is no surprise, since the call on dollars vs yen is simply the put on yen vs dollars. Similarly, call options on stock price in dollar terms can be thought of as put options on dollars in stock price terms as the numeraire. The dividend yield of the stock price is similar to the interest rate of the currency—thus completing the reflexivity. The price of a call or put can be written in terms of one equation [179]:

$$C \text{ (or) } P = \phi[S e^{-dT} N(\phi x_1) - K e^{-rT} N(\phi x_2)] \tag{3.71}$$

where we use $\phi = 1$ for calls and $\phi = -1$ for puts, and use the identity $N(-x) = 1 - N(x)$.

Margrabe Trick

Suppose now we have a payoff for an outperformance option at maturity time T:

$$C_T = \max[S_{2,T} - K S_{1,T}, 0] \tag{3.72}$$

Dividing throughout by $S_{1,T}$, we get

---

6. This may or may not be a symmetry for more general stochastic processes.

$$C_T' = \frac{C_T}{S_{1,T}} = \max\left[\frac{S_{2,T}}{S_{1,T}} - K, 0\right] = \max[S' - K, 0] \qquad (3.73)$$

which looks like the payoff of a standard call in the asset given by the ratio $S_{2,T}/S_{1,T}$ with the corrected volatility $\sqrt{\sigma_1^2 + \sigma_2^2 - 2\rho_{1,2}\sigma_1\sigma_2}$. So the general conclusion is that one can change the numeraire by changing the risk-neutral stochastic process such that the new drift term has the difference of the "dividend yields" (or cost of carry) of the asset and the currency, and the noise term has variance computed with the correct covariance between the asset and the currency in it.

Multiasset Symmetries

Now we catalog some of the symmetries of the multifactor Black-Scholes equation:

$$\frac{\partial C}{\partial t} + \sum_i (r - d_i) S_i \frac{\partial C}{\partial S_i} + \frac{1}{2} \sum_{i,j} \sigma_i \sigma_j S_i S_j \frac{\partial^2 C}{\partial S_i \, \partial S_j} = rC \qquad (3.74)$$

- Temporal Rescaling Invariance:

$$t \to t e^\epsilon$$
$$r \to r e^{-\epsilon}$$
$$d_i \to d_i e^{-\epsilon}$$
$$\sigma_i \to \sigma_i e^{-\frac{1}{2}\epsilon} \qquad (3.75)$$

- Power Law Invariance:

$$S_i \to S_i^{1+\epsilon}$$
$$d_i \to d_i(1+\epsilon) - \epsilon(r + \tfrac{1}{2}(1+\epsilon)\sigma_i^2)$$
$$\sigma_i \to (1+\epsilon)\sigma_i \qquad (3.76)$$

- Asset Recombination:

$$S_i \to S_i(S_k)^\epsilon$$
$$d_i \to d_i(1 + \epsilon) - \epsilon(r - d_k + \rho_{ik}\sigma_i\sigma_k + \tfrac{1}{2}(\epsilon - 1)\sigma_k^2)$$
$$\sigma_i \to \sqrt{\sigma_i^2 + 2\epsilon\rho_{ik}\sigma_i\sigma_k + \epsilon^2\sigma_k^2}$$
$$\rho_{ij} \to \frac{\rho_{ij}\sigma_i + \epsilon\rho_{jk}\sigma_j}{\sqrt{\sigma_i^2 + 2\epsilon\rho_{ik}\sigma_i\sigma_k + \epsilon^2\sigma_k^2}} \qquad\qquad (3.77)$$

- Derivative Rescaling:

$$C \to C(S_k)^\epsilon$$
$$r \to r - \epsilon(r - d_k + \tfrac{1}{2}(\epsilon - 1)\sigma_k^2)$$
$$d_i \to d_i - \epsilon(r - d_k + \tfrac{1}{2}(1 + \epsilon)\rho_{ik}\sigma_i\sigma_k) \qquad (3.78)$$

- Generalized Margrabe Trick:

$$S_i \to \frac{S_i}{S_k} \ \forall i \neq k$$
$$S_k \to \frac{1}{S_k}$$
$$C \to \frac{C}{S_k}$$
$$r \to d_k$$
$$d_k \to r$$
$$\sigma_i \to \sqrt{\sigma_i^2 - 2\rho_{ik}\sigma_i\sigma_k + \sigma_k^2}$$
$$\rho_{ij} \to \frac{\rho_{ij}\sigma_i\sigma_j - \rho_{ik}\sigma_i\sigma_k - \rho_{jk}\sigma_j\sigma_k + \sigma_k^2}{\sqrt{\sigma_i^2 - 2\rho_{ik}\sigma_i\sigma_k + \sigma_k^2}\sqrt{\sigma_j^2 - 2\rho_{jk}\sigma_j\sigma_k + \sigma_k^2}} \ \forall i, \qquad j \neq k$$
$$\rho_{ik} \to \frac{\rho_{ik}\sigma_i - \sigma_k}{\sqrt{\sigma_i^2 - 2\rho_{ik}\sigma_i\sigma_k + \sigma_k^2}} \qquad\qquad (3.79)$$

- Barrier Symmetries: the transformation

$$b \to -b$$
$$\mu_2 \to -\mu_2$$
$$\rho \to -\rho$$

takes the distribution

$$F_+(X_T < X, \tau_b^Y > T) = N\left(\frac{X - \mu_1 T}{\sigma_1\sqrt{T}}, \frac{b - \mu_2 T}{\sigma_2\sqrt{T}}; \rho\right)$$
$$- e^{\frac{2b\mu_2}{\sigma_2^2}} N\left(\frac{X - \mu_1 T - 2\rho b}{\sigma_1\sqrt{T}}, \frac{-b - \mu_2 T}{\sigma_2\sqrt{T}}; \rho\right)$$

into

$$F_-(X_T < X, \tau_b^Y > T) = N\left(\frac{X - \mu_1 T}{\sigma_1\sqrt{T}}, \frac{-b + \mu_2 T}{\sigma_2\sqrt{T}}; -\rho\right)$$
$$- e^{\frac{2b\mu_2}{\sigma_2^2}} N\left(\frac{X - \mu_1 T - 2\rho b}{\sigma_1\sqrt{T}}, \frac{b + \mu_2 T}{\sigma_2\sqrt{T}}; -\rho\right)$$

This points to a simple way of obtaining two-factor up-barrier options from down-barrier options (see below). Also note that the sum of F_+ and F_- is then invariant under this barrier symmetry, and thus should correspond to a barrierless option, i.e., plain vanilla option. The same results work for the single-factor case since the first-passage time density for one asset is the only part above that gets affected by the symmetry.

Symmetry Breaking and Residual Invariances

As mentioned before, the presence of boundary conditions renders some of the symmetries of the original diffusion as nonsymmetries, i.e., it breaks the symmetries. We can then study the remaining symmetry, if any remains, and then *guess* the form of the final solution (since it has to be of the most general form that respects the remaining symmetries).

- Power Option: the payoff is

$$C_T = \max[S_T^{1+\epsilon} - K, 0] \tag{3.80}$$

Using Equation (3.76), we can write down the form of the solution from the plain vanilla price:

$$C = S^{1+\epsilon} e^{-d'(T-t)} N(x_1') - e^{-r(T-t)} N(x_2') \tag{3.81}$$

where

$$d' = d(1 + \epsilon) - \epsilon(r + \tfrac{1}{2}(1 + \epsilon)\sigma^2)$$
$$S' = S^{1+\epsilon}$$
$$\sigma' = (1 + \epsilon)\sigma \tag{3.82}$$

and x_1', x_2' are evaluated using these definitions.

- Outperformance Options:

$$C_T = \max[S_{2,T} - KS_{1,T}, 0]$$
$$= \max\left[\frac{S_{2,T}}{S_{1,T}} - K, 0\right] \tag{3.83}$$

Now, both the differential equation and the boundary condition have the change of numeraire symmetry or the generalized Margrabe symmetry given in Equation (3.79):

$$S_2 \to \frac{S_2}{S_1}$$
$$C \to \frac{C}{S_1}$$
$$r \to d_1$$
$$\sigma_2 \to \sqrt{\sigma_2^2 - 2\rho_{12}\sigma_1\sigma_2 + \sigma_1^2} \tag{3.84}$$

so that the most general form of the price respecting these symmetries is

$$\frac{C}{S_1} = \frac{S_2}{S_1}e^{-d_2(T-t)}N(x_1') - Ke^{-d_1(T-t)}N(x_2') \tag{3.85}$$

where, in the evaluation of the arguments of the cumulative normal densities x_1', x_2', we use

$$S = \frac{S_2}{S_1}$$
$$K = 1$$
$$r = d_1$$
$$d = d_2$$
$$\sigma = \sqrt{\sigma_2^2 - 2\rho_{12}\sigma_1\sigma_2 + \sigma_1^2} \tag{3.86}$$

- Quanto Options: the payoff or boundary condition is

$$C_T = X_T \max[S_T - K, 0]$$

$$\Rightarrow \frac{C_T}{X_T} = \max[S_T - K, 0] \tag{3.87}$$

where X_T is some exchange rate at the terminal date that determines the payoff in the local currency.

Substituting the symmetry relationships from Equation (3.78):

$$C \to \frac{C}{X}$$
$$r \to d_x$$
$$d_s \to d_s - (r - d_x + \rho_{sx}\sigma_s\sigma_x)$$
$$d_x \to 2d_x - r - \sigma_x^2 \tag{3.88}$$

to the standard Black-Scholes price, we get the correct price for the quanto option.

SPREAD OPTIONS

We now return to the pricing of spread options in the multivariate context. Note that the Margrabe symmetry trick we used above for outperformance options can only be used if the strike of the spread option is zero, otherwise the change of numeraire symmetry is completely broken. In this section, we will reduce the two-dimensional integration to a one-dimensional integration that is numerically efficient [162]. We assume that the two assets follow the process

$$dS_{1t} = (\mu_1 - d_1)S_{1t} \, dt + \sigma_1 S_{1t} \, dz_{1t}$$
$$dS_{2t} = (\mu_2 - d_2)S_{2t} \, dt + \rho\sigma_2 S_{2t} \, dz_{1t} + \sigma_2\sqrt{1 - \rho^2}S_{2t} \, dz_{2t} \tag{3.89}$$

where z_{1t} and z_{2t} are standard Brownian motions and S_1 and S_2 are assumed to be jointly lognormal. Then, the value of the European call option on the spread is[7]

$$C = e^{r(T-t)} \int_0^\infty \int_0^\infty \max[S_{2T} - S_{1T} - K, 0] g(S_{2T}|S_{1T}) f(S_{1T}) \, dS_{2T} \, dS_{1T}$$

(3.90)

where $g(S_{2T}|S_{1T})$ is the conditional density of S_{2T} given S_{1T}, $f(S_{1T})$ is the marginal density of S_{1T}, and the product of these two densities is the joint density.

$$f(S_{1T}) = \frac{1}{\sqrt{2\pi(T-t)}\sigma_1 S_{1T}} e^{-\frac{1}{2}\frac{(\ln S_{1T} - m_1)^2}{\sigma_1^2(T-t)}}$$

$$g(S_{2T}|S_{1T}) = \frac{1}{\sqrt{2\pi\sigma}S_{2T}} e^{-\frac{1}{2}\frac{\left(\ln S_{2T} - m_2 - \rho\frac{\sigma_2}{\sigma_1}(\ln S_{1T} - m_1)\right)^2}{\sigma^2}}$$

(3.91)

where

$$\sigma^2 = \sigma_2^2(1-\rho^2)(T-t)$$
$$m_1 = \ln S_{1t} + (r - d_1 - \tfrac{1}{2}\sigma_1^2)(T-t)$$
$$m_2 = \ln S_{2t} + (r - d_2 - \tfrac{1}{2}\sigma_2^2)(T-t)$$

(3.92)

and we define for use below,

$$M_2 = m_2 + \frac{\rho\sigma_2}{\sigma_1}(\ln S_{1T} - m_1)$$

(3.93)

Now, the integration limit for S_{2T} can be used to write the integral as

$$e^{-r(T-t)} \int_0^\infty \int_{\max(S_{1T}+K,0)}^\infty [S_{2T} - S_{1T} - K] g(S_{2T}|S_{1T}) \, dS_{2T} \, f(S_{1T}) \, dS_{1T}$$

(3.94)

---

7. We will discuss the numerical valuation of the American spread option in Chapter 5.

The S_{2T} integral can now be carried out in two parts:

$$\int_{\max(S_{1T}+K,0)}^{\infty} S_{2T} g(S_{2T}|S_{1T}) \, dS_{2T}$$

$$= \int_{\max(S_{1T}+K,0)}^{\infty} \frac{1}{\sqrt{2\pi}\sigma S_{2T}} S_{2T} \, e^{\frac{-\frac{1}{2}(\ln S_{2T} - M_2)^2}{\sigma^2}} \, dS_{2T}$$

$$= \frac{1}{\sqrt{2\pi}\sigma} \int_{\ln\max(S_{1T}+K,0)}^{\infty} e^y \, e^{\frac{-\frac{1}{2}(y - M_2)^2}{\sigma^2}} \, dy$$

$$= \frac{1}{\sqrt{2\pi}\sigma} \int_{\ln\max(S_{1T}+K,0)}^{\infty} e^{\frac{-\frac{1}{2}(y - (M_2 + \sigma^2))^2}{\sigma^2}} \, e^{M_2 + \frac{1}{2}\sigma^2} \, dy$$

$$= \frac{1}{\sqrt{2\pi}} \int_{\frac{\ln\max(S_{1T}+K,0) - (M_2 + \sigma^2)}{\sigma}}^{\infty} e^{-\frac{1}{2}z^2} \, e^{M_2 + \frac{1}{2}\sigma^2} \, dz$$

$$= e^{M_2 + \frac{1}{2}\sigma^2} N(x_1)$$

$$= e^A S_{2t} \left(\frac{S_{1T}}{S_{1t}}\right)^{\frac{\rho\sigma_2}{\sigma_1}} N(x_1) \tag{3.95}$$

where

$$A = \left[r\left(1 - \frac{\rho\sigma_2}{\sigma_1}\right) - \left(d_2 - d_1 \frac{\rho\sigma_2}{\sigma_1}\right) + \frac{1}{2}\rho\sigma_2(\sigma_1 - \rho\sigma_2) \right](T - t)$$

$$x_1 = \frac{M_2 + \sigma^2 - \ln\max(S_{1T}+K,0)}{\sigma}$$

Also,

$$\int_{\max(S_{1T}+K,0)}^{\infty} (S_{1T} + K) g(S_{2T}|S_{1T}) \, dS_{2T}$$

$$= \int_{\ln\max(S_{1T}+K,0)}^{\infty} \frac{S_{1T} + K}{\sqrt{2\pi}\sigma} e^{-\frac{1}{2}\frac{(y - M_2)^2}{\sigma^2}} \, dy$$

$$= (S_{1T} + K) N(x_2)$$

where

$$x_2 = \frac{M_2 - \ln\max(S_{1T}+K,0)}{\sigma} \tag{3.96}$$

Now, with the definition

$$F(S_{1T}) = e^A S_{2t} \left(\frac{S_{1T}}{S_{1t}}\right)^{\frac{\rho\sigma_2}{\sigma_1}} N(x_1) - (S_{1T} + K)N(x_2) \qquad (3.97)$$

the price of the spread option is

$$e^{-r(T-t)} \int_0^\infty F(S_{1T})f(S_{1T})\,dS_{1T} \qquad (3.98)$$

which is now a simple *one-dimensional* integral that can be attacked by a one-dimensional numerical integration routine (see Chapter 5 on numerical techniques for both the bivariate and the univariate integration technique).

CONSTRUCTING THE EXPLICIT DYNAMIC HEDGE

A constant reminder throughout this book will be that the approach to pricing any given product, especially exotic and hybrid options, should begin with a careful consideration of what would be needed to hedge the exposure dynamically once the product is sitting in the books. Frequently, the very exercise of trying to create a theoretical hedge not only enlightens the pricing mechanism, but also forces one to think about the relative advantages of entering into the trade. In the current section, we will go through the exercise of pricing a *differential swap* by constructing an explicit dynamic hedge. Further details of the method are found in Reference [118].

In simplest terms, a differential swap is a product in which the interest rates in two different currencies are settled in one currency. So the interest rate in one currency simply acts as an index. Consider, for example, a diff swap in which, at each payment date, the buyer of the swap pays the seller a U.S. dollar amount equal to a fixed notional amount times the value of a prespecified U.S. floating interest rate. The seller pays the buyer a dollar amount equal to the same notional amount times a prespecified Japanese floating interest rate. If an environment like the one at the time of this writing persists, where the U.S. rates are much higher than the Japanese rates, the buyer will end up paying more than the seller (assuming the same sign in the interest-rate differential for each forward rate), so, at inception, the seller has to give the buyer a cash amount to make the whole trade zero cost. We will find here the value of this upfront cost and the hedging strategy.

At first glance, it might seem that the hedge for the buyer is simply to be short some U.S. interest-rate futures and long some yen-denominated yen interest-rate futures. However, this is not a complete hedge. Assume that the yen rates rise at some point in the future, and at the same time the yen gets stronger vs the dollar. Now, the buyer of the swap loses money on the long yen interest-rate futures, but since the yen is stronger and he has to settle mark-to-market losses during a much stronger yen environment, he loses more than if there was no correlation between the exchange rate and the interest rates. So the correlation hurts him (note that if yen rates were to fall, the same sign of correlation will result in less than the zero-correlation gain also), and thus he will require compensation for the adverse correlation. To hedge the correlation exposure, he needs to have some hedge exposure in the currency; how much, we can determine by creating a local hedge portfolio.

We assume that the correlation between the forward exchange rates and the Japanese forward interest rates is deterministic.[8] We will now proceed to construct a self-financing, dynamically rebalancing trading strategy that replicates the payoff for each period of the diff swap. Then, the initial cost of instituting this strategy should equal the initial price of the diff swap, or an arbitrage opportunity is created.

To construct the hedging strategy at time t consider three times $t \leq T < \tau$ around a single reset and the following strategy: buy $n_{t,\tau}$ number of U.S. τ maturity zero-coupon bonds, short $m_{t,\tau}$ number of τ maturity Japanese zero-coupon bonds, and also buy $m_{t,T}$ number of T maturity Japanese zero-coupon bonds. Set (we will see why this selection is appropriate):

$$n_{t,\tau} = \frac{V_t}{P_{t,\tau}}$$

$$m_{t,\tau} = \frac{V_t}{X_t Q_{t,\tau}}$$

$$m_{t,T} = \frac{V_t}{X_t Q_{t,T}} \tag{3.99}$$

---

8. This can be generalized by building a stochastic correlation model, which some have valiantly attempted. I find the present-generation stochastic correlation models far from satisfactory.

where we use X_t for the exchange rate in dollars per yen, $P_{t,\tau}$ for the time t price of a τ maturity U.S. zero-coupon bond, and $Q_{t,\tau}$ for the time t price of a τ maturity Japanese zero-coupon bond. Now, with this identification, the value of the portfolio at time t is

$$V_t = n_{t,\tau}P_{t,\tau} + X_t(m_{t,T}Q_{t,T} - m_{t,\tau}Q_{t,\tau}) \qquad (3.100)$$

Holding this portfolio for the small time interval dt, we get the instantaneous change dV_t in the dollar value of the portfolio to equal

$$dV_t = n_{t,\tau}\,dP_{t,\tau} + (X_t + dX_t)[m_{t,T}\,dQ_{t,T} - m_{t,\tau}\,dQ_{t,\tau}] \qquad (3.101)$$

which, with the substitutions from Equation (3.99) and using $dX_t\,dY_t = \mathrm{Cov}_t[dX_t, dY_t]$, gives

$$\frac{dV_t}{V_t} = \frac{dP_{t,\tau}}{P_{t,\tau}} + \frac{dQ_{t,\tau}}{Q_{t,T}} - \frac{dQ_{t,\tau}}{Q_{t,\tau}} - \mathrm{Cov}_t\left[\frac{dQ_{t,\tau}}{Q_{t,\tau}} - \frac{dQ_{t,T}}{Q_{t,T}}, \frac{dX_t}{X_t}\right] \qquad (3.102)$$

This equation can now be solved to get

$$V_t \equiv V_{T,\tau}(t) = \frac{P_{t,\tau}Q_{t,T}}{Q_{t,\tau}}\,e^{\int_t^T \mathrm{Cov}\left[\frac{dQ_\tau}{Q_\tau} - \frac{dQ_T}{Q_T}, \frac{dX}{X} + \frac{dQ_\tau}{Q_\tau} - \frac{dP_\tau}{P_\tau}\right]} \qquad (3.103)$$

Note what happens as $t \to T$. The T maturity Japanese bonds have just matured, and their principal can be used to cover the short position in the τ maturity Japanese bonds. Since $V_{T,\tau}(T) = P_{T,\tau}/Q_{T,\tau}$, we are left with $n_{T,\tau} = 1/Q_{T,\tau}$ U.S. τ maturity zero-coupon bonds which can be held to maturity to collect the principal $1/Q_{T,\tau}$ at time τ. This V_t can be thought of as the price of a "quanto roll bond" for all times $t \le T$. Note that another interpretation of the long $n_{t,\tau}$ U.S. bond and short $m_{t,\tau}$ positions, along with the spot exchange transaction in this replicating portfolio, is equivalent to a forward exchange-rate agreement for the τ maturity.

Generalizing the single reset case to n resets, with a slight change of notation (putting maturity into parentheses) to make things clearer, we obtain the value immediately after clearing the payments at time t_{j-1}:

$$P_{t_j}(t)\left(\frac{1}{Q_{t_j}(t_{j-1})} - \frac{1}{P_{t_j}(t_{j-1})}\right) + \sum_{i=j+1}^n (V_{t_{i-1},t_i}(t) - P_{t_{i-1}}(t)) \qquad (3.104)$$

from which it is possible to derive the following hedge for any time t: create a portfolio with a long position of

$$n_i(t) + \frac{m_i(t)X_t Q_{t_i}(t)}{P_{t_i}(t)} \tag{3.105}$$

U.S. t_i maturity bonds and a t_i maturity forward exchange-rate contract to pay

$$\frac{m_i(t)X_t Q_{t_i}(t)}{P_{t_i}(t)} \tag{3.106}$$

dollars and receive $m_i(t)$ yen at time t_i. This is a self-financing portfolio with each diff swap payment financed by the resetting of the hedge.

LONG-DATED FOREX OPTIONS

As discussed briefly in Chapter 1, the pricing and risk management of long-dated foreign exchange options requires the detailed consideration of the interaction between the spot-rate variable and the interest-rate variables in two currencies. Two approaches to modeling the relevant factors will be presented below.

In the first approach, called the composite model here, the relevant variable for option pricing is the volatility of the underlying forward exchange rate. Since the forward exchange rate is obtained by taking the spot exchange rate and adjusting it using the interest-rate differential between the two currencies, we can see immediately that the forward exchange-rate volatility depends not only on the spot exchange-rate volatility, but also on the volatility of the interest-rate differential, which, in its turn, depends on the volatilities of the individual interest rates (the zero-coupon bond prices, to be more accurate) and the correlation between them. It turns out that using three input volatilities and three input correlations (all of which will be shown how to estimate explicitly), one can extract a fairly accurate approximation to the volatility for the foreign exchange forward that can be put into the Black-Scholes pricing framework. This price should locally equal the price obtained using a three-factor process where the spot rate and the two interest rates are correlated random assets. Early work along these lines was done in Reference [98]. This model has to be recalibrated so that the local equivalence can be maintained.

In the second approach, we summarize a full term-structure approach, where the evolution of interest rates, as well as exchange rates, is dictated by a self-consistent framework in which arbitrage between bonds and their derivatives is not possible. Here, the term structure of interest rate and exchange rate volatilities is specified from the very beginning. The benefit of this approach is that futures, options on futures, as well as all types of American and path-dependent foreign exchange exotic contracts, can be valued consistently [4,8].

Composite Model

By interest-rate parity arguments, also known as "covered interest-rate arbitrage," we know that the exchange-rate forward is equal to the spot exchange rate times the ratio of the discount factors in the two currencies under consideration. This is simply a statement of fact that if one currency yields a higher rate of interest on deposits compared with another currency, then one will prefer to hold a deposit in the currency with the higher yields. To avoid riskless profit, the rate at which the currency is repatriated at some future date should then be expected to be more adverse than it is now. We will fix our notation in which U.S. dollars is the local currency and the spot and forward exchange rates, X_S and X_F, respectively, are quoted in terms of the units of foreign currency per U.S. dollar. For instance, in the dollar–yen pair, if $X = 112$, it means that one can get 112 yen per U.S. dollar. We will also assume that all interest rates are quoted in terms of continuous compounding, so that a discount factor for a deposit for time t is given simply by $Z(t) = e^{-r(t)t}$ where $r(t)$ is the appropriate zero-coupon rate for time t to expiration in the appropriate currency. Note that since this is the discounted present value of a unit dollar received at time t, *it is equivalent to the price of a zero-coupon bond in the appropriate currency.* By the parity argument,

$$X_F = X_S \frac{Z_{\text{Dom}}}{Z_{\text{For}}} \qquad (3.107)$$

where X_S is the spot exchange rate, X_F is the forward exchange rate, Z_{Dom} is the price of a domestic zero-coupon bond on the spot date maturing on the forward date, and Z_{For} is the price of a foreign zero-coupon bond on the spot date maturing on the forward date.

Now, if we assume that X_S, Z_{Dom}, Z_{For} are jointly lognormally distributed, the above equation can be used to calculate the variance (volatility squared) of the forward exchange rate *implied* by the following six parameters:

1. The volatility of the spot exchange rate σ_{X_S}.
2. The price volatility of the domestic zero-coupon bond $\sigma_{Z_{Dom}}$.
3. The price volatility of the foreign zero-coupon bond $\sigma_{Z_{For}}$.
4. The correlation between spot exchange rates and the domestic zero-coupon bond price $\rho_{X_S, Z_{Dom}}$.
5. The correlation between spot exchange rates and the domestic zero-coupon bond price $\rho_{X_S, Z_{For}}$.
6. The correlation between the domestic and foreign zero-coupon bond prices $\rho_{Z_{For}, Z_{Dom}}$.

The relationship is given by

$$
\begin{aligned}
\sigma_{X_F}^2 = \sigma_{X_S}^2 &+ \sigma_{Z_{Dom}}^2 + \sigma_{Z_{For}}^2 \\
&+ 2\rho_{X_S, Z_{Dom}} \sigma_{X_S} \sigma_{Z_{Dom}} \\
&- 2\rho_{X_S, Z_{For}} \sigma_{X_S} \sigma_{Z_{For}} \\
&- 2\rho_{Z_{For}, Z_{Dom}} \sigma_{Z_{For}} \sigma_{Z_{Dom}}
\end{aligned}
\tag{3.108}
$$

Once the left-hand side of this equation is known with confidence, we can use it in a variety of option pricing models. For instance, this volatility is the correct volatility to use if we use a single-factor Black-Scholes model for long-dated foreign exchange options. It captures, in essence, the arbitrage-free adjustments required to hedge a portfolio of long-dated options using spot exchange rates and domestic and foreign zero-coupon bonds.

How do we efficiently extract the relevant parameters from market data, i.e., the volatilities and correlations? The correlation parameters have to be estimated using statistical techniques for most currency pairs (though some quanto bonds have started trading in the market that carry implied spot/bond price correlation information). The volatility can be implied from traded derivative products.

Under normal circumstances, we know, with a fair degree of confidence, the volatility implied by option prices in the foreign exchange market from overnight out to 2 years. This gives the σ_{X_S} term. However, temporary perceptions of event risk might drive up the premium on the very short-dated options, so using the volatility implied by them might lead to errors in forecasting σ_{X_F}. Experience tells us that in most situations the implied volatility market in options of 1 month and out is fairly liquid and not subject to liquidity or event risk. So the first modification we make to the above equation is

$$X_{F(t_2)} = X_{F(t_1)} \frac{Z(t_1 \to t_2)_{\text{Dom}}}{Z(t_1 \to t_2)_{\text{For}}} \qquad (3.109)$$

where the zero-coupon bond prices in question are from the forward date t_1 to the forward date t_2. The "spot" exchange rate is replaced by the short-dated forward exchange rate $X_{F(t_1)}$.

This leads to

$$
\begin{aligned}
\sigma^2_{X_{F(t_2)}} = {} & \sigma^2_{X_{F(t_1)}} + \sigma^2_{Z_{\text{Dom}}} + \sigma^2_{Z_{\text{For}}} \\
& + 2\rho_{X_{F(t_1)}, Z_{\text{Dom}}} \, \sigma_{X_{F(t_1)}} \sigma_{Z_{\text{Dom}}} \\
& - 2\rho_{X_{F(t_1)}, Z_{\text{For}}} \, \sigma_{X_{F(t_1)}} \sigma_{Z_{\text{For}}} \\
& - 2\rho_{Z_{\text{For}}, Z_{\text{Dom}}} \, \sigma_{Z_{\text{For}}} \sigma_{Z_{\text{Dom}}}
\end{aligned}
\qquad (3.110)
$$

where all the zero-coupon bond prices volatilities are forward volatilities for date t_1.

Note that all we have done here is to change the spot-rate volatility into a forward exchange-rate volatility that we know. For instance, for t_1 we can use 3 months, for which forex options are very liquid. This also proves to be a judicious choice for extraction of the two zero-coupon bond volatility terms. The forward zero-coupon bond volatilities that we are interested in estimating can be approximated accurately by observing that the interest-rate option market quotes very liquid cap (or Eurodollar options), swaption, and constant maturity treasury (CMT) option volatilities.

For the relatively short-dated foreign exchange options, cap volatilities may be used, and for the longer dated options, swaption and CMT volatilities are used.

Tables 3–1 and 3–2 show sample constant maturity Black model lognormal swap volatilities for different tenors for yen and U.S. dollar European interest-rate swaptions. In the tables, the length of the options increases from top to bottom, and the "tail" of the swap that the option exercises into increases from left to right. For instance, for 3 months, the volatility of a 5-year bond at the money forward swap in yen has an implied volatility of 29 percent.

However, the constant maturity swap volatility is not exactly what goes in Equation (3.110) for two reasons:

T A B L E 3–1

Yen CMT Swap Volatility Matrix

	1 yr	2 yr	3 yr	4 yr	5 yr	7 yr	10 yr
3 mo	75.0	59.0	47.5	35.2	29.1	21.7	18.0
6 mo	66.5	52.0	41.5	30.7	25.6	18.9	16.0
1 yr	58.0	44.0	35.5	26.2	22.6	16.9	15.0
2 yr	44.0	31.5	27.5	20.7	19.6	15.4	14.0
3 yr	33.0	25.4	19.3	18.6	17.6	14.7	13.8

T A B L E 3–2

USD CMT Swap Volatility Matrix

	1 yr	2 yr	3 yr	4 yr	5 yr	7 yr	10 yr
3 mo	18	19.5	19	18.5	18	17	16.3
6 mo	18.8	19.8	19.3	18.8	18.3	17.5	16.5
1 yr	20.3	19.8	19.3	18.8	18.3	17.5	16.5
2 yr	19.9	19.3	18.8	18.3	17.7	17	16.3
3 yr	19.3	18.8	18.4	17.8	17.2	16.2	15.5

1. The volatility given in the tables above is the yield volatility, not the price volatility. We can fix this problem by noting that

$$\sigma_P \approx \frac{D\sigma_y y}{P} \qquad\qquad (3.111)$$

   where D is the duration of the swap under question, σ_y is the yield volatility, and P is the "price" of the swap (which is always struck at par zero net present value).

2. The duration is of a coupon swap, but we need a zero-coupon swap. Again, replacing the duration above with the duration of the full zero-coupon constant maturity swap (which equals the tenor of the option from spot date), we can obtain approximately the zero-coupon price volatility.

Now there are three forward correlations to be estimated:

1. Between forward domestic zero-coupon bond price and the known exchange rate forward $\rho_{X_{F(t_1)}, Z(t_1)_{Dom}}$.

2. Between forward foreign zero-coupon bond price and the known exchange rate forward $\rho_{X_{F(t_1)}, Z(t_1)_{For}}$.

3. Between the forward domestic zero-coupon bond price and the forward foreign zero-coupon bond price $\rho_{Z(t_1)_{For}, Z(t_1)_{Dom}}$.

We can extract these correlations from empirical data.[9] The forward zero-coupon bond prices can be calculated simply from the spot zero-coupon bond prices to the forward date divided by the zero-coupon bond price from the forward date to the end date.

Table 3–3 shows the results of these sample calculations for the long-dated exchange-rate volatilities on the U.S. dollar/Japanese yen cross rate. We see that an upward sloping term structure of forex vols is obtained that incorporates interest-rate spread volatility. Though the long-dated forex options have traditionally been

---

9. On methods for obtaining good correlation estimates, the reader will have to wait until the next chapter.

T A B L E 3–3

Example of Single-Factor Composite Model Approximation for Cross-Market (Dollar–Yen) Implied Long-Dated Forex Volatilities

Tenor	2 yr	3 yr	5 yr	10 yr
3 Mo vol	7.00%	7.00%	7.00%	7.00%
For bond vol	1.27%	2.14%	3.25%	5.66%
Dom bond vol	2.39%	3.65%	6.01%	11.25%
Spot foreign corr	50.00%	50.00%	50.00%	50.00%
Spot dom corr	100.00%	100.00%	100.00%	100.00%
For/dom bond corr	40.00%	40.00%	40.00%	40.00%
Japan	**2 yr**	**3 yr**	**5 yr**	**10 yr**
Yield vol	59.00%	47.50%	29.10%	18.00%
Yield	1.08%	1.50%	2.24%	3.15%
Duration	2	3	5	10
Price	100	100	100	100
Price vol	1.274%	2.138%	3.252%	5.661%
United States	**2 yr**	**3 yr**	**5 yr**	**10 yr**
Yield vol	19.50%	19.25%	18.25%	16.25%
Yield	6.13%	6.32%	6.59%	6.92%
Duration	2	3	5	10
Price	100	100	100	100
Price vol	2.391%	3.650%	6.013%	11.245%
Implied forward vol	8.86%	9.84%	11.90%	16.56%

rather illiquid with wide markets, this analysis, though very rough, is still adequate and should allow the reader to extract value from long-dated forex options.

There are some cases of Equation (3.110) that should be pointed out. Assume that over the period of interest, it is observed that the spot rate and the prices of the two zero-coupon bonds are practically uncorrelated, and that the zero-coupon bonds are exactly correlated (i.e., $\rho_{Z_{Dom},Z_{For}} \sim 1$) so that we are left with

$$\sigma^2_{X_{F(t_2)}} \sim \sigma^2_{X_{F(t_1)}} + \sigma^2_{Z_{Dom}} + \sigma^2_{Z_{For}}$$

$$- 2\sigma_{Z_{For}}\sigma_{Z_{Dom}}$$

$$= \sigma^2_{X_{F(t_1)}} + (\sigma_{Z_{Dom}} - \sigma_{Z_{For}})^2 \qquad (3.112)$$

which implies that the forward volatility

$$\sigma_{X_{F(t_2)}} \sim \sigma_{X_{F(t_1)}} + \frac{1}{2}\left(\frac{\Delta\sigma}{\sigma_{X_{F(t_1)}}}\right)^2 + \cdots \qquad (3.113)$$

when the short-dated forward volatility is large compared with the volatility differential of the zero-coupon bonds. This shows that the long-dated forward rate volatility in this case is

1. Strictly larger than the spot-rate volatility and exceeds it by a term proportional to the squared difference in the volatilities of the two zero-coupon bonds;
2. Vanishes when the spread between the volatilities of the zero-coupon bonds vanishes.

Now, illustrating what was mentioned earlier—that as the tenor of the option increases, the effects of correlations and volatilities of the interest rate instruments can be overwhelming: if we assume that $\sigma_X, \sigma_D,$ and σ_F are mutually uncorrelated,

$$\frac{\partial \sigma_{X_{F(t_2)}}}{\partial \sigma_{X_{F(t_1)}}} = \frac{\sigma_{X_{F(t_1)}} + \rho_{X_{F(t_1)},Z_{Dom}}\sigma_{Z_{Dom}} - \rho_{X_{F(t_1)},Z_{For}}\sigma_{Z_{For}}}{\sigma_{X_{F(t_2)}}}$$

$$\frac{\partial \sigma_{X_{F(t_2)}}}{\partial \sigma_{Z_{Dom}}} = \frac{\sigma_{Z_{Dom}} + \rho_{X_{F(t_1)},Z_{Dom}}\sigma_{X_{F(t_1)}} - \rho_{Z_{For},Z_{Dom}}\sigma_{Z_{For}}}{\sigma_{X_{F(t_2)}}}$$

$$\frac{\partial \sigma_{X_{F(t_2)}}}{\partial \sigma_{Z_{For}}} = \frac{\sigma_{Z_{For}} - \rho_{X_{F(t_1)},Z_{For}}\sigma_{X_{F(t_1)}} - \rho_{Z_{For},Z_{Dom}}\sigma_{Z_{Dom}}}{\sigma_{X_{F(t_2)}}} \qquad (3.114)$$

Observe the first equation in this set for the following special case when the correlation between the exchange rate and both zero-coupon bonds is close to unity. For instance, this has been the recent experience for the correlation between JGBs (Japanese government bonds), U.S. bonds, and the dollar–yen exchange rate. The exchange rate has been positively correlated with both bonds. Then (approximating the short-term forward volatility by the spot volatility):

$$\frac{\partial \sigma_{X_F}}{\partial \sigma_{X_S}} = \frac{\sigma_{X_S} + \sigma_D - \sigma_F}{\sigma_{X_F}} \tag{3.115}$$

which implies that the rate of change of forward volatility with respect to change in spot volatility is higher by the difference of the two bond volatilities. Note that, in this context, the "delta" of the forward volatility with respect to spot volatility is not constant (i.e., equal to 1), but can be different. As spot exchange-rate volatility changes, the forward volatility may change faster or slower than the spot volatility, depending on the correlations between spot levels and the bond volatilities and the actual level of the bond volatilities. This can lead to various shapes of the long-dated forex volatility term structure. In fact, one might go as far as to say that the shape of exchange-rate volatility term structure is mostly dependent on the expectations for interest-rate volatility.

Denoting the forwards with the subscript F and the spot vols with the subscript S, and differentiating Equation (3.110) with respect to the correlations, we get

$$\frac{\partial \sigma_{X_F}}{\partial \rho_{X_S, Z_{Dom}}} = \frac{\sigma_{X_S} \sigma_{Z_{Dom}}}{\sigma_{X_F}}$$

$$\frac{\partial \sigma_{X_F}}{\partial \rho_{X_S, Z_{For}}} = -\frac{\sigma_{X_S} \sigma_{Z_{For}}}{\sigma_{X_F}}$$

$$\frac{\partial \sigma_{X_F}}{\partial \rho_{Z_{For}, Z_{Dom}}} = -\frac{\sigma_{Z_{For}} \sigma_{Z_{Dom}}}{\sigma_{X_F}} \tag{3.116}$$

which shows that the sensitivity of the forward vols to the correlation is proportional to the product of two volatilities. In particular, note that as the correlation between the domestic and foreign bonds becomes smaller (or more negative), then the forward exchange-rate volatility rises rapidly as the bond volatilities rise.

Table 3–4 uses Equation (3.116), for the data given earlier, to tabulate the sensitivity of the forward volatility to the three pairwise correlations (in units of forward forex vol multiplied by a scaling factor). Note that as we look at longer and longer dated options, the forward volatility is increasingly sensitive to the

T A B L E 3–4

Relative Sensitivity of Long-Dated Vol to Correlations

	6 mo	9 mo	1 yr	2 yr	3 yr	5 yr	10 yr
Spot/dom bond	9	17	30	128	169	257	447
Spot/for bond	−20	−51	−81	−174	−288	−475	−888
Dom bond/for bond	0	−1	−4	−36	−78	−196	−637

change in the correlation between the two bonds, as compared with the sensitivity to correlations between the spot and the bonds. Note that this effect arises from the fact that zero-coupon bond price volatility rises with tenor, and the last equation in Equation (3.116) dominates.

If one chooses to manage a long-dated forex option book using this technique, the sensitivity to correlations may be hedged by readjusting the volatility hedges in the short-dated forex option market, as well as the cap and the swaption markets.

Multifactor No-Arbitrage Model

Now, a full term-structure approach will be summarized in which the two interest-rate curves and the spot rate are correlated stochastic variables with an input covariance matrix. Since a detailed discussion of term-structure models will take us too far afield from our main topic, the following is intended to be a compact sketch, with only the essential formulas being displayed. The interested reader may refer to the papers cited below, as well as the recent book by Jarrow [121]. Once the term structure of covariance matrices between the exchange rates and the forward interest rates is given, the complete evolution of the forward exchange-rate distribution is known.

In the notation of References [4] and [102],

$S_d(T)$ = spot price of one unit of foreign currency at time T

$B_d(T)$ = domestic money-market account

$$= e^{\int_0^T r_d(u)\,du}$$

$r_d(t) = f_d(t, t)$

$f_d(t, t)$ = instantaneous riskless domestic interest rate $\qquad$ (3.117)

consider first a European call option on the spot exchange rate, with exercise price K and expiration date T, denoted $C(0, T, K)$. Then,

$$C(0, T, K) = E\left[\max\left[\frac{(S_d(T) - K)}{B_d(T)}, 0\right]\right] \qquad (3.118)$$

It is possible to calculate this expected value in closed form for a European option, under the assumption that the term structure of forward rate volatilities is a deterministic function of time, to obtain

$$C(0, T, K) = P_f(0, T)S_d(0)N(h) - KP_d(0, T)N(h - \zeta) \qquad (3.119)$$

where

$$h = \frac{1}{\zeta}\log\left(\frac{P_f(0, T)S_d(0)}{KP_d(0, T)} + \frac{1}{2}\zeta^2\right) \qquad (3.120)$$

and

$$\zeta^2 = \sum_{i=1}^{i=4}\int_0^T [a_{fi}(v, T) + \delta_{di}(v) - a_{di}(v, T)]^2\,dv \qquad (3.121)$$

Here, $P_f(0, T)$ and $P_d(0, T)$ are, respectively, the foreign and domestic pure discount prices at time $t = 0$ for maturity T given in terms of instantaneous forward rates by

$$P_k(t, T) = e^{-\int_t^T f_k(t,u)\,du} \qquad (3.122)$$

The quantities a and δ correspond to functions of volatilities of interest rates and spot exchange rates. To understand the explicit forms for these, we have to specify explicit forms for the interest-rate stochastic process and the spot-rate process.

The domestic forward interest-rate dynamics are assumed to follow

$$df_d(t, T) = \alpha_d(t, T)\, dt + \sum_{i=1}^{2} \sigma_{di}(t, T, f_d(t, T))\, dW_i(t) \qquad (3.123)$$

and, similarly, the foreign interest-rate dynamics are assumed to follow

$$df_f(t, T) = \alpha_f(t, T)\, dt + \sum_{i=2}^{3} \sigma_{fi}(t, T, f_f(t, T))\, dW_i(t) \qquad (3.124)$$

so that the forward interest-rate dynamics

- Are normal;
- Have two factors that they depend on (in the sense of principal components);
- Have one factor in common that describes the correlation between the interest-rate movements in the two economies. Thus, the covariance between the forward interest-rate movements is

$$\text{Cov}\,(df_d, df_f) = \sigma_{d2}\sigma_{f2}\, dt \qquad (3.125)$$

With these assumptions,

$$a_{di}(t, T) = -\int_t^T \sigma_{di}(t, u, f_d(t, u))\, du$$

$$b_d(t, T) = -\int_t^T a_d(t, u)\, du + \frac{1}{2}\sum_{i=1}^{2}\left[\int_t^T \sigma_{di}(t, u, f_d(t, u))\, du\right]^2 \qquad (3.126)$$

The spot exchange rate is assumed to follow a lognormal stochastic process:

$$dS_d(t) = \mu_d(t)S_d(t)\, dt + \sum_{i=1}^{4} \delta_{di}(t)S_d(t)\, dW_i(t) \qquad (3.127)$$

so that

$$\text{Var}(dS_d(t)/S_d(t)) = \left[\sum_{i=1}^{4} \delta_{di}^2(t) \right] dt$$

$$\text{Cov}(dS_d(t)/S_d(t), df_d(t, T)) = \left[\sum_{i=1}^{2} \sigma_{di}\delta_{di} \right] dt \qquad (3.128)$$

All unknown quantities are now defined and, after fitting for the free parameters, the no-arbitrage prices for all options can be obtained.

"INSIDE" AND "OUTSIDE" BARRIER OPTIONS

This section will discuss the pricing and hedging of barrier options. The simplest kind of barrier options are on a single asset and depend simply on one stochastic process. Thus, whether or not the contingent payoff occurs depends on the path that the asset itself takes at all times between the start and the end of the option expiration period.

On the other hand, if the option payoff depends on one asset class, with extra path-dependent contingencies on other assets, we are forced to consider the time evaluation of all underlying assets. This leads to so-called "outside" barrier options.

In general, these options are simpler to value than American options since the critical boundary that determines the payoff is well known in advance and is specified in the contract describing the option.

All barrier options can be valued using the theoretical framework described in this chapter. In particular, we can use the densities obtained earlier for barriers to explicitly compute the prices and hedge parameters. The classification scheme for both inside barrier and outside barrier options is threefold:

1. Type: put or call.
2. Nature of barrier: in or out, i.e., does the option come alive if the barrier is hit or does it terminate if the barrier is hit?
3. Relationship of spot price to barrier: up or down, i.e., is the spot price above or below the barrier level at the start time?

Thus, there are eight kinds of inside barrier options that can be values in a uniform framework. More complex options with the basic barrier nature (e.g., indexed notional or index amortizing options) can be valued by numerical means using the same general methods. Outside barrier options with any number of variable contingencies can similarly be valued. In special cases, we can reduce this number by using a number of symmetries, i.e., put–call parity, to relate the out options to the in options, or the up options to the down options.

We will describe first the valuation of an "inside," call, in, down barrier option in which the payoff variable and the trigger variable are the same. Then, a simple put–call parity relationship will be illustrated that will be generalized to the outside case and used exhaustively in the discussion of risk management in Chapter 6.

"Inside" Barrier Options

Assume that the density of the natural logarithm of the risk-neutral asset return is

$$f(u) = \frac{1}{\sigma\sqrt{2\pi t}}\, e^{-\frac{1}{2}v^2} \tag{3.129}$$

where

$$v = \frac{u - \mu t}{\sigma\sqrt{t}} \tag{3.130}$$

r and d are the rates of interest and the dividend yield (or foreign currency interest rate), respectively, σ is the volatility of the underlying asset, and t is the time to expiration of the option.

Now, referring to the densities we obtained earlier, or to Appendix J, we can also write down the following "one-touch" density. Given that the underlying asset price first starts at S, above ($\eta = 1$) or below ($\eta = -1$) some barrier H, the density of the natural logarithm of the underlying asset return when the underlying asset price breaches the barrier, but ends below the barrier at expiration, is

$$g(u) = e^{2\frac{\mu}{\sigma^2}\log\frac{H}{S}}\frac{1}{\sigma\sqrt{2\pi t}}e^{-\frac{1}{2}v^2}$$

where

$$v = \frac{\left(u - 2\eta\log\frac{H}{S} - \eta\mu t\right)}{\sigma\sqrt{t}}$$

We will also have the need to use the time derivative for this density. If we differentiate the integral of $g(u)$ with respect to t, we generate probability density for the "first-passage time" τ for the underlying asset to hit the barrier:

$$h(\tau) = -\frac{\eta}{\sigma\tau\sqrt{2\pi\tau}}\log\frac{H}{S}e^{-\frac{1}{2}v^2}$$

where

$$v = \frac{(-\eta\alpha + \eta\mu\tau)}{\sigma\sqrt{\tau}} \tag{3.131}$$

and $\eta = 1$ if the barrier is being approached from above and $\eta = -1$ if the barrier is being approached from below.

Down and in call

The buyer of the option pays the premium up front but does not receive the payoff unless the price of the underlying asset hits a prespecified level H called the knockin boundary. To set the notation, if, for time $\tau \le T$, the underlying asset price hits the barrier, a standard call is received with strike price K and time to expiration $T - \tau$. If, on the other hand, the barrier is never hit, a rebate R is received at expiration. So, if the starting asset price $S > H$, then the payoff is

$$\text{Down-and-in-call payoff} \begin{cases} \max[S_T - K, 0] & \text{if for some } \tau \le T, S_\tau \le H \\ R(\text{at expiry}) & \text{if for all } \tau \le T, S_\tau > H \end{cases}$$

Two cases must now be considered separately according to whether the strike price is greater than or less than the barrier level.

1. $K > H$: The value of the option corresponds to the weighted payoff with the probability that the terminal asset price S_T is larger than the strike K given that it was below the barrier at some interim time τ, given by $P(S_T > K|S_\tau < H)$ and the probability that only the rebate was received, corresponding to $P(S_T > H) - P(S_T > H|S_\tau \leq H)$. Thus, the price is the sum of two integrals:

$$
\begin{aligned}
P_{K>H} = e^{-rT} &\int_{\log(K/S)}^{\infty} (S e^u - K)g(u)\, du + R e^{-rT} \int_{\log(H/S)}^{\infty} [f(u) - g(u)]\, du \\
= &\, S e^{-dT}(H/S)^{2\lambda} N(y) - K e^{-rT}(H/S)^{2\lambda-2} N(y - \sigma\sqrt{T}) \\
&+ R e^{-rT}[N(x_1 - \sigma\sqrt{T}) - (H/S)^{2\lambda-2} N(y_1 - \sigma\sqrt{T})] \quad (3.132)
\end{aligned}
$$

where

$$
\begin{aligned}
\lambda &= 1 + (\mu/\sigma^2) \\
x_1 &= [\log(S/H) - \sigma\sqrt{T}] + \lambda\sigma\sqrt{T} \\
y &= [\log(H^2/SK) + \sigma\sqrt{T}] + \lambda\sigma\sqrt{T} \\
y_1 &= [\log(H/S) + \sigma\sqrt{T}] + \lambda\sigma\sqrt{T}
\end{aligned}
$$

and $N(\cdot)$ denotes the standard normal distribution function.

2. $K < H$: For this case we need the probabilities

$$
P(H \geq S_T > K) = P(S_T > K) - P(S_T > H) \quad (3.133)
$$

and $P(S_T > H|S_\tau \leq H)$. Then, the price is

$$
\begin{aligned}
P_{K<H} = e^{-rT} \Bigg(&\int_{\log(K/S)}^{\infty} (S e^u - K)f(u)\, du \\
&- \int_{\log(H/S)}^{\infty} (S e^u - K)f(u)\, du \\
&+ \int_{\log(H/S)}^{\infty} (S e^u - K)g(u)\, du \\
&+ R e^{-rT} \int_{\log(H/S)}^{\infty} [f(u) - g(u)] \Bigg) du \quad (3.134)
\end{aligned}
$$

where

$$
x = [\log(S/K) + \sigma\sqrt{T}] + \lambda\sigma\sqrt{T} \quad (3.135)
$$

These integrals can again be carried out in closed form using the formulas in Appendix A to obtain

$$P_{K<H} = S e^{-dT}[N(x) - N(x_1) + (H/S)^{2\lambda}N(y_1)]$$
$$+ K e^{-rT}[N(x_1 - \sigma\sqrt{T}) - N(x - \sigma\sqrt{T})$$
$$- (H/S)^{2\lambda-2}N(y_1 - \sigma\sqrt{T})]$$
$$+ R e^{-rT}[N(x_1 - \sigma\sqrt{T}) - (H/S)^{2\lambda-2}N(y_1 - \sigma\sqrt{T})] \quad (3.136)$$

The interested reader should refer to the classic papers [179] for a complete compendium of all "inside" barrier options. Before we pass on to "outside" barrier options, I would like to point out a couple of interesting features of barrier options that make pricing and risk management easier.

Put–Call Parity for Barriers

Assume for a moment that there is no rebate if the barrier is breached and then construct two distinct portfolios. Suppose in our first portfolio we have a long position in a down-and-in-call option. To (partially) hedge this in a static manner, we can sell an ordinary, plain vanilla call option with the same strike price. Then, if the (down) barrier is breached at some interim time, we have no net position after the barrier is breached. However, if the barrier is not breached and the asset goes to a higher price level than the strike, we have to pay, on settlement, the amount that the plain vanilla option is in the money, but we do not make any money on the down and in call.

Now consider a second portfolio where we initiate a short position in a call option with the same strike, but with the contingency that if the asset price hits the same barrier at any interim period in time, the call option "knocks out." Then, if the barrier level is hit, we have to pay nothing at expiration on this option, regardless of the terminal price of the asset price. However, if the barrier level is not hit, we are exposed to the simple payoff from a short vanilla call. The total payoff of this portfolio is thus identical to the one in the previous portfolio.

Since the portfolios are the same at expiration and at interim times if the contingencies are met, they have to be the same at all times.

Thus, assuming that the strike and the barrier levels are identical,

Long position in "in option"
> + Short position in "plain vanilla option"
> = Short position in "out option"   (3.137)

or, rearranging terms, we obtain for the zero-rebate case,

Plain vanilla = down and out + down and in   (3.138)

This is an example of a very simple observation, but, just as for vanilla, nonexotic options, such observations lead to efficient methods for hedging a large exotic book. Even when options on different assets are combined, correlation-driven equivalences between strike and barrier levels in return space can be constructed such that different positions statically effectively hedge each other. We have already seen the mathematical justification of this symmetry earlier in this chapter.

Also note that put–call parity of this kind does not always hold! The correct specification of the option contract has to be carefully considered before applying such symmetry relationships. This can be seen if the rebate is nonzero. Going back to the example, assume that we are long a down and in call and short a regular call. If the barrier is hit, we have no position and we get no rebate. If the barrier is never hit, we will receive a rebate at the end. Now consider the short position in the down and out call that pays a rebate as soon as the barrier is hit. If the barrier is hit, the call is terminated and we have to pay a rebate immediately. If the barrier is never hit, and we end up in the money, we pay no rebate. Hence, the two portfolios are completely different by the uncertainty in when the rebate is received.[10]

"Outside" Barrier Options

Assume that there are two assets, each of which lives in a lognormal environment. We will denote by S the variable on which the payoff directly depends and by R the variable on which the payoff is contingent, i.e., the barrier variable. The terminal date is T and the correlations and volatilities are assumed to be constant. Then,

---

10. The effect of this uncertainty can be valued within our framework by using the density of first exit time.

$$dS = \mu_1 S\, dt + \sigma_1 S\, dz_1$$
$$dR = \mu_2 R\, dt + \sigma_2 R\, dz_2 \qquad (3.139)$$

The key density that we need to value outside barrier options is the joint density of the returns of the payoff variable $\log(S_T/S)$ and R not hitting (or hitting) the barrier H (from above or below) during the option's lifetime.

Denote then by P_+ the joint density of $\log S_T/S$ and R not hitting the barrier H from above during the barrier's lifetime, and by P_- the joint probability of $\log S_T/S$ and R not hitting the barrier H from below during the option's lifetime.

Then, in the notation of Reference [104]:

$$V_{\text{Down-out outside call}} = e^{-rT} \int_{\log K/S}^{\infty} (S\, e^u - K) P_+ \, du$$

$$V_{\text{Down-out outside put}} = e^{-rT} \int_{-\infty}^{\log K/S} (K - S\, e^u) P_+ \, du$$

$$V_{\text{Up-out outside call}} = e^{-rT} \int_{\log K/S}^{\infty} (S\, e^u - K) P_- \, du$$

$$V_{\text{Up-out outside put}} = e^{-rT} \int_{-\infty}^{\log K/S} (K - S\, e^u) P_- \, du \qquad (3.140)$$

Now, using our results for two-factor barrier densities from Equations (3.66) and (3.67):

$$P_{\pm}(u < x) = N\left[\frac{x - \mu_1}{\sigma_1 \sqrt{T}}, \frac{\mp(\log(H/R) - \mu_2 T)}{\sigma_2 \sqrt{T}}; \theta\rho\right] - e^{\frac{2\mu_2 \log \frac{H}{R}}{\sigma_2^2}}$$
$$N\left[\frac{x - \mu_1 T - 2\rho \log(H/R)}{\sigma_1 \sqrt{T}}, \frac{\pm(\log(H/R) + \mu_2 T)}{\sigma_2 \sqrt{T}}; \theta\rho\right]$$

where

$$N[a, b, \rho] = \frac{1}{2\sqrt{1 - \rho^2}} \int_{-\infty}^{a} \int_{-\infty}^{b} e^{\frac{-1}{2(1-\rho^2)}(x^2 + y^2 - 2\rho xy)} \, dx\, dy \qquad (3.141)$$

is the standard bivariate normal distribution with upper limits a and b, and correlation coefficient ρ.

This can now be inserted into the previous equations and evaluated numerically by carrying out numerical integration.

However, if one pushes a little further, these integrals can be performed exactly [104] to obtain:

$$V = \eta S \left(N[\eta\, d_1, \theta e_1; -\eta\theta\rho] - e^{\frac{2(\mu_2 + \rho\sigma_2^2)\log(H/R)}{\sigma_2^2}} N[\eta\, d_1', \theta e_1'; -\eta\theta\rho] \right)$$

$$- \eta\, e^{-rT} K \left(N[\eta\, d_2, \theta e_2; -\eta\theta\rho] - e^{\frac{2\mu_2 \log(H/R)}{\sigma_2^2}} N[\eta\, d_2', \theta e_2'; -\eta\theta\rho] \right)$$

where we define

$$d_1 = \frac{\log(S/K) + (\mu_1 + \sigma_1^2)T}{\sigma_1\sqrt{T}}$$

$$d_2 = d_1 - \sigma_1\sqrt{T}$$

$$d_1' = d_1 + \frac{2\rho\log(H/R)}{\sigma_1\sqrt{T}}$$

$$d_2' = d_2 + \frac{2\rho\log(H/R)}{\sigma_1\sqrt{T}}$$

$$e_1 = \frac{\log(H/R) - (\mu_2 + \rho\sigma_1\sigma_2)T}{\sigma_2\sqrt{T}}$$

$$e_2 = e_1 + \rho\sigma_1\sqrt{T}$$

$$e_1' = e_1 - \frac{2\log(H/R)}{\sigma_2\sqrt{T}}$$

$$e_2' = e_2 - \frac{2\log(H/R)}{\sigma_2\sqrt{T}} \tag{3.142}$$

with $\eta = 1$ for calls, $\eta = -1$ for puts, $\theta = -1$ for down and out, and $\theta = 1$ for up and out options. When $\rho \to 1$, we get the expressions for the single-factor "inside" barrier options of the previous section. When $\rho = 0$, we expect from our discussion of zero-correlation pricing that we should simply get the Black-Scholes price on the nonbarrier asset, times the probability that the barrier asset reaches the barrier.

From the formula, we can also see that the effect of correlation comes out as expected. For down and out calls, as the correlation gets more positive, the call option has less likelihood of being knocked out when it moves more in the money, so higher correlation increases its price. On the other hand, for down and in calls, the likelihood that the option is worth very much when it knocks in is lower, so higher correlation leads to lower prices. For a string of two-factor barrier options, such as caps with a number of caplets over a long-term horizon (as discussed in Chapter 1), the term structure of correlation can have effects of different magnitudes on different caplets.

The shorter the time to maturity, the weaker is the effect of correlation on the price of the barrier option. This has important consequences, in general, on risk management. Correlation plays a role similar to volatility, and we already know from single-asset options that volatility has a more significant effect on longer dated options.

Also note that since in the $\rho = 1$ limit the outside down-and-out-call barrier option is exactly like the inside down-and-out-call barrier option, and its value increases as the correlation becomes more positive, it has to be true that the outside down and out call has its maximum price when $\rho = 1$ and its minimum price when $\rho = -1$. Thus, in general, two-asset down and out calls are cheaper than single-asset down and out calls. In contrast, two-asset down and in calls have their minimum price when $\rho = 1$, so for $\rho < 1$ they are more expensive than single-factor down and in calls.

Thus, to summarize:

- Two-factor down and out calls, up and in calls, down and in puts, and up and out puts all have their maximum value for $\rho = 1$, thus for $\rho < 1$ they are all cheaper than corresponding single-asset barrier options.
- Two-factor down and in calls, up and out calls, down and out puts, and up and in puts all have their minimum value for $\rho = 1$, so for $\rho < 1$ they are more expensive than their single-asset counterparts.

"RAINBOW" OPTIONS

For simplicity and illustration purposes we will consider only two assets. The results may be generalized to any number of assets with the use of general, multidimensional densities [125,201].

"Best-of-two" Options

These options have the terminal payoff, with terminal date T:

$$\max[S_1^T, S_2^T, K] \tag{3.143}$$

where S_1^T and S_2^T are the terminal values of the two assets under consideration.

The value at time zero prior to expiration is given by the discounted expected present value:

$$\mathcal{P}_{\text{Best of two}} = e^{-rT} E[\max[S_1^T, S_2^T, K]] \tag{3.144}$$

Now, the expectation in our jointly lognormal world can be written as

$$\mathcal{P}_{\text{Best of two}} = e^{-rT} \int_{-\infty}^{\infty} \int_{-\infty}^{\infty} \max[S_1 e^x, S_2 e^y, K] f(x, y) \, dx \, dy \tag{3.145}$$

with the standard definitions

$$x = \log(S_1^T/S_1)$$

$$y = \log(S_2^T/S_2)$$

$$f(x, y) = \frac{1}{2\pi\sigma_1\sigma_2\sqrt{1-\rho^2}} e^{-\frac{1}{2}u}$$

$$u = \frac{(x - \mu_1 T)^2}{\sigma_1^2 T} - \frac{2\rho(x - \mu_1 T)(y - \mu_2 T)}{\sigma_1\sigma_2 T} + \frac{(y - \mu_2 T)^2}{\sigma_2^2 T}$$

where $f(x, y)$ is the standard bivariate normal density function.

Now the payoff function can be realized in one of three distinct forms, at expiration, based on the relationship between S_1^T, S_2^T, and K:

1. $S_1^T > K$ and $S_1^T > S_2^T$;
2. $S_2^T > K$ and $S_2^T > S_1^T$;
3. $K > S_1^T$ and $K > S_2^T$.

If we can figure out the conditional densities for each of the above three cases, then we need only to compute the expectation of the relevant largest price (S_1^T, S_2^T, K) with respect to that conditional density to obtain the partial price in that case.

Then, the price of the option is the sum of three conditional expectations:

$$P_{\text{Best of two}} = \underbrace{S_1 e^{-rT} \int_{\log(K/S_1)}^{\infty} \left[\int_{-\infty}^{x-\log(S_2/S_1)} f(y|x)\,dy \right] e^x f(x)\,dx}_{1}$$

$$+ \underbrace{S_2 e^{-rT} \int_{\log(K/S_2)}^{\infty} \left[\int_{-\infty}^{y-\log(S_1/S_2)} f(x|y)\,dy \right] e^y f(y)\,dy}_{2}$$

$$+ \underbrace{K e^{-rT} \int_{-\infty}^{\log(K/S_1)} \left[\int_{-\infty}^{\log(K/S_2)} f(y|x)\,dy \right] f(x)\,dx}_{3} \qquad (3.146)$$

where we have the marginal normal densities

$$f(x) = \frac{1}{\sigma_1\sqrt{2\pi T}} e^{-\frac{1}{2}v_1^2}$$

$$v_1 = \frac{(x - \mu_1 T)}{\sigma_1\sqrt{T}}$$

$$f(y) = \frac{1}{\sigma_2\sqrt{2\pi T}} e^{-\frac{1}{2}v_2^2}$$

$$v_2 = \frac{(y - \mu_2 T)}{\sigma_2\sqrt{T}}$$

and the conditional densities

$$f(x|y) = \frac{1}{\sigma_1\sqrt{2\pi(1-\rho^2)T}} e^{-\frac{1}{2}w_1^2}$$

$$w_1 = \frac{[(x - \mu_1 T) - \rho(\sigma_1/\sigma_2)(y - \mu_2 T)]^2}{(1-\rho^2)\sigma_1^2 T}$$

$$f(y|x) = \frac{1}{\sigma_2\sqrt{2\pi(1-\rho^2)T}} e^{-\frac{1}{2}w_2^2}$$

$$w_2 = \frac{[(y - \mu_2 T) - \rho(\sigma_2/\sigma_1)(x - \mu_1 T)]^2}{(1-\rho^2)\sigma_2^2 T}$$

Then we can carry out the integrals in Equation (3.146) in terms of normal density functions to obtain:

$$\mathcal{P}_{\text{Best of two}} = \underbrace{S_1 e^{-d_1 T} \left(N[y_1] - N_2[-x_1, y_1; \rho_2] \right)}_{1}$$

$$+ \underbrace{S_2 e^{-d_2 T} \left(N[y_2] - N_2[-x_2, y_2; \rho_2] \right)}_{2}$$

$$+ \underbrace{K e^{-rT} N_2[-x_1 + \sigma_1 \sqrt{T}, -x_2 + \sigma_2 \sqrt{T}; \rho]}_{3}$$

where we define

$$x_1 = \left[\log \frac{S_1}{K} + (r - d_1)T + \sigma_1 \sqrt{T} \right] + \frac{1}{2} \sigma_1 \sqrt{T}$$

$$x_2 = \left[\log \frac{S_2}{K} + (r - d_2)T + \sigma_2 \sqrt{T} \right] + \frac{1}{2} \sigma_2 \sqrt{T}$$

$$y_1 = \left[\log \frac{S_1}{S_2} + (d_2 - d_1)T + \Sigma \sqrt{T} \right] + \frac{1}{2} \Sigma \sqrt{T}$$

$$x_2 = \left[\log \frac{S_2}{S_1} + (d_1 - d_2)T + \Sigma - \sqrt{T} \right] + \frac{1}{2} \Sigma \sqrt{T}$$

$$\Sigma^2 = \sigma_1^2 + \sigma_2^2 - 2\rho \sigma_1 \sigma_2$$

$$\rho_1 = \frac{(\rho \sigma_2 - \sigma_1)}{\Sigma}$$

$$\rho_2 = \frac{(\rho \sigma_1 - \sigma_2)}{\Sigma}$$

and use the standard definitions

$$N(a) \equiv \frac{1}{\sqrt{2\pi}} \int_{-\infty}^{a} e^{-\frac{1}{2} x^2} dx$$

$$N_2(a, b; \rho) \equiv \frac{1}{2\pi \sqrt{1 - \rho^2}} \int_{-\infty}^{a} \int_{-\infty}^{b} e^{-\frac{1}{2(1-\rho^2)} (x^2 + y^2 - 2\rho xy)} \, dx \, dy \quad (3.147)$$

for the standard univariate and bivariate joint normal distribution functions.

Option on the Maximum of Two Assets

The general payoff function for these options is

$$\max(0, \phi \max(S_1^T, S_2^T) - \phi K) \qquad (3.148)$$

where $\phi = 1$ for calls and $\phi = -1$ for puts.

We do not need to evaluate the integrals that appear in this problem afresh. We can simply massage the payoff function so as to relate it to the option that delivers the best of two assets or strike that we considered in the last subsection. This is a straightforward application of "max–min" tricks that are described in Appendix E.

Call on the Maximum
Note that

$$\max[0, \max(S_1^T, S_2^T) - K] = \max[S_1^T, S_2^T, K] - K$$
$$= \mathcal{P}_{\text{Best of two}} - K \qquad (3.149)$$

where $\mathcal{P}_{\text{Best of two}}$ has been calculated earlier. So the price of the left-hand side equals the price of the right-hand side, i.e., the only difference is an extra term equal to the present value of the strike.

Note here that the relationship is rather trivial to find. In general, I recommend using the "max–min" algebra, as described in Appendix E, to reduce one option payoff to another known option payoff. It should be emphasized though that there is, in general, no simple substitute for thought—in the above example, from a pure economic point of view, if I am short an option that delivers, on expiry, the payoff of a call on one of two assets, my static option hedge has to deliver to me enough units of the better performing asset, at expiration, so as to meet my obligation of delivery. However, if both assets end up below a strike, I have to protect myself against being delivered an asset trading below the strike price at expiration by shorting money-market instruments that will deliver to me the cash value K at expiration. Thus, the two terms that show up in the price are clearly reasonable from a purely static hedging viewpoint, and could even have been *guessed* from examination of the payoff function without detailed computation.

Put on the Maximum
Similar reasoning as above can be used for puts on the maximum of two risky assets:

$$\max[0, K - \max(S_1^T, S_2^T)] = \max[0, \max(S_1^T, S_2^T) - K] - \max(S_1^T, S_2^T) + K$$
$$= \text{Call on max} - \text{Zero strike best of two} + K$$

which is a "put–call parity relationship."

Note that this put–call parity relationship can be restated in words that justify its origin from the static hedgers viewpoint: If I am long a call option on the maximum of two assets and short a put option on the better of two assets, I have a long position in a forward contract whose value is the better of the two assets at expiry minus the common strike. Thus, if both assets end up below the strike K, I will lose, no matter what. This example can be generalized to most exotic options—*an option on a complex, nonlinear payoff structure is related to simpler "forward-like" payoffs which can be options in their own right.* Development of intuition on the hierarchy of complex payoff structures plays a very important role in the management of exotic multifactor options.

Call on the Minimum

Suppose now that we short a call on the minimum of two assets. To hedge our position, we buy a call on the first asset *and* also buy a call on the second asset. But this is an overhedge because on our short position we pay on only one asset, whereas we are paying premium on two correlated assets. To retrieve the premium, we can sell a call on the maximum. This is clearly true since the sum of a portfolio of a call on the maximum and a call on the minimum equals the sum of calls on two assets, since the portfolio has options on both by construction. So,

$$\max[0, \min(S_1^T, S_2^T) - K] = \max[0, S_1^T - K] + \max[0, S_2^T - K]$$
$$- \max[0, \max(S_1^T, S_2^T) - K]$$
$$= \text{Call on S1} + \text{Call on } S_2$$
$$- \text{Call on the maximum}$$

Put on the Minimum

We now confidently use our generalized put–call parity relationship. A long call on the minimum plus a short put on the minimum must deliver the minimum of two assets plus cash equal to strike. So, rearranging,

$$\max[0, K - \min(S_1^T, S_2^T)] = \max[0, \min(S_1^T, S_2^T) - K]$$
$$- \min(S_1^T, S_2^T) + K$$
$$= \text{Call on } S_1 + \text{Call on } S_2$$
$$- \text{Call on the maximum}$$
$$- \text{Worst of two} + \text{Strike}$$

CONVERTIBLE BONDS WITH STOCHASTIC INTEREST RATES

Convertible bonds are simply bonds that can be converted to equity if certain conditions are met. Usually, these provide an embedded American-style option to the holders. While the proper pricing of these structures again requires a full term-structure model for interest rates, for simplicity we imagine a simpler setup here so that the important correlation issues can be emphasized. We will follow the approach of Reference [215].

We will define our convertible bond to be like an ordinary bond, except for the additional feature that, at any point, the holder of the bond might choose to exercise a conversion option to convert the bond into another asset, usually the common or preferred stock of the bond issuer. First, we assume that interest rates are nonstochastic, so the bond price is some function $V = V(S, t)$. In usual Black-Scholes fashion, if we have a hedged portfolio with $-\Delta$ units of the underlying asset to counteract the local movements of the convertible bond, we get the change in the value of the hedged portfolio to be, using Ito lemma,

$$d\mathcal{P} = \frac{\partial V}{\partial t} dt + \frac{\partial V}{\partial S} dS + \frac{1}{2}\sigma^2 S^2 \frac{\partial^2 V}{\partial S^2} dt - \Delta\, dS + (c(S, t) - d(S, t)\Delta)\, dt$$

(3.150)

where the last term is the difference of the coupon c and the dividend on the stock d. Now we choose as the "delta" the change of the bond price with respect to the underlying stock price S:

$$\Delta = \frac{\partial V}{\partial S}$$

(3.151)

so that the portfolio is riskless.

Then, we have

$$\frac{\partial V}{\partial t} + \frac{1}{2}\sigma^2 S^2 \frac{\partial^2 V}{\partial S^2} + (rS - d(S, t))\frac{\partial V}{\partial S} - rV + c(S, t) \leq 0 \qquad (3.152)$$

since the return on the portfolio cannot be any higher than the risk-free rate. The final condition is that the bond should pull to its par value Z, so

$$V(S, T) = Z \qquad (3.153)$$

and the convertibility option to convert into n shares at any given time is equivalent to

$$V \geq nS \qquad (3.154)$$

Now, the value of the convertible bond is beginning to look like an option pricing problem. Just before maturity the value is

$$\max(nS, Z) \qquad (3.155)$$

with the boundary conditions

$$V(S, t) \sim nS \qquad \text{as } S \to \infty \qquad (3.156)$$

and

$$V(0, t) = Z e^{-r(t-T)} \qquad (3.157)$$

which is exactly the pricing problem for an American option. This can then be solved by using the numerical method of trees, which will be discussed in detail in Chapter 5.

A simplification happens when the bond is really a zero-coupon bond, i.e., it pays no coupon, so that $c = 0$, and the underlying asset into which the bond can be converted is a non-dividend-paying stock, so that $d = 0$. Then, the bond can be priced as a European call option and cash. This is clear because (recall the earlier discussion and review the mechanism of decomposing pay-offs using max–min algebra)

$$\max(S_1, S_2) = S_1 + \max(S_2 - S_1, 0) \qquad (3.158)$$

so that

$$\max(nS, Z) = nS + \max(Z - nS, 0) \qquad (3.159)$$

Now we come to the case when interest rates are not deterministic but random. Then, the correlation between interest rates and the underlying stock price can have an effect on how the convertible bond and the options on it are priced. Then assume that the stock price follows a lognormal random walk and the interest rate follows some general stochastic process:

$$dS = \mu S + \sigma S \, dz_1$$
$$dr = a(r, t) \, dt + b(r, t) \, dz_2 \tag{3.160}$$

Then, as usual,

$$E[dz_1 \, dz_2] = \rho \, dt$$
$$dz_1^2 = dz_2^2 = dt \tag{3.161}$$

and, by Ito lemma,

$$dV = \frac{\partial V}{\partial t} dt + \frac{\partial V}{\partial S} dS + \frac{\partial V}{\partial r} dr$$
$$+ \frac{1}{2}\sigma^2 S^2 \frac{\partial^2 V}{\partial S^2} dt + \rho \sigma S b \frac{\partial^2 V}{\partial S \partial r} dt + \frac{1}{2} w^2 \frac{\partial^2 V}{\partial r^2} dt$$

Now we construct a hedge portfolio consisting of a convertible bond with maturity T_1, $-\Delta_2$ bonds with maturity date T_2, and $-\Delta$ of the underlying asset. Then,

$$\mathcal{P} = V_1 - \Delta_2 V_2 - \Delta S \tag{3.162}$$

To eliminate risk, we have to choose these so that

$$\Delta_2 = \frac{\partial V_1 / \partial r}{\partial V_2 / \partial r}$$
$$\Delta = \frac{\partial V_1}{\partial S} - \frac{\partial V_1 / \partial r}{\partial V_2 / \partial r} \frac{\partial V_2}{\partial S} \tag{3.163}$$

which yields

$$\frac{\partial V}{\partial t} + \frac{1}{2}\sigma^2 S^2 \frac{\partial^2 V}{\partial S^2} + \rho \sigma S b \frac{\partial^2 V}{\partial S \, \partial r} + \frac{1}{2} w^2 \frac{\partial^2 V}{\partial r^2}$$
$$+ rS \frac{\partial V}{\partial S} + (a - b\lambda) \frac{\partial V}{\partial r} - rV = 0 \tag{3.164}$$

where λ is the market price of risk. Once boundary conditions are specified, this equation can be solved numerically.

Note that an interesting feature here is the correlation-dependent cross term $\rho\sigma Sb(\partial^2 V/\partial S\partial r)$, which is like the gamma term for each underlying asset and refers to the mishedge due to local delta-hedging. However, here it is possible, even if there is no change in r, for this term to contribute to changes in the bond price, as well as the bond price hedge, due to movements in the stock price, or even the stock price implied volatility factor. There will be lots to say about hedging these higher, extremely important cross effects later on.

Note, again, that for this special case when the bond pays no intermediate coupons and the stock pays no dividend, the valuation problem reduces to an European option problem, but in two stochastic variables. Then, using the methods described above for the better of two assets, and by performing bivariate integrations, this bond can be valued.

BASKETS AND THE EDGEWORTH EXPANSION

Given n assets $S_i, i = 0, 1, \ldots, n$, a basket $B = \sum_{i=1}^{n} w_i S_i$ can be constructed by taking w_i as the percentage weight of each of the underlying assets, with $\sum_i w_i = 1$. We discussed an important example of this in Chapter 1 when we discussed yield curve basket options. Options on aggregate stock indices, such as the Standard and Poor's 500, are also examples of basket options. We will assume that the volatility of the ith asset is σ_i and the correlation between asset i and asset j is ρ_{ij}.

The simplest and most direct way to value options on baskets is to assume that each asset included in the basket has a lognormal distribution, with each having some correlation with the other assets that determines the future evolution of each variable's distribution. For a large number of underlying assets, this approach can very quickly become difficult to manage numerically. As an alternative, we can model the basket itself as a "pseudo-asset" and price the options according to the time evolution of the distribution of the pseudo-price distribution. Let us now price a call option on the basket. The terminal price of the basket option is given by

$$C(T) = \max\left(\sum_i w_i S_i(T) - K, 0\right) \qquad (3.165)$$

where the strike K is, in general, nonzero. Now the following are defined:

F_i = forward price of asset i

$\dfrac{S_i(T)}{F_i} = S_i'(T)$, the pseudo spot price of the asset i at maturity

$\dfrac{w_i F_i}{\sum_i w_i F_i} = z_i$, the weight of the asset i in the forward price of the basket

$\dfrac{K}{\sum_i w_i F_i} = K'$, the pseudo strike price

$\sum_i z_i S_i'(T) = B'(T)$, the pseudo-basket spot price at time T $\qquad (3.166)$

Then, the price of the call option is

$$C(T) = \max\left(\sum_i w_i S_i(T) - K, 0\right)$$

$$= \sum_i w_i F_i \max\left(\sum_i \frac{w_i F_i}{\sum w_i F_i} \frac{S_i(T)}{F_i} - \frac{K}{\sum_i w_i F_i}, 0\right)$$

$$= \sum_i w_i F_i \max\left(\sum_i z_i S_i'(T) - K', 0\right)$$

$$= \sum_i w_i F_i \max(B'(T) - K', 0) \qquad (3.167)$$

In this equation, the distribution of the pseudo spot prices $S_i'(T)$ is lognormal if the distribution of S_i is lognormal, since F_i values are simply constants.

Now if we can figure out what the closed-form expression is for the terminal distribution of B', then we would be done, since then we could evaluate the price of the basket call in very much the same way as we evaluate the price of an ordinary call option. Since the sum of a number of lognormal variables does not necessarily follow a lognormal distribution, we are not able to proceed in this direction immediately. The approach we take is as follows: assume that there is a good lognormal distribution A, which, when known in terms of a number of parameters, can be used to calculate an option price in closed form. If this distribution is a reasonable approximation to the true distribution for the basket, then we have approximated the price of the actual basket option. The goodness of the approximation can be evaluated in terms of the difference of the prices. Normally, as more terms in the expansion of the true and approximating densities are retained, the error in pricing converges to zero. This is the method of "empirical" distributions (see discussion in Appendix H).

The approach used here for constructing an approximate distribution is called the Edgeworth expansion. The basic idea is to construct an approximation by matching some of the leading moments of the true and the approximating distributions. The terms in the expansion are simple functions of the moments of the true and approximating distributions.

We will use the notation α_j for the jth moment, μ_j for the jth central moment, and κ_j for the jth cumulant of any distribution. Also, $C(F)$ is the price of the basket call at time t according to the true distribution F of the pseudo basket price $B'(T)$, and $C(A)$ is the price of the basket call at time t according to approximating distribution A.

The true value of the basket call is

$$C(F) = e^{-r(T-t)} \sum_i w_i F_i \int_{K'}^{\infty} (y - K') f(y) \, dy \qquad (3.168)$$

where

$$F(x) = \int_{-\infty}^{x} f(y) \, dy \qquad (3.169)$$

is the true distribution of the basket $B'(T)$ and $f(y)$ is the true density.

Let A be a lognormal distribution and ξ be a random variable of this distribution. The distribution is completely determined by two parameters, α and β, respectively corresponding to the expected value and the variance of the lognormal variate:

$$\alpha = E[\ln \xi]$$
$$\beta = \text{Var}[\ln \xi]$$

All moments are given by

$$\alpha_j(A) = e^{j\alpha + \frac{1}{2}j^2\beta} \qquad (3.170)$$

For instance, if $j = 1$, then the first moment, or the mean of the lognormal variable, is simply $e^{\alpha + \frac{1}{2}\beta^2}$, where α and β correspond to the mean of a normal variable that is in the exponential of the density describing the lognormal distribution. Now suppose that A was the distribution of the pseudo-basket B'. Then, using Equation (3.168), the price of the basket call would simply become

$$C(A) = e^{-r(T-t)} \sum_i w_i F_i \int_{K'}^{\infty} (y - K')a(y)\,dy$$

$$= e^{-r(T-t)} \sum_i w_i F_i(\alpha_1(A)N(d_1) - K'N(d_2)) \qquad (3.171)$$

with $a(y)$ representing the density function for F, $N()$ the standard normal distribution function, $d_1 = (\alpha - \ln K' + \beta)/\sqrt{\beta}$, and $d_2 = (\alpha - \ln K')/\sqrt{\beta}$.

Assuming that $\alpha_j(F)$, i.e., the moment of order j exists for F, the difference between the true density f and the approximating density a can be written in terms of a sum:

$$f(y) = a(y) + \sum_{j=1}^{n-1} C_j \frac{(-1)^j}{j!} \frac{\partial^j a}{\partial y^j} + \epsilon(y, n) \qquad (3.172)$$

where the error term $\epsilon(y, n)$ vanishes for all y as $n \to \infty$. Then, the coefficients C_j are found by expanding the left-hand side and then matching orders in the expansion of the moment generating or cumulant generating function:

$$e^{\sum_{j=1}^{n-1} [\kappa_j(F) - \kappa_j(A)] \frac{(it)^j}{j!}} = \sum_{j=0}^{n-1} C_j \frac{(it)^j}{j!} + \mathcal{O}(t^{n-1}) \qquad (3.173)$$

For instance, the first five coefficients are

$$C_0 = 0$$
$$C_1 = \kappa_1(F) - \kappa_1(A)$$
$$C_2 = (\kappa_2(F) - \kappa_2(A)) + C_1^2$$
$$C_3 = (\kappa_3(F) - \kappa_3(A)) + 3C_1(\kappa_2(F) - \kappa_2(A)) + C_1^3$$
$$C_4 = (\kappa_4(F) - \kappa_4(A)) + 4C_1(\kappa_3(F) - \kappa_3(A))$$
$$+ 3(\kappa_2(F) - \kappa_2(A))^2 + 6C_1^2(\kappa_2(F)$$
$$- \kappa_2(A)) + C_1^4 \tag{3.174}$$

where κ_i are the cumulants[11] of the indicated distributions and are defined by expansion:

$$e^{\sum_{j=1}^{n-1} \kappa_j \frac{(it)^j}{j!}} = \sum_{j=0}^{n-1} \alpha_j \frac{(it)^j}{j!} + \mathcal{O}(t^{n-1}) \tag{3.175}$$

For instance, the first four cumulants are

$$\kappa_1 = \alpha_1$$
$$\kappa_2 = \mu_2$$
$$\kappa_3 = \mu_3$$
$$\kappa_4 = \mu_4 - 3\mu_2^2$$

where we have used the notation α_j for the jth moment of the distribution and μ_j for the jth central moment (i.e., subtract the mean from the random variable before computing the moment) of the distribution.

Finally, putting Equation (3.172) into Equation (3.168), and using Equation (3.171), we obtain

$$C(F) = C(A) + e^{-r(T-t)} \sum_i w_i F_i \left(\sum_{j=1}^{n-1} C_j \frac{(-1)^j}{j!} \int_{K'}^{\infty} (y - K') \frac{\partial^j a}{\partial y^j} dy \right.$$
$$\left. + \int_{K'}^{\infty} (y - K') \epsilon(y, n) dy \right) \tag{3.176}$$

---

11. Cumulants can be obtained in the same way as moments, if one uses the logarithm of the moment generating function in the derivative expansion. See Appendix H for details. The reason cumulants are useful is because the logarithm enables one to add cumulants of convolved random variables to get the resultant cumulants.

For a lognormal approximating distribution A:

$$\int_{K'}^{\infty} (y - K') \frac{\partial^j a}{\partial y^j} dy = \frac{\partial^{j-2} a}{\partial y^{j-2}} (K') \qquad (3.177)$$

as long as $j \geq 2$.

Now, if the first cumulant matches, i.e., $\kappa_1(F) = \kappa_1(A)$, then we can write Equation (3.176) as

$$C(F) = C(A) + e^{-r(T-t)} \sum_i w_i F_i \left(\sum_{j=2}^{n-1} C_j \frac{(-1)^j}{j!} \frac{\partial^{j-2} a}{\partial y^{j-2}} (K') \right.$$

$$\left. + \int_{K'}^{\infty} (y - K') \epsilon(y, n) \, dy \right) \qquad (3.178)$$

with the last term vanishing rapidly as higher moments are used.

We can determine the moments α_j for the approximating distribution A from the formula given in Equation (3.170) for lognormal distributions. For the moments of F, we can use simple statistical computations from empirical data, or, as discussed in Chapter 4, occasionally from options on quantos or crosses.

As an example of the use of the method, assume that $\alpha_1(F) = \alpha_1(A) = \sum_i z_i = 1$. Also, the effective basket variance gives β:

$$\beta = \left(\sum_i z_i^2 \sigma_i^2 + \sum_{i,j \neq i} z_i z_j \rho_{ij} \sigma_i \sigma_j \right) (T - t) \qquad (3.179)$$

Now, taking the logarithm of both sides of Equation (3.170), and using $\alpha_1(A) = 1$, we get

$$\alpha = -\tfrac{1}{2}\beta \qquad (3.180)$$

Then, from Equation (3.171),

$$C(A) = e^{-r(T-t)} \left(\sum_i w_i F_i N(d_1) - K N(d_2) \right) \qquad (3.181)$$

where

$$d_1 = \frac{1}{\sqrt{\beta}}(\tfrac{1}{2}\beta - \ln K')$$

$$d_2 = \frac{1}{\sqrt{\beta}}(-\tfrac{1}{2}\beta - \ln K') \qquad\qquad (3.182)$$

Further details and results on these methods are given in References [93], [117], and [210].

GENERALIZED PUT–CALL CONVERSIONS AND STATIC HEDGING

The notion of put–call parity is a familiar and useful one. In its simplest form, the put–call parity relationship relates European calls, with expiration T and strike K, to European puts with the same expiration and strike and the time zero price of a pure zero-coupon bond $B(T)$, and a forward price $F(T)$ for delivery at time T:

$$C(K, T) = (F(T) - K)B(T) + P(K, T) \qquad\qquad (3.183)$$

so that if the options are struck at the money forward, i.e., $F(T) = K$, then $C(K, T) = P(K, T)$. This result may be generalized in terms of "put–call symmetry," which is an equality between put and call prices on opposite sides of the forward. The symmetry holds exactly if zero drift is assumed for the underlying price process diffusion, and, if for any future time t, the local volatility is assumed to be the same for any two forward price levels whose geometric mean equals the current forward, i.e., $\sigma(Fu, t) = \sigma(F/u, t)$. In particular, the symmetry condition holds true when we assume deterministic volatility, as in the Black-Scholes environment of this book, even with "smiles" and "frowns." Given frictionless markets, no arbitrage, zero drift, and the symmetry condition, puts and calls obey the following:

$$\frac{C(K_C)}{\sqrt{K_C}} = \frac{P(K_P)}{\sqrt{K_P}} \qquad\qquad (3.184)$$

where $\sqrt{K_C K_P} = F$. Another way of saying this is that the ratio of prices of calls struck at K_C and puts struck at K_P equals the ratio of the forward price to the put strike. So, a call struck at twice the current forward would have twice the value of a put struck at half the current forward:

$$\frac{C(2F)}{P(\frac{1}{2}F)} = \frac{F}{\frac{1}{2}F} = 2 \qquad (3.185)$$

The power of this result can be appreciated when it is used to infer a static hedge (equivalently a pricing algorithm) for barrier options. A down and out call (DOC) becomes worthless if a lower barrier is hit at any time during the life of the option. Thus, the price of the DOC is always less than the price of a plain vanilla call. When the forward equals the barrier H, the DOC option is clearly worthless. Suppose we hedged the DOC with a vanilla European call option with the same strike K. Clearly, this is an overhedge since the hedge has positive value even when the DOC is knocked out. To compensate for the overhedge, we can go short an instrument that has the same value as the residual value of the European call option when the barrier is hit. At $F = H$,

$$\frac{C(K)}{\sqrt{K}} = \frac{P(K_P)}{\sqrt{K_P}}$$

$$\sqrt{KK_P} = H$$

$$\rightarrow K_P = \frac{H^2}{K} \qquad (3.186)$$

which implies that

$$C(K) = \frac{K}{H} P\left(\frac{H^2}{K}\right) \qquad (3.187)$$

so the initial hedge is to write K/H European vanilla puts struck at H^2/K to have a complete hedge. Hence, the static hedge and the replicating portfolio is

$$DOC(K, H) = C(K) - \frac{K}{H} P\left(\frac{H^2}{K}\right) \qquad \text{for } H < K, F \qquad (3.188)$$

If the barrier is hit before expiration, the calls should be sold and the proceeds used to buy back the puts. If the barrier is not hit, then the long calls give the desired protection and the puts provide the reimbursement for the excess premium spent.

Following Reference [45], a similar formula is derived for up and out calls ($H > K, F$):

$$UOC(K, H) = C(K) - \frac{K}{H}C\left(\frac{H^2}{K}\right) - \left[2(H - K)BC(H) + \frac{H - K}{H}C(H)\right]$$

$$(3.189)$$

where the binary calls are reconstructed from a large number of vertical spreads of standard calls:

$$BC(H) = \lim_{n \to \infty}\left[C(H) - C\left(H + \frac{1}{n}\right)\right] \qquad (3.190)$$

In practice, with a finite number of call spreads, usually three or four strikes, the results converge fast enough to be used for static replication.

We will turn briefly to knockout options with barriers on both sides. Suppose that the initial forward price and the strike of the double-barrier call is between two barriers. The option knocks out if either the upper barrier H or the lower barrier L is hit before expiration. It pays off the payoff of a simple call option if neither barrier is hit. Note that exotic products, such as range floaters, can be valued by using put–call parity on the vanilla option by subtracting a double-barrier put. Double barrier knockins can be computed by taking the difference of a vanilla call and a double-barrier knockout.

To begin constructing a static hedge for the double-barrier knockout call, let us first buy a standard call (which is an overhedge), and subtract off the extra amounts, as done above for each barrier separately. If the forward price reaches the lower barrier before it reaches the upper barrier, then we can nullify the value of the vanilla call residual value by selling K/L puts struck at L^2/K. On the other hand, if the price is assumed to reach the upper barrier first, then the up-and-out pricing procedure tells us to use Equation (3.189). So, as a first cut, we have

$$DBKO(K, L, H) \approx C(K) - \frac{K}{L}P\left(\frac{L^2}{K}\right)$$

$$- \left[\frac{K}{H}C\left(\frac{H^2}{K}\right) + 2(H - K)BC(H) + \frac{H - K}{H}C(H)\right]$$

However, we have not removed the part that takes account of the necessary contingency that if the price hits one of the barriers first, the call at the other barrier is automatically cancelled. For instance, if the forward price hits H first, then the second term in the above equation in effect reduces the price by contributing negative values. To cancel this, we can buy L/H calls struck at H^2K/L^2, and to cancel the negative influence of the third term, we can add binary calls. Since the first-order cancellation is still not enough to remove higher order coupling of the barrier probabilities, we have to keep adding an infinite number of options to replicate the exact price (eventually leading to the result that we derived earlier for double barriers). The contribution of each additional set of cancellation options decreases exponentially, so convergence is rapid. The reader interested in further details and the full form of the infinite sum of options is referred to Reference [45]. Now note that to introduce the dependence on drift, we can make the barriers time dependent, so that

$$L_t = L\, e^{(r-r_f)(T-t)}$$
$$H_t = H\, e^{(r-r_f)(T-t)}$$

for $0 \le t \le T$. Since the upper bound on these barriers is $L e^{(r-r_f)T}$ and $H e^{(r-r_f)T}$, upper and lower bounds on the price can readily be derived [45].

WHICH DISCOUNT CURVE?

Before we leave the discussion of pricing, I would like to recapitulate the important ingredients that enter into any approach. In particular, I would like to draw attention to the discounting assumption that is used for computing the present value of the future payoff.

We can summarize the algorithm for any option pricing problem by breaking it up into three simple questions:

1. What is the payoff for given values of the underlying assets?
2. What is the probability of payoff?
3. What is the discounted value of the probability-weighted payoffs?

The first question is simply a question of arithmetic and is extraneous to the pricing algorithm (though recent events in derivatives suggest that many individuals have a hard time doing this arithmetic when losses mount!). The second question is answered once assumptions about the joint distribution of the asset prices have been specified for all future dates. The third question is really a question of judgment—and is not always easy to answer, though it might appear trivial.

If options can be dynamically hedged continuously, then the discount rate that should be used is the risk-free rate, since, locally, any portfolio can be immunized against adverse moves. On the other hand, if local hedging is not possible, the discount rate at which the probability-weighted payoff is discounted is the *risk-adjusted* discount rate. The risk-adjusted rate is equivalent to the risk-free rate plus or minus the risk premium in rate units for being invested, respectively, in a security that is more or less risky than simple treasury bills.

Nondeliverable Swaps

To illustrate the issues, consider, as an example, the following contract that a hypothetical Philippine corporation may hypothetically enter to tap favorable investor liquidity in U.S. dollars. The corporation issues a dollar-denominated floating-rate bond, but is legally prohibited from converting pesos into dollars to settle at each semiannual settlement date. Since the peso payments cannot be delivered in pesos, the corporation chooses to settle in U.S. dollars, but using the spot exchange-rate fix due days prior to the delivery date, on a notional that is calculated at the start of the swap. So the payments, in dollars, are

$$N_{\text{Peso}} r(t)_{\text{Peso}} X(t) \tag{3.191}$$

where $X(t)$ and $r(t)$ are, respectively, the stochastic exchange rate in U.S. dollars per peso and the stochastic peso interest-rate index on the fixing date prior to the period t settlement. Now,

$$N_{\text{Peso}} = \frac{N_{\$}}{X(0)} \tag{3.192}$$

so that we have payments

$$N_\$ r(t)_{\text{Peso}} \frac{X(t)}{X(0)} \qquad (3.193)$$

Now, normally, we would be able to write the forward exchange rate that is contained in $X(t)$ in terms of the spot exchange rate $X(0)$ plus or minus the forward points that are derived from the difference of the zero-coupon deposit rates. In the present situation, this analysis is not easy because legal restrictions can make it hard to figure out what is the correct zero-coupon yield curve. In many real-life situations, there is a yield curve in the local market that is artificially kept at levels that discourage capital flight. The consequence turns out to be the spontaneous development of an offshore nondeliverable market with a distinct yield curve of its own. This leads to two different forward exchange rates for each future point in time. Which forward exchange rate should be used by the hedger to figure risk? Usually, the solution is to assume that the curves for computation are the ones in which the hedger can reinvest the proceeds, or which he or she can use to finance positions. Clearly, this approach is vulnerable to fluctuations in legal or other capital controls, as well as general liquidity. Even for simple swaplike transactions, since dynamical hedging in the appropriate curve might not be possible, risk-neutral valuation cannot simply be assumed. Hence, volatilities of the curve, as well as correlations between the exchange rates and the two different types of yield curves, may have to be considered.

We really need not look at international markets—even different credit quality issuers in one country really only have recourse to the markets that fit their credit quality profile. Thus, their issuances have the credit risk premia built in. Once the risk premium is separated from the other risks, the mark-to-market valuation and computation of market risk parameters of any embedded options can be carried out at the risk-free rate. This "factorization" of risks is why, after the credit premium is separated and included in the inception gain, a dealer desk hedging a portfolio of options becomes blind to the actual credit quality of the component counterparties.

CHAPTER 4

Correlation

In this chapter, we will discuss topics related to the estimation of the multivariate distribution of assets and its time evolution. The first section deals with techniques, both simple and complex, for the estimation of correlation from historical data. The second section discusses the construction of a reasonable term structure of correlation. The third section deals with methods to extract correlation information from traded options and shows the interrelationships between correlation and volatility. In the fourth section we will reintroduce the concept of random variables as vectors in time, and show how simple vector calculus may be used to compute some useful identities that are used repeatedly while dealing with multiasset options. Finally, in the last section we will show that a very real sample data series of correlated assets shows significant deviation from joint multinormality, and how more complex theoretical distributions might be constructed by the process of *mixing* multivariate distributions.

ESTIMATION

General Remarks

From the point of view of trading and dynamic hedging, it is preferable to have models, even though somewhat rough, that are easy to implement and modify, and whose risk parameters can be effort-lessly translated into hedge positions. This transparency imposes the requirement of faithful mapping between the form and content of model inputs and outputs. This price of simplicity is increased sensitivity to the fundamental inputs whose correct estimation can have long-term effects on the behavior of portfolios.[1]

In this chapter, we will describe some statistical methods that are used to obtain correlation estimates that will be used in the multivariate valuation models.[2] Here, we will restrict ourselves to dependence techniques; in Chapter 6, on risk management, the interdependence techniques, such as principal components decomposition and factor analysis, will be illustrated. In practical terms, the estimation of correlations assumes that there is a time series in which each time point of interest has one or more asset values attached with it, the prices of which are measured in a specific common numeraire. The problem is to figure out to what degree the knowledge of one of the variables enables, *demonstrably*, the determination of the other variables with the same time index. For very large data sets, it is usually possible to show that two variables have association that is statistically significant, even if very weakly so. For small data sets, it becomes hard to figure out if strong association is significant or just a fluke.

The main task at hand is to develop measures for both the *strength* and *significance* of association between two or more distributions, so that probabilistic statements may be made about a portfolio that consists of exposures from two or more of these variables. Since option trading is not a deterministic enterprise, but is deeply statistical, it is also crucial to understand that a specific model used to price and hedge must ultimately consist of an idealized extraction of the true distribution of the variables, and

1. Many trading desks have put trades on their books, based on incorrect estimates of correlations and volatility, only to notice that the increased costs of hedging and the slow spin out of sync with the market eventually take their toll on the bottom line. Avoiding mark-to-market is a "solution," but then the portfolio ends up being speculative and cannot be valued in the risk-neutral framework.
2. A discussion on volatility estimation is included in Appendix F. For dealer desks, the need to estimate volatility from historical data has been somewhat mitigated due to the rapid development of the OTC options market, which provide a ready means for backing out implied values.

that significant deviations are certain to be present, which, though statistically ignorable, may for completeness also have to be captured and quantified.

In its most general form, for n variables, the geometric representation of the degree of association is an n-dimensional table, where for every value of each variable, the measured values of other variables are displayed. Then, a measure of association, called a *statistic*, between the variables may be constructed. For instance, for two different assets, one can build a two-dimensional table and construct the well-known chi-square statistic. Then, to quantify the significance of the association, one can compare the value of the statistic obtained from the empirical table with tabulated values for the chi-square statistic. The chi-square distribution function can be evaluated to give values for the expected probability of finding a given value in a random experiment. If the statistic is significant, i.e., nonrandom, then there is some evidence of nontrivial association. But once the association has been found, how can we quantify the strength of the association? For the tabulated data, one method is to construct measures, based on the entropy of the table, that can be utilized to predict the conditional probability of obtaining a value for one variable once the value for the other variables is known. We will not delve into the tabular method, not only because it is tedious to apply for very large data sets, but also because it does not yield parametric values that have a correspondence in the pricing differential equations and which are familiar to the financial community.

Since our focus is on developing techniques for pricing and hedging option-type structures, we have to be consistent with the models that are used for pricing and hedging multifactor options. As an extension of the single-factor case, the simplest choice to make is to assume that the returns of prices of the variables are independently normally distributed, i.e., the price variables themselves are lognormally distributed. Then, for jointly normally distributed returns, the price variables are jointly lognormally distributed. The correlation parameter that is appropriate to such a description is the statistical correlation of the *returns* and not of the prices themselves—and the returns have all to be specified in a numeraire that makes sense. For example, it makes no sense to quote the correlation coefficient between the performance of the

Nikkei stock index and the U.S. S&P 500 without also specifying which currency they are in. To compare apples with apples, we need to convert them into the same currency (at the spot exchange rate), before computing the correlation of the returns. Otherwise, an error proportional to the correlation between the currency exchange rate and one of the indices will be made in the estimate (more on this when we discuss quantos).

Also recall that pricing models that can be put into the form of equations like the Black-Scholes equation and its generalizations assume that the variables are in continuous time. However, any empirical estimate of association has necessarily to assume that the data series are discrete, even if the discreteness is very fine. As soon as statistical estimates are used for inputs into continuous time models, the assumption of smoothness is being made, i.e., the measure of association is smooth and does not change fundamentally as the continuous limit is taken. However, a smooth limit does not mean that correlations estimated from samples of different discrete size time slices will all yield the same numerical values for the estimates. Clearly, one should not expect correlations calculated with weekly data to be the same as correlations calculated with monthly or quarterly data. However, one would expect that as one moves from smaller time steps to larger time steps, the correlation would behave monotonically, as long as there are no significant outliers.

The reader should also be reminded that to provide a complete description of the statistical comovement of assets, we need to be able to recreate the joint density from an infinite Taylor expansion of the joint moments, i.e., we need to know the joint moment generating function. Using simple assumptions, such as joint normality of returns, it is easy to show that only the first two moments and cross-moments for each pair of assets are needed to recreate the full joint normal distribution. While we will not prove this in any rigor here, the reader can refer to Appendix H to see a proof based on the evaluation of cumulants for the case of a two-asset portfolio. The implication of this completeness result is that for an idealized lognormal universe, which is frequently assumed, only the expected rate of returns, standard deviations, and correlations are required. Once these measures are known, the pricing model is completely specified. The advantage of the simplified approach is that there are only a few parameters to estimate, and their common intuitive meaning is known to all practitioners. But we need to keep in mind that the joint lognormal assumption is an idealization which may or may not be borne out by actual observations—so we have to be ready to refine the distributional assumptions if the market demands them. In the last section, we will show how a very real time series of assets shows significant deviation from joint normality of returns, and how the empirical distribution may be recreated as a "mixed" version of a number of joint lognormals with appropriate weights.

For European options, we are interested in estimating statistical properties of the terminal distribution of variables, such as the mean, the variance, and the cross-correlations. When implied information is not available, estimation from historical time series data is the last resort. Now, if we think of each time path or realization of the asset prices as stochastic processes, there is a unique history. So, in principle, we have only a single terminal price for each asset. How can we then infer the statistical properties of the terminal distribution? For example, we make the leap of faith that the expected return for the stock market at some terminal date will be some percentage r, and we calculate the r value by taking an average of the r values over the single historical path that the stock market has followed over the last year, or whatever the horizon of interest. The answer is that for processes possessing the property of "ergodicity" for a particular statistic, we can estimate the ensemble averages from time averages. Weiner processes are strictly speaking of infinite variance as time goes to infinity, but under nonpeculiar situations the approximations may be used anyway. Thus, it is justifiable to use time averages as substitute estimates for terminal averages.

Simple Linear Correlation Estimation

For pairs of quantities (x_i, y_i), where $i = 1, \ldots, n$ refers to distinct measurements in time, and $\bar{x}, \bar{y}$ refer to the time averages, the linear or Pearson correlation coefficient (this measure of correlation is totally useless if the relationship between the variables is nonlinear, i.e., the regression is not a line, or expected to be significantly nonnormal) is given by

$$R = \frac{\sum_i (x_i - \bar{x})(y_i - \bar{y})}{\sqrt{\sum_i (x_i - \bar{x})^2} \sqrt{\sum_i (y_i - \bar{y})^2}} \qquad (4.1)$$

where $R = 1$ is called perfectly positively correlated, $R = -1$ is called perfectly negatively correlated, and $R = 0$ is called uncorrelated. When two variables are known to be associated significantly, R is a reasonable statistic for determining the strength of the association. However, if the significance is not known, e.g., for sparse data sets, it is impossible to trust R as a good measure of the strength of association. This is simply because, in Equation (4.1), nowhere in the calculation of the statistic is one required to know the distribution of x and y, so it is impossible, in the general case, to say anything about the distribution of R. If we assume that x and y are uncorrelated, and also that they have localized distributions (i.e., quickly decaying tails), then R is approximately normally distributed, with a mean of zero and a standard deviation of $1/\sqrt{n}$. We will come back to a more thorough discussion of the distributional properties of the correlation coefficient at a later point in this chapter.

If it is assumed that the returns of the assets are well modeled by a joint normal distribution, such as the one we have used in the multivariate Black-Scholes extension, then, as we have shown in Equation (3.14), the theoretical joint density leads to a correlation coefficient that equals the covariance term divided by the product of the two standard deviations. For most simple pricing problems, the region of interest is within a few standard deviations of the mean, where most empirical data can be well approximated by a bivariate normal distribution. However, when considering tail events, this approximation might be very bad, and an empirical distribution may have to be used.

Contradictory, confusing, and uncoordinated floods of information on the *robustness* properties of the sample correlation coefficient are scattered in dozens of journals [124]. There is frequently failure to distinguish between non-normality robustness and the robustness with respect to outlying observations. If we define the "influence function" of the correlation statistic as the index of the effect on the distribution of the statistic of a single additional observation with value x, it is found that the distribution of the influence function is unbounded, so that the correlation estimate is very sensitive to outliers [64]. Data cleaning to remove spurious outlying data points might be required to obtain good correlation estimates.

Moving Window Histograms

Coming back to the parameter estimation itself—take the two time series between which correlation estimates are to be made, then calculate the returns to obtain the returns series. Select a time window, say, if the return data is weekly, 30 weeks of data from the two series. Calculate the correlation coefficient by using the standard formula from Equation (4.1), where $n = 30$, and $\bar{x}$ and $\bar{y}$ are the means of the returns of the two data series. This gives the correlation for the first "time-window." Now discard the first data point from each series and include one new data point, then repeat the correlation calculation. Repeating this process until all the data points are used up will give, for a sample length of n in each series, $n - 30 + 1$ separate correlation numbers. Plot these numbers as a histogram. Doing a statistical analysis of the histogram gives some grasp of the nature of variation in the correlation. Repeat the algorithm now for different sized windows. For instance, select chunks of 100 data points at a time instead of 30.

Figure 4–1 shows the histograms for varying window sizes using the Standard and Poor's 500 index and U.S. interest rates as the two data series.

A number of remarks should be made about using the moving window algorithm for calculation of correlation histograms.

- Mathematically, the histogram is the distribution of

$$R_{i,j,t} = \frac{\sigma_{i,j,t}}{\sqrt{\sigma_{i,i,t}\sigma_{j,j,t}}} \tag{4.2}$$

where $\sigma_{i,j}$ represents the covariance matrix

$$\sigma_{i,j,t} = \frac{1}{n}\sum_{k=1}^{n} r_{i,t-k} r_{j,t-k} \tag{4.3}$$

where $r_{i,t}$ is the excess return of asset i, n is the size of the rolling window, and t is the time at which the rolling correlation is evaluated. Thus, there are sharp cutoffs as the

F I G U R E 4–1

S&P 500 vs 3-Month U.S. Libor Correlation Histograms for Different Length Rolling Time Windows (1975–1993)

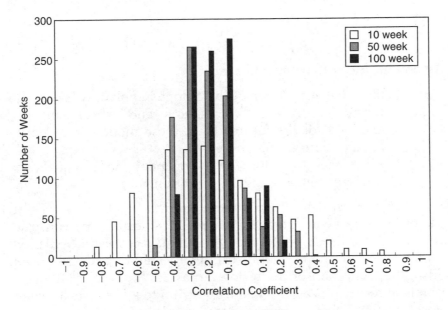

memory of variables is retained for exactly the number of data points equal to the length of the window.

- Correlation computed from smaller moving windows has a more "normal" appearance, and, in general, has a larger spread.

- Correlation computed from longer moving windows shows clustering, which is reflective of the fact that during different periods, variables might show different joint subdistributions. This can be understood as a manifestation of the fact that variables correlate differently under different economic cycles. When we discuss the term structure of correlation, this will have a natural explanation.

Exponential Smoothing

Somewhat more sophisticated than the simple rolling window algorithm is the exponential smoother—essentially, this replaces the variable n corresponding to the length of the window by a parameter λ:

$$\sigma_{i,j,t} = (1 - \lambda)\sigma_{i,j,t-1} + \lambda r_{i,t-1}r_{j,t-1} \qquad (4.4)$$

so that

$$\Delta\sigma_{i,j,t} = \lambda(r_{i,t-1}r_{j,t-1} - \sigma_{i,j,t-1}) \qquad (4.5)$$

Two points need to be made here:

1. Since the expectation of the change in volatility is zero, no further changes in covariances and correlations are expected for the future. Thus, these models intrinsically have no forecasting power.
2. As λ goes to unity, the exponential model equals the ordinary rolling window algorithm.

The problem with the histogram approach is that, in general, the histogram of correlation is not normal, since it is, by construction, truncated at ±1; hence, many techniques of inference that we know, based on the normal distribution, cannot be directly used. Also, the truncation of the histogram at ±1 "squeezes" the end-points in the empirical correlation spectrum to a very small region. For time series that are expected to have high absolute values of correlation, this can be a serious handicap for accurate pricing. If the price has high sensitivity to correlation, then naively adding and subtracting fractions or multiples of the observed standard deviation of the simple distribution might take the resultant esti-mates to domains that do not have similar probabilities of occur-ring in reality. Translated to pricing, a serious error that can be made by using this naive estimation is that near the tails of the distribution, the same bid–offer spread can lead to unreasonably wide markets when compared to zero-correlation pricing.

The Fisher z Transform, Confidence Levels, and Bid–Offers

For the pricing of illiquid multifactor options, it is also important to have a good statistical estimate for the *bid–offer* on correlation. For most correlation options available in the market today, implied correlation information is not available, and historical data has to be used to estimate not only the midpoint, but also the bid and offer on correlation, based on the expected variation of the correlation coefficient over the life of the option.[3] In a Black-Scholes environment where each underlying asset is assumed to follow geometric Brownian motion, the most straightforward estimates of correlation input are usually performed by a statistical analysis of the histogram of correlation of returns of moving, overlapping time windows as in the last section. The simplest technique to determine the bid–offer on correlation is to center the midpoint correlation on the statistical median of the histogram, and then to use a bid–offer spread on correlation that is some fraction or multiple of the empirical standard deviation of the histogram.

To test for the statistical significance of the correlation parameter, as well as to put confidence bounds on the estimates, and thus to produce statistical bid–offers, a useful methodology is to transform the correlation variable so that the distribution behaves like a normal distribution. Then, statistical tolerance and confidence checks can be performed *on the distribution of the transformed variable.* Finally, the transformed variables and confidence bounds are inverted back to the original correlation variable. We will discuss this (purely statistical but enlightening technique) next.

The Fisher transformation[4] smears out the tails of the histogram. Given a set of correlation estimates R for n pairs of values for the underlying variables, the Fisher-transformed correlation variable is

$$R_F \equiv \frac{1}{2} \ln \left(\frac{1 + R}{1 - R} \right) = \tanh^{-1} R \qquad (4.6)$$

and the inverse of this transformation is given by

$$R = \frac{e^{2R_F} - 1}{e^{2R_F} + 1} \qquad (4.7)$$

---

3. For currency crosses, as well as equity indices and some interest-rate futures that trade in a number of currencies, option-implied volatility can be used to extract implied correlation information, as discussed in the next section.

4. In addition to the Fisher transform given here, Harley's arcsine transform $\sin^{-1} R$ and others are also simple and useful.

The motivation behind this transformation is that if one calculates the variance of the ordinary linear correlation parameter, assuming that the underlying joint distribution of the variables is joint log-normal with some correlation parameter ρ, then

$$\text{Var}(R) \sim \frac{1}{n}(1 - \rho^2)^2 \tag{4.8}$$

and

$$\int \frac{1}{1 - \rho^2} d\rho = \frac{1}{2} \log \frac{1 + \rho}{1 - \rho} \tag{4.9}$$

so that the Fisher transformation is a variance-equalizing transform [124].

The moments of the transformed variable are approximately

$$\mu_1(R_F) = \frac{1}{2} \log \frac{1 + \rho}{1 - \rho} + \frac{1}{2} \rho(n - 1)^{-1} \left[1 + \frac{1}{4}(5 + \rho^2)(n - 1)^{-1} \right]$$

$$\mu_2(R_F) = (n - 1)^{-1} \left[1 + \frac{1}{2}(4 - \rho^2)(n - 1)^{-1} \right.$$

$$\left. + \frac{1}{6}(22 - 6\rho^2 - 3\rho^4)(n - 1)^{-2} \right]$$

In these variables, each R_F is approximately normally distributed with a mean value

$$\overline{R_F} = \frac{1}{2} \left[\log \frac{(1 + \rho)}{(1 - \rho)} \right] \tag{4.10}$$

where ρ is the true parent correlation coefficient. The standard deviation of the Fisher-transformed correlation is approximately equal to $R_F = 1/\sqrt{n - 3}$ where n is the number of points for which return data is available; since,

$$(n - 1)^{-1} + \tfrac{1}{2}(4 - \rho^2)(n - 1)^{-2}$$

$$= n^{-1} + n^{-2} + \cdots + \tfrac{1}{2}(4 - \rho^2)n^{-2} \sim n^{-1}[1 + 3n^{-1}]^{-1}$$

$$= (n - 3)^{-1} \tag{4.11}$$

In the limit that $R \to \pm 1$, the Fisher transform $R_F \to \pm\infty$, satisfying the desirable property that the distribution behave like a Normal.

The significance level at which a measured value of R differs from some hypothesized value ρ is then given in terms of the error function:[5]

$$1 - \mathrm{Erf}\left(\frac{|R_F - \overline{R_F}|\sqrt{n-3}}{\sqrt{2}}\right) \tag{4.12}$$

This expression also lets one evaluate the significance of the difference between two correlation coefficients R_1 and R_2 where these are obtained from different length time windows (this is a crucial question in pricing, since the stability of the estimate over time is central for hedging):

$$1 - \mathrm{Erf}\left(\frac{|R_F^1 - R_F^2|}{\sqrt{2}\sqrt{\frac{1}{n_1-3} + \frac{1}{n_2-3}}}\right) \tag{4.13}$$

where n_1 refers to the time window used for the R_1 estimate and n_2 refers to the time window used for the R_2 estimate.

The way to use this to deduce a statistically "fair" value for the correlation bid–offer is best demonstrated by an example. Consider the 30-week correlation between deutschemark libor and the dollar/DM exchange rate extracted from weekly data. The simple (midpoint) correlation of returns for the last 30 weeks of data is 0.10. The question is, with a given degree of confidence, what can be said about this value? The answer to the question is obtained by taking the Fisher transformation of 0.10, using Equation (4.6), which equals roughly 0.10. Now assume that we want 60 percent confidence intervals for this estimate. Using the fact that 60 percent of the probability in a standardized normal distribution is included within 0.84 standard deviations of zero, we can get an estimate of the 60 percent upper and lower confidence bounds of the Fisher-transformed correlation (k_F denotes the number of standard deviations for the required confidence bounds in terms of the Fisher variable):

---

5. Note that the relationship between the familiar standard cumulative normal distribution and the error function is $N(x) = \frac{1}{2}(1 + \mathrm{Erf}(x/\sqrt{2}))$.

$$R_F(\text{Upper,Lower}) = R_F \pm k_F \sigma_F$$

$$= 0.10 \pm 0.84 \, \frac{1}{\sqrt{30-3}} \qquad (4.14)$$

where we have used the fact that the standard deviation of the Fisher transform for 30 weeks of data, i.e., 30 sample points, is $1/\sqrt{27}$.

Inverting these bounding Fisher correlations to normal correlation variables by using the inverse of the Fisher transform given in Equation (4.7), we get the upper and lower bounds on correlation:

$$R(\text{Upper,Lower}) = 0.26, \; -0.06 \qquad (4.15)$$

Assuming that the trader puts bid–offers at the bounds of correlation confidence levels, the fair bid–offer spread at 60 percent confidence level is 0.32 correlation points.

In this example, since the midpoint estimate of correlation was so close to zero, it turned out that the bid and the offer were about the same distance from the midpoint. As the absolute value of midpoint correlation gets closer to unity in absolute value, the bid or offer side, whichever is closer to zero, is further away from the midpoint than the side closer to absolute unity, i.e., the bid–offer is skewed.

Figure 4–2 plots the correlation of moving 30-week windows between deutschemark libor and the dollar–mark rate with the Fisher bands.

In this method there is a trade-off between the confidence levels required and the tightness of the resulting correlation bid–offer spread. A conservative market-maker using this technique would like to be very sure that true correlation lies within the corresponding Fisher bands obtained by his confidence levels, so he will use a higher confidence estimate for the bands, thus forcing the bid–offer spread wider. On the contrary, an aggressive market-maker would want the bands to be tighter, so he would use a lower confidence interval.

Using the above methodology, for low confidence levels (and tighter correlation spreads), the formulas written above give to linear order in $\epsilon = k_F \sigma_F$ the following formula for "fair" correlation bid–offers as a function of the confidence level imposed:

F I G U R E 4–2

Moving Correlation of Deutschemark Libor and Dollar/Mark Exchange Rate with Fisher Bands

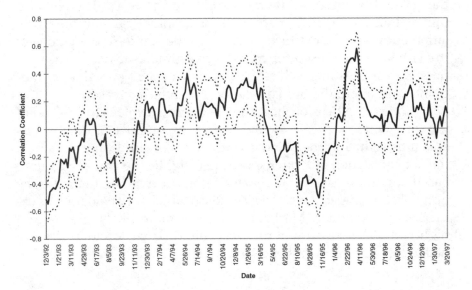

$$\text{Fair correlation spread} = 2\left(\frac{R^2 - 1}{R^2 + 1}\right)^2 \epsilon \qquad (4.16)$$

Since the value of σ_F is fixed for a selection of time-window periods, the correlation bid–offer is directly proportional to the value of k_F. Note that k_F is simply the number of standard deviations in the transformed correlation variable within which a given proportion of all probability lies, so reducing k_F is equivalent to reducing the confidence level in the estimate. It is a little disconcerting that what we call statistically fair depends on specific confidence levels. However, this is really not a problem in markets: as competition increases, the bid–offer spreads in correlation will get tighter, but so will the liquidity and the ability to hedge in implied correlation, and hence the need to rely on estimates of correlation from historical data will be much less. The overall ability of the market to decide the fair value of spread will not depend too much on statistics, but rather on risk appetites.

Figure 4–3 illustrates Equation (4.16): for a given level of confidence, the fair correlation bid–offer is maximum when the absolute correlation midpoint is close to zero and it decreases rapidly as the absolute value of midpoint correlation increases. There is also minimal bias in the bid–offer when the absolute value of the correlation midpoint is close to zero. Also, as the standard deviations of the Fisher variable used for confidence estimates increase, the confidence estimates themselves increase, so for a given value of midpoint correlation, the fair correlation bid–offer increases.

Notice also that for the same confidence level, as the period of the time window increases (increasing the number of data points and thus reducing the standard deviation of the Fisher variable), the fair correlation bid–offer spread gets tighter, i.e., for correlation-based options, it is easier to make a tighter correlation market if the option life is longer. This is clearly reasonable and analogous to the markets in volatility. Market-makers are more likely to charge a higher disaster premium for very short-dated options, i.e., to hedge the gamma risk, hence the higher volatility bid–offers. For

F I G U R E 4–3

Fair Correlation Bid–Offer Spread as a Function of Correlation for Different Confidence Levels

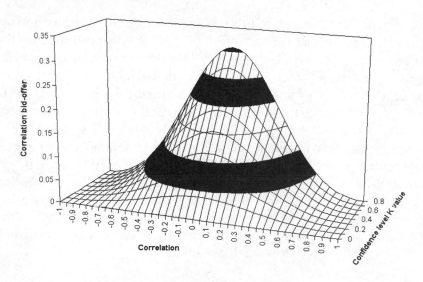

correlation options, very short-lived options rapidly increase the cross-gamma risks, hence requiring higher correlation bid–offers compared with those required for longer dated correlation options. Of course, the statistical estimate for correlation has to be supplemented by a reasonable term structure that has a high confidence level of being statistically significant on forward dates. In a later section we will discuss how both implied and statistical information may be used to construct such a reasonable term structure of correlation.

Distributional Characteristics of the Correlation Coefficient

The point estimate of correlation from n pairs of data points is statistically not completely satisfactory. Assuming joint lognormality, a number of more general results on the distributional characteristics of correlated variables can be obtained. They will be stated without proof here. The interested reader may refer to Reference [124] for further details.

Recall Equation (4.1) for the correlation coefficient based on n pairs of observables. What we want to ask, and what is too frequently not asked in the market where people trade correlation based on point estimates, is the probability that the correlation really is not R, but some other value, i.e., What is the distribution of the estimate? We have already shown how the Fisher transformation can be used to put confidence bounds on estimates. Here, we will state some other general results on the distribution of the correlation coefficient assumed to arise from joint normal returns.

Given the assumption of joint normality of x and y with an assumed bivariate normal density with correlation parameter ρ, the probability density of the correlation parameter for n fixed observations is, for $-1 \leq R \leq 1$:

$$p_R(R) = \frac{(1-\rho^2)^{(n-1)/2}(1-R^2)^{(n-4)/2}}{\sqrt{\pi}\,\Gamma(\tfrac{1}{2}(n-1))\Gamma(\tfrac{1}{2}n-1)}$$
$$\times \sum_{j=0}^{\infty} \frac{[\Gamma(\tfrac{1}{2}(n-1+j))]^2}{j!}(2\rho R)^j \qquad (4.17)$$

An alternative form is given by Fisher in terms of the nth derivative of $\theta = \cos^{-1}(\rho R)$:

$$p_R(R) = \frac{(1 - \rho^2)^{\frac{1}{2}(n-1)}(1 - R^2)^{\frac{1}{2}(n-4)}}{\pi(n - 3)!} \left(\frac{\partial}{\partial\theta}\right)^{n-2} \frac{\theta}{\sin\theta} \qquad (4.18)$$

This can also be expressed in terms of hypergeometric functions, which encapsulate the information on the infinite sum.

The product moment function is a biased estimator of the true correlation coefficient. The bias in R as an estimator of ρ is approximately equal to $-(1/2n)\rho(1 - \rho^2)^2$ so that as n gets large, the bias disappears. Also, for $\rho = \pm 1, 0$, there is no bias. The bias function looks sinusoidal. And, as every correlation trader knows in his gut, the variance of the estimate of ρ is maximum when the correlation is close to zero (and, as we have seen, the bid–offer spread is then widest). The variance of R is approximately equal to $(1/n)(1 - \rho^2)^2$.

Nonparametric Estimation Methods

In estimating the linear correlation coefficient, we are forced to make statements about the individual distributions of the variables, as well as their joint distribution. Now, if one suspects significant deviation from the ideal joint distribution in the observed data, it becomes useful to have an idea of nonparametric association. For hedging purposes, what becomes more important, in practice, is not whether the exact correlation parameter turns out to be 0.55 or 0.6, but whether, for large moves, the assets show an increased tendency to move together or opposite each other. It is useful to have, from the perspective of developing a hedging plan, a measure of the association ranked in terms of the size of moves.

To achieve this aim, we take the same series of asset returns as before, (x_i, y_i), with $i = 1, \ldots, N$, and replace each individual series with its *rank* in the series, so that the largest return moves come at the top and the smallest return moves come at the end. Whenever two data points have the same value, we assign them a mid-rank, defined as the mean of the ranks that they would have had if they were distinct. Note, now, that each series of ranks has a *uniform* distribution (of ranks). So, after this transformation, all we need to do is to create a statistic that can detect correlation between uniformly distributed variables. An added benefit is that for outliers in the data, the rank correlation algorithm is less sensitive than the simple linear correlation.

The Spearman rank–order correlation coefficient is defined in a way similar to linear correlation:

$$R_S = \frac{\sum_i (R_i - \overline{R})(S_i - \overline{S})}{\sqrt{\sum_i (R_i - \overline{R})^2}\sqrt{\sum_i (S_i - \overline{S})^2}} \tag{4.19}$$

where R_i, S_i are now the ranks of the x and y data points. Note that implementing this algorithm is only slightly harder than using the simple correlation formula that one finds in most spreadsheet applications—just rank the series entries before calculating the correlation. In fact, this statistic is closely related to the statistic called *sum-squared difference of ranks*:

$$\sum_i (R_i - S_i)^2 \tag{4.20}$$

Further details on these and the related technique called Kendall's tau can be found in any elementary statistics book. Figure 4–4 shows a scatterplot between linear and rank correlation estimates of the 30-day rolling correlation of weekly returns of the S&P 500 and Nikkei 225 indices from 1970. Though close, the slight scatter indicates that the two correlation estimates are not identical.

Choice of Time Window

The basic variable upon which any correlation computation depends is the time period over which the data series is observed, i.e., the "window" over which interrelationships between two series are to be quantified. If Δt is the time (in years) between independent recordings of market prices, and τ is the observation period, if returns over time intervals are not autocorrelated, then the one standard deviation error in estimation is given by

$$\epsilon_1 = (1 - R^2)\sqrt{\frac{\Delta t}{\tau}} \tag{4.21}$$

Solving for τ gives

F I G U R E 4–4

Scatterplot between Linear Correlation Estimates and Rank Correlation Estimates

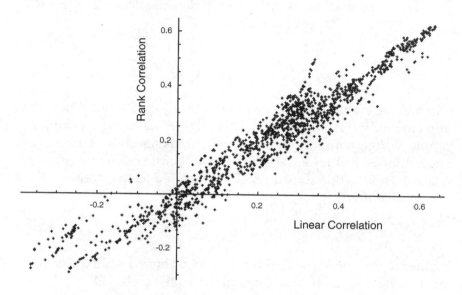

$$\tau = \frac{(1 - R^2)^2 \Delta t}{\epsilon_1^2} \tag{4.22}$$

so that the observation period needed for doubling the level of accuracy (i.e., cutting the error in half) is quadrupled. However, one cannot expect to increase the period indefinitely, because though the estimation error is minimized, the correlation estimate may have too much dependence on history, so it may not be a good reflection of current market conditions. A good statistical estimate of correlation will be accurate numerically but will also be a good representation of current market conditions and comovements.

As the time period included in the window increases, we increase *memory* error as we reduce the *sampling* error [202]. A compromise is needed. The memory error can be estimated by fitting a least-squares regression line to the current correlation estimates, i.e.,

$$R(t) = a + bt \tag{4.23}$$

where t is time from the start of the fitting interval. This corresponds to a memory error $\epsilon_2 = (|b|\tau/2)$ so that the total error from sampling and memory is

$$\epsilon_T = \sqrt{\epsilon_1^2 + \epsilon_2^2} = \sqrt{\frac{b^2\tau^2}{4} + \frac{(1 - R^2)^2 \Delta t}{\tau}} \tag{4.24}$$

The period for which the total error is minimum is

$$\tau_m = \left(\frac{2(1 - R^2)^2 \Delta t}{b^2}\right)^{1/3} \tag{4.25}$$

and the minimum error is

$$\epsilon_{min} = \sqrt{3}\left(\frac{(1 - R^2)^2 \Delta t |b|}{4}\right)^{1/3} \tag{4.26}$$

While this method, discussed in more detail in Reference [202], provides a good starting point, in practice there is no substitute for a careful scrutiny of the data and the special economic conditions present that may have influenced the correlation estimates. Unfortunately, good judgment is still an important ingredient in making good choices for how much data should be included in forming a good correlation statistic.

Synchronicity Adjustments

A typical options book that deals in different asset classes cannot avoid having exposures that depend on markets which operate in different time zones. For instance, while the U.S. stock market is open during the normal daylight hours in the United States, the Japanese equity market is closed. While COMEX gold is trading, London gold has been fixed for that day. Even within one country, there are markets that are open at different hours and that can have significant effects on each other.

What is the effect of computing correlations with data that is nonsynchronous? What adjustments can be made so that the correlation estimates from nonsynchronous data are close to the "true" estimate of correlation?

Let us look at the New York and Tokyo stock markets more closely for purposes of example. The reader can generalize this to futures markets on three continents, or even to cash markets that do not trade synchronously. The New York market is open from 9:30 A.M. to 4 P.M. EST. The Tokyo market for the next calendar day opens at 7 P.M. EST and remains open until 1 A.M. the next morning. So the total overlap between the two markets for a given day is in the period after New York closes *and* Tokyo closes, i.e., about 8.5 hours, which is about 30 percent of the total. Now, if we were to do a correlation analysis between the two markets and used only the returns computed from the closing data for each market, we would be missing a lot of the covariance in the two markets. If, however, we could capture some of the missing covariance by systematically incorporating the effect of the time lags, we could add it to the ordinary covariance to get an adjusted covariance. The variance for each individual market does not get affected by the lag, so in computing an adjusted correlation from nonsynchronous data, we need to know only the covariance adjustment. By estimating the autocovariances, it is possible to measure the 1-day lead and lag effects across series of returns. This is because of partial information overlap—current and past information in one data series is correlated with current and past information in another data series. One simple way of describing the adjustment process is to write the observed returns as a weighted sum of true past returns and unobserved current returns, and then to compute the covariances. Then, in terms of observed returns, we obtain

$$R_{jk,t} = \frac{\mathrm{Cov}(r_{j,t}r_{k,t-1}) + \mathrm{Cov}(r_{j,t}r_{k,t}) + \mathrm{Cov}(r_{j,t-1}, r_{k,t})}{\sigma_{j,t}\sigma_{k,t}} \qquad (4.27)$$

When we apply this to the Nikkei and S&P data from 1990, we find that the synchronous correlation is 0.10, whereas the asynchronous contribution with Nikkei leading is close to zero, but with S&P leading it is almost 0.25! Thus, more than 60 percent of the total correlation between the data series comes from the first-order lagged return. We also repeat the exercise by taking correlations between 30-day rolling windows over the last 7 years (from 1990), and find that, on the average, the synchronous correlation is about 0.10, the average correlation with S&P leading (by a day) is 0.20, and the average with Nikkei leading is almost zero. While the magnitude of these relationships is quite surprising, the fact that considering only synchronous returns underestimates the covariance should not be too surprising, since there is only partial (30 percent) information overlap between the two markets. Also, the fact that the Nikkei is correlated to leading S&P, more than the other way around, shows that there is clear causal flow of information, i.e., the larger U.S. market leads the Japanese market. While I have not been too rigorous in the preceding statistical analysis, I hope that it has enlightened the importance of making synchronicity adjustments when considering correlation and other similar summary statistics.

Nonlinear Correlation Models

One of the major shortcomings of using the linear correlation approach is that it totally misses nonlinear association. If, for example, there is a sinusoidal relationship between two variables, which is usually the case when cyclically related variables are at hand, simple linear correlation will tend to give the wrong result—that the two variables are uncorrelated over a large number of cycles.

Recall how the linear correlation coefficient is calculated. We regress the dependent variable on the independent variable:

$$Y = \alpha + \beta x + \epsilon \qquad (4.28)$$

where β equals $R\sigma_X/\sigma_Y$ for the value that minimizes $E[Y - (\alpha + \beta X)]^2$. Now, if we generalize the linear regression to a nonlinear regression where the curve that we fit to is not a line but a general smooth curve, then the interpretation of the correlation coefficient is necessarily local, i.e., dependent on the value of the independent variable. This is the natural measure of association when the strength of association depends on the *level* of the variates. For linear correlation, geometrically the slope of the regression line, equal to the inverse tangent of the angle the line forms with the x axis, is a measure of the correlation coefficient. For the nonlinear case, the tangent of the line at each point is different, and yields a *correlation curve* with the local measure of association dependent on the level of the x variable.

In practice, implementation of nonlinear correlation estimation is no more difficult than linear correlation estimation. All that is needed is to have a fitting algorithm that can do nonlinear fits. If one chooses, a parametric form for the model may be specified with the value of the parameters obtained from the least-squares fit. More details of nonlinear correlation estimation and examples are given in Reference [25].

Smoothing and Savitzky-Golay Filters

A useful concept in the statistical description of data is one of filters. To reduce noisy data, and the effect of outliers, one uses algorithms such as moving averages, weighted moving averages, and such. In general, filters take a data point f_i and replace it with a linear combination of itself and some chunk of data surrounding it (usually the preceding data to protect causality). So the new data points are $g_i = \sum_n c_n f_{i-n}$. The trade-off is always between smoothness of the data and the resolution that is lost as a result of the smoothing. As everyone knows, if the neighboring data moves around a lot, simple averaging (including weighted schemes) does not work too well in keeping the structure of the original data.

We can describe a nontrivial smoothing function here. Pick some data point f_i and assume a normal distribution with mean at that point and some arbitrary standard deviation σ about that point. Now, for a normal distribution, we can easily calculate how much probability lies between the previous data-point index $i-1$ and i based on this assumption (since i is normalized with mean zero and variance σ^2). For instance, choosing $\sigma = 1$, we get 0.34 as the probability between $x = \pm 1$ and $x = 0$. Clearly, as σ increases, the amount of probability between these points falls as the distribution has higher dispersion. Now, by definition, the value of all these partial cumulative probabilities should sum to unity. Hence, these partial cumulative probabilities can be used to construct a weighting scheme. For example, with $\sigma = 2$, for steps that lie a given number of steps (in first column below) before or after the central point, we would use symmetric weights given in the second column:

```
0   0.191462468
1   0.149882273
2   0.091848031
3   0.044057167
4   0.016540382
5   0.004859713
6   0.001117294
7   0.000200987
8   3.13989E-05
```

The values in the right-hand column add up to a half since we are using a smoothing algorithm based on the standard normal distribution. Note that this scheme uses data points that come both before and after the data point whose value is being smoothed. This is not a problem for causality as long as the size of the span is small compared with the forecast period.

The usual procedure is to plot the original discrete data and the smoothed version on the same chart, and then to vary the free parameter, for instance σ in the above discussion, until a reasonable trade-off between smoothing and dispersion is achieved. Once this parameter is settled on, the smoothed data points can be used to estimate correlations and volatilities.

Savitzky-Golay filters use a least-squares fit on the window of surrounding data to compute the value of the data point of interest. For each new point in the original data series, the same fit is made over the new shifted window. Such fitted data points can then be used to compute a new series from which volatility and correlation can be calculated [164].

The Risk-Metrics Approach

Building on work done by many groups within a number of organizations, JP Morgan has recently attempted to create some standardization for the construction and use of covariance matrices for a variety of applications. In this section, some of the important features of their approach will be summarized, though we will steer clear of the controversies surrounding the universal applicability of the techniques [239,240].

In the simplest scheme described so far, each point in the data series is weighed equally, so that if X denotes a $T \times N$ data series of mean subtracted returns, with N assets, and T returns for each asset, then the covariance matrix can be defined by

$$\text{Covariance matrix} \equiv \Sigma = \frac{X^T X}{T} \tag{4.29}$$

which is $N \times N$. Now, Risk-Metrics uses an exponential weighting scheme, with the older data weighted less than the newer data. The exponential weighting factors are estimated separately.

In this notation, the exponentially weighted return series is written in matrix notation as

$$\tilde{X} = \begin{bmatrix} r_{11} & \cdots & \cdots & \cdots & r_{1N} \\ \sqrt{\lambda}r_{21} & \cdots & \cdots & \cdots & \sqrt{\lambda}r_{2N} \\ \cdots & \cdots & \sqrt{\lambda^{ii}}r_{ii} & \cdots & \cdots \\ \cdots & \cdots & \cdots & \cdots & \cdots \\ \sqrt{\lambda^{T-1}}r_{T1} & \cdots & \cdots & \cdots & \sqrt{\lambda^{T-1}}r_{TN} \end{bmatrix} \tag{4.30}$$

so that the covariance matrix is

$$\tilde{\Sigma} = \frac{\tilde{X}^T \tilde{X}}{\sum_{i=1}^{T} \lambda^{i-1}} \tag{4.31}$$

To calculate the exponentially weighted correlation matrix, we can define the standardized data matrix

$$\tilde{Y} = \begin{bmatrix} \dfrac{\tilde{r}_{11}}{\sigma_1} & \cdots & \cdots & \cdots & \dfrac{\tilde{r}_{1N}}{\sigma_N} \\ \cdots & \cdots & \cdots & \cdots & \cdots \\ \cdots & \cdots & \dfrac{\tilde{r}_{ii}}{\sigma_i} & \cdots & \cdots \\ \cdots & \cdots & \cdots & \cdots & \cdots \\ \dfrac{\tilde{r}_{T1}}{\sigma_1} & \cdots & \cdots & \cdots & \dfrac{\tilde{r}_{TN}}{\sigma_N} \end{bmatrix} \tag{4.32}$$

where

$$\sigma_j = \frac{\sqrt{\sum_{i=1}^{T} \lambda^{i-1}\tilde{r}_{ij}^2}}{\sum_{i=1}^{T} \lambda^{i-1}} \tag{4.33}$$

so that the correlation matrix is

$$\tilde{R} = \frac{\tilde{Y}^T \tilde{Y}}{\sum_{i=1}^T \lambda^{i-1}} \tag{4.34}$$

The advantage of using an exponential moving average where more recent data affects the computation of volatility and correlation more than older data is that volatility and correlation can respond to shocks much faster, as they should. Also, this is a good approximation to what is observed in reality, i.e., the effects of shocks decay only slowly. Contrast this with the unweighted or simple moving average, where the effects of shocks fall off abruptly as the moving window crosses over that data point.

Note that as the number of data points gets large, i.e., $T \rightarrow \infty$, we can use

$$\sum_{t=1}^T \lambda^{i-1} \sim \frac{1}{1-\lambda} \tag{4.35}$$

so that we can replace the old definition of σ with

$$\sigma \sim \sqrt{(1-\lambda)\sum_{t=1}^T \lambda^{t-1}(r_t - \bar{r})^2} \tag{4.36}$$

Similarly, the covariance equation for a large number of data points is simply (see Equation (4.4))

$$\sigma_{jk}^2 = (1-\lambda)\sum_{t=1}^T \lambda^{t-1}(r_{jt} - \bar{r}_j)(r_{kt} - \bar{r}_k) \tag{4.37}$$

Now, note that these equations can be used to derive recursion relations which are usable for forecasting. Thus, the volatility forecast for time $t+1$, given all the information up to and including time t, for the jth asset, is

$$\sigma_{j,t+1|t} = \sqrt{\lambda\sigma_{j,t|t-1} + (1-\lambda)r_{j,t}^2} \tag{4.38}$$

and, similarly, the covariance forecast is

$$\sigma_{jk,t+1|t}^2 = \lambda\sigma_{jk,t|t-1}^2 + (1-\lambda)r_{jt}r_{kt} \tag{4.39}$$

which gives the *1-day* correlation forecast

$$R_{jk,t+1|t} = \frac{\sigma^2_{jk,t+1|t}}{\sigma_{j,t+1|t}\sigma_{k,t+1|t}} \tag{4.40}$$

This can be straightforwardly extended to multiday forecasts by combining a sequence of single-day forecasts. We obtain

$$\sigma^2_{j,t+T|t} = \sqrt{T}\sigma_{j,t+1|t}$$

$$\sigma^2_{jk,t+T|t} = T\sigma^2_{jk,t+1|t}$$

$$R_{jk,t+T|t} = \frac{T\sigma^2_{jk,t+1|t}}{\sqrt{T}\sigma_{j,t+1|t}\sqrt{T}\sigma_{k,t+1|t}} = R_{jk,t+1|t} \tag{4.41}$$

so that the variance and covariance forecasts increase with time as T, and the correlation forecast never changes. So, in this framework, as the time horizon gets larger, the forecast volatility "blows up," and there is no possibility of having a correlation term structure. These are major shortcomings of this approach for longer term forecasting applications.

Cointegration

One of the major shortcomings of the unconditional correlation coefficient that we have computed above is that it is a purely static concept. The same correlation coefficient is obtained whatever the ordering of the simultaneous data points in the two time series. So if a time point is taken with all the variable values and reinserted, at random, at some other point, the correlation coefficient will not change. Cointegration is a method to extract the *long-run* dynamical relationships between two or more time series. Thus, it has been claimed to be able to quantify causal flows of information between different asset classes. The working definition of two or more cointegrated series is as follows:

- Each individual series is a random walk.
- A linear combination of these series is stationary.

Note that a series is stationary if it has constant mean, finite variance, and autocorrelation that depends only on the lag between the two series. The testing for stationarity is closely related to the existence of "unit roots." Suppose we have a model

$$Y_t = \beta Y_{t-1} + \epsilon_t, \qquad t = 0, 1, 2, \ldots \qquad (4.42)$$

where β is some real number and ϵ_t is a sequence of independent normal zero-mean random variables with variance σ^2. The series Y_t is stationary if $|\beta| < 1$. If $|\beta| = 1$, then the series is not stationary, since then the variance of Y_t is $\sigma^2 t$ and increases with time. This is the random walk. Clearly, when $|\beta| > 1$, the series is nonstationary also. When $|\beta| = 1$, then

$$Y_t - Y_{t-1} = \epsilon_t \qquad (4.43)$$

and the series is said to have a unit root. Since the first difference is equal to ϵ_t, which is stationary by assumption, this differenced process is stationary.

In general, a series x_t is said to be integrated of order d if the series becomes stationary after differencing d times. Then,

$$x_t = I(d) \qquad (4.44)$$

Now suppose we have two time series, p_t and q_t, where

- both are integrated to the same order d (this is crucial, and if the series are not integrated to the same order to begin with, it makes no sense to look for a cointegrating vector), and
- some linear combination of p_t and q_t is integrated to order $b < d$,

then the two series are said to be *cointegrated* to order (d, b), with the vector of coefficients of the linear combination known as the *cointegrating vector*. This can be easily extended to cases where more than two time series are considered together. For $N > 2$, the cointegrating vector does not have to be unique.

One simple way for retrieving the cointegrating vector is to do a simple least-squares regression over all possible combinations until the one that makes the combination stationary is obtained. Once a stationary linear combination has been found, it can be reasoned that this implies the existence of long-term equilibrium relationships between the two time series since the changes in one variable are compensated by scaled changes in the other variables in the combination. Further details of these techniques, such as the Dickey-Fuller test and Johansen's method, can be found in a number of excellent papers on this topic [77,238].

CORRELATION TERM STRUCTURE

For simple, European-style multifactor options, e.g., European-style spread options, the term structure of correlation, i.e., the variation of correlation with respect to time, is not of much direct interest. Once the correlation coefficient is given (either by statistical techniques or by extraction from market variables), the terminal joint distribution is completely specified. However, for path-dependent options, the interim value of correlations can affect the evolution of the paths. Within the joint lognormal framework, the term structure of correlation is a priori unconstrained, and can lead to unrealistic results for option prices. Fortunately, the correlation coefficient can often be controlled by relating its value to the effect on the dispersion of the time evolution of the parent distributions.

Volatility Constraints

As a heuristic example of the correlation curve being constrained by volatility, consider a yield spread option. The starting point for pricing a spread option using the Gaussian model for spreads assumes that the spread is a Weiner process S with continuous sample paths, stationary independent increments (i.e., the distribution of $S_t - S_s$ for time $t > s$ depends only on $t - s$), and $S_t N(0, t)$, where $N(0, t)$ is the standard normal distribution with zero mean and variance t. Heuristically, this assumes that the variance of the distribution of the spread increases with time as t, or the standard deviation increases with time as $\sqrt{t}$. However, this would imply that as the time for expiration increases, the two components could move arbitrarily far from each other. Obviously, macroeconomic considerations preclude this. It is extremely unlikely, if not impossible, for one sector of yields to be too far away from another sector. In terms of correlation, this imposes the constraint that for longer times the yields have to get highly positively correlated so that the spread cannot get too large.

To find an explicit quantitative relationship we will consider the spread of two assets with forwards F_1, F_2 within a two-factor joint lognormal model. Then, the variance of the spread itself is[6]

$$\sigma(T)_S^2(T) = F_1^2[e^{\sigma(T)_1^2 T} - 1] + F_2^2[e^{\sigma(T)_2^2 T} - 1]$$
$$- 2F_1 F_2[e^{\rho(T)\sigma(T)_1 \sigma(T)_2 T} - 1] \qquad (4.45)$$

This should be compared with the results of a model where the spread is assumed to be a Gaussian variable. The variance within the Gaussian model is

$$\frac{1}{\sigma(T)_G \sqrt{2\pi T}} \int_{-\infty}^{\infty} S_T^2 e^{-\frac{1}{2}[(S_T - S_F)/\sigma_G(T)\sqrt{T}]^2} \, dS_T = \sigma_G(T)^2 \qquad (4.46)$$

Equating the variances obtained in these two different ways, we obtain a relationship between the correlation and the Gaussian volatility, i.e.,

$$\rho(T) \sim \frac{1}{\log \sigma_G(T)} \qquad (4.47)$$

This shows the roughly inverse relationship between the correlation and the Gaussian volatility of the spread. If one has a good idea of what the term structure of Gaussian spread volatility is for a given time horizon, under another model which has the same local pricing, the correlation estimate for that time horizon is also known. The way correlation effects are incorporated in single-factor effective models is by creating an effective volatility term structure which gives the correct pricing to the market. In this sense, one dealer might use a completely different number for volatility than another dealer, and the proprietary volatility structures depend on their individual pricing models.

In the exotic market, there are weakly and strongly correlation-dependent products that trade. By pricing all trades in the same book with a common framework and by using reasonable interpolation schemes, it is possible to construct a reasonable implied term structure of correlation. However, it is crucial to recalibrate frequently, as the correspondence between implied

---

6. See derivation in Chapter 6.

volatilities and implied correlations is only valid locally. Disastrous consequences of not following this maxim were evident in early 1994 when end-users pricing index-amortizing swaps with single-factor models with an implied volatility curve did not recalibrate after the first interest-rate hike by the U.S. Fed. The consequence was that the term structure of correlation for the libor yield curve changed almost overnight, leading to a drastically different pricing for indexed structures (which, after all, are barrier options). Since the single-factor models' volatility has exponential sensitivity to the change in correlation, and since the calibration was way off after the Fed move, when the dust had settled it was realized that the portfolios implicitly dependent on these models had suffered huge mark-to-market losses.

The Correlation Cone

One can get a visual idea of the time dependence of correlation by plotting the high, low, median, and mean correlations against time, as in Figures 4–5 and 4–6, the trade underlying which was discussed as the very first example in Chapter 1. Since the long-term range between high and low correlations is much smaller than the short-term range, this type of figure goes by the name of a correlation "cone." The advantage of a picture such as this is that it succinctly summarizes the relationship of the current value of correlation for a given time horizon to its historical statistics, as well as to the presence of outliers, if any. If the current value is significantly different than history, it will immediately point to the specialness of the situation and to the wisdom of entering into the particular trade. Also, a significant trend over time in either the lower or upper bound of the range points to long-term targets that can be confidently assumed for the estimate and which should be used as inputs. The median and mean correlations point to the average correlation for that period, and the *average deviation*, which equals the average value of the absolute deviation from the mean, quantifies that the short-term correlation is usually much more volatile than the long-term correlation.

F I G U R E 4–5

Yen Libor vs Nikkei 225 Correlation Cone, 1986–1997

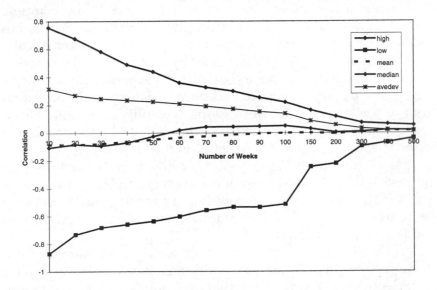

F I G U R E 4–6

Yen Libor vs Dollar/Yen Exchange-Rate Correlation Cone, 1986–1997

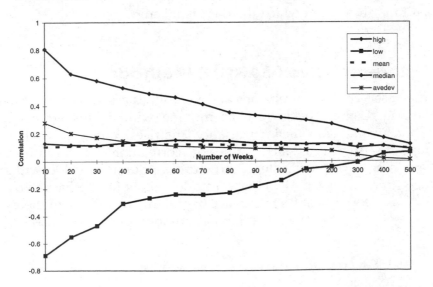

Stepping

The stepping algorithm is straightforward to describe. Take two price series and compute the return data series. Now compute the volatilities and correlations using not all the data points, but a subset of the original data series. The subset can be systematically extracted from the original data series by stepping, i.e., by ignoring all the intermediate data points between some predetermined steps. Figure 4–7 displays computed stepped volatility and correlation from 1 week out to 50 week steps (volatility is in annualized terms) for weekly return data for the Standard and Poor's 500 (asset 1) and the Nikkei 225 (asset 2) indices from 1975.

As is clear from Figure 4–7, volatility falls as the time step increases—this is a classic sign of mean reversion. Also, the correlation is fairly constant, so a flat correlation term structure is probably appropriate for a product that requires correlation between Nikkei and S&P 500 as an input.

As a special method of sampling, we can take samples from random points in two data series and then calculate the correlation coefficient. Then, in the limit that the number of such random samples becomes large, the sample correlation coefficient should be a good approximation to the true correlation coefficient. Note that there are two dimensions to this approach—we can decide to vary the number of points chosen randomly, as well as the length of the time slices from which the data is taken.

Autoregressive (GARCH) Methods

It is observed that correlations and volatilities are, in general, time varying. Using models such as moving window histograms or exponentially smoothed covariance matrices, one can, at best, hope to predict a static value of correlation for the future. Obtaining a correlation term structure is thus impossible within these frameworks. GARCH-type[7] models allow for stochastic volatility and correlation from the very beginning, so, at least in theory, they should perform a better job at hedging option portfolios [80].

---

7. Generalized Autoregressive Conditional Heteroskedasticity.

FIGURE 4-7

Stepping for Volatility and Correlation

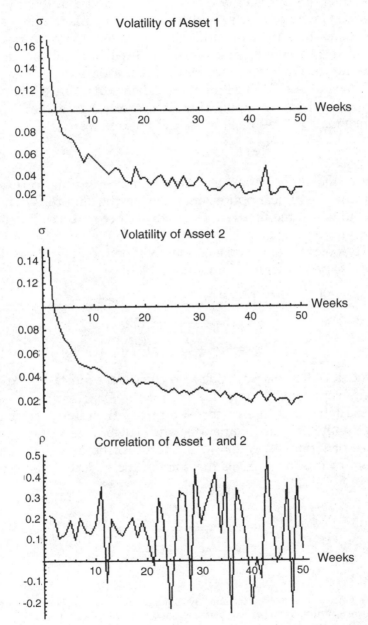

As pointed out in the literature [76,79], autocorrelation in squared returns points to time-varying volatility. Similarly, using the product of returns of two assets, it is found that there is auto-correlation in the products of returns, which points to time-varying correlation. This can be quantified in terms of the Box-Ljung statistic [142]. It is observed that the relevant Box-Ljung statistics indicate strong autocorrelation of the covariance matrices.

The simplest GARCH model is called scalar GARCH and is a generalization of the exponential smoother given earlier. The covariance matrix is assumed to follow the process

$$\sigma_{i,j,t} = \omega_{i,j} + \alpha r_{i,t-1} r_{j,t-1} + \beta \sigma_{i,j,t-1} \tag{4.48}$$

where α and β are parameters determined by fitting to historical data using a nonlinear optimizer, and $\omega_{i,j}$ is the long-run covariance matrix to which the times series of covariance matrices is expected to converge.[8]

To forecast the covariance matrix k periods ahead on time t, take the expected value of Equation (4.48):

$$
\begin{aligned}
E_t[r_{i,t+k} r_{j,t+k}] &= E_t[\sigma_{i,j,t+k}] \\
&= \omega_{i,j} + (\alpha + \beta) E_t[\sigma_{i,j,t+k-1}] \\
&= \overline{\sigma}_{i,j} + (\alpha + \beta)^{k-1} (\sigma_{i,j,t+1} - \overline{\sigma}_{i,j})
\end{aligned}
\tag{4.49}
$$

then the deviation from the one-step covariance forecast is expected to decay exponentially with a parameter $\alpha + \beta$.

The term structure of correlation can then be determined in terms of the forward variances and covariances since, in the absence of serial correlation in the returns, the expected value of the sum of products equals the sum of the expected value of the squares:

$$
R_{i,j,t}^{(k)} = \frac{\sum_{l=1}^{k} \sigma_{i,j,t+l/t}}{\sqrt{\sum_{l=1}^{k} \sigma_{i,t+l/t} \sum_{l=1}^{k} \sigma_{j,t+l/t}}}
\tag{4.50}
$$

---

8. Scalar GARCH models have the same dynamics for all variances and covariances, and there is no distinction between permanent and transitory volatilities. There is also no feedback mechanism from the volatility of one asset to another asset.

There will now be a brief description of an approximation known as the "multivariate orthogonal factor GARCH model" [3], which fits nicely within the index approach framework for managing a large correlation book (see Chapter 6). Despite some problems in dealing with weakly correlated assets, this approximation is attractive since (1) it requires only univariate GARCH models for estimation; (2) the amount of noise can be controlled by keeping a subset of the principal components, thus leading to more stable forecasts; and (3) it can deal efficiently with very large numbers of assets. The period t return for the ith asset is reconstructed in terms of an m-dimensional subset of the full set of principal components $P_{j,t}$, $j = 1, \ldots, k$ (equal to the total number of assets k):

$$Y_{i,t} = \mu_i + \sum_{j=1}^{m} \phi_{ij} P_{j,t} + \epsilon_{i,t} \qquad (4.51)$$

where μ_i are the sample means of the returns, and $\epsilon_{i,t}$ is the error term that includes the error due to the exclusion of some of the components. The coefficients $\phi_{ij} = w_{ij}\sigma_i$ consist of the factor weights w_{ij}, determined by the standard principal component algorithm (see Appendix G), and the sample standard deviation for each return series σ_i.

Now, taking variances of both sides of Equation (4.51), we get

$$\text{Var}(\mathbf{Y}) = \mathbf{\Phi} D \mathbf{\Phi}^T + \boldsymbol{\sigma}_\varepsilon \qquad (4.52)$$

where D is the diagonal matrix of variances of the principal components, and $\boldsymbol{\sigma}_\varepsilon$ is the variance–covariance matrix of the errors. Now, the residual variance is ignored (an approximation), and a conditional variance–covariance matrix $\mathbf{V}_t$ is constructed using a diagonal conditional variance–covariance matrix $\mathbf{D}_t$ containing the GARCH conditional variance of each of the principal components. Thus,

$$\mathbf{V}_t \approx \mathbf{\Phi} D_t \mathbf{\Phi}^T \qquad (4.53)$$

Since the components are independent of each other, their GARCH variance can be forecast from simple scalar GARCH models. Then, using Equation (4.53), the approximate full variance–covariance matrix for all k factors $\mathbf{V}_t$ is obtained. Note also that since the principal components are only unconditionally orthogonal, the diagonal matrix $\mathbf{D}_t$ is only an approximation to the conditional variance–covariance matrix of the principal components. However, as discussed in Reference [3], when considering systems with high correlation, the approximation works pretty well.

In principle, this is all there is to the algorithm for forecasting the full variance–covariance matrix for any number of assets. However, much work has been done to improve the simple algorithm, and the interested reader is directed to the literature for more detail [26,78–80,147]. In practice, a key shortcoming of the GARCH methodology is that it provides very little intuition about the meaning of the numerous parameters that are obtained from fitting to historical data, and hence it has made little progress on trading desks.

In conclusion, while determining the correlation term structure is almost an art, as a general rule of thumb, long-dated correlation is best thought of as the value of the correlation that will most likely be obtained, on the average, over a period of that tenor. An analogy with interest rates will be helpful. Long-term interest rates can be thought of as the expected value of short-term rates for the long tenor. Then, the best expectation of the long-term rate is simply the expected value of all such rates at forward dates linked together. Similarly, long-term correlation is the "average" of all the short-term correlations expected over that period. A practical analogy on how the market for the term structure of correlation will evolve is best explained by looking at the market for interest-rate caps. The convention in the current market for options such as interest-rate caps and floors is to quote the volatility input parameter as a single number for which the sum of prices of the Black model caplets equals the price of the full cap. However, since a cap is a portfolio of these caplets, each caplet is priced by using an appropriate forward volatility parameter appropriate for that forward time slice. Hence, there is a need for a forward volatility curve or a volatility term structure. Options on Eurodollar futures of different maturities enable the extraction of these forward volatilities. Similarly, the correlation term structure can be built up as the sequence of self-consistent values of forward correlations that leads to the correct expected values for long-term correlation. Suppose that the full forward term structure of correlation was known and the individual forward pieces of the option were priced according to this forward correlation curve. In the same sense as described for volatility, a single flat correlation can be backed out such that the price of the option turns out to be the same. So, even though in the guts of the pricing model a full correlation term structure is being used, for quotational simplicity a single correlation number can be used for pricing.

TRADING CORRELATION WITH VOLATILITY

Using options, an end-user can take a view on anticipated volatility in the market without taking a view on the direction of the market. This is done by buying or selling option straddles and/or strangles and hedging the delta of the position in the underlying assets. Using options in two or more interrelated markets, the end-user can also implement views on how the correlation between these markets will evolve over time. In other words, correlation can be traded with volatility in many cases [20]. While, in principle, there is no restriction to the implementation of this strategy in any set of interrelated markets, the foreign exchange markets have provided the most liquid arena for correlation strategies.

Recall the no-arbitrage relationship for exchange rates: (1) the dollar is exchanged for deutschemarks and then, (2) deutschemarks are exchanged for yen. Then, the final result is the same if dollars are directly exchanged for yen (allowing for bid–offer spreads and slippage). Similarly, there is a "triangle" relationship in the volatility markets, with standard option straddles being the simplest vehicle for execution.

The relationships are easily described in terms of the Black-Scholes volatility of the underlying options, which can be depicted in geometrical terms. Let us say we have the DM/USD, yen/USD, and DM/yen exchange-rate trio with percentage Black-Scholes volatilities of 18 percent, 16.6 percent, and 14.4 percent, respectively, for 1-month long options. To obtain the implied correlation for the next month between DM/USD and yen/USD, follow this recipe: construct a triangle as in Figure 4–8 with three vertices labeled USD, DM, and JY (yen) such that the length of the edges is in proportion to these volatilities. Then, the correlation between any pair of exchange rates is calculated by taking the cosine of the

FIGURE 4-8

Volatility-Correlation Triangle

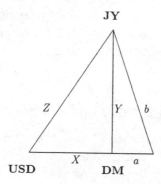

angle between the two edges that connect them. The justification is given below.

The Geometry of Implied Correlation

Consider

$$\sigma_{DM/\$} = X$$
$$\sigma_{DM/JY} = Y$$
$$\sigma_{JY/\$} = Z$$

so that,[9]

$$Y^2 = X^2 + Z^2 - 2\rho XZ \qquad (4.54)$$

where ρ is the correlation between \$/DM and \$/JY.

Now, from Figure 4–8 we can show that

$$\rho = \cos(\theta) = \frac{X + a}{Z} \qquad (4.55)$$

by noting

---

9. See the section on vector algebra for correlation if this variance–covariance relationship is not familiar.

$$(X + a)^2 + b^2 = Z^2$$
$$a^2 + b^2 = Y^2$$
$$2X(X + a) = X^2 + Z^2 - Y^2$$
$$\Rightarrow \frac{X + a}{Z} = \frac{X^2 + Z^2 - Y^2}{2XZ} \tag{4.56}$$

The last equation, on comparison with Equation (4.54), yields Equation (4.55).

With the volatilities mentioned above this recipe gives an implied month-long positive correlation between USD/DM and USD/yen of 78 percent (0.78). Note that changing the order of the quotation, i.e., DM/USD vs USD/DM, changes the sign of the correlation since the angle is now 180 degrees minus the previous angle.

A trader who believes that the correlation between USD/DM and USD/yen over the next month should decrease down to 50 percent can implement the view by doing the inverse of the above, i.e., by constructing a triangle with an angle between the DM/USD and yen/USD edges that corresponds to 50 percent correlation (i.e., by calculating the inverse cosine of 50 and creating a triangle with that angle between the two relevant sides), assuming that in that period the USD/DM and USD/yen volatilities will not change appreciably. This gives a new volatility for the DM/yen options of 17.34 percent. Geometrically, this makes sense since the reduction in the correlation corresponds to the angle becoming more close to a right angle. To complete the triangle, the third side then has to be longer, which corresponds to a higher volatility for that cross. Keeping this geometrical analogy in mind, the trader who thinks that the correlation is going to be lower in the future can implement his strategy by "buying the third side of the triangle," i.e., by buying straddles on the DM/yen cross. In recent history, this strategy was successfully used by option players in the case of the British pound sterling crisis in the exchange-rate mechanism (ERM) by betting against the artificial positive correlation of European currencies maintained as a consequence of exchange-rate bands. Out-of-the-money strangles provided a cheap way to go short the correlation between the sterling and other European currencies.

The geometrical construction described above highlights the fact that given three currencies, the implied volatility of their exchange rates and their pairwise correlations should always lead to a closed triangle (otherwise there is an arbitrage opportunity lurking). It is also easy to generalize this to four and more currencies with higher dimensional geometrical constructs. For example, with four currencies, we would get a tetrahedron. The generalization of the consistency condition to higher dimensions is that the covariance matrix between any number of assets should be positive definite, i.e., the eigenvalues should be real and positive. If this is not the case, then the higher dimensional "triangle" equality is not satisfied and there is a possibility of arbitrage.

Exactly the same construct can be used to relate the volatilities and correlations between the Nikkei stock index futures options (or Euroyen) traded in yen in SIMEX, the Nikkei futures (or Euroyen) options traded in IMM in dollars, and options on the futures on the dollar vs yen exchange rate traded in the IMM. The IMM Nikkei options are, however, too illiquid for large volumes of correlation trades to be executed.

Assuming normal models, a similar relationship can be derived between the volatilities and correlations of different maturity yields in the yield curve. By using the recent CBOT yield curve spread options, yield curve correlations can then be traded with yield volatility instruments.

An interesting generalization is to indices that have a large number of components. For example, options on the S&P 500 or the new Dow Jones options will satisfy the following relationship in terms of the returns and volatilities of their n-weighted components:

$$r_{\text{Index}} = \sum_{i}^{n} w_i r_i$$

$$\sigma_{\text{Index}}^2 = \sum_{i=1}^{n} \sum_{j=1}^{n} w_i w_j \rho_{ij} \sigma_i \sigma_j \tag{4.57}$$

Now, even though it is not possible to invert all the correlations from just this one equation, it is extremely useful to assume that there is an *average correlation*

$$\overline{\rho} = \frac{\sigma_{\text{Index}}^2}{\sum_{i=1}^{n} \sum_{j=1}^{n} w_i w_j \sigma_i \sigma_j} \tag{4.58}$$

which can be used to trade and manage portfolios of index options against options on the components.

Note that in all these examples we clearly see the interrelationship between the volatility and the correlation variables. We have also already seen the mathematical underpinnings of the volatility–correlation transmutability in our discussion of yield curve spread options and long-dated forex options. These are not coincidences; they are reflections of the fact that both volatility and correlation are pieces of the same parent object—the covariance matrix—which, for any reasonable distribution, is tightly constrained.

Finally, note that if an underlying asset is positively correlated with interest rates, then there is an advantage to holding long futures positions as compared with forwards. On the other hand, if the correlation is negative, it is better to hold short futures positions. In the positive-correlation case, as the price of the asset rises, the gains on the futures positions are reinvested at a higher interest rate, whereas losses are financed at lower interest rates. By comparing the futures and forwards for a given asset, a value for the correlation between interest rates and the commodity price can be calculated. Further details on these studies are found in the literature [48,73,110].

VECTOR ALGEBRA FOR CORRELATION

The starting point for calculating all combinations of correlations is to think of consecutive occurrences of the random variable as coordinates of a vector. Then, any random variable can be thought of as a vector in a space where the number of occurrences corresponds to the dimensionality of the vector space:

$$\mathbf{z} = (z_{t_1}, z_{t_2}, \ldots, z_{t_n}) \tag{4.59}$$

Then, the variance of the random variable is simply

$$\mathbf{z} \cdot \mathbf{z} = z^2 \tag{4.60}$$

and thus the standard deviation is the magnitude of the length of the vector, $|z|$.

Given two such vectors, $\mathbf{w}$ and $\mathbf{z}$, the correlation is given by

$$\rho_{w,z} = \frac{\mathbf{w} \cdot \mathbf{z}}{|w||z|} = \cos\theta \tag{4.61}$$

where the last part is reminiscent of the correlation geometry discussion.

For option pricing within a lognormal price or normal return framework, the random variables are taken to be $\mathbf{A} \equiv \log w$ and $\mathbf{B} \equiv \log z$.

Then,

$$\mathbf{A} \cdot \mathbf{A} = |\mathbf{A}|^2 = (\log w)^2 = \sigma_w^2$$
$$\mathbf{B} \cdot \mathbf{B} = |\mathbf{B}|^2 = (\log z)^2 = \sigma_z^2$$
$$\mathbf{A} \cdot \mathbf{B} = \rho_{w,z} \log w \log z = \rho_{w,z}\sigma_w\sigma_w \tag{4.62}$$

where σ_w and σ_z correspond to the volatility[10] of *returns* of the price variables.

Now, w and z correspond to the market traded prices. For example, for currency markets the exchange rates can be assigned as follows:

$$\frac{\text{DM}}{\text{USD}} \equiv w$$

$$\frac{\text{YEN}}{\text{USD}} \equiv z$$

$$\frac{\text{DM}}{\text{YEN}} = \frac{w}{z} \tag{4.63}$$

Then, to find the volatility of the cross DM/YEN, note that

$$\sigma_{\frac{\text{DM}}{\text{YEN}}} = \sigma_{\frac{w}{z}} = \sqrt{\left(\log\frac{w}{z}\right)^2} \tag{4.64}$$

However,

$$\log\frac{w}{z} = \log w - \log z \tag{4.65}$$

so

---

10. Henceforth, the technical definition of volatility will be exactly this: the non-negative square root of the variance of the logarithm of price ratios.

$$\left(\log\frac{w}{z}\right)^2 = (\log w - \log z)^2$$
$$= (\mathbf{A} - \mathbf{B}) \cdot (\mathbf{A} - \mathbf{B})$$
$$= (\mathbf{A} \cdot \mathbf{A} + \mathbf{B} \cdot \mathbf{B} - 2\rho_{w,z}|\mathbf{A}||\mathbf{B}|)$$
$$= \sigma_w^2 + \sigma_z^2 - 2\rho_{w,z}\sigma_w\sigma_z$$
$$\sigma_{DM/YEN}^2 = \sigma_{DM/USD}^2 + \sigma_{YEN/USD}^2 - 2\rho_{w,z}\sigma_{DM/USD}\sigma_{YEN/USD}$$

This can be solved for the correlation to yield

$$\rho_{\frac{DM}{USD},\frac{YEN}{USD}} = \frac{\sigma_{\frac{DM}{USD}}^2 + \sigma_{\frac{YEN}{USD}}^2 - \sigma_{\frac{DM}{YEN}}^2}{2\sigma_{\frac{DM}{USD}}\sigma_{\frac{YEN}{USD}}} \tag{4.66}$$

which we saw earlier in this chapter.[11]

A slightly nontrivial example of a correlation calculation is to get a similar relationship when four currencies are included. Define

$$u = DM/AUD$$
$$v = YEN/AUD$$
$$w = DM/USD$$
$$z = USD/AUD \tag{4.67}$$

and

$$A = \log DM/AUD$$
$$B = \log YEN/AUD$$
$$C = \log DM/USD$$
$$D = \log USD/AUD \tag{4.68}$$

Let us find the correlation

$$\rho(DM/USD, YEN/AUD) = \rho\left(\frac{DM/AUD}{USD/AUD}, YEN/AUD\right) \tag{4.69}$$

Symbolic manipulation gives

---

11. Note that if we flip the currency and countercurrency units for one currency, the sign of the correlation will flip also.

$$\mathbf{C} \cdot \mathbf{B} = 2\rho_{w,v} \log w \log v$$
$$= 2\rho_{w,v}\sigma_w\sigma_v$$
$$= (\mathbf{C} - \mathbf{D}) \cdot \mathbf{B}$$
$$2\rho_{u/z,v} = \log(u/z)\log(v)$$
$$= 2\rho_{u,v}\log u \log v - 2\rho_{z,v}\log z \log v$$
$$= 2\rho_{u,v}\sigma_u\sigma_v - 2\rho_{z,v}\sigma_z\sigma_v \tag{4.70}$$

which implies

$$\rho_{w,v} = \frac{\rho_{u,v}\sigma_u - \rho_{z,v}\sigma_z}{\sigma_w} \tag{4.71}$$

and thus, finally,

$$\rho_{\text{DM/USD,YEN/AUD}} = \frac{1}{\sigma_{\text{DM/USD}}}(\rho_{\text{DM/AUD,YEN/AUD}}\sigma_{\text{DM/AUD}}$$
$$- \rho_{\text{USD/AUD,YEN/AUD}}\sigma_{\text{USD/AUD}}) \tag{4.72}$$

The following is another example that is applicable when pricing spread options: let

$$w = \text{10-year CMT yield}$$
$$z = \text{2-year CMT yield} \tag{4.73}$$

and let us assume we want the correlation of actual changes of the spread 10-year CMT − 2-year CMT with 10-year CMT. Note that here we are assuming that the individual variables, i.e., the spread and the yield, are *normal* variables. Make the assignment

$$\text{10-year CMT} - \text{2-year CMT} = \mathbf{A}$$
$$\text{10-year CMT} = \mathbf{B} \tag{4.74}$$

So we want the correlation of $\mathbf{A}$ with $\mathbf{B}$.

With the usual recipe,

$$\rho = (\mathbf{A} - \mathbf{B}) \cdot \mathbf{A}$$
$$= A^2 - \mathbf{B} \cdot \mathbf{A}$$
$$= \sigma_{\text{10-year yield}}^2 - 2\rho_{\text{10-y,2-y}}\sigma_{\text{10-y}}\sigma_{\text{2-y}} \tag{4.75}$$

Using this simple technology, any set of joint moments can be readily computed.

Higher Moment Correlations and Price's Theorem

When a correlation-dependent option position is hedged using options on individual component assets, the optimal hedging decision depends on the interrelationship of the asset volatilities in addition to the interrelationship of the asset returns. Thus, we need to know the comovement of the second moments of the two assets. Fortunately, if the distribution is assumed to be joint lognormal, these moments are known in terms of the means, variances, and correlations of the asset prices. However, when empirical or fitted distributions are used, these moments may be independent and will have to be determined from data.

When two returns, x and y, are known to be jointly normal, then the expected value of some function $g(x, y)$ is

$$I(C) = E[g(x, y)] = \int_{-\infty}^{\infty} \int_{-\infty}^{\infty} g(x, y) f(x, y) \, dx \, dy \qquad (4.76)$$

where the integral is a function $I(C)$ of the covariance C between x and y and the four parameters specifying the joint density. It can be shown [165] that if $g(x, y) f(x, y) \to 0$ as $(x, y) \to 0$, then

$$\frac{\partial^n I(C)}{\partial C^n} = \int_{-\infty}^{\infty} \int_{-\infty}^{\infty} \frac{\partial^{2n} g(x, y)}{\partial x^n \partial y^n} f(x, y) \, dx \, dy = E\left[\frac{\partial^{2n} g(x, y)}{\partial x^n \partial y^n}\right] \qquad (4.77)$$

This result is known as Price's theorem.

We will now compute the correlation of the second moments. Set $g(x, y) = x^2 y^2$. Applying Price's theorem with $n = 1$, we get

$$\frac{\partial I(C)}{\partial C} = E\left[\frac{\partial^2 g(x, y)}{\partial x \, \partial y}\right] = 4E[xy] = 4C \qquad (4.78)$$

so that

$$I(C) = 2C^2 + I(0) \qquad (4.79)$$

Now, when $C = 0$, the two random variables are independent, hence $I(0) = E[x^2 y^2] = E[x^2]E[y^2]$, so inserting this in Equation (4.79), we obtain, finally,

$$E[x^2 y^2] = E[x^2]E[y^2] + 2E^2[xy] \qquad (4.80)$$

hence the correlation of variances is expected to be proportional to the sum of the product of the variances and the square of the covariance term. The same technique can be used to figure out the relationships between higher moments in terms of known parameters, i.e., coskewness, cokurtosis, etc.

DEVIATIONS FROM MULTINORMALITY

Instead of generating our stochastic processes from a joint multivariate lognormal assumption as assumed in Chapter 3, it is entirely reasonable to extract a joint multivariate density by matching moments, and to use this empirical distribution. Details of this method are discussed in Appendix H. In this section, some empirical results that use the statistical location, shape, and multivariate dispersion-association properties will be presented to illustrate the significant deviation of observations from the idealized multinormal distribution.

   To motivate this, we will first explore some features of multiple time series, i.e., statistical characteristics obtained by standard multivariate statistical manipulations. The aim is to illustrate that significant deviations from joint normality of returns can exist, hence the very assumptions that allow lognormal valuation might be flawed. This has a somewhat relieving consequence for those who are frustrated in their search for closed-form solutions to multivariate pricing and hedging problems. In general, assumptions of joint normality or lognormality are most likely to yield nontrivial yet analytically tractable results. However, if analytical results are not what we ultimately desire, but simply a fairly accurate depiction of reality, we might not be too far off base in using simple-minded but accurate numerical algorithms. Numerical methods that employ empirical distributions are no harder, in principle, to implement than normal- or lognormal-based techniques. So what we might be giving up in terms of analytic, so-called "closed-form" results, we might be compensating for in terms of more accurate results. A simple test of violation of joint normality is to compute the multivariate skewness which ought to vanish for normal distributions.

   The sample data set that we use for our analysis is the same one that we will use for construction of the index approach in

Chapter 6. The data series are daily data for approximately 300 trading days for nine representative markets, i.e.:

1. Gold Handy-Harmon fix
2. Silver Handy-Harmon fix
3. U.S. 10-year constant maturity yield
4. Japanese 10-year constant maturity yield
5. Yen per dollar exchange rate
6. Deutschemark per dollar exchange rate
7. Swiss franc (SF) per dollar exchange rate
8. Nikkei 225 stock index
9. S&P 500 stock index

We first compute the returns by taking the relative changes for each data series and then taking the mean out. Recall that a standard single-variable normal distribution has no skew. In general, skewness corresponds to the statement that the mean and median are not coincident. If the median is less than the mean, the distribution is called positive skew, and if the median is greater than the mean, the distribution is called negative skew. Thus, skewness corresponds to unequal probabilities lying above and below the mean. The coefficient of univariate skewness is calculated by

$$E\left(\frac{X - \mu}{\sigma}\right)^3 \tag{4.81}$$

where σ corresponds to the standard deviation. Univariate kurtosis is the fourth central moment and is given by

$$E\left(\frac{X - \mu}{\sigma}\right)^4 - 3 \tag{4.82}$$

and signifies the sharpness of a peak of the distribution. A high-kurtosis distribution is called leptokurtic, and one with low kurtosis is called platykurtic. A normal distribution has kurtosis of 3.

The results are shown in Table 4–1, which shows that each return above is seen to be more peaked than the normal distribution. The Nikkei and the S&P 500 returns show opposite skewness, while the currency exchange-rates returns vis-à-vis the dollar are all negatively skewed compared with the normal distribution (for the time horizon of the data under consideration).

T A B L E   4–1

Univariate Statistics (Skewness and Kurtosis) of Returns from a
Collection of Assets

Asset	Skewness	Excess Kurtosis
Gold	0.128	2.90
Silver	−0.153	1.21
U.S. 10	0.609	2.915
Jap 10	0.032	0.3607
$/yen	−0.498	1.673
$/DM	−0.40	2.009
$/SF	−0.636	3.096
Nikkei 225	0.344	1.17
S&P 500	−0.7	2.327

Even at the level of univariate statistics, it is clear that the joint distribution is not multinormal, because for a joint distribution to be multinormal, it is necessary, but not sufficient, that the univariate marginal distributions be normal. So the univariate shape statistics clearly indicate significant deviations from joint multinormality.

The multivariate skewness coefficient (a generalization of the univariate coefficient), defined in terms of the covariance matrix C, is

$$\frac{1}{n^2} \sum_i \sum_j [(x_i - \bar{x})^T C^{-1} (x_j - \bar{x})]^3 \qquad (4.83)$$

and is computed from the data to be 6.39756 (and, of course, it would be zero if the actual distribution was normal). The multivariate kurtosis excess over the multivariate normal,

$$\frac{1}{n} \sum_i \sum_j [(x_i - \bar{x})^T C^{-1} (x_j - \bar{x})]^2 - p(p+2) \qquad (4.84)$$

for p data series, is 19.00. So the return data for the time horizon under consideration is not jointly normal! This can be further tested by looking at the generalized location statistics, such as multivariate simplex medians, etc. In fact, the deviation is fairly large. The question then presents itself is how much pricing and hedging error can we make by using idealized multivariate joint lognormal density function to model illiquid hybrid/correlation products?

Taking a step backward, note that the same question may also be asked for single-factor options, i.e., even the simplest stock option. Even a cursory look at the statistics of the simplest behavior of any stock price is likely to show significant deviations of the price from lognormal behavior. But lognormal valuation is still quite popular. Are we making substantial errors? The answer there is rather simple—stock options are traded in liquid markets, so any *deviations from lognormal behavior can be hedged*[12] and at least quantified precisely in terms of liquidity premia (e.g., volatility skews, etc.). So the lognormal approximation is simply a benchmark, with adjustments made by the book-runner to reflect the true nature of the underlying price dynamics. This is not so for illiquid options—they are not as liquid; thus they are, in general, warehoused in books for a much longer time. Hence, not using empirical adjustments is likely to cause *significant* errors that compound in large hedging costs over time. One compromise is to use a combination of theoretical distributions with known functional forms, and then to fit the free parameters by matching statistics.

Mixing Multivariate Distributions

While the details of the mixing methodology are deferred to Appendix H, the discussion in the previous section sets the stage for an introduction to the key motivations behind multivariate mixing distributions.

We usually assume for computational simplification that two or more markets might be distributed in a joint lognormal fashion, but this assumption might not be borne out by the data. For instance, in the previous section we computed the individual and joint statistics of a set of nine different assets, which shows large deviations from multivariate joint lognormality. We might choose to proceed by totally surrendering the assumption of joint lognorm-

---

12. Though using the wrong distribution will eventually lead to accumulated excess hedging costs.

ality and using an empirical distribution to calculate probabilities. This is clearly too extreme and the optimal approach lies somewhere in between. The markets can be assumed to be roughly jointly lognormal, but with some "contamination" so that there is some deviation from joint lognormality.

To quantify the contamination, we need to make assumptions about the contaminating distribution, create a mixed density, and then estimate the parameters in the mixed density. Note that, in mixing, we take linear combinations of the distributions. This is very different from taking linear combinations of random variables from different densities, where the solution is a convolution of densities.

Using $\Phi(\mu_x, \mu_y, \sigma_x, \sigma_y, \rho)$ to denote a general cumulative density function (CDF) of two assets, x and y, with correlation ρ, we can write down a mixed CDF:

$$\alpha\Phi(\mu_{x1}, \mu_{y1}, \sigma_{x1}, \sigma_{y1}, \rho_1) + (1 - \alpha)\Phi(\mu_{x2}, \mu_{y2}, \sigma_{x2}, \sigma_{y2}, \rho_2) \quad (4.85)$$

Suppose we choose 98 percent of the first ($\alpha = 0.98$) and 2 percent of the second. Assume also that all the means are zero: $\mu_{x1}, \mu_{x2}, \mu_{y1}, \mu_{y2} = 0$, and the second distribution has three times as much marginal volatility as the first, so that

$$\sigma_{x1} = \sigma_{y1} = 1$$
$$\sigma_{x2} = \sigma_{y2} = 3$$

and the first distribution has nonvanishing correlation $\rho_1 = \rho$ whereas the second distribution has zero correlation $\rho_2 = 0$. This is the kind of situation that we expect to find when there are outliers, i.e., large correlated shocks. In such cases, the bias effect is quite large and toward zero. For example, with $\rho = 0.8$ and $n = 50$, a simulated set of data give an average estimate of $R = 0.688$ [16].

The higher moments of the distribution of Equation (4.85) for $\mu_{x1} = \mu_{x2} = \mu_{y1} = \mu_{y2} = 0$ and $\sigma_{x1} = \sigma_{x2} = \sigma_{y1} = \sigma_{y2} = 1$, but $\rho_1 \neq \rho_2$, yield zero skewness but nonzero kurtosis (thus, mixed or contaminated bivariate distributions can lead to redistribution of the probability toward the center, i.e., fatter or thinner tails) [135]:

$$\text{Mixed kurtosis} = [\alpha(1 - \alpha)]^2(3A_1^2 + 3A_2^2 + 2A_1 + A_2) \quad (4.86)$$

where

$$A_1 = \frac{(1 + \rho_2)^2 - (1 + \rho_1)^2}{\alpha(1 + \rho_1)^2 + (1 - \alpha)(1 + \rho_2)^2}$$

$$A_2 = \frac{(1 - \rho_2)^2 - (1 - \rho_1)^2}{\alpha(1 - \rho_1)^2 + (1 - \alpha)(1 - \rho_2)^2}$$

The kurtosis is maximal when ρ_1 and ρ_2 are apart.

Thus, the main motivation for mixing distributions is that it allows more general distributions to be generated, which might be a better fit to observations and may possess novel properties, such as more skew or higher kurtosis. If intuition suggests that the underlying dynamics of a number of assets is a combination of different distributions, then an initial guess of the weights and forms can be a starting point. By fitting, the values of the fundamental free parameters may then be obtained, leading to a better theoretical and practical model on which to base computations.

CHAPTER 5

Numerical Methods

$\mathbf{T}$he job of an exotic options trader is made difficult because of the lack of exact solutions to a large fraction of pricing and hedging issues. It is not always possible to find formulas like Black-Scholes into which the values of certain key inputs can be put to get the theoretical prices and risk factors. Actual computation requires, in many cases, sophisticated mathematical algorithms, augmented with an intelligent intuition of limiting cases that may be used as checks. On the other hand, once these technical difficulties are overcome, and a basic set of working tools becomes available, the trader can then savor the luxury of working in a relatively rarified environment, where the natural absence of competition provides for better returns for the same amount of risk.

The process of translating a theoretical model into a pricing and risk management tool usually consists of the following steps:

- Decide on the fundamental variables in the model. Make assumptions regarding which of these will be assumed to be stochastic, and which will be deterministic.

- Settle on a pricing environment, i.e., are asset prices lognormal, or normal, or driven from some empirical distribution? Given the choice of the environment, decide on the exact form of the stochastic differential equations, if they can be derived.

- Can the payoff be decomposed into pieces whose pricing is known? Are exact solutions available? If so, stop and use them, otherwise proceed.
- Is the payoff path dependent? Is the path dependence continuous or discrete? Are there American, i.e., early exercise, features?
- Select, based on the above, whether to use numerical integration, Monte-Carlo simulation, or trees and lattices and their higher dimensional extensions.
- Based on the method of choice in the previous step, use the most efficient algorithms for the purpose at hand, i.e., a process that yields outputs that are practically useful for repricing and hedging.

The exotic trading desk is usually staffed with traders or analysts who have some familiarity with programming principles. With the current generation of tools available on even the most modest of personal computers, it is an almost trivial task to program in the basic pricing tools that can be rolled into systems if the product becomes "hot." I have found higher level programming packages to be extremely useful as a trader's tool. The two tools that are especially useful are Mathematica and later versions of Microsoft Excel, which have the advantages of (1) allowing compact and natural programming concepts, (2) excellent graphics, (3) interfaces that are an integrated part of the trading environment, (4) portability to other traders and desks, and (5) the ability to communicate with each other and thus act as complementary tools. Mathematica has state-of-the-art numerical integration routines in multidimensions, as well as multidimensional random number generators. It also has superb list-manipulation algorithms that make sorting and searching through "nodes" in trees and lattices an easy task. Excel has the benefit of having an integrated Visual Basic programming toolkit, which can be used to write high-level code that refers to the data in related spreadsheets, thus making the input–output process of programming a simple job. Code for American-style trees in multidimensions in

Mathematica can be written in a few lines (see below), which Excel can call as a function using its Mathlink feature. Though simple and elegant, Mathematica's programming constructs are just as rigorous as state-of-the-art programs written in other higher level languages. It is also relatively easy to store user-defined functions as "modules," which can then be imported into other contexts and other platforms—including production level C or Fortran code [145,218].

The methods of choice for multifactor options, when exact solutions are not available, are numerical integration, wherever it can be used; Monte-Carlo, whenever the number of assets is large and there are no early exercise features;[1] and lattices or trees, whenever there are American features. Note that experience teaches traders to become lazy, i.e., the first thing to try before embarking on a stand-alone numerical model for pricing a customized product is to see if the structure is decomposable into simpler structures, or at least into structures that give upper or lower bounds for prices, which should then be used for intuition as well as for simplification. For exotic products, this comes with a warning—intuition is frequently wrong, and it is recommended highly that the following adage then be used as a thinking tool:

You can price what you can hedge!

Simple as it sounds, most traders agree that when faced with a complex structure, if they approach the problem by thinking from the point of view of how they can "lay off the risk," even the pricing problem becomes rapidly clearer.

The purpose of this chapter is to give a self-contained exposition of useful numerical methods, as well as to point out the relevance of certain parameters to which the outputs of the algorithms are intrinsically sensitive, and which may affect the accuracy and the reliability of results. While the tools are available, it is useful to know exactly what goes on "under the hood," so that the limits of the algorithms are known for real-time applications.

---

1. Although, a number of researchers have recently claimed that they can value American-style options fairly accurately using modified Monte-Carlo simulation algorithms, and this will be discussed later.

NUMERICAL INTEGRATION

The pricing of a complex European option, or, for that matter, any linear or nonlinear payoff product, consists of a simple single step. Assuming that the variables have a joint probability density $f(x_i)$, and the payoff of the contract on terminal date is $P(x_i)$, the price of the structure is simply

$$\text{Present value} \quad \sum_{\text{All values for each } x_i} f(x_i)P(x_i) \qquad (5.1)$$

Going to continuous time, we replace the sum by an integral. Then, one can proceed with a number of numerical integration routines as described in Reference [164].

In Mathematica, numerical integration can be performed by calling the function NIntegrate. For example, Figure 5–1 shows the time taken to evaluate numerically on a Pentium 200 MHz PC the single-variable and multivariable densities (that, by construction, have to evaluate to unity).

While we will not go into the details of numerical integration routines, some remarks about multidimensional integration are in order. The number of functional evaluations needed to sample an N-dimensional space increases as the Nth power of the number needed to do a one-dimensional integral. Also, the boundaries might be terribly complicated. If there are symmetries in the

F I G U R E 5–1

Numerical Integration of Univariate and Multivariate Densities

```
Timing[NIntegrate[1/Sqrt[2 Pi]*Exp[-x^2/2], {x, -Infinity, Infinity}]
{0.331 Second,1.}
```

and for the bivariate density

```
p=0.5;
Timing[NIntegrate[(1/(2*Pi*Sqrt[1-p^2]))*
     Exp[(1/(2*(1-p^2)))*(-x^2-y^2+2*p*x*y)],
{x,-Infinity,Infinity},
   {y,-Infinity,Infinity}]
]
{9.39 Second,1.}
```

original equations that lead to the integral, the symmetries are preserved in the integrals, and should be used to reduce computation time drastically. Random sampling of points in the integration region can be carried out using the Monte-Carlo integration algorithm. The Mathematica built-in function can perform the integrals with choices for the `Method` option ranging over `GaussKronrod`, `DoubleExponential`, `Trapezoidal`, `Oscillatory`, `Multi-Dimensional`, `MonteCarlo`, or `QuasiMonteCarlo`. The `GaussKronrod` method is adaptive, and recursively subdivides the integration region to obtain desired accuracy. For speeding up the integrals, it is usually preferred to set the `MaxRecursion` variable to a low number, such as 5, as long as the integrand is smooth.[2] Also, for high-dimensional integrals, the `QuasiMonteCarlo` option, which uses a quasi-random Halton-Hammersley-Wozniakowski algorithm, is preferred to recursive quadrature.

Figure 5–2 gives code for the numerical computation of a European spread option with different numbers of recursive subdivisions. As can be seen, the integral converges rather rapidly as the number of maximum subdivisions or recursions increases.

MULTIVARIABLE MONTE-CARLO SIMULATION

The simplest numerical approach for pricing complex European options in many dimensions is an approach based on simulation. Essentially, all one needs to do is to generate enough scenarios for the coevolution of a set of variables, value the option payoffs at terminal dates for this set of "random" states of the world, and then discount the expected value of the payoff to the pricing date.

Mathematically, this is a reverse of the numerical integration approach. By sampling enough points, it is expected that a discrete sum of probability-weighted values of the target function is a good approximation to the integral. Hence, one replaces a continuous average by a suitably good discrete average.

---

2. If this choice is not made carefully, wrong answers can be obtained, such as the integration of the delta function over the real line computing to zero instead of 1! Since delta functions are used in the pricing of binary and barrier options, wrong pricing is easy to obtain if caution is not exercised.

F I G U R E 5-2

European Spread Option by Numerical Integration at Different Numbers of Recursive Subdivisions

```
F1=5.50; (* First Asset Forward *)
sigma1=0.17;(* First Asset Vol *)
F2=4.50; (* Second Asset Forward *)
sigma2=0.25;(* Second Asset Vol *)
rho=0.60; (* Correlation *)
time=0.5; (* Time to Maturity *)
strike=0.50;(* Option Strike *)
TableForm[Table[Timing[NIntegrate[
Max[F1*Exp[-0.5*sigma1^2*time+sigma1*Sqrt[time]*x]-
    F2*Exp[-0.5*sigma2^2*time+sigma2*Sqrt[time]*y]-strike,0]*
(1/(2*Pi*Sqrt[1-rho^2]))*
Exp[-(1/(1-rho^2))*(x^2+y^2-2*rho*x*y)],
{x,-Infinity,Infinity},{y,Infinity,Infinity},
MaxRecursion->n]],{n,1,5}]
]

(* Outputs *)

{1.35999999999999987 Second, 0.275133019146255097},
{4.06200000000000027 Second, 0.275007975564518591},
{11.9530000000000002 Second, 0.274914937879449983},
{41,9380000000000041 Second, 0.274915696929913755},
{59.3590000000000017 Second, 0.274915673370672619}
```

Thus,

$$I(f) = \int_D f(x)\,dx$$

$$\approx U_n(f) = \frac{1}{n}\sum_{i=1}^{n} f(t_i) \tag{5.2}$$

where $D = [0, 1]^d$ is the d dimensional unit cube.

The expected error of the Monte-Carlo algorithm for a function f is

$$E_n(f) = \sqrt{\int_{D^n} (I(f) - U_n(f))^2 dt_1 \ldots dt_n}$$

$$= \frac{\sigma(f)}{\sqrt{n}} \tag{5.3}$$

where

$$\sigma^2(f) = I(f^2) - I^2(f) \tag{5.4}$$

so that if the variance of the integrand is reduced, the expected error in the simulation method would also decrease. This is the main idea behind the various *variance reduction* schemes used in combination with the Monte-Carlo algorithm, i.e., importance sampling, control variates, antithetic variables, etc., [127] to which we will come shortly.

Random Number Generation

How does one generate random numbers from a computer which is deterministic since it can only follow some predefined algorithm? The notion of a true random number really does not exist for computation purposes. The best one can do is come up with a statistical notion. The working definition of a random number is that one has obtained a statistically reasonable random number generator if, given a number of random number generators, the results of the program based on any of these random number generators are statistically indistinguishable from the results generated from any of the other generators.

The simplest procedure for generating random numbers in most vendor-provided libraries is known as *linear congruential generators* or Lehmer's algorithm. It consists of generating a sequence of integers, $I_1, I_2, I_3, \ldots$, each between 0 and the largest random number that can be generated in the system by a recurrence relation of the kind [164]

$$I_j = f(I_{j-1}) \tag{5.5}$$

where the function f is some linear function. The "minimal standard" generator of Park and Miller provides a good benchmark and is reasonably good for simple applications:

$$I_{j+1} = aI_j \bmod m \tag{5.6}$$

where $a = 7^5 = 16807$ and $m = 2^{31} - 1 = 2{,}147{,}483{,}647$ is one example of the parameters.

Once a sequence of pseudo-random numbers is generated between 0 and some maximum integer, they can be scaled by division by the maximum random number to generate random numbers between 0 and 1. Note that the sequence will repeat itself with a period that is no greater than m. One of the biggest problems in implementing random number generating routines on PC-type systems is that the value returned by the rand() function call is an integer which takes up two bytes or sixteen bits, making the largest value equal to $2^{15} - 1 = 32,767$. What this means is that if the trader thinks that he is running a million different simulations, i.e., equal to 10^6, he is fooling himself drastically—because at best what he is doing is running $10^6/32,767 = 30$ copies of the same set of random numbers!

A linear congruential generator can be implemented in Mathematica with a simple recursion relation:

```
a=16807;
m=2147483647;
Ir[j_]:=N[Mod[a*Ir[j-1],m]];
Ir[1]=1;
```

A counterpoint to the speed and efficiency of this method is the problem that there is autocorrelation in the random numbers so generated. This can be quite dangerous when pricing multi-factor options by simulation. Assume that three different factors are driving the underlying price of the option. Since random numbers for each asset are generated from the same table, the number of distinct random number sequences available before repetition is now only a third of what is available for single-factor options. So even if there is no observable market correlation between the three factors, the method of evaluation of scenarios introduces correlation between the assets and may lead to wrong results.

Mathematica's integer random number generator, i.e., numbers returned by the call Random[Integer,min,max] is based on a different approach derived from cellular automata [217]. For machine precision real numbers, the functions Random[] or Random[Real] are based on Reference [150] and have much higher period of 10^{445}.

Transformation to Other Distributions

Assuming that the random number generator generates uniformly distributed random numbers over a given interval with the possibility of some period exhaustion known in advance, we now want to translate them into random numbers over distributions that are closer to the distributions assumed in the stochastic process used for pricing and hedging. For instance, in the Black-Scholes framework,

$$dS = S\mu \, dt + S\sigma \, dz \tag{5.7}$$

which integrates for constant σ to

$$S_T = S_0 \, e^{(\mu - \frac{\sigma^2}{2})t + \sigma\sqrt{t}z} \tag{5.8}$$

where z is a *normal* random variable with mean of zero and variance of unity.

Now there will be a description of how to get random variables for distributions that are related to the uniform distribution by some kind of transformation of variables. The next subsection will describe the method to obtain random numbers from distributions if there is no known transformation rule to take one from the uniform distribution to the distribution of choice.

We know from the discussion in the previous section that the probability of generating a number between x and $x + dx$ from a uniform density $p(x)$ is given by $p(x)\,dx$:

$$p(x)\,dx = \begin{cases} dx & 0 < x < 1 \\ 0 & \text{otherwise} \end{cases}$$

For normalization, we have $\int_{-\infty}^{\infty} p(x)\,dx = 1$, which remains unchanged under transformations. This result may be used to change variables. Suppose we take a function $y(x)$ of the uniform deviate x. Then, the density of y is given by

$$p(y) = p(x)\left|\frac{dx}{dy}\right| \tag{5.9}$$

This can now be generalized to higher dimensions. If $x_1, x_2, \ldots, x_n$ are random deviates from some *joint* probability

$$f(x_1, x_2, \ldots, x_n)\,dx_1\,dx_2\ldots dx_n \tag{5.10}$$

and if we make a change of variables to $y_1, y_2, \ldots, y_n$, then the joint probability distribution of the y values is

$$f(y_1, y_2, \ldots, y_n)\, dy_1\, dy_2 \ldots dy_n = f(x_1, x_2, \ldots, x_n)|J|\, dy_1\, dy_2 \ldots dy_n$$
(5.11)

where

$$J = \left| \frac{\partial(x_1, x_2, \ldots, x_n)}{\partial(y_1, y_2, \ldots, y_n)} \right|$$
(5.12)

corresponds to the Jacobian determinant, i.e., the determinant of the matrix of partial derivatives of the x variables with respect to the y variables.

Normal Random Variables

The standard method for obtaining normal random variables from uniform random variates is called the *Box-Muller* method. We want to generate random numbers with the probability density $f(y) = (1/\sqrt{2\pi})\, e^{-\frac{1}{2}y^2}$. Draw two uniform random variates in the interval $(0, 1)$ and make the change of variables

$$x_1 = e^{-\frac{1}{2}(y_1^2 + y_2^2)}$$

$$x_2 = \frac{1}{2\pi} \tan^{-1} \frac{y_2}{y_1}$$
(5.13)

The Jacobian is

$$|J| = -\frac{1}{\sqrt{2\pi}} e^{-\frac{1}{2}y_1^2} \frac{1}{\sqrt{2\pi}} e^{-\frac{1}{2}y_2^2}$$
(5.14)

which is the square of the density we need using Equation (5.11). However, this is a product of two marginal normal densities, and is itself a joint normal density with zero correlation between y_1 and y_2. Thus, inverting the above equations, we get two normal variates from two uniform variates:

$$y_1 = \sqrt{-2 \ln x_1} \cos 2\pi x_2$$

$$y_2 = \sqrt{-2 \ln x_1} \sin 2\pi x_2$$
(5.15)

which is used in the code examples below.

In Mathematica, this is already built in (as a matter of fact, a function that returns an array of random numbers according to any specified distribution can also be returned). For instance,

```
Get["Statistics'NormalDistribution'"]
randnormal:=Random[NormalDistribution[0,1]]
Table[randnormal,{1000}]
```

can be used to generate a table of a thousand random variates from the standard normal distribution.

An improvement to this was proposed by Marsaglia and Bray [151] as follows: let U_1 and U_2 be uniformly distributed on $(-1, 1)$ subject to the condition that $U_1^2 + U_2^2 \leq 1$. Thus, the joint density p_{U_1,U_2} is a disk of uniform height and radius 1, centered at the origin, and is given by

$$p_{U_1,U_2}(u_1, u_2) = \frac{1}{\pi} \quad \text{for} -1 \leq u_1, u_2 \leq 1, 0 \leq u_1^2 + u_2^2 \leq 1 \quad (5.16)$$

Then, the variables X_1 and X_2 given below are independent standard normal:

$$X_1 = U_1 \sqrt{\frac{-2 \ln(U_1^2 + U_2^2)}{U_1^2 + U_2^2}}$$

$$X_2 = U_2 \sqrt{\frac{-2 \ln(U_1^2 + U_2^2)}{U_1^2 + U_2^2}}$$

Random Variates from Empirical Distributions

Very frequently, the joint distributions of market variables are quite far away from any sort of joint lognormality or general analytic form. In such cases, especially if the hedging is infrequent, there is a possibility of large errors due to the mis-specification of the underlying stochastic processes. The best approach to calibrate the pricing and hedging error is to reconstruct the empirical joint distribution from the underlying joint statistics, fit a multidimensional volume to the empirical distribution to obtain a parametric analytic form, and then generate random variates from this empirical fit to use for subsequent pricing.

To implement this, in practice, we can use the "Rejection Method" [164]. Basically, the method consists of the following steps:

1. Given a fitted form for the probability density $f(x)$ with the lower and upper limits of x (support) equal to L, U, choose a comparison function $c(x)$ with known indefinite integral such that $c(x) > f(x)$ for all values of x.

2. Since the indefinite integral of c is known, set $\int_L^U c(x)\,dx = A$ and, using a random number generator, generate a *uniform* random number between 0 and A and call it $R(c, A)$.

3. Solve $\int_L^x c(x)\,dx = R(c, A)$ for x by inversion (since c has known analytic integral).

4. Pick a second uniform random variable $S(c, x)$ between 0 and $c(x)$. If the second random variate is larger than $f(x)$, then reject it, otherwise accept it.

Note that the rejection method can also be used when the functional form for the distribution at hand is known, but cannot be obtained by a transformation from the simple uniform distribution. Mathematica code is included in Figure 5–3, which uses the Gaussian density to generate random numbers from an inverse quadratic (Lorentzian) density below between the bounds $(-2, 2)$. As is clear from this discussion, the method really consists of generating random numbers from the inverse cumulative density function, known as the percentile transformation method, but it is more general since the inverse does not have to be computed analytically.

Generating Correlated Random Numbers

It is now possible to give the recipe for generating a set of random numbers that have a predefined correlation coefficient between them. Note that all we need to do is to specify the functional form for the joint density between the variables, and then to draw uniform random numbers from the hypervolume under the graph of the density function in the multidimensional space. It turns out that this process can be simplified in terms of some well-known techniques for manipulating symmetric matrices.

F I G U R E 5–3

Example of Rejection Method: Random Number Generation for
Generalized Distribution

```
Get["Statistics'NormalDistribution'"]
a=1;
b=0.5;
(* "Empirical Distribution" *)
gendens[x_]:=(1/Pi)*(1/(a+b*x^2));
(* "Known Distribution" *)
normdens[x_]:=(1/Sqrt[2 Pi]) Exp[-0.5*x^2];
lowerbound=-2;
upperbound=2;
AreaNorm=CDF[NormalDistribution[0,1],upperbound]-
    CDF[NormalDistribution[0,1],lowerbound];

(* Rejection Algorithm *)
randgen[]:=Module[{firstrand,xcoord,secondrand},
firstrand=Random[Real,{0,AreaNorm}];
xcoord=N[Sqrt[2]*InverseErf[2*firstrand]];
secondrand=Random[Real,{0,normdens[xcoord]}];
If[gendens[xcoord]-secondrand>=0 ,secondrand]
]
(*function called below*)
randgen[]
```

To be specific, let us assume that the task at hand is to generate
two random variables which are both marginally in $N[0,1]$, i.e.,
they both have a mean of zero and a variance of unity. Also,
assume that the correlation between the two variables is ρ. We
can think of these two variables as representing the returns on
two lognormally distributed assets after the mean has been taken
out and the variance has been normalized to unity. This is usually
the stage at which Monte-Carlo algorithms are started in real pricing problems.

- The covariance matrix is

$$C = \begin{bmatrix} 1 & \rho \\ \rho & 1 \end{bmatrix} \qquad (5.17)$$

- The inverse of the covariance matrix is

$$C^{-1} = \frac{1}{1-\rho^2}\begin{bmatrix} 1 & -\rho \\ -\rho & 1 \end{bmatrix} \tag{5.18}$$

- The quadratic form that appears in the exponential in the joint density of $N[0, 1, 0, 1; \rho]$ is

$$Q = X^T C^{-1} X \tag{5.19}$$

where $X = (x, y)$ is a vector of correlated random variables that we are interested in generating for our simulations.
- We can write this in terms of its Cholesky decomposition matrix U and its transpose matrix U^T as $C^{-1} = U^T U$. Then,

$$\begin{aligned} Q &= X^T U^T U X \\ &= (UX)^T (UX) \\ &= Y^T Y \end{aligned} \tag{5.20}$$

where $Y = UX = (w, z)$ and the Cholesky decomposition U of C^{-1} is

$$U = \begin{bmatrix} \frac{1}{\sqrt{1-\rho^2}} & \frac{-\rho}{\sqrt{1-\rho^2}} \\ 0 & 1 \end{bmatrix} \tag{5.21}$$

- With $Y = UX$, we get the two *uncorrelated* random variables[3]

$$w = x\frac{1}{\sqrt{1-\rho^2}} - \rho y \frac{1}{\sqrt{1-\rho^2}}$$

$$z = y \tag{5.23}$$

---

3. Check that $w \cdot z = 0$ by direct substitution:

$$\begin{aligned} w \cdot z &= \left(x \cdot y \sqrt{\frac{1}{1-\rho^2}} - y \cdot y \frac{\rho}{\sqrt{1-\rho^2}} \right) \cdot z \\ &= \rho\sqrt{\frac{1}{1-\rho^2}} - 1 \times \frac{\rho}{\sqrt{1-\rho^2}} \\ &= 0 \end{aligned} \tag{5.22}$$

which can be inverted to get the familiar expressions for correlated random variables x and y:

$$x = w\sqrt{1 - \rho^2} + \rho z$$
$$y = z \tag{5.24}$$

- So, to generate a simulation, we can draw uncorrelated random variables from independent normal distributions $N[0, 1]$ and then use Equation (5.24) to get the correlated random variables as in Figure 5–4.

For general random variables with non unit variances, we can generalize the above procedure simply:

- The covariance matrix is

$$C = \begin{bmatrix} \sigma_x^2 & \rho\sigma_x\sigma_y \\ \rho\sigma_x\sigma_y & \sigma_y^2 \end{bmatrix} \tag{5.25}$$

- The inverse of the covariance matrix is

$$C^{-1} = \frac{1}{\sigma_x^2\sigma_y^2(1 - \rho^2)} \begin{bmatrix} \sigma_y^2 & -\rho\sigma_x\sigma_y \\ -\rho\sigma_x\sigma_y & \sigma_x^2 \end{bmatrix} \tag{5.26}$$

FIGURE 5–4

Mathematica Generation of Two Random Variables with General Covariance Matrix from Two Uncorrelated Standard Normal Variates

```
Get["LinearAlgebra'Cholesky'"]

X={x,y};
Covmat={{1,p},{p,1}};
InvCovmat=Inverse[Covmat];
Q=X.InvCovmat.X;
DecompInvCovmat=CholeskyDecomposition[InvCovmat];
Y={w,z};
Simplify[Solve[X==Inverse[DecompInvCovmat].Y,{x,y}]]
```

- The relevant quadratic form is

$$Q = X^T C^{-1} X \tag{5.27}$$

where $X = (x, y)$ is a vector of correlated random variables that we are interested in generating for our simulations.
- We can write this in terms of its Cholesky decomposition matrix U and its transpose matrix U^T as $C^{-1} = U^T U$. Then,

$$\begin{aligned} Q &= X^T U^T U X \\ &= (UX)^T (UX) \\ &= Y^T Y \end{aligned} \tag{5.28}$$

where $Y = UX = (w, z)$ and the Cholesky decomposition U of C^{-1} is

$$U = \begin{bmatrix} \frac{1}{\sigma_x \sqrt{1-\rho^2}} & \frac{-\rho}{\sigma_y \sqrt{1-\rho^2}} \\ 0 & \frac{1}{\sigma_y} \end{bmatrix} \tag{5.29}$$

- Finally, we get the correlated random variables x and y:

$$\begin{aligned} x &= w\sigma_x \sqrt{1 - \rho^2} + \rho\sigma_x z \\ y &= \sigma_y z \end{aligned} \tag{5.30}$$

The code in Figure 5–5 generalizes this algorithm to the three-variable case in Mathematica. Further generalization to higher dimensions is straightforward.

The three-variable case gives a set of three correlated random vectors x_i in terms of three uncorrelated univariate normal variables y_i as follows (note that the symmetry of the covariance matrix is used to make the appropriate replacements, $\rho_{12} = \rho_{21}$, etc.):

$$C = \begin{bmatrix} 1 & \rho_{12} & \rho_{13} \\ \rho_{12} & 1 & \rho_{23} \\ \rho_{13} & \rho_{23} & 1 \end{bmatrix}$$

which, with the algorithm above, gives

F I G U R E 5–5

Mathematica Generation of Three Random Variables with General Covariance Matrix from Three Uncorrelated Normal Variates

```
Get["LinearAlgebra'Cholesky'"]

X={x1,x2,x3}; Covmat={{1,p12,p13},{p12,1,p23},{p13,p23,1}};
InvCovmat=Inverse[Covmat];
Q=X.InvCovmat.X;
DecompInvCovmat=CholeskyDecomposition[InvCovmat];
Y={y1,y2,y3};
Simplify[Solve[X==Inverse[DecompInvCovmat].Y,{x1,x2,x3}]]
```

$$x_1 = \frac{y_1}{a} + \sqrt{\frac{1}{1 - \rho_{23}^2}} \, (\rho_{12} - \rho_{13}\rho_{23})y_2 + \rho_{13}y_3$$

$$x_2 = y_2\sqrt{1 - \rho_{23}^2} + \rho_{23}y_3$$

$$x_3 = y_3$$

where

$$a = \sqrt{\frac{1 - \rho_{23}^2}{1 - \rho_{12}^2 - \rho_{23}^2 - \rho_{13}^2 + 2\rho_{12}\rho_{13}\rho_{23}}} \qquad (5.31)$$

This result is also used in Appendix D where the Visual Basic code is given for a three-factor Monte-Carlo simulation engine.

Monte-Carlo Pricing and Hedging of Options

Due to the simplicity of its implementation, the Monte-Carlo algorithm is extremely popular for the pricing of exotic and hybrid options. Assuming that the technical issues have been appropriately taken care of, according to the algorithms described above, all we need to do is to simulate repeatedly sets of paths for the time evolution of each underlying asset in a risk-neutral world according to the stochastic process that defines them, as shown in Figure 5–6. To be completely general and to avoid arbitrage, it is important to remember that if interest rates are directly one of the assets with

F I G U R E 5-6

Three-Factor Monte-Carlo Engine in Mathematica

```
Get["Statistics'NormalDistribution'"]

(* Set correlations *)
corr12=0.80;
corr23=0.70;
corr13=0.60;
(* Set number of paths *)
paths=1000;
(* Set number of time steps *)
steps=100;
(* Set length of time for each step *)
months=3;
(* Assign forward term structure *)
forward1=Table[5.8,{steps}];
forward2=Table[6.0,{steps}];
forward3=Table[6.4,{steps}];
(* Assign vol term structure *)
vol1=Table[0.22,{steps}];
vol2=Table[0.18,{steps}];
vol3=Table[0.16,{steps}];
(* Generate Random Numbers *)
For[{sumz1=0,sumz2=0,sumz3=0};p=1,p<=paths,p++,
For[s=1,s<=steps,s++,
z3[s]=Random[NormalDistribution[0,1]];
e1[s]=Random[NormalDistribution[0,1]];
e2[s]=Random[NormalDistribution[0,1]];
z2[s]=corr23*z3[s]+Sqrt[1-corr23^2]*e2[s];
z1[s]=e2[s]*((corr12-corr13*corr23)/Sqrt[1-corr23^3])+e1[s]*(Sqrt[(1+2*corr12*
corr13*corr23-corr12^2-corr13^2-corr23^2)
/(1-corr23^3)])+corr13*z3[s];
(* Store path dependence information *)
sumz1=sumz1+Sqrt[months/12]*z1[s];
sumz2=sumz2+Sqrt[months/12]*z2[s];
sumz3=sumz3+Sqrt[months/12]*z3[s];
(* Do computation for forward asset price matrix *)
ndata[p,s]={forward1[[s]]*Exp[vol1[[s]]*sumz1-0.5*vol1[[s]]^2*s*months/12],
forward2[[s]]*Exp[vol2[[s]]*sumz2-0.5*vol2[[s]]^2*s*months/12],
forward3[[s]]*Exp[vol3[[s]]*sumz3
0.5*vol3[[s]]^2*s*months/12]}
]
]
```

time evolution, then the value of the option payoff at each point in each path is discounted back to time zero at the correct (i.e., stochastic) interest rate along that path. Thus,

$$V_t = E[V_T e^{-\bar{r}(T-t)}] \tag{5.32}$$

where V_T is the value along the given path at time T, and $\bar{r}$ is the average instantaneous risk-free rate between times t and T. The expected value is under the risk-neutral measure, i.e., the average risk-free rate is used for growth and discounting. This assumes that continuous hedging of the position is possible at each stage in the time evolution of the assets. If the securities under consideration are not tradable securities, then we have to reduce the drift rate by the risk-adjusted market price of risk, i.e., by $\lambda\sigma$.

For n variables, now we define S_i to be the ith variable, with σ_i the volatility, μ_i the growth rate in a risk-neutral world, and ρ_{ij} the instantaneous correlation between asset i and asset j. We divide the life of the option to be valued into N subintervals, each of length Δt. Then, in discrete terms, the process is (assuming joint lognormal evolution)

$$\Delta S_i = \mu_i S_i \Delta t + \sigma_i S_i \epsilon_i \sqrt{\Delta t} \tag{5.33}$$

where ϵ_i is drawn from the standard joint normal distribution described above. For each variable, N such random variates can be drawn and stored.

The hedge parameters in the Monte-Carlo algorithm are also obtained by brute force recalculation. Assume that the price of the security with respect to asset i in state S_i is P_S. Then, the price in the state S_i' is $P_{S'}$. Thus, the delta with respect to the ith asset is

$$\frac{P_{S'} - P_S}{S_i' - S_i} \tag{5.34}$$

assuming that the same random number streams are used for both pricing runs. This can be insured in Mathematica with the command SeedRandom[n], where n is some integer. It is usually more practical to let Mathematica pick its own seed, but after each call to the random number generator, store the random state of the internal random number generator by the assignment s = $RandomState and then recall it during the hedge computation run by using the recall statement $RandomState = s. This ensures that the random number generator is in the same state each time. Of course, one can choose simply to generate a random number table once and for all, and this can be stored and used for daily revaluation reports.

Improving the Simulation

If we make N Monte-Carlo runs for the valuation of a security, the error of the correct price decreases as the inverse square root of N, i.e., the standard error of the Monte-Carlo estimate is $1/\sqrt{N}$. The so-called *antithetic variable* technique can reduce this by a factor of 2: for every ϵ_i, regard $-\epsilon_i$ as a good random variate from the joint normal distribution. In the *control variate* technique, one assumes that an exotic security with a complicated payoff function can be approximately priced by comparison with another security with an exact analytic solution. Then, both securities are valued using simulation. The difference in the price of the two securities obtained by simulation can then be added to or subtracted from the analytic price of the security with known analytic price to obtain a control variate approximation for the exotic one. A rapid summary of these improvement techniques will be provided. The reader may refer to any number of excellent references on simulation methods, e.g., [127], for further details.

Antithetic Variables

Assume that we want to calculate the expectation $E[P_d(z)]$ where P_d is the discounted payoff and z is a normal random variable. We replace P_d by $g(z) = P_d(z) + \alpha[P_d(z) - P_d(-z)]$, where α is a constant and is chosen to minimize the variance of g, which leads to $\alpha = 0.5$. So the expected value can be replaced by $\frac{1}{2}[P_d(z) - P_d(-z)]$, which has variance $\frac{1}{2}\text{var}(P_d)(1 + \rho)$ where ρ is the correlation between $P_d(z)$ and $P_d(-z)$. If ρ is less than 1, the variance of the antithetic technique is less than the variance of the original procedure. This will be useful if the variance of $\frac{1}{2}(P_d(z) + P_d(-z))$ is, at most, half the variance of $P_d(z)$, since one now has to calculate both $P_d(z)$ and $P_d(-z)$. Note that whenever P_d is a monotonic function of z, then ρ is negative, and the antithetic approach leads to an efficiency factor of $1 + \rho < 1$.

Control Variates

In this technique, we replace the discounted payoff $P_d(z)$ by $g(z) = P_d(z) + \alpha(h(z) - E(h))$, where $h(z)$ is the control variate with some known expectation. Again, α is selected to minimize the variance of g. This is achieved if $\alpha = \text{Cov}(P_d, h)/\text{Var}(h)$, where the covariance can be estimated by simulation. Then, $\text{Var}(g) = \text{Var}(P_d)(1 - \rho^2)$ where ρ^2 is the correlation between $P_d(z)$ and the control variate $h(z)$. Since, for all values of ρ, the variance of g is less than the variance of the original discounted payoff function, we will always have fewer cycles before the Monte-Carlo converges. Now, if the computation time required to compute $h(z)$ is some fraction f of the time for $P_d(z)$, we will benefit if $|\rho| > \sqrt{f/(1+f)}$. In particular, if it takes the same amount of time to compute P_d and h, we gain if the absolute value of the correlation between the original variables and the control variates is larger than about 0.7071. The more time needed to compute the control variate, the more correlated in absolute value the control variate and the original variable have to be. For this reason, control variates have to be chosen very carefully. The choice has to be dictated by reasons of fast computation and dome intrinsic relationship to the original pricing problem. For example, a natural control variate for pricing an arithmetic average option is a geometric average option for which the price is known in closed form.

Functional Method

In this method, the approach is to multiplicatively replace the payoff function with a modified function whose variance can be reduced. Note that if the stochastic process for an asset is

$$dS_t = a_t\, dt + b_t\, dw_t \tag{5.35}$$

and if we are interested in the expectation $E[P_d(S_T)]$, we can consider the two stochastic processes

$$dS'_t = (a_t - \alpha_t b_t)\, dt = b_t\, dw_t$$
$$dg_t = g_t \alpha_t\, dw_t \tag{5.36}$$

so that the terminal expectation is

$$E[P_d(S_T)] = \frac{1}{g_0} E[P_d(S'_T)g_T] \tag{5.37}$$

where the last equation follows from the change of measure or Girsanov formula (see Appendix I).

Low-Discrepancy Sequences

Whereas a detailed exposition of this topic is beyond the scope of this book, I would like to highlight some essential features and motivation behind using low-discrepancy or quasi-random or sub-random sequences for pricing higher dimensional options [161, 229].

The motivation behind using Monte-Carlo algorithms is to sample just enough points in the space of terminal payoffs such that a reasonably good value for the average payoff, or expected value, can be computed. In a very direct sense, the simulation paths terminate at the final target on expiry in a number of price points which, if the simulation is good, will "fill up" the final state. Monte-Carlo algorithms get better as the number of paths or points increase, but only at the rate of the square root of the number of paths. The problem is that some of the paths start clustering together and oversampling a given region, at the cost of ignoring other equally important regions.

One way around this problem is to use a predefined lattice of points on which the terminal payoff can be evaluated. But this is not too efficient, because the lattice itself has no knowledge of the behavior of the function, i.e., it will blindly compute values even where the value is zero.

Quasi-random sequences are not really random in any sense. They are a systematic way of generating a lattice such that the points know how to avoid each other and further recursion stops as some predefined convergence or accuracy criterion is met. Thus, the sequence of points so generated fills up n space better and more uniformly than random numbers generated from an algorithm like the ones described above.

Halton's sequence is a simple one to describe. In one dimension, generate the jth number in the following way:

1. Write j as a number in base b where b is some prime.
2. Reverse the digits and put a decimal point before the first digit.
3. This is H_j, the jth Halton number.

These numbers can then be used in simulations. These methods give robust simulation prices for higher dimensional problems.

MULTIVARIATE TREES AND LATTICES

Discretization

The use of discrete lattices and trees will be motivated as appropriate discretizations of the continuous densities. We need the result known as the DeMoivre-Laplace theorem:

$$\binom{n}{k}p^k q^{n-k} \simeq \frac{1}{\sqrt{2\pi npq}}e^{\frac{-(k-np)^2}{2npq}} \tag{5.38}$$

for k in the $\sqrt{npq}$ neighborhood of np. As $n \to \infty$, the two expressions above tend to equality. The proof of this result is based on Stirling's formula:

$$n! \simeq n^n e^{-n}\sqrt{2\pi n} \quad n \to \infty \tag{5.39}$$

Note that the probability of obtaining the discrete value k, given that the random variable $\mathbf{x}$ is normal, is simply

$$P(x = k) = \int_{-\infty}^{\infty} e^{-\left(\frac{x-np}{\sqrt{npq}}\right)^2} \delta(x - k)\,dx = e^{-\left(\frac{k-np}{\sqrt{npq}}\right)^2} \tag{5.40}$$

which equals the probability of obtaining exactly k successes in n trials. By setting $m \to 2k - n$, we can see explicitly how, in the limit $n \to \infty$, the Equation (5.38) leads to the normal density.

The generalization of this result to r variables (events) is

$$\frac{n!}{k_1!k_2!\dots k_r!}p_1^{k_1}\dots p_r^{k_r} \simeq \frac{e^{-\frac{1}{2}\left[\frac{(k_1-np_1)^2}{np_1}+\dots+\frac{(k_r-np_r)^2}{np_r}\right]}}{\sqrt{(2\pi n)^{r-1}p_1\dots p_r}} \tag{5.41}$$

Suppose $p = q = \frac{1}{2}$. Also, let $m = 2k - n$. Then, the left-hand side of Equation (5.38) equals $\binom{n}{k}(1/2^n)$, which is the probability of k heads in n tosses. So we can think of the discretization of the ordinary normal density in terms of coin tosses, where we move up for heads and down for tails. For the multidimensional joint normal density, note that we can change variables using the Cholesky decomposition to eliminate cross-correlation terms. Then, the overall joint density is simply a product of single-variable densities of uncorrelated variables. Each of these terms can be discretized, using Equation (5.38), into combinatoric factors which represent simultaneous coin tosses of more than one coin, with each coin being responsible for moves in one dimension. Then, for N coins, we can represent the move in an N-dimensional lattice, where we move up if the coin responsible for that dimension shows up heads.

Using this discretization, we will first summarize the single-factor tree approach.

The Single-Factor Tree

Assuming that the initial stock price is S, and the probability in a small time interval Δt of an up move to state Su is p, and that of a down move to state Sd is $1 - p$, we get

$$S e^{r \Delta t} = pSu + (1 - p)Sd \tag{5.42}$$

Also, since the variance of the stock price in a small time interval is $S^2 \sigma^2 \Delta t$,

$$S^2 \sigma^2 \Delta t = pS^2 u^2 + (1 - p)S^2 d^2 - S^2[pu + (1 - p)d]^2 \tag{5.43}$$

and, for the lattice recombining property to be maintained,

$$u = \frac{1}{d} \tag{5.44}$$

Solving the above system,

$$p = \frac{e^{r \Delta t} - d}{u - d}$$

$$u = e^{\sigma \sqrt{\Delta t}}$$

$$d = e^{-\sigma \sqrt{\Delta t}} \tag{5.45}$$

Now suppose the life of an option on a non-dividend-paying stock is divided into N subintervals, each with length Δt. Here, f_{ij} is the value of the option at the (i, j) node, i.e., at time $i \Delta t$ when the stock price is $u^j d^{i-j}$ for $0 \leq i \leq N$ and $0 \leq j \leq i$. For example, for an American put, at expiration the payoff is $\max(K - S_T, 0)$, so

$$f_{Nj} = \max[K - Su^j d^{N-j}, 0] \qquad \text{for } j = 0, 1, \ldots, N \tag{5.46}$$

and at other nodes

$$f_{ij} = e^{-r\,\Delta t}[pf_{i+1,j+1} + (1-p)f_{i+1,j}] \tag{5.47}$$

for $0 \le i \le N-1$ and $0 \le j \le i$. Taking early exercise into account, we compare this with the intrinsic value of the option at each node to obtain the recursive formula

$$f_{ij} = \max[K - Su^j d^{i-j}, e^{-r\,\Delta t}[pf_{i+1,j+1} + (1-p)f_{i+1,j}]] \tag{5.48}$$

For currencies, we replace $e^{r\,\Delta t}$ in the expression for p by $e^{(r-r_f)\,\Delta t}$ to capture the loss of interest, where r_f is the foreign currency rate. This also works for dividend-paying stocks if we use the dividend yield in place of r_f. For trees that model interest-rate processes, the stochastic value of r is used also for the period-to-period growth and discounting. For time- and level-dependent volatility, $\sigma(S,t)$, the full "volatility surface" of strike and maturity is used [63,72,188]. A simple implementation of a single-factor tree is given in Figure 5–7.

The Multifactor Pyramid

This can be generalized in a straightforward way to the multivariate case [178]. Geometrically, we now have a pyramid, in which at each time step n, $(n+1)^2$ new nodes are generated. Just as before, the first asset can move up, with return u, or down, with return d. However, we now assume that the moves are with equal probability, so as to make the book-keeping easier. Simultaneously, if the first asset return is u, the second asset is restricted to have returns A or B; and if the first asset moves to d, the second asset can have only returns C or D, with equal probability. Also, to keep the pyramid recombining, we assume that $AD = BC$. To be able to represent generic correlations, $A \ne C, B \ne D$. Now we can build up the tree of returns. Suppose the first return (now indexed with two asset returns) is (u, A). Then, the second return can be generated from any of the four $(u, A), (u, B), (d, C), (d, D)$ to get the possible states $(u^2, A^2), (u^2, AB), (ud, AC), (ud, AD)$ with equal probability of $\frac{1}{4} \times \frac{1}{4} = \frac{1}{16}$. Figure 5–8 shows explicitly the node values for a three-step pyramid.

F I G U R E 5–7

Single-Factor Binomial Tree in Mathematica with Sample Output

```
(*Normal Tree: Probabilities are all 0.5, but the forwards
have the 1/2 sigma^2 t term in it
This is simpler and easier to implement *)
Module[{n,F,S,sigma,t,strike,mu,z,x,i,j,tree,f,prob},
n=5;F=100;S=100;sigma=0.40;t=1;r=0.0;strike=50;prob=0.5;
mu=(1/t)Log[F/S];
z[i_,j_]:=(j-(i-j))/Sqrt[i+0.000001];
p[i_,j_]:=(1/2)^i*(i!/ (j! (i-j)!));
x[i_,j_]:=(mu-sigma^2/2)(i*t/n)+sigma Sqrt[i*t/n]*z[i,j];
For[j=0,j<=n,j++,
f[n,j]=Max[S*Exp[x[n,j]],0]
];
f[i_,j_]:=f[i,j]=Max[S*Exp[x[i,j]],Exp[-r*t/n]*(prob*f[i+1,j+1]+
(1-prob)*f[i+1,j])];
tree=TableForm[N[Table[f[i,j],{i,0,n},{j,0,i}]]]
(* Print[TableForm[Table[p[i,j],{i,0,n},{j,0,i}]]] *)
]
```

100.

82.2929   117.69

67.7212   96.8507   138.51

55.7297   79.7012   113.984   163.012

45.8616   65.5884   93.8005   134.148   191.85

37.7409   53.9746   77.1911   110.394   157.879   225.788

With

$$\Delta t = t/n$$
$$\mu_1 = r - \tfrac{1}{2}\sigma_1^2$$
$$\mu_2 = r - \tfrac{1}{2}\sigma_2^2$$

F I G U R E 5–8

Moves for a Three-Step Binomial Pyramid

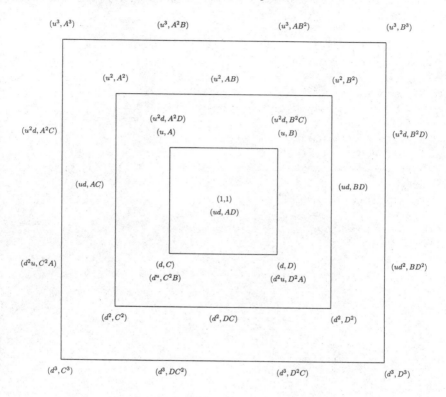

we get

$$u = e^{\mu_1 \Delta t + \sigma_1 \sqrt{\Delta t}}$$

$$d = e^{\mu_2 \Delta t - \sigma_1 \sqrt{\Delta t}}$$

$$A = e^{\mu_2 \Delta t + \sigma_2 \sqrt{\Delta t}(\rho + \sqrt{1-\rho^2})}$$

$$B = e^{\mu_2 \Delta t + \sigma_2 \sqrt{\Delta t}(\rho - \sqrt{1-\rho^2})}$$

$$C = e^{\mu_2 \Delta t - \sigma_2 \sqrt{\Delta t}(\rho - \sqrt{1-\rho^2})}$$

$$D = e^{\mu_2 \Delta t - \sigma_2 \sqrt{\Delta t}(\rho + \sqrt{1-\rho^2})}$$

with $AD = BC$.

We can now implement this for the option of choice. For an American spread option,

$$C = \max[(S_2 - S_1) - K, 0] \qquad (5.49)$$

and we have, for a three-step tree (and $(3+1)^2 = 16$ terminal nodes),

$$C(u^3, A^3) = \max[(S_2 A^3 - S_1 u^3) - K, 0]$$
$$C(u^3, A^2 B) = \max[(S_2 A^2 B - S_1 u^3) - K, 0]$$
$$C(u^3, AB^2) = \max[(S_2 AB^2 - S_1 u^3) - K, 0]$$
$$C(u^3, B^3) = \max[(S_2 B^3 - S_1 u^3) - K, 0]$$
$$C(u^2 d, A^2 C) = \max[(S_2 A^2 C - S_1 u^2 d) - K, 0]$$
$$C(u^2 d, A^2 D) = \max[(S_2 A^2 D - S_1 u^2 d) - K, 0]$$
$$C(u^2 d, B^2 C) = \max[(S_2 B^2 C - S_1 u^2 d) - K, 0]$$
$$C(u^2 d, B^2 D) = \max[(S_2 B^2 D - S_1 u^2 d) - K, 0]$$
$$C(d^2 u, C^2 A) = \max[(S_2 C^2 A - S_1 d^2 u) - K, 0]$$
$$C(d^2 u, C^2 B) = \max[(S_2 C^2 B - S_1 d^2 u) - K, 0]$$
$$C(d^2 u, D^2 A) = \max[(S_2 D^2 A - S_1 d^2 u) - K, 0]$$
$$C(u d^2, BD^2) = \max[(S_2 BD^2 - S_1 u d^2) - K, 0]$$
$$C(d^3, C^3) = \max[(S_2 C^3 - S_1 d^3) - K, 0]$$
$$C(d^3, DC^2) = \max[(S_2 DC^2 - S_1 d^3) - K, 0]$$
$$C(d^3, D^2 C) = \max[(S_2 D^2 C - S_1 d^3) - K, 0]$$
$$C(d^3, D^3) = \max[(S_2 D^3 - S_1 d^3) - K, 0]$$

Now we can start to *roll back* through the pyramid. At the penultimate time step, the value of the option is the higher of the discounted value of the probability-weighted (with equal probabilities $\frac{1}{4}$) option value or the intrinsic value from exercise:

$$C(u^2, A^2) = \max[(S_2A^2 - S_1u^2) - K,$$
$$e^{-r\Delta t}\tfrac{1}{4}[C(u^3, A^3) + C(u^3, A^2B) + C(u^2d, A^2C) + C(u^2d, A^2D)]]$$
$$C(u^2, AB) = \max[(S_2AB - S_1u^2) - K,$$
$$e^{-r\Delta t}\tfrac{1}{4}[C(u^3, A^2B) + C(u^3, AB^2) + C(u^2d, A^2D) + C(u^2d, B^2C)]]$$
$$C(u^2, B^2) = \max[(S_2B^2 - S_1u^2) - K,$$
$$e^{-r\Delta t}\tfrac{1}{4}[C(u^3, AB^2) + C(u^3, B^3) + C(u^2d, B^2C) + C(u^2d, B^2D)]]$$
$$C(ud, AC) = \max[(S_2AC - S_1ud) - K,$$
$$e^{-r\Delta t}\tfrac{1}{4}[C(u^2d, A^2C) + C(u^2d, A^2D) + C(d^2u, C^2A) + C(d^2u, C^2B)]]$$
$$C(ud, AD) = \max[(S_2AD - S_1ud) - K,$$
$$e^{-r\Delta t}\tfrac{1}{4}[C(u^2d, A^2D) + C(u^2d, B^2C) + C(d^2u, C^2B) + C(d^2u, D^2A)]]$$
$$C(ud, BD) = \max[(S_2BD - S_1ud) - K,$$
$$e^{-r\Delta t}\tfrac{1}{4}[C(u^2d, B^2C) + C(u^2d, B^2D) + C(d^2u, D^2A) + C(ud^2, BD^2)]]$$
$$C(d^2, C^2) = \max[(S_2C^2 - S_1d^2) - K,$$
$$e^{-r\Delta t}\tfrac{1}{4}[C(d^2u, C^2A) + C(d^2u, C^2B) + C(d^3, C^3) + C(d^3, DC^2)]]$$
$$C(d^2, DC) = \max[(S_2CD - S_1d^2) - K,$$
$$e^{-r\Delta t}\tfrac{1}{4}[C(d^2u, C^2B) + C(d^2u, D^2A) + C(d^3, DC^2) + C(d^3, D^2C)]]$$
$$C(d^2, D^2) = \max[(S_2D^2 - S_1d^2) - K,$$
$$e^{-r\Delta t}\tfrac{1}{4}[C(d^2u, D^2A) + C(d^3, D^2C) + C(ud^2, BD^2) + C(d^3, D^3)]]$$

Rolling to the first time step, next we get

$$C(u, A) = \max[(S_2A - S_1u) - K,$$
$$e^{-r\Delta t}\tfrac{1}{4}[C(u^2, A^2) + C(u^2, AB) + C(ud, AC) + C(ud, AD)]]$$
$$C(u, B) = \max[(S_2B - S_1u) - K,$$
$$e^{-r\Delta t}\tfrac{1}{4}[C(u^2, BA) + C(u^2, B^2) + C(ud, BC) + C(ud, BD)]]$$
$$C(d, C) = \max[(S_2C - S_1d) - K,$$
$$e^{-r\Delta t}\tfrac{1}{4}[C(du, CA) + C(du, CB) + C(d^2, C^2) + C(d^2, CD)]]$$
$$C(d, D) = \max[(S_2D - S_1d) - K,$$
$$e^{-r\Delta t}\tfrac{1}{4}[C(du, DA) + C(du, DB) + C(d^2, DC) + C(d^2, D^2)]]$$

and, finally, to the origin:

$$C = \max[(S_2 - S_1) - K, e^{-r\Delta t}\tfrac{1}{4}[C(u, A) + C(u, B) + C(d, C)$$
$$+ C(d, D)]] \tag{5.50}$$

To get the sensitivities of the option, we give the recipes to calculate these directly from the pyramid (note that A and C are the "up" moves for the second asset):

$$\Delta(S_1) = \frac{\frac{1}{2}[C(u, A) + C(u, B) - C(d, C) - C(d, D)]}{S_1 u - S_1 d}$$

$$\Delta(S_2) = \frac{[C(u, A) + C(d, C) - C(u, B) - C(d, D)]}{S_2 A + S_2 C - S_2 B - S_2 D}$$

The Mathematica code in Figure 5–9 shows a recursive general multivariate pyramid algorithm that can be used to value American-style spread options, etc.

F I G U R E 5–9

Two-Factor American Pyramid Code

```
Normal tree, i.e., all probabilities are the same = 0.25
Terminal forwards have variance term 0.5 sigma^2 t in them

pyramid[n_:5,f1_:6.5,f2_:6.5,s1_:6.5,s2_:6.5,
sigma1_:0.18,sigma2_:0.15,corr_:0.80,t_:1,r_:0.05]:=
Module[{mu1,mu2,i,j,k,z,p,q,x,y,f},
mu1=(1/t) Log[f1/s1];
mu2=(1/t) Log[f2/s2];
w[i_,j_,k_]:=(j-(i-j))/Sqrt[i+0.0001]; (*Square root of i is to keep variance
equal to 1*)
z[i_,j_,k_]:=((corr*(j-(i-j))+Sqrt[1-corr^2](k-(i-k))))/Sqrt[i+0.0001];
p[i_,j_]:=(1/2)^i (i! / (j! (i-j)!));
q[i_,k_]:=(1/2)^i (i!/ (k! (i-k)!));
x[i_,j_,k_]:= (mu1 -(0.5*sigma1^2))(i*t/n) + sigma1 Sqrt[i*t/n] w[i,j,k];
y[i_,j_,k_]:= (mu2-(0.5*sigma2^2)) (i*t/n) + sigma2 Sqrt[i*t/n] z[i,j,k];
For[j=0,j<=n,j++,
For[k=0,k<=n,k++,
f[n,j,k]=Max[s2 Exp[y[n,j,k]] - s1 Exp[x[n,j,k]],0];
]
];
f[i_,j_,k_]:=f[i,j,k]= Max[s2 Exp[y[i,j,k]] - s1 Exp[x[i,j,k]],
Exp[-rt/n]*0.25*(f[i+1,j+1,k+1]+f[i+1,j,k+1]+f[i+1,j,k]+f[i+1,j+1,k])];
tree=TableForm[N[Table[f[i,j,k],{i,0,n},{j,0,i},{k,0,i}]]];
N[f[0,0,0]]
]
```

FINITE DIFFERENCE METHODS

The finite difference method approaches the problem of option valuation directly, i.e., by trying to find a numerical solution to the partial differential equations that describe the evolution of the option price with given boundary and/or initial conditions. For complex options products, finite difference methods have other added benefits. To calculate the hedge ratios, the pricing algorithm does not have to be rerun. Consider an option that depends on three underlying market variables with their volatility term structures. Just to calculate the "delta" risks, a Monte-Carlo simulation has to be run three times, in addition to the pricing run. To calculate second derivatives, including cross-gammas, many further runs are needed. In the finite difference method, the value of the option for different initial values is known from the very beginning, so the calculation of hedge parameters boils down to taking the difference of option values for adjacent starting points. Finite difference methods can easily handle American exercise problems also, so they provide one consistent means for valuing a large class of products within the same framework.

Consider the generalized multidimensional Black-Scholes equation,

$$\frac{\partial O}{\partial t} + \sum_i S_i \frac{\partial O}{\partial S_i}(\mu_i - \lambda_i \sigma_i) + \frac{1}{2}\sum_{i,j}\rho_{ij}\sigma_i\sigma_j S_i S_j \frac{\partial^2 O}{\partial S_i\, \partial S_j} = rO \qquad (5.51)$$

which has only first-order time derivatives and second-order derivatives with respect to the assets S_i.

If we wish, we can first reduce this equation to the canonical multidimensional diffusion equation (using the transformations given in Chapter 3),

$$\frac{\partial f}{\partial t} + \sum_i \frac{\partial^2 f}{\partial S_i^2} = 0 \qquad (5.52)$$

with some boundary conditions, i.e., conditions for various limiting values of S_i, and initial conditions, i.e., limiting conditions for $t = 0$. The diffusion equation, which describes the distribution of temperature in a rod in many dimensions, has been studied extensively in physics, and many canned algorithms for its numerical solution

exist. Once the solution is found, we can translate all resultant outputs back into the original variables. However, to make things very
transparent, we will deal directly with the full Black-Scholes equation.

Single-Variable Finite Differences

This section will illustrate the application of the finite difference
method in one dimension in the case of the American put on a
non-dividend-paying stock.

The option satisfies the Black-Scholes form of the diffusion
equation

$$\frac{\partial O}{\partial t} + rS\frac{\partial O}{\partial S} + \frac{1}{2}\sigma^2 S^2 \frac{\partial^2 O}{\partial S^2} = rO \tag{5.53}$$

We can choose N subdivisions of the time axis to be equally spaced
between the current time and maturity T, with $\Delta t = T/N$, and a
finite number of prices of the underlying asset with $\Delta S = S_\infty/M$,
where we have chosen S_∞ to represent some high asset price that is
sufficiently far away. Next, we construct an $(M+1)$ by $(N+1)$
lattice with an arbitrary point given by (i, j) corresponding to
time $i\,\Delta t$, asset price $j\Delta S$, and option price $O_{i,j}$. We are interested
in finding, for pricing and hedging purposes, $O_{0,\alpha\Delta S}$ where α corresponds to a value of the index j such that $j\Delta S$ equals the current
asset price. Once the value of the option for each (i, j) on the grid is
known, the risk parameters *delta*, *gamma*, and *theta*, corresponding
to the change in option price and option hedge with respect to the
underlying asset and time, can be calculated by taking the slope
with respect to the prices adjacent to the current gridpoint.

For the time derivative, we use a forward difference approximation,

$$\frac{\partial O}{\partial t} = \frac{O_j^{i+i} - O_j^i}{\Delta t} \tag{5.54}$$

For the asset derivative we use a symmetric difference,

$$\frac{\partial O}{\partial S} = \frac{O_{j+1}^i - O_{j-1}^i}{2\,\Delta S} \tag{5.55}$$

and for the second derivative, a centered difference,

$$\frac{\partial^2 O}{\partial S^2} = \frac{O_{j+1}^i - 2O_j^i + O_{j-1}^i}{\Delta S^2} \tag{5.56}$$

so that we get

$$O_j^{i+1} = a_j O_{j-1}^i + b_j O_j^i + c_j O_{j+1}^i \tag{5.57}$$

where

$$a_j = \tfrac{1}{2}rj\,\Delta t - \tfrac{1}{2}\sigma^2 j^2\,\Delta t$$
$$b_j = 1 + \sigma^2 j^2\,\Delta t + r\,\Delta t$$
$$c_j = -\tfrac{1}{2}rj\,\Delta t - \tfrac{1}{2}\sigma^2 j^2\,\Delta t$$

For an American put, the boundary conditions are

$$O_j^N = \max[K - j\Delta S, 0] \qquad \text{for } j = 0, 1, \ldots, M$$
$$O_0^i = K \qquad \text{for } i = 0, 1, \ldots, N$$
$$O_M^i = 0 \qquad \text{for } i = 0, 1, \ldots, N \tag{5.58}$$

which are essentially the three conditions for the option price at the three edges of the lattice.

Now we can start solving the system backward. Since the payoff function at expiration determines O_j^N, and also $O_0^{N-1} = K$ and $O_M^{N-1} = 0$, we get

$$a_j O_{j-1}^{N-1} + b_b O_j^{N-1} + c_j O_{j+1}^{N-1} = O_j^N \tag{5.59}$$

for $j = 1, 2, \ldots, M - 1$. We are left with $M - 1$ equations to solve for the $M - 1$ unknowns $O_1^{N-1}, O_2^{N-1}, \ldots, O_{M-1}^{N-1}$. Compare each solution with the intrinsic value for the American put, $K - j\Delta S$. If $O_j^{N-1} < K - j\Delta S$, early exercise at the penultimate time is optimal and, for that gridpoint, we can set $O_j^{N-1} = K - j\Delta S$. Once all the values for O_j^{N-1} are determined in this way, we can repeat the step for the O_j^{N-2}, etc., until we have determined all the values $O_1^0, \ldots, O_{M-1}^0$. Since one of these asset prices corresponds to the current value, we have then determined the corresponding option price.

F I G U R E 5–10

Finite Difference in One Dimension

```
n=7;
m=7;
deltaS=14.285;
deltat=0.0595;
sigma=0.40;
r=0.10;
K=50;
For[j=0,j<=m,j++,O[n,j]=Max[K-j deltaS,0]];
For[i=0,i<n,i++,O[i,0]=K];
For[i=0,i<n,i++,O[i,m]=0];
Solve[
Flatten[
Table[O[i,j]==
(0.5 r j deltat - 0.5 sigma^2 j^2 deltat) O[i-1,j-1]+
(1+sigma^2 j^2 deltat + r deltat) O[i-1,j] +
(-0.5 r j deltat - 0.5 sigma^2 j^2 deltat) O[i-1,j+1],{j,1,m-1},{i,1,n}
]
]
]
```

The Mathematica code in Figure 5–10 shows the application of this algorithm for the computation of a 7×7 lattice.

Tridiagonal Matrix Equations

Now that the application of the simple finite difference algorithm has been illustrated, I would like to generalize it to a bivariate lattice. However, before we go on to general formulas for a multivariate lattice, I would like to summarize the above methodology in terms of matrix equations. The reason for this is that the numerical solution of matrix equations is radically simplified when the matrix equations have tridiagonal forms, i.e., the only nonzero elements are the elements that are on the main, sub, and super diagonals. The boundary and initial conditions, as well as the equations for the intermediate time steps for diffusion-like partial differential equations, such as the Black-Scholes equation, can be compactly expressed in terms of such tridiagonal matrix equations.

First, note that in the backward difference scheme we have the derivatives for the i, j lattice point as

$$\frac{\partial O}{\partial t} = \frac{O_j^{i+1} - O_j^i}{\Delta t}$$

$$\frac{\partial O}{\partial S} = \frac{O_{j+1}^{i+1} - O_{j-1}^{i+1}}{2\,\Delta S}$$

$$\frac{\partial^2 O}{\partial S^2} = \frac{O_{j+1}^{i+1} - 2O_j^{i+1} + O_{j-1}^{i+1}}{(\Delta S)^2} \tag{5.60}$$

whereas in the forward difference scheme we have

$$\frac{\partial O}{\partial t} = \frac{O_j^{i+1} - O_j^i}{\Delta t}$$

$$\frac{\partial O}{\partial S} = \frac{O_{j+1}^i - O_{j-1}^i}{2\,\Delta S}$$

$$\frac{\partial^2 O}{\partial S^2} = \frac{O_{j+1}^i - 2O_j^i + O_{j-1}^i}{(\Delta S)^2} \tag{5.61}$$

where

$$i = 0, 1, \ldots, N$$
$$j = 0, 1, \ldots, M \tag{5.62}$$

In the Crank-Nicholson scheme, we use an average of the backward and forward difference schemes, and this leads to better accuracy in the finite difference scheme. Taking the average and representing the Black-Scholes Equation (5.53), we obtain the Crank-Nicholson representation,

$$a_{j+1}O_{j+1}^{i+1} + b_{j+1}O_{j+1}^i + c_{j+1}O_{j-1}^{i+1} + a_jO_{j+1}^i + d_jO_j^i + c_jO_{j-1}^i = 0 \tag{5.63}$$

where

$$a_j = \left(\frac{r}{4}j + \frac{\sigma^2}{4}j^2 \right) \Delta t$$

$$b_j = \left(1 - \frac{\sigma^2}{2}j^2 \, \Delta t \right)$$

$$c_j = \left(-\frac{r}{4}j + \frac{\sigma^2}{4}j^2 \right) \Delta t$$

$$d_j = b_j + r \, \Delta t \tag{5.64}$$

We will write this in terms of matrices and vectors:

$$\mathbf{C}v^{i+1} = \mathbf{D}v^i + B^i \tag{5.65}$$

where

$$v^{i+1} = \begin{bmatrix} O_0^{i+1} \\ O_1^{i+1} \\ \vdots \\ O_M^{i+1} \end{bmatrix} \tag{5.66}$$

and

$$v^i = \begin{bmatrix} O_0^i \\ O_1^i \\ \vdots \\ O_M^i \end{bmatrix} \tag{5.67}$$

and

$$C = \begin{bmatrix} c_2 & b_2 & a_2 & 0 & \cdots & \cdots & \cdots \\ 0 & c_3 & b_3 & a_3 & \cdots & \cdots & \cdots \\ 0 & 0 & c_4 & b_4 & \cdots & \cdots & \cdots \\ \cdots & \cdots & \cdots & \cdots & \ddots & \cdots & \cdots \\ \cdots & \cdots & \cdots & \cdots & c_M & b_M & a_M \end{bmatrix} \tag{5.68}$$

and

$$D = \begin{bmatrix} c_1 & d_1 & a_1 & 0 & \cdots & \cdots & \cdots \\ 0 & c_2 & d_2 & a_2 & \cdots & \cdots & \cdots \\ 0 & 0 & c_3 & b_3 & \cdots & \cdots & \cdots \\ \cdots & \cdots & \cdots & \cdots & \ddots & \cdots & \cdots \\ \cdots & \cdots & \cdots & \cdots & c_{M-1} & d_{M-1} & a_{M-1} \end{bmatrix} \tag{5.69}$$

and B^i is the zero vector.

At this stage, we can use the boundary conditions to reduce the dimensionality of the matrix and also to put it into tridiagonal form. For example, in the case of an American put, we have

$$O_j^N = \max(K - j \, \Delta S, 0)$$
$$O_0^i = K$$
$$O_M^i = 0$$

so that we can write, in terms of reduced *tridiagonal* matrices,

$$C = \begin{bmatrix} b_2 & a_2 & 0 & 0 & \cdots & \cdots & \cdots \\ c_3 & b_3 & a_3 & 0 & \cdots & \cdots & \cdots \\ 0 & 0 & b_4 & c_4 & \cdots & \cdots & \cdots \\ \cdots & \cdots & \cdots & \cdots & \cdots & \cdots & a_{M-1} \\ \cdots & \cdots & 0 & \cdots & \cdots & c_M & b_M \end{bmatrix} \tag{5.70}$$

and

$$D = \begin{bmatrix} d_1 & a_1 & 0 & 0 & \cdots & \cdots & \cdots \\ c_2 & d_2 & 0 & 0 & \cdots & \cdots & \cdots \\ 0 & 0 & \cdots & \cdots & \cdots & \cdots & \cdots \\ \cdots & \cdots & \cdots & \cdots & \cdots & \cdots & a_{M-2} \\ \cdots & \cdots & 0 & \cdots & \cdots & c_{M-1} & d_{M-1} \end{bmatrix} \tag{5.71}$$

with

$$B^i = \begin{bmatrix} c_2 O_0^{i+1} + c_1 O_0^i \\ \vdots \\ a_M O_M^{i+1} + a_{M_1} O_M^i \end{bmatrix} \tag{5.72}$$

and

$$v^i = \begin{bmatrix} O_1^i \\ \vdots \\ O_{M-1}^i \end{bmatrix} \tag{5.73}$$

Note that for an American put, we have the boundary conditions (when asset price is close to zero)

$$O_0^i = K \ \forall \ i \tag{5.74}$$

and (when asset price is large)

$$O_M^{i+1} = 0 \ \forall \ i \tag{5.75}$$

so that

$$B_{\text{Put}}^i = \begin{bmatrix} K(c_2 + c_1) \\ \vdots \\ 0 \end{bmatrix} \tag{5.76}$$

In this form, all the equations for intermediate values, as well as boundary and initial conditions, are subsumed under one matrix equation which can be solved inductively by a variety of numerical techniques. At any time step i, only the information contained in one time step ahead is needed for the "roll back."

Now, in principle, the original matrix equation $Cv^{i+1} = Dv^i + B^i$ can be solved by inverting C and doing the matrix multiplication $v^{i+1} = C^{-1}(Dv^i + B^i)$, but this does not take advantage of the fact that the reduced matrices C and D are actually tridiagonal. The solution using tridiagonal matrices is much faster and more memory efficient.

Multidimensional Finite Differences

In this section, the analytics of the previous section will be generalized to multiple dimensions. We will address only the two-dimensional case since the generalization to more than two dimensions is straightforward. The two-dimensional case illustrates all the complex issues that one might confront while trying to implement a finite difference algorithm that prices hybrid securities. The form of the equations presented in this section is sufficient for numerical computation, but, due to the coupling effect of many dimensions, it is not very efficient. The next section will touch briefly on a method that can make the solution of the system of equations more tractable.

We have as our example the two-factor Black-Scholes equation:

$$\frac{\partial O}{\partial t} + rS_1 \frac{\partial O}{\partial S_1} + rS_2 \frac{\partial O}{\partial S_2} + \frac{1}{2}\sigma_1^2 S_1^2 \frac{\partial^2 O}{\partial S_1^2} + \frac{1}{2}\sigma_2^2 S_2^2 \frac{\partial^2 O}{\partial S_2^2}$$

$$+ \rho\sigma_1\sigma_2 S_1 S_2 \frac{\partial^2 O}{\partial S_1 \partial S_2} - rO = 0 \qquad (5.77)$$

Instead of using Crank-Nicholson here, we will use a simple explicit finite difference scheme which can be easily generalized to a more sophisticated differencing scheme. We will assume the space on which we discretize the equation to represent, geometrically, a three-dimensional cuboid with time along the z axis and the two asset prices along the x and y axes. We assume N partitions of the time to expiry, and M partitions for both asset price ranges.

Then, representing the value of the option at some intermediate node in terms of the time index i, and asset indices j, k for the two assets, we get

$$\frac{\partial O}{\partial t} = \frac{O_{j,k}^{i+1} - O_{j,k}^{i+1}}{\Delta t}$$

$$\frac{\partial O}{\partial S_1} = \frac{O_{j+1,k}^{i} - O_{j-1,k}^{i}}{2\,\Delta S_1}$$

$$\frac{\partial O}{\partial S_2} = \frac{O_{j,k+1}^{i} - O_{j,k-1}^{i}}{2\,\Delta S_2}$$

$$\frac{\partial^2 O}{\partial S_1^2} = \frac{O_{j+1,k}^{i} - 2O_{j,k}^{i} + O_{j-1,k}^{i}}{2\,\Delta S_1^2}$$

$$\frac{\partial^2 O}{\partial S_2^2} = \frac{O_{j,k+1}^{i} - 2O_{j,k}^{i} + O_{j,k-1}^{i}}{2\,\Delta S_2^2}$$

$$\frac{\partial^2 O}{\partial S_1 \partial S_2} = \frac{O_{j+1,k+1}^{i} - O_{j+1,k-1}^{i} - O_{j-1,k+1}^{i} + O_{j-1,k-1}^{i}}{4\,\Delta S_1 \Delta S_2}$$

It can be checked that the differencing scheme is consistent in that interchanging the order of the S_1 and S_2 derivatives leaves the representation unchanged. So the scheme is fully symmetric.

Putting all of this into the original equation, we obtain the difference approximation to the differential equation:

$$
\begin{aligned}
0 = \; & O^{i+1}_{j,k} + O^i_{j,k}[-1 - \tfrac{1}{2}j^2\sigma_1^2 \, \Delta t - \tfrac{1}{2}k^2\sigma_2^2 \, \Delta t - r \, \Delta t] \\
& + O^i_{j+1,k}[j \, \Delta t + \tfrac{1}{4}j^2\sigma_1^2 \, \Delta t] \\
& + O^i_{j,k+1}[k \, \Delta t + \tfrac{1}{4}k^2\sigma_2^2 \, \Delta t] \\
& + O^i_{j,k-1}[-\tfrac{1}{2}k \, \Delta t + \tfrac{1}{4}k^2\sigma_2^2 \, \Delta t] \\
& + O^i_{j-1,k}[-\tfrac{1}{2}j \, \Delta t + \tfrac{1}{4}j^2\sigma_1^2 \, \Delta t] \\
& + O^i_{j+1,k+1}[\tfrac{1}{4}\rho\sigma_1\sigma_2 \, \Delta t] \\
& + O^i_{j+1,k-1}[-\tfrac{1}{4}\rho\sigma_1\sigma_2 \, \Delta t] \\
& + O^i_{j-1,k-1}[\tfrac{1}{4}\rho\sigma_1\sigma_2 \, \Delta t] \\
& + O^i_{j-1,k+1}[\tfrac{1}{4}\rho\sigma_1\sigma_2 \, \Delta t]
\end{aligned}
\tag{5.78}
$$

which can be written symbolically as

$$
\begin{aligned}
O^{i+1}_{j,k} = \; & aO^i_{j,k+1} + bO^i_{j,k} + cO^i_{j,k-1} \\
& + uO^i_{j+1,k+1} + vO^i_{j+1,k} + wO^i_{j+1,k-1} \\
& + xO^i_{j-1,k+1} + yO^i_{j-1,k} + zO^i_{j-1,k-1}
\end{aligned}
\tag{5.79}
$$

where the coefficients have suppressed indices j, k (see Equation (5.78)) that represent their positions in the cuboid and using which their values can be computed.

The most important thing to note about this equation is that the time evolution of the option price depends on nine values of the option at the previous time step. In the two-dimensional case, the nine points that contribute are all the ones in a plane and the nearest neighbors of the next time point. If the correlation is exactly zero, the "diagonal" moves are irrelevant, and only the knowledge of five point in the previous time plane is needed. In that case, the terms $O^i_{j+1,k+1}, O^i_{j+1,k-1}, O^i_{j-1,k-1}, O^i_{j-1,k+1}$ are zero and need not be considered.

The correct application of boundary conditions and initial values is still critical. Now the value of the option has to be known on five of the six planes before the option price at initial time can be calculated. As an example, consider an option on a basket of two assets with payoff function

$$P_{\text{Basket}} = \max(K - (aS_1 + bS_2), 0) \qquad (5.80)$$

with $a, b > 0$. We can write down the boundary and initial conditions:

$$O_{j,k}^N = \max(K - aj\,\Delta S_1 - bk\,\Delta S_2, 0)$$
$$O_{0,k}^i = \max(K - bk\,\Delta S_2, 0)$$
$$O_{j,0}^i = \max(K - aj\,\Delta S_1, 0)$$
$$O_{M,k}^i = 0$$
$$O_{j,M}^i = 0 \qquad (5.81)$$

Now the problem is completely specified along with boundary conditions, and by matrix inversion, as in the previous section, the solution can be iteratively found.

Operator Splitting Methods

The discretization obtained above can be used to find solutions to the pricing and hedging problem in multidimensions. Given sufficient computing power, no further modification of the above equations is needed. However, note that due to the coupling between the different asset classes, the equations have no simplification in terms of "tridiagonal" type of equations, even though the evolution is described by tensors that are very sparse. An elegant way to break the difference equations into simpler pieces is to assume that each full-length move on the lattice is made up of fractional smaller moves. A full exposition of this can be found in Reference [164].

Application: Differential Swaptions

A popular multifactor transaction is the "diff" or differential swap, which was described in Chapter 1. In this structure, counterparties exchange interest-rate liabilities without exchanging currency liabilities. For instance, assume that counterparty A is receiving floating payments in yen on some investment. Assume also that yen rates are at historically low levels, as they were in the mid 1990s. Compared with these levels, the dollar interest rates provide very attractive returns. One way for counterparty A to enhance its assets is to enter into a transaction whereby it passes along the floating yen receivables to a swap counterparty B, and in exchange receives dollar libor minus some margin, payable in yen. So it essentially uses the dollar interest-rate market as an index on which to peg its receivables. Note that at each settlement rate, the exchange rate which is current on that date is used to calculate the amount that B would have to pay on the next date. Now as long as the dollar receivables minus the diff swap margin exceeds the yen payments, the investor is better off, since the return to his assets are calculated based on the higher receivables.

The nature of risk is better understood if we consider carefully what the hedge for B has to be. Since B needs to pay dollars on each settlement date, he has to be short some number of Eurodollar contracts to match his potential future dollar interest-rate liability. At the same time, since the payments are in yen, he has to be hedged in the currency forwards market to convert the dollars into yen. Now, if dollar interest rates are negatively correlated to the exchange rate (i.e., as dollar rates rise, the dollar gets weaker), then to deliver the appropriate yen, B has the risk that he might have to convert his dollars from hedge settlement at an adverse exchange rate. So, for negative correlation, he would expect to require a premium, i.e., the floating rate that he would be willing to pay would be less than the dollar libor flat.

To price an American option to enter into such a swap, we are forced to solve the equation numerically using a multidimensional lattice. At each point on the lattice, we assume that the decision to enter into such a swap is optimal as compared with the decision not to enter into the swap just yet but to wait for a future period.

Recent work on pricing differential swaptions and related applications using finite differences can be found in References [7], [58], and [116].

ADVANCED NUMERICAL TECHNIQUES

Path-dependent options that depend on several sources of uncertainty are notoriously hard to model numerically. As long as the number of assets is less than three or four, it is not hard to generalize the binomial lattice scheme to higher dimensional lattices. However, this is not too efficient if the interest is in modeling a whole book, such as a hybrid book with 30 or 40 different asset exposures, since the memory requirement grows exponentially with the number of risk sources. Alternatively, consider a specific pricing example such as the multidimensional American puts given in Chapter 1.

Recently, there has been significant progress in applying simulation-type techniques to the valuation of multidimensional American-style options. Note that the common lore of derivatives has held the belief for a long time that American options cannot be valued by Monte-Carlo. This is not true in principle, though it has been true in practice because of numerical limitations. In principle, it is possible to sample the future for each point on the early exercise time line and to check if early exercise is optimal. However, this, in its most brute force form, would require running independent "mini-Monte-Carlos" for each future point.

An early attempt to overcome the optimal exercise decision problem was published by Tilley [205]; this introduces the first "bundling" algorithm into Monte-Carlo for the American put.

Stratified State Aggregation

This section focuses on a specific approach to the valuation of American-style claims in many dimensions and uses a special way of partitioning the method of the underlying asset space called the *Stratified State Aggregation (SSA)* [11–13] algorithm.

The price of an American contingent claim is the maximum over all possible cash-flow monitoring schemes of the associated present values of cash flows; i.e., for an American option, we could, in principle, calculate the maximum over all possible early exercise strategies of the corresponding present values.

The philosophy behind the stratified state aggregation algorithm is to partition the space of underlying assets into a tractable number of cells, and then to compute an approximate early exercise strategy that is constant over these cells. If the cells are carefully chosen, the approximation should be fairly close to the actual strategy.

The price of an American option on asset(s) X (a vector) can be written as

$$C(X_t, t) = \max_u E_t \left[\int_t^\infty \frac{f(u(X_\tau, \tau), X_\tau, \tau)}{P(t, \tau)} d\tau \right] \qquad (5.82)$$

where $f(u, X, t) dt$ is the cash flow generated by the American security during the time dt, e.g., for a put option $f(X, t) = \max(0, K - S(X, t))$, $u(X_t, t)$ is some decision that influences the cash flow and the expected value is computed over the risk-neutral process. Here, $P(t, T) = e \int_t^T r(X, s) ds$ is the value of a dollar invested at time t in the money-market, where $r(X, t)$ is the riskless short rate. The maximization is over all strategies u. For American options, $u(X, t)$ for any given time can only have one of two possible values, i.e., exercise or do not exercise. Also, since exercise can only happen once, if $u(X, t_1)$ corresponds to exercise, then for all $t > t_1$, $u(X, t)$ has to have the value no-exercise. Now, numerical solution of the pricing problem is possible because of the "Markov" assumption, i.e., that the optimal exercise strategy at time t depends only on the price at time t, and t itself. The recursive equation derived from the maximization problem is what we have already shown how to solve in the previous sections using trees and lattices. Since for higher dimensional problems that scheme is not efficient, we will now turn to the simulation-based approaches.

To construct a good simulation-based approximation to multi-dimensional American options, we need to create "reasonable" partitions (called cells in Reference [11]) of the sample space of asset prices, and then create a recursive algorithm to compute expected payoffs and discounted probabilities to roll back. In the SSA approach, the partitions are created based on stratification maps, i.e., choose a function of the underlying variables that influences the optimal strategy in a given problem, and within which the optimal strategy is constant. For most American option problems, the obvious function that influences the exercise strategy is the payoff function itself.

To illustrate this with an example, suppose we try to price an American option on the maximum of n assets using the SSA approach. For an American call, denoting by X the state of the variables, we can write the payoff as

$$\max(S(X) - K, 0) \qquad (5.83)$$

with K being the strike price. The start of the option period is at time 0 and the expiration is at time T. Choose a constant number, $k = 100$, of partitions $Q_i(t)$ for all times such that

$$Q_1(t) = (-\infty, A(t))$$

$$Q_i(t) = (A(t)\, e^{B(t)(i-2)}, A(t)\, e^{B(t)(i-1)}) \qquad \text{for } i = 2, \ldots, 99$$

$$Q_{100}(t) = (A(t)\, e^{B(t)(k-2)}, \infty) \qquad (5.84)$$

are the intervals within which the payoff function falls for a given state X. Note that the partitions are defined not in terms of the state of the underlying variables, but in terms of the payoff functions, or, in general, in terms of the stratification map. The numbers $A(t)$ and $B(t)$ are chosen so that a very small fraction of probability falls in the first and last partitions, usually less than 0.5 percent.

Now, with the joint lognormality assumption, we generate Monte-Carlo paths using (setting dividends equal to zero for simplicity)

$$S_i(t + \Delta t) = S_i(t)\, e^{(r - \frac{1}{2}\sigma_i^2)\Delta t + \sum_{j=1}^{n} \sigma_{ij}\sqrt{\Delta t}\, z_j^t} \qquad (5.85)$$

where the z_j^t values are independent standard normal variables and σ_{ij} is the covariance matrix between asset i and asset j returns. For d time steps and M paths, we need to generate $M \times d \times n$ standard normal variates.

Now, all that remains to be done is an evaluation of the number of paths crossing a given partition, and the payoff function for each of these paths. The optimal exercise equation can then be applied for each partition as we roll back. Defining by $a_i(t)$ the total number of paths going through partition i at time t, by $b_{ij}(t)$ the sum over all discount factors between times t and $t + \Delta t$ between partitions i and j, and by $c_i(t)$ the sum of the payoffs from the paths crossing the ith partition at time t, we get

$$C(i, T) = \frac{c_i(T)}{a_i(T)}$$

$$C(i, T - \Delta t) = \max \left[\frac{c_i(T - \Delta t)}{a_i(T - \Delta t)}, \sum_{j=1}^{k} C(j, T) \frac{b_{ij}(T - \Delta t)}{a_i(T - \Delta t)} \right] \qquad (5.86)$$

In Reference [11], it is reported that while for low dimensions (i.e., single-asset case), the scheme is inferior to the tree approach, for higher dimensions, i.e., three dimensions, it is six times as fast as the multidimensional lattice approach. For higher than three dimensions, this approach is the only viable one since the computation time grows as n^2 compared with 2^n for the multidimensional lattice approach.

Other Algorithms

There has been other related work by other researchers in pricing American-style options using Monte-Carlo algorithms under the names of "error-bound" algorithms [37] and "functional optimization" [140]. In the Broadie-Glasserman "error-bound" approach [37], an asset price tree is first generated using b branches at each time step. Then, working backward from maturity, at each step the option value is replaced by the greater of the intrinsic value and the present value of the expected one-step-ahead value. This gives an upper estimate U for the option price, which is biased high due to perfect forward view. Then, the dynamic programming exercise is modified with $b_1 < b$ branches of the tree at each step to decide whether to exercise early, and the remaining $b - b_1$ branches are used to compute the holding value of the option. This gives a lower estimate L of the option price since the partial tree decision is sub-optimal. Then, as $b \to \infty$, it is proved in Reference [37] that the lower and upper estimates converge to the true option value.

CHAPTER 6

Strategic Risk Management

It is obvious to anyone trading options that they provide a means of transferring risk for a price. Once the risk is transferred, the amount of money that the seller of the option gets to keep depends largely on the nature of the probability distribution of gains and losses of the risky portfolio. However, it is inefficient to use the full distribution every time a summary description of risks is desired. Thus, there arises a need to develop measures of communicating essential aspects of the dispersion in the distribution. There is no best way of looking at risk, though one hopes that there is a best hedge, once the risk has been explored in all possible ways. Risk *aggregation* helps to summarize and clarify the coarse behavior of the trading book, and suggests trades that are more suitable and appropriate with the implied views of the book. Risk *disaggregation*, on the other hand, is useful for accurate description of the portfolio at security-level detail, and is essential for practically implementing the views that are found to be optimal from the aggregation exercise.

It is possible to take too microscopic a view of a correlation book and end up incurring losses in delta-hedging a portfolio that may be largely self-hedging. The value of a portfolio of options which is the sum of individual options may not be the same as the sum of the values of individual options if transaction costs are taken into consideration. This happens because of the nonlinear

218

nature of time evolution of a portfolio of options. Option risk is not additive, even though the practice of dynamical hedging assumes that it is. This nonlinearity is fortunate for investors and hedgers, because it allows them to deal with a complex profile of risk by buying a customized product. It has the potential of becoming a headache for the risk manager, but a well-balanced and well-managed portfolio of exotics can be largely *self-hedging* due to automatic diversification. The recognition and exploitation of the full set of symmetries of the fundamental pricing equations and boundary conditions is an extremely useful tool in enabling the portfolio to "hedge itself."

The purpose of this chapter is to focus on risk management rather than risk monitoring. As such, it is necessary to omit detailed discussion of Value at Risk (VaR)[1] methodologies. The important point to understand is that due to the relative illiquidity of customized options, managing a portfolio of exotics and hybrids cannot be separated from position taking. The expected excess returns that one expects to gain have to be evaluated in the light of the potential higher and unhedgeable volatility.

This chapter begins with some general principles for selecting trades that contribute positively to the existing portfolio. We will discuss new types of cross risks that arise with options that contain more than one underlying asset. This proceeds to a systematic exploration of the issue of costs incurred in the process of hedging individual options and portfolios of options. Next, we will explicitly construct a set of indices using multivariate interdependence techniques (principal components) for risk aggregation. Due to the special features that arise from the relative illiquidity of complex options, the important topic of market price of risk is discussed next. There is a brief discussion of static hedging, which is still quite an active field of research. The last two sections present an

---

1. Simply put, VaR is the size of the loss that occurs with a specified probability over a given period of time. Thus, it is parametrized by two numbers—the required probability and the time horizon. For instance, a good measure that may be used by a risk manager overseeing an exotic portfolio would be the amount of capital that the desk is expected to lose no more than once per year in a given day. This, on the basis of the VaR distribution for the underlying assets and positions in the portfolio, should be considered to be a statistically normal event in the course of risk management.

example of extraction of market-implied joint probability densities and how one can use this information, along with an algorithm based on preferences, beliefs, and the current state for managing risk systematically.

TRADE SELECTION

Before we go deep into the details of hedging and hedging costs, it is important to understand some details on the incremental benefit of entering into a transaction that entails new risks for a portfolio of exotic options. In new markets, such as the one for exotic options, it is frequently very hard, if not outright impossible, to "lay off" risks in the market. Static hedging, even when available, is usually so expensive that it is possible, if the hedges are not chosen carefully, to lose a substantial portion of the spreads earned as costs of hedging. Dynamical or delta-hedging is the usual practice, with the option buyer compensating the option seller for the labor and the risks of hedging movements that cannot be hedged for infinitesimal movements of the underlying assets. However, it is easy for a book that has a number of correlated assets to very quickly become dangerously unhedged as small changes accumulate.

Experience teaches us that it is impossible for an exotic book to be completely delta-hedged at all times without accumulating substantial rehedging costs. It then becomes imperative for the bookrunner to take educated risks, i.e., to align the book in such a way that the risks are clear and exactly the ones that he wants to take. When the opportunity of a new transaction occurs, it should not be judged simply on the merit of how much instant profit (i.e., from the midprice to the transaction price) it results in, but also on whether it suits the risks of the book, the constraints imposed by limits, and the estimated accumulated hedging costs over time. In short, what are the marginal impacts of adding a new trade, and, once a new trade is added, the impacts of altering its contribution to the risks of the portfolio by increasing or decreasing the size of the position? We will try to find the answers to some of these questions by using the concept of the marginal risk decomposition of a portfolio [141].

While it is true that the total risk of a portfolio is not the sum of individual positions, the total risk is the sum of marginal impacts on portfolio risk from small percentage increases in each of the portfolio's positions. Whether we use volatility or VaR as the basis for making risk-management decisions, then, as all position sizes are increased by the same factor, the risk, as measured by either one of these measures, is also increased by the same factor. This can be used to decompose the total risk in terms of the marginal impacts. Suppose we have the risk measure $R(\vec{p})$, where $\vec{p}$ is an n-dimensional vector of positions. Now let us scale all the positions by the number $k > 0$ to get the new measure $R(k\vec{p})$. But this, by the linearity of volatility, equals $kR(\vec{p})$. So, by differentiation of the two sides of this equation with respect to k, we obtain

$$R_1(\vec{p})x_1 + R_2(\vec{p})x_2 + \ldots + R_n(\vec{p})x_n = R(\vec{p}) \qquad (6.1)$$

where $R_i(\vec{p})$ is the partial derivative of the risk function R with respect to the ith position x_i. Now each term in the product $R_i(x)x_i$ is the marginal rate of change in risk per unit change in the position times the position size itself, so it corresponds to the rate of change in risk with respect to a small percentage change in the size of the position. Thus, the total risk is the sum of the rates of change in risk with respect to percentage changes in each of the positions. Then the quantity $100R_i(\vec{p})x_i/R(\vec{p})$ is the percentage contribution of the ith position to the risk of the portfolio. Note that since we are describing marginal effects, it is crucial to have a nonvanishing position in order for it to have even a marginal impact on the risk of the portfolio.

We will also need some basic results from modern portfolio theory [74]. Given some assets S_i, S_j, and the "market" index M,[2] we can write, in terms of the market's return R_M and variance σ_M^2:

$$E(R_i) = \alpha_i + \beta_i E(R_M) + e_i$$
$$\sigma_i^2 = \beta_i^2 \sigma_M^2 + \sigma_{ei}^2$$
$$\sigma_{ij} = \beta_i \beta_j \sigma_M^2 \qquad (6.2)$$

---

2. Later in this chapter it will be shown how to construct a set of such indices for a correlation book.

so that the correlation between any two securities can be expressed in terms of their beta as

$$\rho_{ij} = \frac{\sigma_{ij}}{\sigma_i \sigma_j} = \frac{\beta_i \beta_j \sigma_M^2}{\sigma_i \sigma_j} \qquad (6.3)$$

Now suppose that the second asset is the market index itself, so that $\beta_M = 1$. Then, the correlation of the ith asset with the market is

$$\rho_{iM} = \frac{\beta_i \beta_M \sigma_M^2}{\sigma_i \sigma_M} = \frac{\beta_i \sigma_M}{\sigma_i} \qquad (6.4)$$

which gives back the usual definition of the β:

$$\beta_i = \frac{\rho_{iM} \sigma_i}{\sigma_M} = \frac{\rho_{iM} \sigma_i \sigma_M}{\sigma_M^2} = \frac{\text{Cov}(S_i, M)}{\text{Var}(M)} \qquad (6.5)$$

which will be used in the computation of "beta" responses to the indices developed below.

Marginal Risk Decomposition

There are two distinct questions that one needs to ask when adding a new exotic trade to a book. The first one is whether such a trade should be added at all. The addition of a new security to an existing portfolio is attractive if, and only if, this increases the portfolio's Sharpe ratio, i.e., the ratio of excess return to standard deviation of the return. This, of course, assumes that the new trade is not extremely skewed, or does not change the higher moments of the return distribution drastically. The second question is related to how much of the new security should be added. If one decides to increase the weight of the security in the portfolio, a higher Sharpe ratio would result only if the security's ratio of excess return to its beta with the existing portfolio exceeded the existing portfolio's excess rate of return, i.e., $R/\beta_0 > R_P$. At some point, this inequality is no longer true, and adding more of the new exotic will result in worse portfolio performance for the same amount of risk.

To formalize this, consider a portfolio P [23,154]. If we can find an asset S which has a beta $\beta_{S,P}$ with this portfolio such that the expected excess return R_S (i.e., over the risk-free rate) on S is higher than the expected excess return on the portfolio R_P times $\beta_{S,P}$, then it is attractive to add that asset to the portfolio. Before the asset is added, suppose the excess return on the portfolio is R_P and the standard deviation is σ_P. Then, denote the Sharpe ratio, or risk–reward profile by

$$\psi_P = \frac{R_P}{\sigma_P} \tag{6.6}$$

Now reassemble the portfolio so that the asset S forms a weight w of the whole. Then the Sharpe ratio of this new portfolio, denoted P', is

$$\psi_{P'} = \frac{wR_S + (1-w)R_P}{\sigma_P'} \tag{6.7}$$

where

$$\sigma_P' = \sqrt{w^2\sigma_S^2 + (1-w)^2\sigma_P^2 + 2w(1-w)\rho_{SP}\sigma_S\sigma_P} \tag{6.8}$$

and we have used ρ_{SP} for the correlation between the new asset and the old portfolio. Now calculate the beta with respect to the new portfolio:

$$
\begin{aligned}
\beta_{S,P'} &= \frac{\mathrm{Cov}(S, P')}{\mathrm{Var}(P')} \\
&= \frac{S \cdot (wS + (1-w)P)}{(wS + (1-w)P) \cdot (wS + (1-w)P)} \\
&= \frac{w\sigma_S^2 + w(1-w)\rho_{SP}\sigma_S\sigma_P}{w^2\sigma_S^2 + (1-w)^2\sigma_P^2 + 2w(1-w)\rho_{SP}\sigma_S\sigma_P}
\end{aligned} \tag{6.9}
$$

The hurdle that the new asset has to pass to be added in the portfolio, and for the critical weighting to be achieved, is

$$R_S > R_{P'}\beta_{SP'} \tag{6.10}$$

Let us give an example of the use of this approach. Suppose we have a portfolio to begin with that is yielding a high (but not unreasonable for the exotic market) excess return of 10 percent above the risk-free rate. Suppose the standard deviation of this return is 20 percent. Now we suddenly discover that there is a structure out there in the market that has zero correlation to our existing portfolio, and at the same time offers twice as much excess return, i.e., 20 percent above the risk-free rate, with expected standard deviation of 40 percent (also twice as much as the original portfolio). At first glance, this is an attractive proposition, and when we try to satisfy the inequality given in Equation (6.10), we find that the weighting we need for the new asset in the new portfolio is exactly a third. This new asset then has a beta of 1.49 with respect to the new portfolio (we are assuming it is uncorrelated to the original portfolio).

As Figure 6–1 shows, altering the mix is suboptimal. It is indeed possible to generate better returns by having higher weights of the higher yielding asset, but while the excess returns increase linearly, the volatility of the portfolio increases much more rapidly, leading to lower Sharpe ratios.

In general, then, any trade whose returns are negatively correlated with the returns of the portfolio will, at the margin, reduce risk. The negative contribution to risk can be utilized in terms of the position size. As the size of this particular trade is increased, it will result in the reduction of overall portfolio risk. At some point, the

F I G U R E 6–1

Optimal Risk–Reward Profile of Risk, Excess Return, and Sharpe Ratio

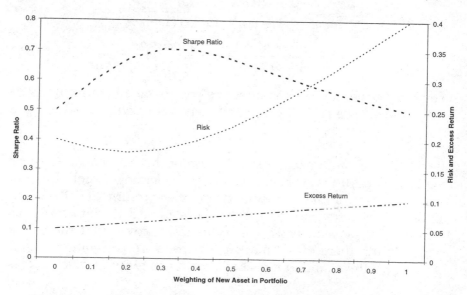

size of the position will be so large that its returns will become uncorrelated with the portfolio. At this stage, a marginal increase in the position does not affect the risk of the portfolio. In our earlier notation, the partial derivative of the risk function vanishes at this point with respect to the position, and, holding all other positions fixed, this is the best or optimal hedge position for that asset in the portfolio. After we have developed the index approach, we will be able to return to the problem of characterization of risk in terms of essentially independent market factors, so that a measure of the total size of the exposure can be efficiently quantified.

CROSS RISKS

Consider a simple correlation option that depends on two securities, A and B. The payoff is simply a function of A, but can be "knocked out" if B hits a preset level. Now, if we know the correlation between A and B, why not hedge only in asset A by a correlation-adjusted amount? Why is there a need to hedge in asset B at all? As long as the correlation is high in absolute value, approximate asset substitution works, e.g., hedging exposure in the 2-year sector with 5-year treasuries. However, when the absolute correlation is low, it is hard to estimate the hedge ratios purely statistically. Since the statistical hedge really is the expected future relationship based on past relationship, the full time-dependent joint density is needed. But since we use identically independently distributed joint normals for returns, with zero autocorrelation from the very beginning, our Black-Scholes environment theoretical framework is inadequate. The joint density between past correlation and expected future correlation can be determined by computing the empirical autocorrelation in the correlation series.[3] With this prologue on the necessity of having underlying positions in as many assets as the number of degrees of freedom in the problem, we turn to exploring the risks that a correlation trader gets paid for managing—i.e., "cross-gamma" risk.

---

3. Proponents claim that cointegrated factor analysis methods do provide the means to hedge in a minimal number of underlying assets. This is because if a set of assets are cointegrated, then the order in which they may vary in time is, in principle, predictable.

Cross-Gamma Hedging

In a well-developed market for correlation options, one would be able to carry out a static hedge of an option portfolio by buying and selling other correlation options. However, as long as the market for cross-asset correlation is underdeveloped, one has to replicate the exotic or hybrid option position by taking positions in the underlying market *and* in simpler single-factor options in the underlying markets. The quantity and ratios of these hedges changes as the correlation changes. The method is a local projection of multifactor risk into the individual variables and their options. Obviously, even after a multifactor option is hedged in this manner using the individual assets and options, the hedge is not static. It has to be rebalanced every day as time passes, even though the markets might not move. Hedging correlation options requires that dynamic hedging be carried out with both underlying assets *and* options on them, just as for single-factor options, dynamic hedging has to be carried out with the underlying assets. This is a direct consequence of the transmutability of correlation and volatility.

For a single-asset option trader the reward-vs-risk trade-off comes from a prudent balance of the book's gamma position versus the time-decay position. In other words, the hedging scheme has to be chosen in a way that minimizes the variance of the book without incurring high transaction costs. A short option position, dynamically hedged, will lose money if there is a large movement in the underlying variable. However, it will earn money through time decay if the moves are not too large. In a similar way, for multifactor options the hedge in one underlying asset generally changes not only with movements that are directly relevant to it, but also due to changes in the other variables. So a prudent management of a correlation book balances the cross-gamma-driven gains and losses against the net time value earned or paid.

It is tempting for a single-asset option book-runner to be short very short dated out-of-the-money options, since the rewards under stable market conditions are quick. However, if the portfolio has delta risk limits, the trader is forced to hedge if there is a large move in the underlying variable. So from the point of view of market timing, the short-gamma position always buys and sells at the worst time. The buys are all done at the highs and the sells are all done at the lows. If the market turns out to be very volatile in the short term, the slippage at each transaction can add up to be larger than the premium received! The other alternative is to be short options and not hedge according to any continuous system, but only to hedge at preset technical levels. This is dangerous for the reason that, in the short term, it is impossible to tell whether the market is going to revert to some mean (recall the discussion in Chapter 3 that the "tails" of the asset distributions are usually fatter for short time horizons) or whether there has been a structural change.

In the same way as the fair price of an option position on one underlying variable can be thought of as the cumulative sum of all the gamma-driven losses or gains, the fair price of an option on many assets can be thought of as the cumulative sum or losses of each of the individual gamma hedges plus the cross-gamma hedges.

Experience quickly teaches that correlation can be very volatile in the short term, and hedging to any point correlation number is full of danger. Surviving correlation trading books are averse to having too many short-term deals on his book, because of the high transaction cost associated with hedging the cross-gamma exposures. As with single-factor options, the option seller has to believe that the underlying factors are not only mean-reverting over some horizon to their individual means, but at the same time also to a conditional mean with respect to all the other variables included, so that rehedging in any underlying asset may be done one at a time.

When in doubt, a rule of thumb that works well is to consider correlation as having inverse effects on pricing when compared with volatility, but having the same order of magnitude sensitivity. For example, we know that longer dated options are more sensitive to volatility than shorter dated options. Similarly, longer dated cross-market options are, in general, more sensitive to correlation changes than shorter dated cross-market options. This even holds true for more complex options such as barriers, which were discussed in Chapter 3.

First, consider the two-variable case [5]. Each underlying variable is assumed to follow geometric Brownian motion:

$$dS_i = \mu_i S_i \, dt + \sigma_i S_i \, dz_i \qquad \text{for } i = 1, 2 \tag{6.11}$$

with $dz_1 \, dz_2 = \rho \, dt$. An option $\mathcal{O}$, dependent on these assets, can be valued by solving the two-dimensional Black-Scholes equation with appropriate boundary conditions for the payoff under consideration.

The sum of the option plus hedges, which consist of the underlying *as well as vanilla options* on each underlying variable, is

$$\mathcal{P} = \mathcal{O} + \alpha_1 S_1 + \alpha_2 S_2 + \beta_1 v_1 + \beta_2 v_2 \tag{6.12}$$

where the v_i values are the fair values of vanilla options on asset i, S_i is the value of that asset, and we have β_i vanilla options and α_i shares of the assets; $\mathcal{O}$ is the multifactor option.

With the delta-neutrality condition for each asset,

$$\frac{\partial \mathcal{O}}{\partial S_i} + \alpha_i + \beta_i \frac{\partial v}{\partial S_i} = 0 \tag{6.13}$$

and using the one-dimensional Black-Scholes equations to get rid of the individual time derivatives, the variance of the stochastic differential $d\mathcal{P}$ can be shown to be (to order dt^2)

$$\begin{aligned}
\sigma_{d\mathcal{P}}^2 = 2\big[& (\xi_{11} + \beta_1 \lambda_1)^2 + (\xi_{22} + \beta_2 \lambda_2)^2 \\
& + 2\rho^2 (\xi_{11} + \beta_1 \lambda_1)(\xi_{22} + \beta_2 \lambda_2)^2 \\
& + 4\rho \xi_{12}(\xi_{11} + \beta_1 \lambda_1) + 4\rho \xi_{12} \\
& + (\xi_{22} + \beta_2 + \lambda_2) + 2\xi_{12}^2 (1 + \rho^2) \big] \, dt^2
\end{aligned} \tag{6.14}$$

where

$$\xi_{ij} = \frac{1}{2} \sigma_i \sigma_j S_i S_j \frac{\partial^2 \mathcal{O}}{\partial S_i \, \partial S_j}$$

$$\lambda_i = \frac{1}{2} \sigma_i^2 S_i^2 \frac{\partial^2 v_i}{\partial S_i^2} \tag{6.15}$$

Minimizing the variance with respect to β_i leads to two equations for the β_i:

$$\beta_1 = -\frac{(2\rho\xi_{12} + (1 + \rho^2)\xi_{11})}{\lambda_1(1 + \rho^2)}$$

$$\beta_2 = -\frac{(2\rho\xi_{12} + (1 + \rho^2)\xi_{22})}{\lambda_2(1 + \rho^2)} \tag{6.16}$$

which gives the minimum variance of the portfolio,

$$\sigma_m^2 = \frac{4\xi_{12}^2(1 - \rho^2)^2}{1 + \rho^2} dt^2 \tag{6.17}$$

Compare Equation (6.17) with the variance where only the individual gammas are hedged but not the cross-gammas:

$$\sigma^2 = \frac{4\xi_{12}^2(1 + \rho^2)^2}{1 + \rho^2} dt^2 \tag{6.18}$$

So, ignoring the cross-gamma increases the overall portfolio volatility over its minimum value by $(1 + \rho^2)/(1 - \rho^2)$ in the two-factor case. Note that for zero correlation, the variance of the portfolio hedged with cross-gamma is the same as the one hedged without. However, when correlation is large and positive, without the cross-gamma hedging the portfolio has a much higher variance than it would otherwise. In Reference [5], a short position in the outperformance, or zero-strike spread or Margrabe option

$$V(T) = \max[S_1(T) - S_2(T), 0] \tag{6.19}$$

is hedged using a call on S_1 and a put on S_2. With $S_1 = S_2 = 100$, $K_1 = K_2 = 100$, $\sigma_1 = 0.25$, $\sigma_2 = 0.15$, $r = 0.05$, $\rho = 0.25$, and time to expiration is 6 months, hedging without the cross-gamma term gives a variance of almost 30 percent more than the proper hedge with the cross-gamma adjustment.

Misestimation of the correlation parameter can thus have nasty consequences. If the correlation is assumed to be zero when it is not, and no cross-gamma hedging is done (since the model will show no need to do it), over time, extra hedges due to the increased variance of the portfolio will take their toll in the form of transaction costs, as well as the usual "buy at the top, sell at the bottom effect" for short option positions.

For N stochastic variables,

$$\sigma_{dP}^2 = 2 \left(\sum_{i,j,k,l=1}^{N} \xi_{ij} \rho_{jk} \xi_{kl} \rho_{il} \right.$$

$$+ 2 \sum_{i,j,k=1}^{N} \xi_{ij} \beta_k \lambda_k \rho_{ik} \rho_{jk}$$

$$\left. + \sum_{i,j=1}^{N} \beta_i \lambda_i \rho_{ij}^2 \beta_j \lambda_j \right) dt^2 \tag{6.20}$$

Minimizing with respect to β_r, N linear equations in N unknowns are obtained:

$$\sum_{i=1}^{N} \lambda_i \beta_i \rho_{ri}^2 + \sum_{i,j=1}^{N} \xi_{ij} \rho_{ri} \rho_{rj} = 0 \tag{6.21}$$

for $1 \le r \le N$. In matrix terms,

$$\vec{\beta} = -\Lambda^{-1} \vec{\Psi} \tag{6.22}$$

where

$$\Lambda_{ij} = \lambda_j \rho_{ij}^2$$

$$\Psi_i = \sum_{m,n=1}^{N} \rho_{im} \xi_{mn} \rho_{ni}$$

HEDGING COSTS

Simple symmetry relationships, as well as the linearity of local risk parameters, may be used to create portfolios that are good hedges for a plethora of exotic options. Using the prices of traded options in the markets, we can create call and put spreads. Using an appropriate number of these spreads, a locally riskless hedge can be created. Then the cost of hedging is related to the expected cumulative transaction costs for hedging the synthetically constructed hedge product over its life.

The cost of an option within the Black-Scholes framework really comes from the assumption of being able to construct a continuous hedge for the option position, i.e., the limit that $dt \to 0$. In general, a large book has economies of scale, i.e., there is internal diversification in the book, so that the requirement of having to hedge continuously is reduced. Thus, the price of hedging in a large book is, in general, lower than in a small book. Contrary to the basic Black-Scholes approach, *there might then be no unique option price* but a price that depends on the frequency of hedging, which, in turn, depends on the size and nature of the larger portfolio within which the particular option will be valued [57, 232].

Hedging Costs for Single-Factor Options

Suppose a simple option depending on an asset price S and time t has value $\mathcal{O}(S, t)$. Then the fundamental differential equation for the incremental change in the value of the option is

$$d\mathcal{O} = \sigma S \frac{\partial \mathcal{O}}{\partial S} dz + \left(\mu S \frac{\partial \mathcal{O}}{\partial S} + \frac{1}{2} \sigma^2 S^2 \frac{\partial^2 \mathcal{O}}{\partial S^2} + \frac{\partial \mathcal{O}}{\partial t} \right) dt \qquad (6.23)$$

Now a portfolio consisting of one unit of the option and a number $-\Delta$ of the underlying asset has the value

$$\mathcal{P} = \mathcal{O} - \Delta S \qquad (6.24)$$

and it changes in a unit time step dt by

$$d\mathcal{P} = d\mathcal{O} - \Delta \, dS \qquad (6.25)$$

so that

$$d\mathcal{P} = \sigma S \left(\frac{\partial \mathcal{O}}{\partial S} - \Delta \right) dz + \left(\mu S \frac{\partial \mathcal{O}}{\partial S} + \frac{1}{2} \sigma^2 S^2 \frac{\partial^2 \mathcal{O}}{\partial S^2} + \frac{\partial \mathcal{O}}{\partial t} - \mu \Delta S \right) dt$$

$$(6.26)$$

so that if we choose a delta hedge

$$\Delta = \frac{\partial \mathcal{O}}{\partial S} \qquad (6.27)$$

at the start of the time step, then we have a riskless change in the value of the incrementally hedged portfolio:

$$d\mathcal{P} = \left(\frac{\partial \mathcal{O}}{\partial t} + \frac{1}{2} \sigma^2 S^2 \frac{\partial^2 \mathcal{O}}{\partial S^2} \right) dt = r\mathcal{P} \, dt \qquad (6.28)$$

Now let us assume that we *cannot* hedge continuously. Rather, we list the full set of new assumptions:

- As usual, we assume

$$dS = \sigma S \phi \sqrt{dt} + \mu S\, dt \tag{6.29}$$

  with ϕ drawn from $N[0, 1]$.
- The portfolio of options is rehedged discretely every dt.
- Transaction costs are proportional to the "size" or monetary value of the transaction. Thus, if n units are bought $(n > 0)$ or sold $(n < 0)$ at price S, then transaction costs are $k|n|S$ where k depends on the trader.

Then, instead of Equation (6.26), we obtain

$$dP = \sigma S \left(\frac{\partial O}{\partial S} - \Delta \right) \phi \sqrt{dt}$$
$$+ \left(\frac{1}{2} \sigma^2 \frac{\partial^2 O}{\partial S^2} \phi^2 + \mu S \frac{\partial O}{\partial S} + \frac{\partial O}{\partial t} - \mu \Delta S \right) dt - kS|n| \tag{6.30}$$

where the transaction costs are subtracted since they are always negative.

Now, as before, the hedge is to choose

$$\Delta = \frac{\partial O}{\partial S}(S, t) \tag{6.31}$$

which changes to

$$\frac{\partial O}{\partial S}(S + dS, t + dt) \tag{6.32}$$

so that the change in the number of asset units that are bought or sold in the finite time interval is

$$n = \frac{\partial O}{\partial S}(S + dS, t + dt) - \frac{\partial O}{\partial S}(S, t) \tag{6.33}$$

which, on Taylor expansion for small dS and dt, becomes

$$n = \frac{\partial^2 O}{\partial S^2}(S, t)\, dS \simeq \frac{\partial^2 O}{\partial S^2} \sigma S \phi \sqrt{dt} \tag{6.34}$$

which leads to the equation for expected transaction costs $E[kS|n|]$ (by integrating over the normal density):

$$\sqrt{\frac{2}{\pi}} k\sigma S^2 \left| \frac{\partial^2 \mathcal{O}}{\partial S^2} \right| \sqrt{dt} \qquad (6.35)$$

If this incremental change were to replicate a riskless dt period deposit, then,

$$\frac{\partial \mathcal{O}}{\partial t} + \frac{1}{2}\sigma^2 S^2 \frac{\partial^2 \mathcal{O}}{\partial S^2} - \sqrt{\frac{2}{\pi}} \frac{k\sigma S^2}{\sqrt{dt}} \left| \frac{\partial^2 \mathcal{O}}{\partial S^2} \right| + rS\frac{\partial \mathcal{O}}{\partial S} - r\mathcal{O} = 0 \qquad (6.36)$$

where the additional term is proportional to the gamma, $\Gamma = \partial^2 \mathcal{O}/\partial S^2$, and is an indication of the mishedging that takes place at the beginning of the time interval, and hence is the required correction to the transaction costs to correct the mishedging. Note also that if the model input σ is lower than the actual volatility, increased transactions will incur added hedging costs.

One consequence of this result is that, in the absence of continuous hedging, a trader not aware of the different types of nonlinear cancellations in his book might actually end up paying transaction costs to hedge exactly offsetting positions (which offset nonlinearly) and actually come out worse off than if he did not delta-hedge! We will see that individual asset hedging of a correlation book leads to exactly this problem—increased transaction costs, even though the portfolio is self-hedging. This is another reason to explore carefully, on a regular basis, the different symmetry-driven relationships between positions in the book.

Note that with the definition

$$\sigma'^2 = \sigma^2 - 2\sqrt{\frac{2}{\pi}} \frac{k\sigma}{\sqrt{dt}} \qquad (6.37)$$

as the new volatility, we get the original Black-Scholes equation. Thus, the effect of transaction costs is to reduce the apparent volatility of a long option position.

Hedging Costs for Multifactor Options

The general multifactor process is given by

$$dO = \left[\frac{\partial O}{\partial t} + \sum_i \mu_i S_i \frac{\partial O}{\partial S_i} + \frac{1}{2} \sum_{i,j} \rho_{ij}\sigma_i\sigma_j \frac{\partial^2 O}{\partial S_i\,\partial S_j}\right] dt + \sum_i \sigma_i S_i \frac{\partial O}{\partial S_i} dz_i$$

(6.38)

Now a portfolio consisting of one unit of the option and a number $-\Delta_i = (\partial O/\partial S_i)$ of the underlying asset has the value

$$\mathcal{P} = O - \Delta_i S_i$$

(6.39)

so that if we choose a delta hedge

$$\Delta_i = \frac{\partial O}{\partial S_i}$$

(6.40)

at the start of the time step, then we have a riskless change in the value of the incrementally hedged portfolio:

$$d\mathcal{P} = \left(\frac{\partial O}{\partial t} + \cdots + \frac{1}{2}\rho_{ij}\sigma_i\sigma_j S_i S_j \frac{\partial^2 O}{\partial S_i\,\partial S_j}\right) dt = r\mathcal{P}\,dt$$

(6.41)

Now let us assume that we *cannot* hedge continuously. Rather, the assumptions are:

- With ϕ_i drawn from a general, multidimensional standard joint normal distribution, the stochastic process is assumed to be

$$dS_i = \sigma_i S_i \phi_i \sqrt{dt} + \mu_i S_i\,dt$$

(6.42)

- The portfolio of options is rehedged discretely every dt.
- Transaction costs are proportional to the "size" or monetary value of the transaction. Thus, if n_i units of asset i are bought ($n_i > 0$) or sold ($n_i < 0$) at price S_i, then transaction costs are $k_i|n_i|S_i$ where k_i depends on the trader's "access" to that market.

Then, as in the previous section, we obtain

$$d\mathcal{P} = \cdots - k_i S_i |n_i|$$

(6.43)

where the transaction costs are subtracted since they are always negative, and the dots correspond to all the usual terms in the incremental change in the portfolio.

Now, as before, the hedge is to choose

$$\Delta_i = \frac{\partial \mathcal{O}}{\partial S_i}(S_j, t) \tag{6.44}$$

where j runs over all the assets (including the ith one), which changes to

$$\frac{\partial \mathcal{O}}{\partial S_j}(S_j + dS_j, t + dt) \tag{6.45}$$

so that the change in the number of ith asset units that are bought or sold in the finite time interval is

$$n_i = \frac{\partial \mathcal{O}}{\partial S_i}(S_j + dS_j, t + dt) - \frac{\partial \mathcal{O}}{\partial S_i}(S_j, t) \tag{6.46}$$

which, on Taylor expansion for small dS_j and dt, becomes

$$n_i = \frac{\partial^2 \mathcal{O}}{\partial S_i^2} dS_i + \frac{\partial^2 \mathcal{O}}{\partial S_i \, \partial S_j} dS_j \simeq \frac{\partial^2 \mathcal{O}}{\partial S_i^2} \sigma_i S_i \phi_i \sqrt{dt} + \frac{\partial^2 \mathcal{O}}{\partial S_i \, \partial S_j} \sigma_j S_j \phi_j \sqrt{dt} \tag{6.47}$$

which leads to the equation for expected transaction costs $E[k_i S_i | n_i |]$ (by integrating over the joint normal density):

$$\sqrt{\frac{2}{\pi}} k_i \sigma_i S_i^2 \left| \frac{\partial^2 \mathcal{O}}{\partial S_i^2} \right| \sqrt{dt} + \sqrt{\frac{2}{\pi}} k_i \sigma_j S_i S_j \left| \frac{\partial^2 \mathcal{O}}{\partial S_i \, \partial S_j} \right| \sqrt{dt} \tag{6.48}$$

where an additional term proportional to the "cross-gamma," $\Gamma_X = \partial^2 \mathcal{O}/\partial S_i \, \partial S_j$, is generated, and is an indication of the mis-hedging that takes place at the beginning of the time interval due to a change in all the other assets in the incremental time. This is an extra adjustment that is needed in the transaction cost calculation.

Again, the consequence is that a trader not aware of the different types of nonlinear *correlation-driven* cancellations in his book might actually pay transaction costs to hedge exactly self-diversifying positions (nonlinearly) and actually come out worse off than if he did not delta-hedge.

Implied Hedge Costs and Leveraged Microdigitals

The smallest building block for any derivatives strategy is the microdigital (see References [36], [107], and [163]). The payoff of a microdigital can be chosen to be one unit of cash if the asset or combination of assets exactly equals some level X. Since the price of a microdigital is exactly equal to the discounted probability that the assets equal the prespecified level X, the microdigital is equivalent to a pure probability position (and is used for density or Green function calculations in partial differential equation methods). The simplest example of replication of a position using microdigitals is a forward position. Suppose the forward is bought at a price of 100 and the asset underlying it moves in 0.10 increments. Then, the profit or loss from the forward can be exactly replicated by buying a portfolio of 0.10 microdigitals struck at 100.10, 0.20 struck at 100.20, 0.30 struck at 100.30, etc., and by shorting 0.10 struck at 99.90, 0.20 struck at 99.80, and so on. A call option can be replicated simply by buying the microdigitals above 100, and the puts by selling the microdigitals below 100. Proceeding in this way, any payoff function can be decomposed in terms of microdigitals. For example, the range option which accrues some coupon C_i if the price remains within a range for a specified period and C_o if the price falls outside of the range can be replicated by evaluating the total probability times payoff of a sequence of microdigitals for each day in the term of the deal.

Leveraged microdigitals may be used to compute the *implied* hedging costs that should be charged for hedging specific option positions that *are consistent with all the factors that influence hedging costs in the market.*[4]

The following is an example of the use of a microdigital for hedging costs. Suppose that gold is trading at 350 an ounce, and we want to hedge an option in which the deal pays a dollar coupon of c

---

4. If microdigitals are so useful, why are they not traded in the exchange traded market? The reason is simple—they can be reconstructed (almost exactly) by combining option positions. Call spreads, put spreads, and butterflies are simple ways of creating micro-digitals. The reason this is not exact is because standard option strikes are separated by discrete intervals, so the integrated value of the probability of achieving the two separate strikes is what is replicated.

if the price of gold is below 400 an ounce on expiration, and nothing otherwise. This is an "outside" barrier option. Suppose, first, that the correlation between interest rates and gold is zero. Then, to get a very coarse idea of what the market's implied probability is of gold exceeding 400 on expiration, we can take the 390 calls and 410 calls (or we can take the 390, 400, 410 call butterfly). The spread between the two strikes is 20, and suppose the difference in the price of the calls is 5 dollars. By paying 5 dollars, I can make 20 dollars, so the rough discounted probability that we are much higher than 400 on expiration is 0.25. This can then be used to multiply the coupon c and be subtracted from the risk-neutral return to get the premium. Of course, correlation cannot be assumed to be zero, so to evaluate the effect of the correlation, the same computation has to be done using the joint bivariate density.

The fact that, in the construction of a call spread as a static hedge, we have to initiate positions in two different call options gives us an idea of what the hedging cost associated with the exotic option position will be. We will be forced to transact in these options if we were to immunize ourselves against sharp price movements, so the cost of hedging in the market should really be proportional to the bid–offer (or bid-to-mid, if netting is done against pre-existing positions) implicit in putting the call spread hedge in place.

If the position is large, then the total hedge cost can be obtained by creating a very tight option spread position that replicates the microdigital, and then buying enough of the spreads so as to match the total contingent payoff, i.e., by "leveraging" the microdigitals. Then the hedging cost is simply the leverage multiple times the bid-to-mid, or bid-to-offer as the case might be, depending on whether or not a counterbalancing position already exists in the book.

In many cases, what makes prices of one book-runner superior to those of another is the fact that one is sufficiently diversified to enable netting of microdigitals against pre-existing positions, thus lowering (i.e., he can charge bid-to-mid as compared with bid-to-offer) hedging costs. This leads to a truism of exotic books that superior hedging leads to superior pricing leads to superior hedging.

Optimal Hedging

In a sequence of classic papers, Hodges and Neuberger [109] and Davis et al. [56] show that the optimal hedging algorithm is to rehedge only when the delta moves by a certain amount, depending on the utility function and risk aversion of the hedger. The amount is a function of both asset price and time and can be determined as the solution of a free boundary problem. Though the free boundary problem, in general, is hard to solve, if the hedging costs are assumed to be small, then it is shown in References [214], [225], and [237] that if transaction costs are assumed to be a function $K(S, U)$ of trading U shares with price S, then the "hedging band-with" around the Black-Scholes delta (Δ) is given by

$$\Delta - A(S, t) \leq y \leq \Delta + A(S, t) \tag{6.49}$$

The optimal rebalance points are $y = \pm B(S, t)$, where, to find the positions A and B, we need to solve, in terms of the Black-Scholes gamma (Γ) and the risk-aversion parameter γ of the hedger in his utility function (for instance, an exponential utility function):

$$\frac{\gamma}{3 e^{-r(T-t)}\Gamma^2} AB(A + B) = \frac{\partial K}{\partial U}(S, A - B)$$

$$\frac{\gamma}{12 e^{-r(T-t)}12\Gamma^2}(A + B)^3(A - B) = K(S, A - B)$$

Higher γ corresponds to more risk aversion and leads to tighter bounds.

When the costs are proportional, i.e.,

$$K(S, U) = a|U|S \tag{6.50}$$

then the bandwidth is

$$\Delta - \left(\frac{3aS\, e^{-r(T-t)}\Gamma^2}{2\gamma}\right)^{1/3} \leq y \leq \Delta + \left(\frac{3aS\, e^{-r(T-t)}\Gamma^2}{2\gamma}\right)^{1/3} \tag{6.51}$$

As the hedger becomes more risk averse, both ends converge to the Black-Scholes delta. Also, note that as the gamma gets larger, the bandwith gets wider.

When the costs are fixed, i.e.,

$$K(S, U) = b \tag{6.52}$$

then

$$\Delta - \left(\frac{12bS\,e^{-r(T-t)}\Gamma^2}{\gamma}\right)^{1/4} \leq y \leq \Delta + \left(\frac{12bS\,e^{-r(T-t)}\Gamma^2}{\gamma}\right)^{1/4} \tag{6.53}$$

What this means is that, even though in an idealized Black-Scholes world everyone may agree on the value of an option, in the real world different participants may assign different values to the same option. As the participant becomes more risk averse, the bandwidth gets narrower, and the accumulated hedging costs increase, thus making the real price quite different than the idealized Black-Scholes price. In a sense (see Chapter 7), it is the presence of distinct risk-aversion levels that makes the exotic and hybrid option markets exist in the first place.

Hedge Conservation Laws and Sum Rules

If we assume that the price of an option is nothing but the sum of the values of the components of the replicating portfolio, and if we assume that we only hedge dynamically, i.e., delta-hedge, then

$$\mathcal{O} = \sum_{i=0}^{n} S_i\,\Delta_i = \sum_{i=0}^{n} S_i\,\frac{\partial\mathcal{O}}{\partial S_i} \tag{6.54}$$

where we use the index $i = 0$ for the numeraire.

Consequently, for each asset j, we have the "gamma-sum rule"

$$\sum_i S_i\,\frac{\partial\Delta_i}{\partial S_j} = \sum_i S_i\Gamma_{ij} \tag{6.55}$$

where Γ_{ij} is the matrix of "gammas." For example, for the simple outperformance option with payoff

$$\max[S_2^T - S_1^T, 0] \tag{6.56}$$

we have the solution

$$\frac{\mathcal{O}}{S_1} = \frac{S_2}{S_1}e^{-d_2(T-t)}N(x_1') - K^{-d_1(T-t)}N(x_2') \tag{6.57}$$

where, in the evaluation of the arguments of the cumulative normal densities x_1', x_2', we use

$$S = \frac{S_2}{S_1}$$
$$K = 1$$
$$r = d_1$$
$$d = d_2$$
$$\sigma = \sqrt{\sigma_2^2 - 2\rho_{12}\sigma_1\sigma_2 + \sigma_1^2} \qquad (6.58)$$

Then, the hedges are

$$\Delta_0 = 0$$
$$\Delta_1 = -e^{-d_1(T-t)}N(x_2')$$
$$\Delta_2 = e^{-d_2(T-t)}N(x_1') \qquad (6.59)$$

Thus, the gamma sum rule says

$$S_1\Gamma_{11} + S_2\Gamma_{12} = 0$$
$$S_1\Gamma_{21} + S_2\Gamma_{22} = 0 \qquad (6.60)$$

i.e., the rate of change of the delta hedge in one asset with respect to the same asset is exactly opposite to the cross-gamma of that asset times the ratio of the assets. This can be generalized to any number of assets.

Suppose now that we have the sensitivity with respect to a nonasset parameter η. Then,

$$\frac{\partial \mathcal{O}}{\partial \eta} = \sum_{i=0}^{n} S_i \frac{\partial \Delta_i}{\partial \eta} \qquad (6.61)$$

For instance, if we consider the time decay of the option

$$\frac{\partial \mathcal{O}}{\partial t} = \sum_{i=0}^{n} S_i \frac{\partial \Delta_i}{\partial t} \qquad (6.62)$$

Thus, the total time decay of the option equals the price-weighted sum of the time decay of the delta hedges!

This can be used to derive a first-order PDE for the Black-Scholes delta hedge [227]:

$$\sum_{i=0}^{n} S_i \frac{\partial \Delta_i}{\partial t} = \sum_{i=0}^{n} d_i S_i \Delta_i - \frac{1}{2} \sum_{i,j=0}^{n} \rho_{ij} \sigma_i \sigma_j S_i S_j \frac{\partial \Delta_i}{\partial S_j} \qquad (6.63)$$

THE INDEX APPROACH AND OPTIMAL RISK AGGREGATION

The problem with hedging a correlation book with reference only to individual pairs of correlations is twofold. Not only might the pairwise process lead to inefficient and tedious hedging that translates into increased transaction costs, but also there might indeed exist logical impossibilities when the bid–offers of each pair are taken into account, i.e., some correlations might be bid or offered with absolute values larger than unity. While the pairwise correlation approach is sufficient for hedging the correlation risk of a small book with few asset types and deal variations, and these two problems might be avoided by scrutiny, it is not at all practical for managing the risks of a large institutional "hybrid" book. This is analogous to the complexity of managing a large portfolio of stocks. Clearly, once the number of stocks in the portfolio gets large, it makes no sense to try to manage it by considering each stock's interrelationship with every other stock. A more appropriate method is to create a set of "sector" indices, and to consider the "betas" with respect to them. This section will show in explicit detail how cross-asset indices like these can be constructed for risk management of a multifactor or hybrid option portfolio. The method has long been used in the construction of "factor models" for the yield curve. The basic idea is to decompose the movements of the yield curve in terms of linear combinations of the different maturity yields based on historical data. Once the components thus retrieved are identified with "parallel shifts," "twists," and "butterfly" movements, then the portfolio's sensitivity to the various magnitude and shape changes can be hedged in true vectorial nature.

Traditional correlation estimates, such as the ones discussed in Chapter 3, are quantified in terms of regression parameters like "R^2," which refers to the goodness of fit of a curve in the sense of minimization of least-square errors. However, this is intrinsically a *dependence* technique, in which one variable is subjugated to another. For a book with many different market factors, it is not sensible to talk of one variable as dominating another. The appropriate technique in this situation is an *interdependence* technique, such as principal components analysis or factor analysis.

The approach taken here is to give only the essential features of principal components analysis as applicable to a fairly generic hybrid book, and to focus on the construction of measures that may be used to quantify *aggregated* risks of a correlation book in a systematic and transparent manner. Also described will be the notion of "factor sensitivities" that can be used to capture hedge ratios against which correlation risk limits are assigned. A good recent reference for principal components and other multivariate techniques is Reference [195].

The Search for a Good Tool

A correlation risk-management tool that serves the purpose of allowing maximum transparency in hedging a book exposed to many factors will have the following properties:

- *Dimensional Reduction*   The technique will naturally categorize the risk factors into groupings that make sense, e.g., risk to precious metals, risk to long-duration bonds, risk to short interest rates, risk to equity sector, risk to the strength of the dollar, etc. Then, depending on the level of micromanagement needed, these representative groups may be further decomposed. Principal components is one of the best techniques used to reduce a large set of data to a set of representative composite indices.

- *Orthogonality or Elimination of Redundancy and Multicollinearity*   An added benefit of principal components is that it decomposes the variance in a large initial data set systematically in terms of factors which are responsible for progressively decreasing variance and which contribute additively to the total variance. The variance accounted for each subsequent leading factor is part of the variance not already accounted for by the leading factor. The set of components thus obtained is nonredundant.

- *Maximization of Variance*   The principal components algorithm is especially useful because the risk components are obtained by *maximizing* the variance explained by each factor. Hence, the retained factors explain more of the variance of the portfolio than does any individual original market factor (see Appendix G for details).

- *Index Construction*   The output of the principal components algorithm is in terms of "component weights," which will be described below. Using them, one can create indices that capture the independent risks of the portfolio. This may be used to construct risk betas in much the same way as an equity portfolio manager can calculate betas of his portfolio with respect to the Standard and Poor's 500 index, or a bond manager benchmarks to the Lehman or Salomon bond index. A systematic set of multiasset "hybrid-risk indices" will be derived below.

Using the standard methodology for principal components decomposition [195,236], and with the help of the code in Figure 6–2, we compute, for instance, the matrix of component weights in Equation (6.64). The principal components are along the rows in decreasing order based on their contribution to the total variance, and the column labels correspond to the weighting for the market factors.

F I G U R E 6–2

Mathematica Codelet for Principal Components Decomposition of the Hybrid Return Time Series Discussed in the Text

```
(* Read in Price Data from file marketdata and assign to array *)
prices=Partition[Map[First,ReadList["marketdata.csv",{Number,Character}]],8];
(* Number of days of prices *)
days=Length[prices];
(* Create Return Series, Subtract Mean and Create Transpose Vector*)
rawdata=Table[N[Log[prices[[k+1]]/prices[[k]]]],{k,1,days-1}];
meanrawdata=Mean[rawdata];
data=Table[rawdata[[k]]-meanrawdata,{k,1,days-1}];
transdata=Transpose[data];
(* Eigenvalues of Covariance Matrix *)
pcompe=Eigenvalues[(1/days)*transdata.data]
(* Relative Probabilities of Components Occurring *)
probs=pcompe/Apply[Plus,pcompe]
(* Principal Components *)
pcompv=Eigenvectors[(1/days)*transdata.data]
```

	Gold	Silver	US10	JY10	$/Yen	$/DM	$/CHF	Nikkei	$&P500
P1	-0.0436	-0.0505	-0.2338	-0.0316	0.4509	0.5714	0.5779	0.1839	0.2051
P2	-0.5800	-0.5728	-0.3765	-0.1987	-0.1191	-0.1373	-0.1235	-0.0579	0.3199
P3	-0.3921	-0.4014	0.5474	0.2535	0.0908	0.1665	0.1556	-0.1471	-0.4890
P4	0.0475	0.0681	-0.0075	-0.7743	0.1463	0.0670	0.0524	-0.5375	-0.2754
P5	0.0386	0.0917	0.0575	0.3465	-0.2763	0.1903	0.1645	-0.7386	0.4258
P6	0.0921	-0.0745	-0.3353	0.3675	0.6968	-0.2520	-0.2578	-0.3215	-0.1392
P7	0.1519	-0.1152	-0.6031	0.1841	-0.4366	0.1613	0.1653	-0.0509	-0.5650
P8	-0.6848	0.6881	-0.1538	0.08098	0.01157	-0.0596	0.0555	-0.0137	-0.1423
P9	-0.0599	0.0511	-0.0228	0.00323	0.000609	0.7021	-0.7069	0.0206	-0.0097

$$(6.64)$$

The matrix shown in Equation (6.64) is calculated from the correlation matrix of the returns of the market factors displayed in Equation (6.65).

$$
\begin{bmatrix}
1. & 0.577 & 0.141 & 0.074 & 0.030 & 0.026 & -0.009 & 0.036 & -0.133 \\
0.577 & 1. & 0.162 & 0.056 & 0.008 & 0.001 & 0.013 & 0.0157 & -0.104 \\
0.141 & 0.162 & 1. & 0.206 & -0.135 & -0.112 & -0.137 & -0.117 & -0.411 \\
0.075 & 0.056 & 0.206 & 1. & -0.069 & 0.021 & 0.019 & 0.090 & 0.005 \\
0.031 & 0.008 & -0.135 & -0.069 & 1. & 0.493 & 0.498 & 0.188 & 0.017 \\
0.026 & 0.001 & -0.112 & 0.021 & 0.493 & 1. & 0.889 & 0.112 & 0.143 \\
-0.009 & 0.013 & -0.137 & 0.018 & 0.498 & 0.889 & 1. & 0.139 & 0.149 \\
0.036 & 0.015 & -0.117 & 0.090 & 0.188 & 0.112 & 0.139 & 1. & 0.044 \\
-0.133 & -0.104 & -0.411 & 0.005 & 0.017 & 0.144 & 0.149 & 0.044 & 1.
\end{bmatrix}
$$

$$(6.65)$$

The percentage of variance, along with the magnitude of the eigenvalue of the normalized variables, amounted to by each of these factors is given in Table 6–1.

Now how many of these factors should be kept? We will use the simple "eigenvalue greater than unity" rule [195]. The rule is that for a factor to be considered relevant, its contribution to the variance of the full set should be at least as large as one of the original market variables. Since the variances of the original variables in the correlation basis are unity, selection of the factors with eigenvalues greater than unity satisfies this rule. This allows only the retention of the first four factors and they are expected to replicate at least 72 percent of the total variance.[5]

Table 6–2 tabulates the *factor loadings* calculated by taking the correlation of the original return data with the principal component returns. We may characterize the factors, which can then be used as

---

5. In general, more sophisticated methods of factor selection add a little bit more new information to the rudimentary analysis presented here.

T A B L E 6–1

Principal Component Contribution and Eigenvalues for Components of Equation (6.65)

Component	Percentage	Eigenvalue
P1	26.9	2.4
P2	19.8	1.77
P3	13.1	1.17
P4	11.9	1.06
P5	10.5	0.947
P6	6.4	0.578
P7	5.6	0.507
P8	4.6	0.418
P9	1.2	0.107

qualitative indicators. For instance, the first component signifies the long-term yield and forex effects for the yen, whereas the last component is a pure forex indicator.

The index method may also be used as a substitute for the traditional multivariate methodology for pricing multifactor options. Once principal components or indices have been created, the pricing problem is rather trivial because of factorization of the joint density of the factors. For all European-style options, the integration of the payoff over all points in the terminal multivariate distribution reduces to a product of single-factor integrations. All American options are valued by trees that are products of single-factor trees in the principal components. Also, since the principal components or indices are uncorrelated, there are no cross-gamma issues when hedging in terms of the components. However, to hedge using traded instruments, appropriate projections in terms of market variables have to be extracted.

Index-Based Risk Factors

Once an option is priced using the principal component variables, the risk is naturally in terms of individual deltas with respect to

T A B L E 6–2

Characterization of Principal Components

Principal Component	Dominant Weights
P1	−Yen 10-year rates + $/yen
P2	−Silver − U.S. 10-year rates + Nikkei + S&P 500
P3	Silver + Nikkei
P4	U.S. 10 + $/yen + Nikkei
P5	$/yen + $/DM + $/CHF

each of the principal components. To hedge the risk in a market where only the original market factors trade and not the principal components, we have to find the relationships between the two methods of hedging.

With the notation

$$
\begin{aligned}
\mathcal{O} &= \text{option value} \\
v_i &= \text{the } i\text{th original variable} \\
F_{ij}^{-1} &= \text{the inverse of the factor-loading matrix } F \\
p_j &= \text{the } j\text{th principal component}
\end{aligned}
\qquad (6.66)
$$

we have the relationship for factor sensitivities, assuming n original variables,

$$
\frac{\partial \mathcal{O}}{\partial p_j} = \sum_{i=1}^{n} \frac{\partial \mathcal{O}}{\partial v_i} F_{ij}^{-1}
\qquad (6.67)
$$

For example, the risk with respect to the first principal component is

$$
\begin{aligned}
\Delta_{P1} = &- 0.049 * \Delta_{\text{Gold}} - 0.124 * \Delta_{\text{Silver}} + 0.179 * \Delta_{\text{US}10} \\
&- 0.082 * \Delta_{\text{JY}10} - 0.0116 * \Delta_{\$/\text{yen}} + 0.04 * \Delta_{\$/\text{DM}} \\
&- 0.042 * \Delta_{\$/\text{CHF}} - 0.966 * \Delta_{\text{Nikkei}} - 0.0771 * \Delta_{\text{S\&P500}}
\end{aligned}
$$

which can be hedged in the market by buying or selling the appropriate number of units of each underlying security. Similar equations can be derived for the other local sensitivities with respect to volatility, time, etc.

Note that Equation (6.67) can be inverted to obtain the risk in terms of hedgeable factors from the components

$$\frac{\partial \mathcal{O}}{\partial v_i} = \sum_{j=1}^{n} \frac{\partial \mathcal{O}}{\partial p_j} F_{ij} \tag{6.68}$$

directly by using the factor-loading matrix.

Before we can use these results for risk management of a portfolio, two questions need to be answered:

1. *How strong* is the dependence of the portfolio on the indices, if any?
2. *What is the form* of the dependence of the portfolio on the indices?

As in the Capital Asset Pricing Model (CAPM) approach, we can estimate this to linear order by regression of the portfolio returns against each of the indices constructed above. The first question is answered by looking at the R^2, t-stats, etc., and the second question is essentially the slope of the regression line. We are effectively computing the quantity $\text{Cov}(I, S_i)/\text{Var}(S_i)$ where I is the generalized index and S_i are the assets under scrutiny, as in Equation (6.5).

Note that, in general, we can assign appropriate dollar values to the weighting in our portfolio and calculate the regressions for general portfolios. Option sensitivities can be obtained by combining the results of the previous section on dollar deltas and then performing the regression. The use of the component method to obtain regression-based factor "betas" is best decribed by making up three examples and observing that the results make intuitive sense.

Example 1: Flat Long Portfolio

Assume that we invest $100 in each of the nine assets mentioned earlier. Then the results of the regression with respect to each of the factors gives the results shown in Table 6–3.

T A B L E 6–3

Dependence of "Flat Long"
Portfolio on Historical
Components

Index	Slope	R^2
P1	−139.165	0.445
P2	18.59	0.005
P3	166.85	0.341
P4	2.163	0

Example 2: Typical Cross-Asset Hedge Portfolio

Take a sample position which has a number of hedges and trades
mixed together as shown in Table 6–4. The dependence on the
components is shown in Table 6–5.

T A B L E 6–4

A Sample Portfolio with Mixed
Positions (Trades and Hedges)

Asset	Position	Dollar Value
Gold	Long	100
Silver	Short	−100
U.S. 10 rates	Short	−100
JY 10 rates	Long	100
$/yen	Short	−100
$/DM	Long	100
$/CHF	Short	−100
Nikkei	Long	100
S&P 500	Short	−100

T A B L E 6–5

Mixed Position Index Risk

Index	Slope	R^2
P1	−73.15	0.2353
P2	116.181	0.38
P3	−11.43	0.003
P4	61.64	0.06

Example 3: Japanese Security Portfolio

We make a portfolio with the allocation of Table 6–6 that has principally Japanese exposure.

We should expect this portfolio to be sensitive to P1, the first factor, since P1 has been categorized as being an index capturing effects from this sector. Performing the regressions, we get the expected results shown in Table 6–7.

T A B L E 6–6

Japanese Rates and Currency
Portfolio

Asset	Position	$ Value
Gold	Long	0
Silver	Short	0
U.S. 10 rates	Short	0
JY 10 rates	Long	30
$/yen	Short	−30
$/DM	Long	0
$/CHF	Short	0
Nikkei	Long	50
S&P 500	Short	0

T A B L E 6–7

Japanese Rates and Currency
Portfolio Dependence on
Principal Components

Index	Slope	R^2
P1	−33.12	0.477
P2	26.25	0.1927
P3	22.75	0.1199
P4	24.43	0.1066

Benchmarking

The above analysis might be generalized in a straightforward manner to the case when we want the risk of the portfolio not in terms of some statistically constructed indices, but in terms of securities that we pick as benchmarks. These might be, for instance, the most liquid forwards or futures trading in that asset class, or they might even be options or other exotics. For example, if the book has a large degree of digital or barrier risk, it does not serve the purpose of hedging too well to try to express the risk of the portfolio in terms of some general market indices, or even in terms of arbitrarily selected underlying securities. The most appropriate expression is in terms of call spreads and put spreads of sufficiently close strikes. The decomposition of the portfolio in terms of such synthetic digitals across the different asset classes is the most direct way of capturing the risk that is ultimately of concern, i.e., the high gamma risk.

We already have the mathematical apparatus to do this. What we want to do is to express the risk of the portfolio in terms of securities S_i, which might, for instance, be option spreads. Now, we assume that we have a model with n separate parameters x_i that are fixed by calibration, or by extraction of implied information from the market. Also, we assume that the risk of each one of our benchmark securities can be computed in terms of these parameters, i.e., we know all the derivatives $\partial S_j/\partial x_i$. Suppose the sensitivity of the portfolio to these parameters is given by a vector dP/dx_i. In practice, these portfolio sensitivities are calculated simply by adding up the corresponding sensitivities for all the products that compose the portfolio.

Now we select n benchmark securities that we expect to be relevant for the hedging exercise. What we want to do is to express $\partial P/\partial x_i$ in terms of $\partial P/\partial S_j$ and $\partial S_j/\partial x_i$. This is expressed in terms of the vector equation

$$\frac{\partial P}{\partial x_i} = \sum_{j=1}^{n} \frac{\partial S_j}{\partial x_i}\frac{\partial P}{\partial S_j}$$

$$\Delta_P^x = \Lambda\Delta_P^S \tag{6.69}$$

so by multiplying the left-hand side with Λ^{-1}, we get the risk in terms of our user-selected securities:

$$\Lambda^{-1}\Delta_P^x = \Delta_P^S \tag{6.70}$$

I have found this technique extremely useful in getting a clear picture of the risk in different dimensions, i.e., given S_i that have different maturities, we obtain maturity-specific risk, or if the S_i

correspond to options with different strikes or barrier levels, we obtain strike- or barrier-level specific risk.

MARKET PRICE OF RISK FOR HYBRIDS

Whenever an option is written on a set of assets that can be traded, it is possible to create a locally riskless portfolio by holding a position in that asset equal to its delta. Consider, on the other hand, trying to hedge a position in a specific bond. It is impossible to hedge the bond other than by holding a number of other bonds as hedges. In other words, there is no perfect local hedge, and there is some premium associated with holding a certain kind of bond. This is the market price of risk. It also holds for options that cannot be hedged in any perfect underlying variable. For instance, consider a call option on a Japanese equity in dollar terms. While it is possible to hedge the equity exactly in Japanese terms, it is impossible to do so in dollar terms if it does not trade in the dollar market. As another example, consider a contract that exchanges a certain number of bonds for stock index units. Since it is not possible to hedge this contract in the market, the market price of risk is introduced.

Let us calculate the market price of risk for one very well-known contract—the Nikkei futures that trade in the IMM in Chicago as well as in SIMEX and in Tokyo. The IMM Nikkei futures have a movement value of $5 per tick per contract. That is, if the contract moves from 20,000 to 20,001, we make $5 if we are long one contract. On the other hand, the SIMEX Nikkei contract has a value of 500 yen per tick. If the dollar/yen exchange rate is greater than a hundred, this means that the SIMEX contract moves less for the same amount of movement in the underlying Nikkei index, in actual dollar terms. On the other hand, if a dollar buys less than a hundred yen, the SIMEX Nikkei contract is a larger contract than the IMM contract. So, clearly, as the exchange rate moves around, one would expect the relationship to change, and the higher the volatility of the exchange rate, the higher the costs involved in hedging the SIMEX contract with the IMM contract. A person who is long the Nikkei index in dollar terms has to quantify the market price of risk that he is undertaking.

Before we go on to derive the form of the market price of risk equation, I would like to point out clearly what variables in our valuation equations this concept will affect. The risk-neutral valuation framework is encompassed in the substitution

$$\mu \to r \tag{6.71}$$

where μ is the growth rate of the asset and r is the risk-free rate, e.g., the rate on a treasury bill of the same horizon. What risk-neutral valuation says is that if locally a position can be hedged, i.e., if a person holding a derivative asset can at any moment have a replicating portfolio that has no risk to the movements of the underlying asset, then the derivative can be valued with discounting at the risk-free interest rate in the market. To formalize this, consider the time t forward price of some asset S given by

$$F_t = E_t[S] \tag{6.72}$$

i.e.,

$$F_t = \frac{1}{\sigma\sqrt{2\pi t}} \int_{-\infty}^{\infty} S_0\, e^{(\mu - \frac{\sigma^2}{2})t + \sigma\sqrt{t}z} dz \tag{6.73}$$

which equals

$$F_t = S_0\, e^{\mu t} \tag{6.74}$$

as we know. If we can set up a portfolio in which we are short the left-hand side and long the right-hand side, then to avoid risk-free gain it has to be true that the rate at which the stock price is expected to grow is exactly equal to r. But what if the portfolio could not be set up? Then there is some finite value μ, which might or might not equal r, at which the underlying asset will be expected to grow. The only reasonable choice is that

$$(\mu - r) \propto \sigma \tag{6.75}$$

i.e., the amount of excess expected gain of the underlying variable is proportional to the amount of risk present in the underlying variable. We can then write this as

$$\mu - r = \lambda\sigma \tag{6.76}$$

where λ is a positive or negative number.

Note that

- $r = \mu - \lambda\sigma$ so the risk-neutral valuation can now be done as usual as long as the growth rate is risk adjusted.

- When $\lambda = 0$, then we have the usual result on risk-neutral valuation. This simply means that a perfect local hedge in traded securities can be set up. This will be crucial, because there are cases in the pricing of hybrids (usually when the correlation is zero) when the market price of risk can be ignored and the pricing and hedging problem simply factorizes.

- When $\lambda > 0$, then the risk premium requires the expected return to be adjusted down. When $\lambda < 0$, then the expected return is adjusted up due to reduction of overall risk.

Coming back to our old portfolio of a long position in Nikkei futures in dollar terms, let us try to figure out what quantity we should identify with λ. Suppose that we are in an environment in which as the value of the index rises, the dollar also gets stronger. Then, when we sell the index contract in yen and convert the proceeds back to dollars, we get an amount that is larger than the amount we would have received if the exchange rate had remained unchanged. However, the cost of this jackpot has to be paid in terms of larger losses when the index declines, since the dollar is more likely to get weaker too. Compare this with the scenario in which as the index rises, the dollar gets weaker, and as the index falls, the dollar gets stronger. Some degree of protection is automatically provided to the portfolio in the second scenario, i.e., the one with negative correlation between the index returns and the currency returns. Referring back to the equation above, we then ask—if σ and μ correspond to the return of the dollar-denominated index, in which case is λ expected to be positive, and in which case is it expected to be negative? Clearly, we would expect the lower risk case to yield lower returns, so that a negative λ should be associated with negative correlation between the index and the exchange level. This will be made explicit in the calculation below.

Example: The Nikkei Contracts

Consider the specification of the underlying stock in yen terms. We get

$$\text{Value in yen} = \frac{\text{Yen}}{\text{Share}} \tag{6.77}$$

When we translate this into dollar holdings, we have

$$\text{Value in dollars} = \frac{\text{Yen}}{\text{Share}} \frac{\text{Dollars}}{\text{Yen}} \tag{6.78}$$

If we calculate the expected value of the stock price in yen terms, we obtain

$$F_t(\text{in yen}) = S_0(\text{in yen})\, e^{\mu t} \tag{6.79}$$

What, then, is the expected forward value of the stock price in dollar terms?

Assuming that the stock price and the exchange rate (in units of dollars per yen) are jointly lognormally distributed with some correlation ρ, we get (see Equation (6.103) below)

$$
\begin{aligned}
F_t(\text{in dollars}) &= F_t(\text{in yen})X_t\, e^{\rho\sigma_s\sigma_x t} \\
&= S_0 X_0\, e^{(\mu_s + \mu_x + \rho\sigma_s\sigma_x)t} \\
&= S_0(\text{in dollars})\, e^{(\mu_s + \mu_x + \rho\sigma_s\sigma_x)t}
\end{aligned}
\tag{6.80}
$$

so that the rate of growth for the dollar-denominated stock price is not simply the sum of the rate of growths of the yen-denominated stock price and the exchange rate of growth, but has an extra term proportional to the covariance of the exchange rate and the stock price in yen terms. This term gives a value for the market price of the risk of holding a dollar-denominated yen share. As mentioned above, if the correlation term ρ is negative, the forward price of the dollar-denominated index is lower than the forward price of the currency-adjusted yen index, simply because there is a price for the automatic diversification that this negative correlation buys. In short, the price of the diversification is paid through a lower expected value. In the exteme case, when the correlation is highly negative and the foreign exchange rate is very volatile, it is completely possible for this last term to dominate so much that the expected return from holding a foreign share valued in dollar terms is very small.

STATIC HEDGING

Until recently, most research on hedging methodologies has focused on dynamical hedging strategies [203], i.e., the hedger uses the underlying assets, but not, in general, options on the assets and their combinations for purposes of insulating himself against adverse price movements. In the dealer community, the dynamical hedging procedure is usually the only admissible one since it is the cheapest and keeps the dealer from losing a significant portion of his mark-up to another dealer from whom the secondary insurance is bought. However, this ends up severely limiting how much volume the dealer can write, since a large movement in asset prices might wipe him out if the position in any one exotic is too large. This occasionally translates into rejecting business from customers who are likely to provide automatic diversification in the future and a good source of flow. For this, and other reasons, dealers might find that they really do not mind paying some "reinsurance" premium themselves to hedge part of their business using option-like products. In general, the dealers might not want to buy customized exotics in the over-the-counter market, either because they do not want to divulge the composition of their portfolio, or because they do not want to pay the additional risk-premia that exotic products command.

A good intermediate solution is to try to use standard option products to hedge part or whole of the underlying exotic exposure. For instance, in Chapter 1 we went into detail for the hypothetical risk of a yen interest-rate cap that knocks out on the Nikkei index entails. The major risks there (from the perspective of the owner of the cap), were falling yen interest rates and rising Nikkei. The simplest dynamical hedge is to buy Euroyen contracts and buy Nikkei contracts denominated in yen. However, this hedge is clearly vulnerable not only to changes in the correlation between the Nikkei index and yen interest rates, but also to changes in the individual volatilities of these two assets. Given that both yen interest rates and the Nikkei were indeed very volatile in the middle to late 1990s, one is tempted to buy more stable, option-like hedges. One possibility is simply to buy a binary option that is struck exactly at the same trigger level as the knockout trigger, with the same maturity, and one that delivers an amount of cash equal to the value on the yen interest-rate cap based on the model. This is a difficult problem, but solvable, in terms of the usual methods for solving barrier option problems. Once this *conversion* is done, the intrinsic short Nikkei call position is neutralized. One can go a step further and even sell out a portion of the interest-rate cap (calculated based on the probability of knockout), thus getting rid of all the optionality.

The problem is that as the correlation changes, the amount of Nikkei options (or binaries) that one wants to hold changes also, and it is simply too expensive to hedge the position by buying and selling binaries. One would like to be able to replicate the binaries using standard calls and puts on the Nikkei index that trade in the SIMEX or the IMM, or even in the OTC index option market.

This indeed turns out to be possible for both path-independent and path-dependent options. As proved in References [35] and [42], when the stopping time is deterministic, as in standard European-type exotics, the time t value of the payoff f is (for $t < T$ and T the expiration of the option)

$$V_t = f(\kappa)B_t + f'(\kappa)I_t(\kappa) + \int_0^{\kappa} f''(K)P_t(K)\,dK + \int_{\kappa}^{\infty} f''(K)C_t(K)\,dK$$

(6.81)

where B_t is the time t value of a unit bond, $I_t(\kappa)$ is the time t value of a forward contract with delivery price κ, and out-of-the-money puts and calls $P_t(K)$, $K \le \kappa$, and $C_t(K)$, $K \ge \kappa$ are used.

Hedging Timing Risk

The question then remaining is: What is a good static hedge that would enable the hedger to hedge the uncertainty of a barrier being breached using only simple puts and calls when the stopping time is not deterministic. Let V_t again denote the value of the option position to be determined for some time t, and assume a payoff that is a function of k assets. Then, if $V_\tau = \sum_{k=0}^{n} a_k S_{k\tau}$, where $S_{k\tau}$ is the time τ price of the kth asset, for all times $t \le \tau$, the absence of arbitrage requires the linearity result $V_t = \sum_{k=0}^{n} a_k S_{kt}$ for constants a_k.

Using this linearity result, it can be shown [42] that it is possible to reconstruct the American binary call, which pays a dollar as soon as the barrier is hit, in terms of a portfolio of "up-and-in" bond calls and 1/barrier "share-or-nothing" calls struck at the barrier, with weightings dependent on the barrier. If the barrier is hit during the life of the option, the portfolio can be immediately liquidated for a dollar (note that the bond is nothing but the discounted value of a terminal dollar). If the barrier is not hit, both portfolios end up worthless. By using this procedure, the path-dependent option is decomposed in terms of path-independent options, for which static hedges can be constructed using Equation (6.81).

IMPLIED JOINT PROBABILITIES

The prices of traded options contain the aggregated views of all market participants. There has been considerable work [196,234] in developing tools for structuring trades that optimally capture the difference between the market-implied probability distribution and the proprietary probability distribution of the trader.

Presented in this section is an example of the extraction of implied probabilities from multifactor options. Take, for instance, the three currency pairs yen/DM, DM/USD, and yen/USD. Then, as described in Chapter 4, we can extract the correlations between any two pairs by inserting the volatilities and using Equation (4.54). We also know that once these fundamental inputs are known, the evaluation of the terminal joint distribution gives us the probability, implied by the option prices, that the currencies will jointly exceed given levels.

For example, Figure 6–3 shows a snapshot of the foreign exchange forwards and implied option volatilities for these three currency pairs (with yen/USD spot rate at 84.67 and DM/USD at 1.40825). Based on these inputs, we can compute the probabilities, implicit in the option prices, that in *1-year* the yen/USD exchange rate will be below 85 and the DM/USD rate will be below 1.41 of 44.15 percent. The full matrix of these joint cumulative probabilities, computed from the joint distribution, is given in Figure 6–4. Table 6–8 shows the *term structure* of probability for the same levels. Figures 6–5, 6–6, and 6–7 show, as two-dimensional plots for different maturities, the joint probabilities of exceeding spot levels.

F I G U R E 6–3

Forward Exchange Rates and Implied Volatilities

Spot

	Yen	DM	YEN/DM
	84.67	1.40825	60.12427

USD DEPOS

	BID	OFFER
1	5.91	6.06
2	5.91	6.06
3	5.81	6.06
6	5.85	6
12	5.85	6

YEN

TENOR	BID	ASK	DIFFERENTIALS BID	ASK	POINTS BID	ASK	FORWARDS BID	OFFER	MID	VOLS BID	ASK	MID
1	1.18	1.25	-0.38833	-0.40667	-0.3288	-0.34432	84.3412	84.32568	84.33344	0.136	13.8	6.968
2	1.15	1.21	-0.78333	-0.81833	-0.66325	-0.69288	84.00675	83.97712	83.99193	13.55	13.75	13.65
3	1.12	1.18	-1.1575	-1.235	-0.98006	-1.04567	83.68994	83.62433	83.65714	13.65	13.8	13.725
6	1.06	1.12	-2.365	-2.47	-2.00245	-2.09135	82.66755	82.57865	82.6231	13.5	13.7	13.6
12	1.03	1.09	-4.76	-4.97	-4.03029	-4.2081	80.63971	80.4619	80.5508	13.4	13.5	13.45

DEM

	DEPOS BID	ASK	DIFFERENTIALS BID	ASK	POINTS BID	ASK	FORWARDS BID	ASK	MID	BID	ASK	MID
1	4.38	4.53	-0.115	-0.14	-0.00162	-0.00197	1.406631	1.406278	1.406454	14.4	14.8	14.6
2	4.35	4.5	-0.235	-0.285	-0.00331	-0.00401	1.404941	1.404236	1.404589	14.25	14.5	14.375
3	4.35	4.5	-0.3275	-0.4275	-0.00461	-0.00602	1.403638	1.40223	1.402934	13.9	14.1	14
6	4.33	4.46	-0.695	-0.835	-0.00979	-0.01176	1.398463	1.396491	1.397477	13.2	13.4	13.3
12	4.41	4.54	-1.31	-1.59	-0.01845	-0.02239	1.389802	1.385859	1.38783	12.65	12.8	12.725

DEM/JY

	DIFFERENTIALS BID	ASK	POINTS BID	ASK	FORWARDS BID	ASK	MID	BID	ASK	MID
1	-0.27917	-0.26083	-0.16785	-0.15682	59.95642	59.96744	59.96193	9.7	10	9.85
2	-0.55833	-0.52333	-0.33569	-0.31465	59.78857	59.80962	59.7991	9.9	10.2	10.05
3	-0.845	-0.7925	-0.50805	-0.47648	59.61622	59.64778	59.632	10.1	10.4	10.25
6	-1.7	-1.605	-1.02211	-0.96499	59.10216	59.15927	59.13071	10.3	10.6	10.45
12	-3.51	-3.32	-2.11036	-1.99613	58.01391	58.12814	58.07102	10.5	10.7	10.6

The term structure of probabilities is not monotonic, but this is not inconsistent since special-event risk can increase the probability of large movements to a specified terminal date. However, if the proprietary distribution suggests that these specific event risks are less important, then an obvious correlation trade is suggested. In the present case, the middle part of the probability could be bought by purchasing cheap straddles on the cross, and the short- and long-term straddles could be sold as hedges. As the probability curve flattens out, this "straddle butterfly" position would profit.

TRADING ALGORITHMS AND RISK MEASURES

Whether one is taking a position with options in a single market or a combination of many markets, the logical decision process usually identifies risk–reward *preferences* and *beliefs*, and expectations in the context of the current state of the world. Preference

F I G U R E 6–4

Joint Probability Distribution for Dollar/Mark, and Dollar/Yen Exchange Rates for 1-Year Period

Implied Probabilities for DM and Yen								
months	**12**							
yen forw	80.5508							
yen vol	0.1345							
dm forw	1.38783							
dm vol	0.12725							
yen level	85							
dm level	1.41							
prob	0.441055							
corr	0.67							
dem/yen	0.106							
0.44105515	70	72	74	76	78	80	82	84
1	0.00	0.00	0.00	0.00	0.00	0.00	0.00	0.00
1.16	0.04	0.05	0.05	0.06	0.06	0.07	0.07	0.07
1.2	0.06	0.07	0.08	0.09	0.10	0.10	0.11	0.11
1.24	0.08	0.09	0.11	0.13	0.14	0.15	0.16	0.16
1.28	0.09	0.12	0.14	0.16	0.18	0.20	0.21	0.22
1.32	0.10	0.14	0.17	0.20	0.23	0.25	0.27	0.29
1.36	0.11	0.15	0.19	0.23	0.27	0.30	0.33	0.35
1.4	0.12	0.16	0.21	0.26	0.30	0.34	0.38	0.41
1.44	0.13	0.17	0.22	0.27	0.33	0.38	0.42	0.46
1.48	0.13	0.18	0.23	0.29	0.35	0.40	0.46	0.51
1.52	0.13	0.18	0.24	0.30	0.36	0.42	0.48	0.54
1.56	0.13	0.18	0.24	0.30	0.37	0.44	0.50	0.56
1.6	0.13	0.18	0.24	0.31	0.37	0.44	0.51	0.57
1.64	0.13	0.18	0.24	0.31	0.38	0.45	0.52	0.58
1.68	0.13	0.18	0.24	0.31	0.38	0.45	0.52	0.59
1.72	0.13	0.18	0.24	0.31	0.38	0.45	0.52	0.59
1.76	0.13	0.18	0.24	0.31	0.38	0.45	0.52	0.59
1.8	0.13	0.18	0.24	0.31	0.38	0.45	0.53	0.60

T A B L E 6–8

Implied Probability Term Structure for Yen/USD < 85 and DM/USD < 1.41 Computed from Inputs of Figure 6–3

1 month	0.470638
2 month	0.426114
3 month	0.424323
6 month	0.429097
12 month	0.441055

specification means simply identification of the utility function of the participant as a function of the participant's wealth. Belief specification means identifying the probability density, i.e., the likelihood that a certain event will happen within some prescribed

FIGURE 6-5

Joint Probability Distribution for Dollar/Mark, and Dollar/Yen Exchange Rates for 1-Month Period

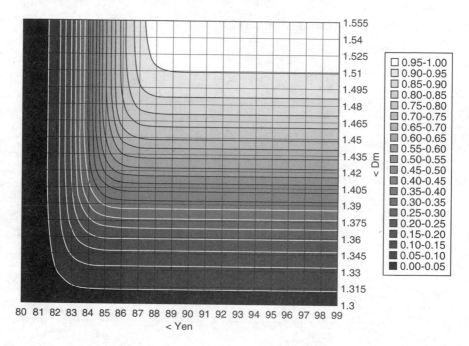

value of the assets. Given the preference specification and the beliefs, the optimal local position is well defined and can be calculated by maximizing utility.

In practice, belief specification might not be carried out at the level of specifying the full probability densities, but rather at the level of individual moments. Thus, the participant might choose to specify the mean, the variance, and perhaps even the skewness and kurtosis of his belief distribution vis-à-vis the implied moments from the market. He will choose to enter into a trade only if his beliefs lead him to believe that there is positive expected return from the trade given his personal (proprietary) beliefs. So the algorithm can be boiled down to the following choices:

1. Decide your risk–reward profile (utility specification):
   a. Limited risk, limited reward
   b. Limited risk, unlimited reward

F I G U R E 6–6

Joint Probability Distribution for Dollar/Mark, and Dollar/Yen
Exchange Rates for 3-Month Period

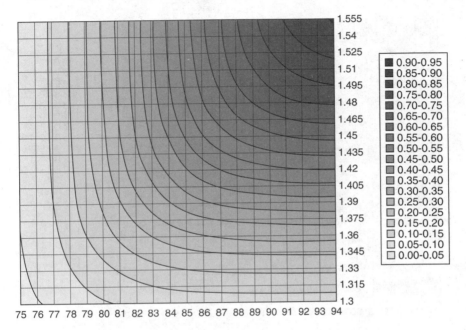

c. Unlimited risk, limited reward
  d. Unlimited risk, unlimited reward
2. Decide your market view (belief specification):
   a. Bullish
   b. Neutral
   c. Bearish
3. Decide if each point on the term structure of implied/
   historical volatility level is (moment level specification of
   current state):
   a. High
   b. Moderate
   c. Low
4. Decide if each point on the term structure of implied/
   historical correlation level is (cross-moment level

F I G U R E 6–7

Joint Probability Distribution for Dollar/Mark, and Dollar/Yen Exchange Rates for 1-Year Period

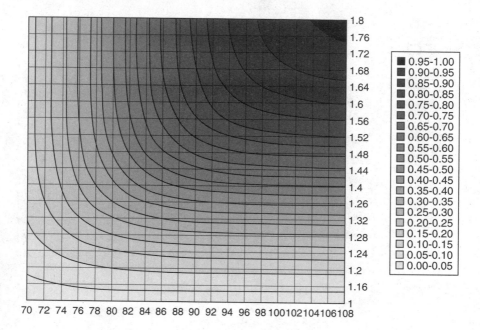

specification of current state):

a. High

b. Moderate

c. Low

5. Decide on a full term-structure-dependent strategy that fits the risk–reward profile, market view, and volatility and correlation levels (optimization).[6]

---

6. An added advantage of this systematic framework is that it might not be possible to identify a strategy that meets all the preference and/or belief specifications. The vacuum usually leads to the design and growth of a new generation of customized products.

Since the basis of risk-taking in any market is the expectation of reward that is some multiple of the total value that can be lost under given assumptions, this means it is necessary to have some measure of the variance (and higher moments, such as skewness) of a given portfolio of assets. The usual practice of taking the volatility of returns as a measure of risk is not always the most useful method for trading, since actual day-to-day dollar value fluctuation is a more important concept for risk management on a trading desk. We will first discuss the question of finding an optimal profile and then return to computing variance measures for some common hybrids.

Optimality

Assume that we have a utility profile that is well described by the exponential utility function as a function of wealth $\tilde{W}$, i.e.,

$$U[\tilde{W}] = -e^{-a\tilde{W}} \qquad (6.82)$$

where a is some constant, and $\tilde{W}$ is a function of the stochastic returns, investment decisions, and the initial wealth W_0. This is a specification of our risk preferences. Computing $-U''[W]/U'[W] = a$, we see that there is constant absolute risk aversion. In other words, the inverse $1/a$, which is also a constant, specifies that we have constant absolute risk tolerance. For the kinds of trades that a large dealer desk engages in, this utility function is not all that bad since most dealer desks like to develop to a stage where they can put away a significant portion of their flow profits, which are essentially risk-free, into deferral accounts, and take new risks with a more or less constant dollar amount. Now suppose we have two risky assets and a risk-free asset. What is our optimal position in each of the risky assets and the riskless asset based on this preference specification?

Note that at this stage we have to specify our beliefs. We assume that the assets are jointly lognormal and have a correlation ρ between them. The stochastic wealth is

$$\tilde{W} = W_0(1 + \alpha x + \beta y + (1 - \alpha - \beta)r) \qquad (6.83)$$

where r is the risk-free return rate and x and y are the stochastic returns on the two correlated risky assets.

Then, the optimization problem can be specified as the maximum of the expected utility over the fractions invested in the risk assets:

$$\max_{\alpha,\beta} E[U[\tilde{W}]] \tag{6.84}$$

which, with our preferences and beliefs, equals

$$\max_{\alpha,\beta} \frac{1}{2\pi\sigma_1\sigma_2\sqrt{1-\rho^2}} \int_{-\infty}^{\infty} \int_{-\infty}^{\infty} e^{-aW_0(1+\alpha x+\beta y+(1-\alpha-\beta)r)}$$
$$\Phi[\mu_1,\mu_2,\sigma_1,\sigma_2,\rho]\,dx\,dy \tag{6.85}$$

where $\Phi[\mu_1,\mu_2,\sigma_1,\sigma_2,\rho]$ is the joint bivariate normal density,

$$\Phi[\mu_1,\mu_2,\sigma_1,\sigma_2,\rho] = e^{-\frac{1}{2}\frac{1}{1-\rho^2}\left[\left(\frac{x-\mu_x}{\sigma_x}\right)^2+\left(\frac{y-\mu_y}{\sigma_y}\right)^2-2\rho\frac{(x-\mu_x)(y-\mu_y)}{\sigma_x\sigma_y}\right]} \tag{6.86}$$

This maximization problem can be solved by setting the first derivatives with respect to α and β equal to zero:

$$\frac{\partial E[U]}{\partial \alpha} = \frac{\partial E[U]}{\partial \beta} = 0 \tag{6.87}$$

which, for the α equation, gives

$$\int_{-\infty}^{\infty} \int_{-\infty}^{\infty} (x-r)\,e^{-aW_0(1+\alpha x+\beta y+(1-\alpha-\beta)r)}\Phi[\mu_1,\mu_2,\sigma_1,\sigma_2,\rho]\,dx\,dy = 0 \tag{6.88}$$

Making the usual transformation

$$\frac{x-\mu_x}{\sigma_x} = w$$
$$\frac{y-\mu_y}{\sigma_y} = z$$

we obtain

$$\int_{-\infty}^{\infty} \int_{-\infty}^{\infty} (w\sigma_x+\mu_x-r)\,e^{-aW_0(1+\alpha(w\sigma_x+\mu_x)+\beta(z\sigma_y+\mu_y)+(1-\alpha-\beta)r)}$$
$$\times e^{-\frac{1}{2}\frac{1}{1-\rho^2}(w^2+z^2-2\rho wz)}\,dw\,dz = 0 \tag{6.89}$$

and, finally, with the Cholesky decomposition

$$w = u\sqrt{1 - \rho^2} + \rho v$$

$$z = v \tag{6.90}$$

we can get rid of the correlation term in the quadratic exponential. Ignoring the constant exponential factors (since the right-hand side is zero), we get

$$\int_{-\infty}^{\infty} \int_{-\infty}^{\infty} (\sigma_x u\sqrt{1 - \rho^2} + \sigma_x \rho v + \mu_x - r)$$

$$\times e^{-aW_0(\alpha\sigma_x\sqrt{1-\rho^2}u + \alpha\sigma_x\rho v + \beta\sigma_y v)} e^{-\frac{1}{2}(u^2+v^2)} \, du \, dv = 0 \tag{6.91}$$

Now use the formulas

$$\frac{1}{\sqrt{2\pi}\sigma} \int_{-\infty}^{\infty} x e^{-bx} e^{-\frac{1}{2}\frac{(x-\mu)^2}{\sigma^2}} dx = (\mu - b\sigma^2) e^{-b\mu + \frac{1}{2}b^2\sigma^2}$$

$$\frac{1}{\sqrt{2\pi}\sigma} \int_{-\infty}^{\infty} e^{-bx} e^{-\frac{1}{2}\frac{(x-\mu)^2}{\sigma^2}} dx = e^{-b\mu + \frac{1}{2}b^2\sigma^2} \tag{6.92}$$

for $\mu = 0, \sigma = 1$, to get the solution (noting that the exponential is a constant that cannot vanish):

$$\alpha_{\text{Optimal}} = \frac{\mu_x - r}{aW_0\sigma_x^2} - \frac{\beta\rho\sigma_x\sigma_y}{\sigma_x^2}$$

$$= \frac{\mu_x - r}{aW_0\sigma_x^2} - \frac{\beta\rho\sigma_y}{\sigma_x} \tag{6.93}$$

Since there is no difference a priori between the symbols for x and y, we can use symmetry of the integration in $x \leftrightarrow y$ and the simultaneous change in $\alpha \leftrightarrow \beta, \mu_x \leftrightarrow \mu_y, \sigma_x \leftrightarrow \sigma_y$ to get

$$\beta_{\text{Optimal}} = \frac{\mu_y - r}{aW_0\sigma_y^2} - \frac{\alpha\rho\sigma_x\sigma_y}{\sigma_y^2}$$

$$= \frac{\mu_y - r}{aW_0\sigma_y^2} - \frac{\alpha\rho\sigma_x}{\sigma_y} \tag{6.94}$$

The first term is recognized as the classic measure of risk–reward, the Sharpe ratio. The second term is the covariance or correlation effect. Note that if the correlation is positive, and if we have invested some fraction of wealth in one asset, the optimal asset allocation requires that we have less of the other asset than we would have in the absence of the correlated asset. On the other hand, with negative correlation, we can increase the proportion in both assets.

Price-Based Risk Measures

Single-Asset Price-Based Risk Measures

We can compute the expected value of the stochastic price S_T in terms of the forward F:

$$\bar{S}_T = \frac{1}{\sigma\sqrt{2\pi T}} \int_{-\infty}^{\infty} S_T \frac{1}{S_T} e^{-\frac{1}{2}\left[\frac{\ln\frac{S_T}{S_0} - \left(\mu - \frac{\sigma^2}{2}\right)T}{\sigma\sqrt{T}}\right]^2} dS_T$$

$$= \frac{1}{\sqrt{2\pi}} \int_{-\infty}^{\infty} S_T e^{-\frac{1}{2}x^2} dx$$

$$= \frac{1}{\sqrt{2\pi}} F e^{\frac{-\sigma^2}{2}T} \int_{-\infty}^{\infty} e^{\sigma\sqrt{T}x - \frac{1}{2}x^2} dx$$

$$= F \tag{6.95}$$

where we use $F = S_T e^{-\frac{1}{2}\sigma^2 T + \sigma\sqrt{T}z}$ for the forward. The variance is

$$\sigma_{S_T}^2 = \frac{1}{\sigma\sqrt{2\pi T}} \int_{-\infty}^{\infty} (S_T - F)^2 \frac{1}{S_T} e^{-\frac{1}{2}\left[\frac{\ln\frac{S_T}{S_0} - \left(\mu - \frac{\sigma^2}{2}\right)T}{\sigma\sqrt{T}}\right]^2} dS_T$$

$$= \frac{1}{\sigma\sqrt{2\pi T}} \int_{-\infty}^{\infty} (S_T^2 + F^2 - 2S_T F) \frac{1}{S_T} e^{-\frac{1}{2}\left[\frac{\ln\frac{S_T}{S_0} - \left(\mu - \frac{\sigma^2}{2}\right)T}{\sigma\sqrt{T}}\right]^2} dS_T$$

$$= \frac{1}{\sqrt{2\pi}} \int_{-\infty}^{\infty} (S_T^2 + F^2 - 2S_T F) e^{-\frac{1}{2}x^2} dx$$

$$= \frac{1}{\sqrt{2\pi}} \int_{-\infty}^{\infty} (F^2 e^{-\sigma^2 T + 2\sigma\sqrt{T}x} + F^2 - 2F^2 e^{-\frac{1}{2}\sigma^2 T + \sigma\sqrt{T}x}) e^{-\frac{1}{2}x^2} dx$$

$$= F^2(e^{\sigma^2 T} + 1 - 2)$$

$$= F^2(e^{\sigma^2 T} - 1) \tag{6.96}$$

The results above are quite intuitive, since the expected value of the asset price should simply be the forward at terminal value. Also, the variance of the terminal price should be larger than zero as long as the returns have any amount of uncertainty. Note that the second result on the variance of the price can be inverted to get the volatility of the returns in terms of the volatility of the price:

$$\sigma_{\text{Returns}} = \sqrt{\frac{1}{T} \ln \left(\frac{\sigma_S^2}{F^2} + 1 \right)} \tag{6.97}$$

Multiple-Asset Price-Based Risk Measures

I find the following results useful in the bivariate computations that follow:

$$\overline{S}_i = F_i$$

$$\sigma_{S_i} = F_i \sqrt{e^{\sigma_i^2 t} - 1}$$

$$\text{Price correlation} = \frac{e^{\sigma_1 \sigma_2 \rho t}}{\sqrt{e^{\sigma_1^2 t} - 1} \sqrt{e^{\sigma_2^2 t} - 1}}$$

in terms of return correlation ρ. Then, by performing the usual bivariate integrations, we can obtain the following results.

Ratios This might be the case, for example, when one considers currency crosses like DM/yen. Consider the expected value of the ratio A/B where $A = $ DM/dollar and $B = $ yen/dollar. Then the ratio is, again, simply the value of DM/yen. If we use

$$\sigma_1 = \text{volatility of DM/dollar}$$
$$\sigma_2 = \text{volatility of yen/dollar}$$
$$F_1 = \text{forward for DM/dollar}$$
$$F_2 = \text{forward for yen/dollar}$$

then the expected value of the ratio is calculated to be

$$\frac{F_1}{F_2} e^{\sigma_2^2 T - \sigma_1 \sigma_2 T} \tag{6.98}$$

and the variance is

$$\frac{F_1}{F_2} e^{\frac{1}{2}\sigma_2^2 T - \sigma_1 \sigma_2 \rho T} \left(\sqrt{e^{\sigma_1^2 T + 2\sigma_2^2 T - 2\sigma_1 \sigma_2 \rho T} + e^{\sigma_2^2 T} - 2} \right) \tag{6.99}$$

Spreads   Assume we have a spread position in forwards on two different asset classes, i.e., forwards on the S&P 500 and the 5-year treasury note. Then let us say we have n_1 units of the first asset and n_2 units of the second unit. The payoff on a spread position is, with the superscript zero representing the value of the forward at time zero:

$$n_1(F_1^T - F_1^0) - n_2(F_2^T - F_2^0) \tag{6.100}$$

The expected value of the payoff is obviously zero since the expected value of the forward is simply the forward.

What is the variance of this portfolio and how do we minimize it by choosing n_1 and n_2 judiciously?

By performing a simple integral for the variance over the bivariate lognormal density, we get the spread price variance:

$$\text{Portfolio variance} = n_1^2 F_1^2 (e^{\sigma_1^2 T} - 1) + n_2^2 F_2^2 (e^{\sigma_2^2 T} - 1)$$

$$- 2n_1 n_2 F_1 F_2 (e^{\rho \sigma_1 \sigma_2 T} - 1) \tag{6.101}$$

Choosing $n_1 = 1$, which takes care of the units, and minimizing the variance with respect to n_2, we get

$$n_2^m(n_1 = 1) = \frac{F_1}{F_2} \left(\frac{e^{\rho \sigma_1 \sigma_2 T} - 1}{e^{\sigma_2^2 T} - 1} \right)$$

$$\sim \rho \frac{F_1 \sigma_1}{F_2 \sigma_2} \tag{6.102}$$

Quantos   Imagine some stock trading in $S = $ dollars/share, but whose payout is in yen/share. Then, to convert from dollar-denominated units to yen-denominated units, we need to multiply the stock price by $X = $ yen/dollar exchange rate. Then, the expected value is

$$\overline{Q} = \frac{1}{\sqrt{2\pi(1 - \rho^2)}} F_S F_X \, e^{\frac{1}{2}(-\sigma_S^2 T - \sigma_X^2 T)}$$

$$\times \int_{-\infty}^{\infty} e^{\sigma_S \sqrt{T} x + \sigma_X \sqrt{T} y} \, e^{-\frac{1}{2(1-\rho^2)}(x^2 + y^2 - 2\rho xy)} \, dx \, dy$$

$$= F_S F_X \, e^{\sigma_S \sigma_X T \rho} \tag{6.103}$$

which has been used earlier in the discussion of the market price of risk.

The variance is

$$\sigma_{F_Q}^2 = F_S F_X (e^{\sigma_S^2 T + \sigma_X^2 T - 4\sigma_S \sigma_X T \rho} + e^{2\sigma_S \sigma_X T \rho} - 2 e^{\sigma_X^2 T + \rho \sigma_S \sigma_X T \rho}) \qquad (6.104)$$

Note that there are a number of nonvanishing partial derivatives that have option-like characteristics even though this is a forward:

$$F_Q = F_X F_S \, e^{\sigma_S \sigma_X \rho T}$$

$$\text{"Time decay"} = F_Q \sigma_S \sigma_X \rho$$

$$\text{Cross-gamma} = \frac{\partial^2 F_Q}{\partial F_X \, \partial F_S} = e^{\sigma_S \sigma_X \rho T} = \frac{F_Q}{F_X F_S} \qquad (6.105)$$

This is useful, for instance, in trading quantos, e.g., the Nikkei futures that are traded on the CME (denominated in dollars) and the ones traded in SIMEX (denominated in yen).

Asset Allocation Example

We will now construct a trading portfolio for a ratio trade and show how options positions in the individual assets can be used to implement the view. Assume that we have sold one contract of the S&P 500 and bought a certain number of treasury notes. The minimum variance portfolio is determined by minimizing Equation (6.101) with respect to n_1, n_2. Assuming $n_1 = 1$, minimization with respect to n_2 gives

$$n_2 = \frac{F_1}{F_2} \left[\frac{e^{\rho \sigma_1 \sigma_2 T} - 1}{e^{\sigma_2^2 T} - 1} \right] \qquad (6.106)$$

which, for small time T, approximates to

$$n_1 = \frac{\rho \sigma_1 F_1}{\sigma_2 F_2} \qquad (6.107)$$

Using the relationship that the assets really are holdings of a certain amount of notional contract value, where

$$\text{Treasury contract value} = 1000 \times \text{Contract price}$$
$$\text{S\&P 500 contract value} = 500 \times \text{Contract price} \qquad (6.108)$$

we may obtain the "minimum variance" ratios. Figure 6–8 shows the required hedge ratios (made up from hypothetical spot levels for the S&P 500) for a portfolio which consists of short one S&P 500 futures contract on the IMM and long a given number of fixed-income contracts traded on the CBOT. The volatility- and correlation-adjusted amounts are the ones that would, given a correlation level, leave a theoretically hedged portfolio flat for small moves in the two markets. For instance, if you believe that the correlation

F I G U R E 6–8

Example of Bond and Note Future Hedges for S&P 500 Futures

Hedge Units of Minimum Variance Portfolio Per S&P Unit					
Tenor	0.001				
	S&P	2ynotes	5ynotes	10ynotes	bonds
Forward	$322,500.00	$205.562.50	$105,281.25	$106,812.50	$108,062.00
Vol	15%	2.15%	5%	7.25%	10%
Index	645.00	102 25/32	105 9/32	106 26/32	108 2/32
Notional	500.00	200000.00	100000.00	100000.00	100000.00
corr	1				
−1		−10.95	−9.19	−6.25	−4.48
−0.9		−9.85	−8.27	−5.62	−4.03
−0.8		−8.76	−7.35	−5.00	−3.58
−0.7		−7.66	−6.43	−4.37	−3.13
−0.6		−6.57	−5.51	−3.75	−2.69
−0.5		−5.47	−4.59	−3.12	−2.24
−0.4		−4.38	−3.68	−2.50	−1.79
−0.3		−3.28	−2.76	−1.87	−1.34
−0.2		−2.19	−1.84	−1.25	−0.90
−0.1		−1.09	−0.92	−0.62	−0.45
0		0.00	0.00	0.00	0.00
0.1		1.09	0.92	0.62	0.45
0.2		2.19	1.84	1.25	0.90
0.3		3.28	2.76	1.87	1.34
0.4		4.38	3.68	2.50	1.79
0.5		5.47	4.59	3.12	2.24
0.6		6.57	5.51	3.75	2.69
0.7		7.66	6.43	4.37	3.13
0.8		8.76	7.35	5.00	3.58
0.9		9.85	8.27	5.62	4.03
1		10.95	9.19	6.25	4.48

between the S&P 500 and the 5-year note futures is going to be 0.40, you should be long 3.68 5-year note futures for every short S&P 500 contract.

To take advantage of the added fact that S&P 500 volatilities will most likely rise when the price falls (as reflected in the skews and explained in terms of the correlation between price and volatility, as discussed in Appendix F), we would like to be long puts on the S&P 500. Similarly, vols of the 5-year note options are expected to rise on a rapid drop in rates or rise in prices. Then we need to sell the required number of put options on the 5-year notes that give a delta that matches the one given from the minimum variance portfolio.

An index $I = S/B$, where S is the level of the S&P 500 futures and B is the level of the fixed-income futures, may be devised. Portfolio hedgers can get into contracts to buy or sell a given number of these units, i.e., to exchange a given amount of S&P 500 notional for fixed-income notionals. Also, they can buy or sell options on these units. This will automatically take advantage of the fact that the price convexity and increased demand for safety in fixed income works when it is needed most, i.e., during sharp sell-offs in the S&P 500. To hedge this position in the vanilla market, we may take option spread positions in the individual markets dictated by the hedge ratios we have derived.

CHAPTER 7

Epilogue

Innovation in financial markets is never a straight-as-an-arrow phenomenon. The jagged path to optimal solutions of risk-management issues is a necessary feature in the marketplace. New markets start by being full of transactions costs, illiquidity, and friction. As competition increases, the underlying variables become commoditized, and start being transacted in their own right.

The infant markets in stocks and bonds led to forwards and futures, which, in turn, were further refined through the introduction of options. While the markets in stocks and bonds allow one to transact in cash assets, the introduction of forwards and futures allows the transaction of time value, i.e., cash flows. The options markets allow all this and also the transaction of uncertainty within a single asset class, i.e., "volatility." The correlation market allows one to deal in the underlying variable, the value of time, and uncertainty, *plus* interrelationships between different asset classes. It is an ever-more-encompassing pyramid, in which each new type and class of product can be combined in various strategies to create risk profiles that pre-exist, and, in addition, to allow new strategies to be created.

One new direction that can be imagined as correlation joins the group of commoditized variables is the incorporation of economic variables directly in pricing models. There is a dichotomy in the pricing paradigm of the day—while market variables are assumed to be stochastic, economic variables, which eventually are the driving factors for market variables, are assumed, and to a certain degree controlled (e.g., by central banks), to be deterministic. What is the price of inflation? What is the price of a bond that is linked to the rate of inflation? While, just a few years ago, these questions were impossible to answer within a risk-neutral framework, the introduction of inflation-indexed bonds has made it possible to trade inflation in very much the same way as one trades ordinary stocks and bonds. For the first time, we are seeing products that require use of the technology that I have tried to develop in this book to capture the pricing consequences of interrelationships between fundamental economic variables and market processes.

UTILITY (OR FUTILITY?) OF HEDGING WITH CUSTOMIZED PRODUCTS

Every new product introduced in the financial markets commands a risk premium. The buyer of protection compensates the seller of protection above and beyond the expected magnitude of loss. This can only be explained in terms of utility theory. The buyer of insurance pays a premium in one form or another to change the probability distribution that represents risk. If the buyer is not forced to buy this insurance, he buys it only when he discovers that the transaction will bring him into a risk situation that he prefers to his original one. The customized-option market allows the buyers and sellers to design probability distributions that suit them both. In other words, if the buyer has a preferential ordering of probability distributions, then the seller can design products that take advantage of this preferential ordering for mutual benefit. In other words, buyers and sellers of options are both risk averse, so even if the expected value of the loss was known and agreed upon by both, the option buyer would have to compensate the seller by paying a premium above the fair "actuarial" value.

 To formalize this, in general, assume that the buyer has a utility function $U_B(x)$ where x represents his wealth or "money" at any given point. Also, assume that $U(x)$ increases with x, i.e., the buyer prefers having more wealth to less, and $U''(x) < 0$. Suppose his initial wealth is W_B and he is exposed to some risk that can cause a loss, which we assume to be a random variable with a "loss density" $f(x)$. Then, the expected utility for the buyer is

$$E[U_B] = \int_0^\infty U_B(W - x)f(x)\,dx \qquad (7.1)$$

If the buyer can pay a premium P to completely get rid of the risk, he would do so if

$$U_B(W_B - P) \geq E[U_B] \qquad (7.2)$$

With the assumption that $U''(x) < 0$, we can use Jensen's inequality to assert that[1]

$$E[U(x)] < U(E[x]) \qquad (7.3)$$

or

$$E[U_B] = \int_0^\infty U_B(W - x)f(x)\,dx < U_B(W - E[x]) \qquad (7.4)$$

so that for some premium value $\overline{P} > E[x]$, the two sides are equal, i.e., the buyer is willing to pay more than the expected loss to have the risk covered by insuring against it.

Now consider the option writer. Let his utility function be $U_S(x)$ and his initial wealth be W_S. He is not exposed to the risk to begin with, but he is willing to take on the risk in exchange for some premium P as long as his expected utility from the transaction is higher than his initial utility:

$$U_S(W_S) \leq \int_0^\infty U_S(W_S + P - x)f(x)\,dx \qquad (7.5)$$

If both inequalities in Equations (7.5) and (7.2) can simultaneously be satisfied, the buyer and seller can get into a contract so that both their expected utilities increase, so, clearly, the correct premium is determined not simply by the risk-neutral fair value, but also by the individual utility of the buyers and the sellers. It is only when the market becomes liquid, and the number of buyers and sellers is large enough, that local hedging becomes possible. In this situation,

---

1. Jensen's inequality says, in simple terms, that if f is a convex function on some space X, and x is some random variable with expected value $E(x)$, then $E(f(x)) \geq f(E(x))$.

the utility-independent price is a reasonable approximation to the risk-neutral fair price.

One consequence of this asymmetry arises in the different management of option positions by the longs and the shorts. The party that is short options has already earned part of the hedging cost by charging a premium over the fair value, and needs to protect it to justify being in the trade in the first place. So in the day-to-day process of hedging, it has to use stop-loss orders. On the other hand, the party that is long the option position, if it chooses to hedge dynamically at all, can trade using limit orders, ensuring that no slippage occurs. Another related result, whose proof is easy but beyond the scope of this book, is that it is never optimal for a hedger to hedge only part of his risk. If a hedge increases his utility function, than he is better off doing it completely.

Under certain idealized conditions, such as continuously open markets, continuous price processes, zero transactions costs, absence of leverage and short selling constraints, simple volatility structures, and symmetric information, it can be shown that the addition of derivatives like simple calls and puts does not enhance the investment possibility beyond that already achievable by trading in the underlying instruments. Clearly, if continuous dynamic hedging were possible in all markets, correlated or not, there would be no use for options, let alone exotics and hybrids. The investor or hedger can completely control his wealth simply by trading in the primitive assets [153]. Ross [177] and the literature spawned from his research study the welfare gains achieved by introducing options into an economy.

In this whole book, as in most finance textbooks, the valuation of options is performed assuming risk-neutral valuation, i.e., by calculating the price of options for utility functions that are linear with vanishing second derivatives. This is due to the ability to hedge dynamically. However, the very reason that an exotic option market exists, and is extremely active during periods of financial turmoil, is that people are not risk neutral, especially when it comes to hedging their own very customized and specific exposures. Then, the interaction of the utility functions of the sellers and the buyers of financial insurance determines the price and the course of a line of products. A very nice discussion of the optimal payoff structures, once beliefs and preferences are specified, has been given recently by Carr and Madan [46]. They also show that derivatives are not extraneous; in fact, they are necessary to complete the market.

DEFERRED PROFITS

Whenever a firm embarks on a new business, it estimates the return on the risks and capital it commits based on some statistical measures. Since statistical measures are useful only if they represent the outcomes of a "normal" course of events, while providing some ability to capture deviations from normalcy, they are woefully inadequate in assisting one to make decisions on reservation of resources towards extreme unforeseen events. Thus, general rules of thumb have been used by various organizations in putting away the "profits" that are earned from unprecedented activity such as the running of an exotic options book.

Some firms take the conservative extreme where all profit (from the midpoint) is deferred at inception, after taking out immediate hedging cost adjustments. The remaining profit then drips in at a constant rate over the life of the transaction. The life of the transaction is usually taken to be the contractual life, *i.e., the length of time the contract would survive if it were not terminated by one of the contingencies in the specification of the contract.* Clearly, for exotic options, with various kinds of knockout features, very few contracts are expected to survive to maturity unaltered. Thus, the average drip is not commensurate with the incremental hedging costs incurred by the trader managing the positions. In some cases, a large outlying event may trigger a barrier without allowing for any rehedging. In such cases, the book might realize a large profit or loss from the trade being, for instance, knocked out, but without realizing the compensating gain or loss from the dynamical hedges that were planned but could not be implemented. Various other firms do not defer the inception profits at all but consider the present value as realized profits. This is clearly extremely aggressive accounting, because hedging costs are only realized over time, and in an essentially nonlinear way. Depending on the change of the levels and covariances of the assets, more or less frequent hedging at better or worse levels may have to be undertaken. It is impossible to predict, especially in illiquid markets, what the integrated value of the hedging costs will be over the expected life of the transaction, so some reserves have to be set aside for the uncertainties.

Personal experience suggests that the speed of drip should be indexed to the expected life of the deal plus all hedges at any given point in time. Thus, the rate at which profits are realized at any given point in time can change. If a trader chooses to undertake static hedging of the book by trading exotic products that match or mimic the trade that is being hedged, and if he can do so at better prices, then obviously he should get to keep the spread for exploiting market inefficiency. On the other hand, if the trader is "cheap" and decides to take a large portion of the risk himself (gamma and cross-gamma risks), by engaging in delta-hedging, then the profit realized in a given unit of time should correspond to the difference in the value of the optimally hedged portfolio revaluation and the actually realized portfolio revaluation. While cost saving from dynamical hedging, optimally, will be rewarded, mishedging would be penalized. At the same time, the hedge cost and drip become a dynamical process, recalculated based on the risk profile of the portfolio of transactions plus existing hedges.

Note that these issues are not purely academic. In the very beginning stages of exotic option businesses, the back-office teams and risk-control groups lag just a little bit behind in the practical aspects of managing risk on a day-to-day basis. The eventual result is an oversimplification of how the profits are realized. Based on a linear drip, the following deferral arbitrage situation can very easily develop. Suppose a trader is short a long-dated transaction that knocks out if one of the underlying assets touches a trigger level. Assume further that the trigger level is below the level at which that asset is initially trading ("down and out"). On consummation of the trade, the profit is deferred for the full life of the trade, and slowly drips in every day in a linear way. Now it is a fact of life that large events do happen once in a while. For instance, a 3 to 5 sigma event can be expected to happen once or twice a year. Suppose such an event does happen very soon after the trade is put on the books, and the trigger variable moves closer to the knockout trigger. Now consider the situation of the trader who is expected to hedge this movement of prices to maximize economic gain, i.e., minimize realized hedging losses. Any model recommends that he should increase his position by shorting more of the trigger security.

However, the trader knows that if the trigger is hit, he gains back all his deferral immediately, rather than over a period of many years. On the other hand, if the trigger is not hit, and the trigger variable bounces up to its original level again, he would have lost this opportunity to obtain the deferral. The only rational way for him to now hedge his personal gain, i.e., monetize the oppportunity, is to hedge himself *against the loss of the deferral realization*! So he goes long the trigger variable, which is exactly the opposite direction of the hedge that the risk-management model dictates. If the trigger is indeed breached, he can always liquidate this extra long position, at a slight loss, just below the trigger on a stop-loss order. While this strategy results in no economic gain to the firm over its long horizon, due to the asymmetric nature of profits versus losses, it does result in a short-term gain to the trader over his short-term horizon. Clearly the "arbitrage" here is not real, i.e., it leads to no expected positive riskless economic gain, but it is simply an extreme case manifestation of inconsistent and wrong accounting practices. Any sensible accounting and deferral policy would have mechanisms built in to avoid such situations.

THE DOCTRINE OF EFFECTIVE DYNAMICS

In the discussions above, it has often been remarked that once a product becomes popular, it takes on a life of its own and starts trading without reference to the components of which it is made up. For example, a trader trading futures or options on the S&P 500 stock index does not really need to reference the individual components. In principle, he can choose to reconstruct the dynamics of the aggregate from the dynamics and covariances of each of the components, as is done by index arbitrageurs, but if he wants to take a view on, or trade options on, the general direction of the market, he is much better off trading the basket as an asset in itself. *This is not simply a matter of convenience.* The simplification of markets by aggregation and synthesis of trading instruments, to construct *effective instruments*—which has its analogues in all fields of science—actually leads to the rapid development of the markets by providing a more abstract and more fundamental set of tools with which to express views. If the reader refers to the discussion of construction of risk indices, he will see that the only way to manage practically and benefit from the plethora of markets and products is to use a scheme of aggregation such as the ones expressed by stock indices. In physics, an analogue is found in the description of the flow of water. Unless one is interested in special behavior, such as turbulent flow, there really is no need to describe the flow of water in terms of the microscopic behavior and interaction of water molecules. Macroscopic fluid mechanics is enough for macroscopic applications. Similarly, while description of planetary motion in terms of atomic and subatomic first principles is intellectually exciting, there is no real need to do so—Newtonian physics is more or less sufficient.

The evolution of exotic products such as baskets, spreads, knockouts and knockins, barriers, digitals, outperformance options, etc., is also simply an intermediate step in further development. The important thing is that these products can be used to form the basis for further development. As these markets develop, there will be less and less need to refer back to the underlying cash or even vanilla option assets to hedge and to price. A property of the markets that enjoy an extended set of tools, such as the bond market, is that the option market becomes larger than the underlying market.

I can also respond to an obvious criticism of this book using the doctrine of effective dynamics. Readers may have frequently wondered why I chose to address specific pricing problems from particular asset combinations in special payoff structures. A top-down approach, in contrast to the one used here, would begin with a general framework in which all the details of every market, their forward curves, their volatilities and their covariances, are given and calibrated as a whole—and then the specific computations are performed as special cases. This is surely a commendable approach, since it is consistent and economical by construction. However, it lacks two features that make it of little practical use in a trading environment. First, grand unified pricing schemes are computationally too hard to implement, and the choices that are usually made to speed them up end up in losing detail. Since the trading market is nothing if not detail, the top-down approach ends up doing too much labor where it is not needed, and does little labor where it is crucial. Second, every market and trade has special economic motivations and quirks behind it, and a trader pricing and doing a deal needs to get to know each aspect intimately. In dealing with less-liquid products, it is impossible to make uniform idealized assumptions, such as lack of market friction and low transaction costs. When markets are correlated, it is frequently observed that the illiquidity of one component of the correlation trade affects the other components too. If the trade is on large notional amounts, these effects are even more magnified. Thus, focusing on the individual trades while maintaining a flexible hierarchy of models for management of portfolio risk is the only pragmatic method that has any hope of leading to efficiency and profitability.

References

[1] Y. Akahiro, Some Formulae for a New Type of Path-Dependent Option, *Annals of Applied Probability*, 5, p. 383, 1995.

[2] C. O. Alexander (Editor), *The Handbook of Risk Management*, Wiley, New York, 1996.

[3] C. O. Alexander and A. M. Chibumba, *Multivariate Orthogonal Factor GARCH*, School of Mathematical Sciences, University of Sussex, U.K., Aug. 1996.

[4] K. I. Amin and R. A. Jarrow, Pricing Foreign Currency Options under Stochastic Interest Rates, *Journal of International Money and Finance*, 10, p. 310, 1991.

[5] J. Ashraff, J. Tarczon, and W. Wu, Safe Crossing, *Risk*, 8(7), p. 56, 1995.

[6] D. F. Babbel and L. K. Eisenberg, Quantity Adjusting Options and Forward Contracts, *Journal of Financial Engineering*, 2, p. 89, 1993.

[7] S. H. Babbs, *The Valuation of Cross-Currency Interest-Sensitive Claims with Application to "Diff" Swaps*, Midland Global Markets Working Paper, 1994.

[8] G. S. Bakshi and Z. Chen, Equilibrium Valuation of Foreign Exchange Claims, *Journal of Finance*, 52(2), p. 799, June 1997.

[9] D. B. Ball, *Financial Failure and Confederate Defeat*, University of Illinois Press, Urbana, 1991.

[10] R. Barakat, Sums of Independently Lognormally Distributed Variables, *Journal of the Optimization Society of America*, 66, p. 211, 1976.

[11] J. Barraquand and D. Martineau, Numerical Valuation of High Dimensional Multivariate American Securities, *Journal of Financial and Quantitative Analysis*, 30, pp. 383–405, Sept. 1995.

[12] J. Barraquand, Numerical Valuation of High Dimensional Multivariate European Securities, *Management Science*, 41, p. 1882, Dec. 1995.

[13] J. Barraquand and T. Pudet, Pricing of American Path-Dependent Contingent Claims, *Mathematical Finance*, 6, p. 17, Jan. 1996.

[14] J. Barrett, G. Moore, and P. Wilmott, Inelegant Efficiency, *Risk*, 5, p. 82, Oct. 1992.

[15] E. N. Barron, The Bellman Equation for Control of the Running Max of a Diffusion and Application to Look-Back Options, *Applicable Analysis*, 48, p. 205, 1993.

[16] A. C. Bebbington, A Method of Bivariate Trimming for Robust Estimation of the Correlation Coefficient, *Applied Statistics*, 27, pp. 221–228, 1978.

[17] R. Benson and N. Daniel, Up, Over and Out, *Risk*, 4, p. 17, 1991.

[18] Y. Z. Bergman, Pricing Path Dependent Contingent Claims, *Research in Finance: A Research Annual*, 5, p. 229, JAI Press, New York, 1985.

[19] P. Bernstein, *Against the Gods*, Wiley, New York, 1996.

[20] V. Bhansali, Trading Correlation with Volatility, *Derivatives Week*, June 5, 1995.

[21] V. Bhansali and B. Seeman, Interest Rate Basket Options or Yield Curve Options, *Derivatives Week*, Sept. 20, 1993.

[22] V. Bhansali, Price/Volatility Correlation and Vol Skews, *Derivatives Week*, June 24, 1996.

[23] F. Black and R. Litterman, Global Asset Allocation with Equities, Bonds and Currencies, *Goldman Sachs Fixed Income Research*, 1991.

[24] G. W. Blazenko, P. P. Boyle, and K. E. Newport, Valuation of Tandem Options, *Advances in Futures and Options Research*, 4, p. 39, 1990.

[25] S. Blythe, Out of Line, *Risk*, 9(10), p. 82, 1996.

[26] T. Bollerslev, Generalized Autoregressive Conditional Heteroskedasticity, *Journal of Econometrics*, 31, p. 307, 1986.

[27] L. Bouaziz, E. Briys, and M. Crouhy, The Pricing of Forward Starting Asian Options, *Journal of Banking and Finance*, 18, p. 823, 1994.

[28] J. Bowie and P. Carr, Static Simplicity, *Risk*, 7(8), p. 44, 1994.

[29] P. P. Boyle, J. Evnine, and S. Gibbs, Numerical Evaluation of Multivariate Contingent Claims, *Review of Financial Studies*, 2, p. 241, 1989.

[30] P. P. Boyle, New Life Forms on the Options Landscape, *Journal of Financial Engineering*, 2, p. 217, 1993.

[31] P. P. Boyle and S. M. Turnbull, Pricing and Hedging Capped Options, *Journal of Futures Markets*, 9, p. 41, 1989.

[32] P. P. Boyle and S. H. Lau, Bumping up Against the Barrier with the Binomial Method, *Journal of Derivatives*, 1, p. 6, 1994.

[33] P. P. Boyle, The Quality Option and Timing Option in Futures Contracts, *Journal of Finance*, 44, p. 101, 1989.

[34] P. P. Boyle and Y. K. Tse, An Algorithm for Computing Values of Options on the Maximum or Minimum of Several Assets, *Journal of Financial and Quantitative Analysis*, 25, p. 215, June 1990.

[35] D. Breeden and R. Litzenberger, Prices of State Contingent Claims Implicit in Option Prices, *Journal of Business*, 51, pp. 621–651, 1978.

[36] E. Briys and M. Crouhy, Creating and Pricing Hybrid Foreign Currency Options, *Financial Management*, 17, p. 59, Winter 1988.

[37] M. Broadie and P. Glasserman, Pricing American-Style Securities Using Simulation, *Journal of Economic Dynamics and Controls*, 21(8–9), p. 1323, 1997.

[38] M. Broadie and J. DeTemple, American Capped Call Options and Dividend Paying Assets, *Review of Financial Studies*, 8, p. 161, 1995.

[39] R. Brooks, A Lattice Approach to Interest Rate Spread Options, *Journal of Financial Engineering*, 4, p. 281, 1995.

[40] R. Brooks, Multivariate Contingent Claims Analysis with Cross-Currency Options as an Illustration, *Journal of Financial Engineering*, 1, p. 1071, 1992.

[41] G. Burghardt, J. Greco, and W. Hoskins, Yield Curve Spread Futures and Options, *Dean Witter Institutional Futures*, Oct. 15, 1996.

[42] P. Carr, *Static Hedging of Timing Risk*, Morgan Stanley Working Paper, 1997.

[43] P. Carr, A Note on the Pricing of Commodity Linked Bonds, *Journal of Finance*, 42, p. 1071, Sept. 1987.

[44] P. Carr, The Valuation of Sequential Exchange Opportunities, *Journal of Finance*, 43, p. 1235, 1988.

[45] P. Carr, K. Ellis, and V. Gupta, Static Hedging of Exotic Options, Johnson Graduate School of Management Publication, Cornell University, Ithaca, NY, 1996.

[46] P. Carr and D. Madan, *Optimal Positioning in Derivative Securities*, Preliminary version obtained from the authors.

[47] A. P. Carverhill and L. J. Clewlow, Flexible Convolution, *Risk*, 3, p. 25, 1990.

[48] E. C. Chang, Returns to Speculators and the Theory of Normal Backwardation, *Journal of Finance*, 40, pp. 193–208, 1985.

[49] O. Cheyette, Pricing Options on Multiple Assets, *Advances in Futures and Options Research*, 4, p. 69, 1990.

[50] N. Chriss and M. Ong, Digitals Defused, *Risk*, 8, p. 56, 1995.

[51] A. Conze and R. Viswanathan, European Path Dependent Options: The Case of Geometric Averages, *Finance*, 12, p. 7, 1991.

[52] A. Conze and R. Viswanathan, Path-Dependent Options: The Case of Lookback Options, *Journal of Finance*, 46, p. 1893, 1991.

[53] C. Joy, P. P. Boyle, and K. S. Tan, Quasi-Monte Carlo Methods in Numerical Finance, *Management Science*, 42, p. 926, 1996.

[54] M. Curran, Beyond Average Intelligence, *Risk*, 5, p. 60, 1995.

[55] A. Dassios, The Distributions of the Quantile of a Brownian Motion with Drift and the Price of Related Path-Dependent Options, *Annals of Applied Probability*, 5, p. 389, May 1995.

[56] M. Davis and H. Lee, Coping with Model Error in Hedging Interest Rate Derivative Products, *Global Derivatives Conference Proceedings*, Paris, 1996.

[57] M. H. A. Davis, V. G. Panas, and T. Zariphopoulou, European Option Pricing with Transaction Costs, *Society for Industrial and Applied Mathematics Journal of Control and Optimisation*, 31, p. 470, 1993.

[58] M. Dempster, *Improving the Pricing and Hedging of Complex Cross-Currency Derivatives Through The Use of Finite Differences*, Judge Institute of

Management Studies Working Paper, University of Cambridge, U.K., 1995.

[59] E. Derman and I. Kani, The Ins and Outs of Barrier Options, *Goldman Sachs Quantitative Strategies Research Notes*, June 1993.

[60] E. Derman, D. Ergener, and I. Kani, Forever Hedged, *Risk*, 7, p. 139, 1994.

[61] E. Derman and I. Kani, Valuing and Hedging Outperformance Options, *Goldman Sachs Quantitative Research Strategy Notes*, January 1992.

[62] E. Derman, P. Karasinski, and J. Wecker, Understanding Guaranteed Exchange Rate Contracts in Foreign Stock Investments, *International Equity Strategies, Goldman, Sachs and Co.*, 1990.

[63] E. Derman, I. Kani, and M. Kamal, Trading and Hedging Local Volatility, *Goldman Sachs Quantitative Strategies Research Notes*, August 1996.

[64] S. J. Devlin, R. Gnanadesikan, and J. R. Kettenring, Robust Estimation and Outlier Detection with Correlation Coefficients, *Biometrika*, 62, p. 531, 1975.

[65] J. N. Dewynne, A. E. Whalley, and P. Wilmott, Path Dependent Options and Transaction Costs, *Philosophical Transactions of the Royal Society of London A*, 347, p. 517, 1994.

[66] J. N. Dewynne and P. Wilmott, A Note on Average Rate Options with Discrete Sampling, *SIAM Journal on Applied Mathematics*, 55, p. 267, 1995.

[67] J. N. Dewynne and P. Wilmott, Partial to the Exotic, *Risk*, 6, p. 38, March 1993.

[68] A. Dravid, M. Richardson, and T. Sun, Pricing Foreign Index Contingent Claims: An Application to Nikkei Index Warrants, *Journal of Derivatives*, 1, p. 33, Fall 1993.

[69] Z. Drezner, Computation of the Bivariate Normal Integral, *Mathematics of Computation*, 32, p. 277, Jan. 1978.

[70] L. E. Dubins, L. A. Shepp, and A. N. Shiryaev, Optimal Stopping Rules and Maximal Inequalities for Bessel Processes, *Theory of Probability and its Applications*, 38(2), p. 226, 1993.

[71] J. D. Duffie and J. M. Harrison, Arbitrage Pricing of Russian Options and Perpetual Lookback Options, *Annals of Applied Probability*, 3, p. 641, 1993.

[72] B. Dupire, Pricing with a Smile, *Risk*, 7(1), p. 18, 1994.

[73] K. Dusak, Futures Trading and Investor Returns: An Investigation of Commodity Risk Premiums, *Journal of Political Economy*, 81, pp. 1387–1406, 1973.

[74] E. Elton and M. Gruber, *Modern Portfolio Theory and Investment Analysis*, Wiley, New York, 1995.

[75] P. Embrechts and G. Samorodnitsky, Sample Quantiles of Heavy Tailed Stochastic Processes, *Stochastic Processes and Their Applications*, 59, p. 217, 1993.

[76] R. Engle, Autoregressive Conditional Heteroscedasticity with Estimates of the Variance of United Kingdom Inflation, *Econometrica*, 50, p. 987, 1982.

[77] R. F. Engle and C. W. Granger, Cointegration and Error Correction: Representation, Estimation and Testing, *Econometrica*, 55, p. 251, 1987.

[78] R. Engle and J. Mezrich, Grappling with GARCH, *Risk*, 8(9), p. 112, 1995.

[79] R. Engle and J. Mezrich, GARCH for Groups, *Risk*, 9(8), p. 36, 1996.

[80] R. F. Engle and J. Rosenberg, GARCH Gamma, *Journal of Derivatives*, 2, p. 47, 1995.

[81] S. Fischer, Call Option Pricing When the Exercise Price is Uncertain and the Valuation of Index Bonds, *Journal of Finance*, 33, p. 169, 1978.

[82] D. Ford, *Mastering Exchange Traded Equity Derivatives: A Step-By-Step Guide to the Markets, Applications and Risks*, Pitman, New York, 1996.

[83] J. C. Francis, W. Toy, and G. Whittaker, *The Handbook of Equity Derivatives*, Irwin, New York, 1994.

[84] E. Fruchard, C. Zammouri, and E. Willems, Basis for Change, *Risk*, 8(10), p. 70, 1995.

[85] Q. Fu, On the Valuation of An Option to Exchange One Interest Rate for Another, *Journal of Banking and Finance*, 20, p. 645, 1996.

[86] M. Garman, Spread the Load, *Risk*, 5, p. 68, 1992.

[87] M. B. Garman, Recollection in Tranquility, *Risk*, 2, p. 16, 1989.

[88] M. B. Garman, Perpetual Currency Options, *International Journal of Forecasting*, 3(1), p. 179, 1987.

[89] G. G. Gay and S. Manaster, The Quality Option Implicit in Futures Contracts, *Journal of Financial Economics*, 13, p. 353, 1984.

[90] H. Geman and A. Eydland, Domino Effect, *Risk*, 8, p. 65, 1995.

[91] H. Geman and M. Yor, Bessel Processes, Asian Options and Perpetuities, *Mathematical Finance*, 3, p. 349, 1993.

[92] H. Geman, N. El Karoui, and J. C. Rochet, Changes of Numeraire, Changes of Probability Measure and Option Pricing, *Journal of Applied Probability*, 32, p. 443, 1995.

[93] D. Gentle, Basket Weaving, *Risk*, 6, p. 51, June 1993.

[94] H. U. Gerber and E. S. W. Shiu, Martingale Approach to Pricing Perpetual American Options on Two Stocks, *Mathematical Finance*, 6, p. 303, 1996.

[95] R. Geske, The Valuation of Compound Options, *Journal of Financial Economics*, 7, p. 63, 1979.

[96] M. B. Goldman, H. B. Sosin, and M. A. Gatto, Path Dependent Options: Buy at the Low, Sell at the High, *Journal of Finance*, 34, p. 1111, 1979.

[97] M. B. Goldman, H. B. Sosin, and L. A. Shepp, On Contingent Claims that Insure Ex-Post Optimal Stock Market Timing, *Journal of Finance*, 34, p. 401, 1979.

[98] J. O. Grabbe, The Pricing of Call and Put Options on Foreign Exchange, *Journal of International Money and Finance*, 2, p. 239, 1983.

[99] J. D. Hamilton, Time Series Analysis, Princeton University Press, 1994.

[100] I. Hart and M. Ross, Striking Continuity, *Risk*, 7, p. 46, 1991.

[101] J. M. Haykov, A Better Control Variate for Pricing Standard Asian Options, *Journal of Financial Engineering*, 2, p. 207, 1993.

[102] D. Heath, R. Jarrow, and A. Morton, Contingent Claim Valuation with a Random Evolution of Interest Rates, *The Review of Financial Markets*, 1990.

[103] B. A. Heenk, A. G. Z. Kemna, and A. C. F. Vorst, Asian Options on Oil Spreads, *Review of Futures Markets*, 9(3), p. 511, 1990.

[104] R. Heynen and H. Kat, Crossing Barriers, *Risk Magazine*, 7(6), p. 46, 1994.

[105] R. C. Heynen and H. M. Kat, Partial Barrier Options, *Journal of Financial Engineering*, 3, p. 253, 1994.

[106] R. Heynen and H. Kat, Selective Memory, *Risk*, 7, p. 73, Nov. 1994.

[107] R. Heynen and H. Kat, Brick by Brick, *Risk*, 9, p. 58, June 1996.

[108] J. E. Hilliard, J. B. Kau, D. C. Keenan, and W. J. Muller III, Pricing a Class of American and European Path Dependent Securities, *Management Science*, 41, p. 1892, Dec. 1995.

[109] S. D. Hodges and S. A. Neuberger, Optimal Replication of Contingent Claims Under Transaction Costs, *Review of Futures Markets*, 8, p. 222, 1989.

[110] H. S. Houthaker, Can Speculators Forecast Prices?, *Review of Economics and Statistics*, 39, pp. 143–151, 1957.

[111] J. Huang, M. G. Subrahmanyam, and G. G. Yu, Pricing and Hedging American Options: A Recursive Integration Method, *Review of Financial Studies*, 9(1), p. 277, Spring 1996.

[112] M. Hudson, The Value in Going Out, *Risk*, 4, p. 29, 1991.

[113] J. C. Hull, *Options, Futures and Other Derivative Securities*, Prentice-Hall, New York, 1996.

[114] J. C. Hull and A. White, Efficient Procedures for Valuing European and American Path Dependent Options, *Journal of Derivatives*, 1, p. 21, 1995.

[115] J. C. Hull and A. White, The Impact of Default Risk on Options and Other Derivative Securities, *Journal of Banking and Finance*, 19, p. 299, 1995.

[116] J. P. Hutton, Fast Pricing of Derivative Securities, Ph.D. Thesis, Department of Mathematics, University of Essex, 1995.

[117] C. B. Huynh, Back to Baskets, *Risk*, 7, p. 59, May 1994.

[118] F. Jamshidian, Price Differentials, *Risk*, 6(7), p. 48, 1993.

[119] F. Jamshidian, Corralling Quantos, *Risk*, 7, p. 46, June 1994.

[120] F. Jamshidian, Hedging Quantos, Differential Swaps and Ratios, *Applied Mathematical Finance*, 1, p. 1, Sept. 1994.

[121] R. Jarrow, *Modelling Fixed Income Securities and Interest Rate Options*, McGraw-Hill Finance Guide Series, McGraw-Hill, New York, 1995.

[122] R. Jarrow, The Pricing of Commodity Options with Stochastic Interest Rates, *Advances in Futures and Options Research*, 2, p. 19, 1995.

[123] R. A. Jarrow and S. M. Turnbull, Pricing Derivatives on Financial Securities Subject to Credit Risk, *Journal of Finance*, 50, p. 53, 1995.

[124] N. Johnson, S. Kotz, and N. Balakrishnan, *Continuous Univariate Distributions*, Wiley, New York, 1995.

[125] H. Johnson, Options on the Maximum or Minimum of Several Assets, *Journal of Financial and Quantitative Analysis*, 22, p. 277, 1987.

[126] H. Johnson and R. Stulz, The Pricing of Options with Default Risk, *Journal of Finance*, 42, p. 267, 1987.

[127] M. H. Kalos and P. A. Whitlock, *Monte-Carlo Methods*, Vol. 1, Wiley, New York, 1986.

[128] I. Karatsas and S. E. Shreve, *Brownian Motion and Stochastic Calculus*, Springer Verlag, New York, 1991.

[129] H. Kat and L. Verdonk, Tree Surgery, *Risk*, 8, p. 53, 1995.

[130] H. M. Kat, Contingent Premium Options, *Journal of Derivatives*, 1, p. 44, Summer 1994.

[131] H. H. Kat, Pricing Lookback Options Using Binomial Trees: An Evaluation, *Journal of Financial Engineering*, 4, p. 375, 1995.

[132] M. Kelly, Stock Answer, *Risk*, 7(8), p. 40, 1994.

[133] A. G. Z. Kemna and A. C. F. Vorst, A Pricing Method for Options Based on Average Asset Values, *Journal of Banking and Finance*, 14, p. 113, 1990.

[134] N. Kishimoto, Pricing Contingent Claims Under Interest Rate and Asset Price Risk, *Journal of Finance*, 44, p. 571, July 1989.

[135] K. Kocherlakota and S. Kocherlakota, On the Distribution of *r* in Samples from the Mixture of Bivariate Normal Populations, *Communications in Statistics—Theory and Methods*, 10, pp. 1943–1966, 1981.

[136] D. O. Kramkov and E. Mordecky, Integral Option, *Theory of Probability and its Applications*, 39, p. 162, 1995.

[137] N. Kunitomo and M. Ikeda, Pricing Options with Curved Boundaries, *Mathematical Finance*, 2, p. 275, 1992.

[138] E. Levy, Asian Arithmetic, *Risk*, 3, p. 7, 1990.

[139] E. Levy and S. Turnbull, Average Intelligence, *Risk*, 5, p. 53, 1992.

[140] B. Li and G. Zhang, *Functional Optimization Problem for Pricing Portfolio Options*, Working paper, Merrill Lynch Quantitative Analysis, 1995.

[141] R. Litterman, Hot Spots and Hedges, *The Journal of Portfolio Management*, Special Issue, Fall 1996. Also *Risk*, Vol. 10, No. 3, p. 42, 1997.

[142] G. Ljung and G. Box, On a Measure of Lack of Fit in Time Series Models, *Biometrika*, 66, p. 67, 1978.

[143] F. A. Longstaff, Hedging Interest Rate Risk with Options on Average Interest Rates, *Journal of Fixed Income*, 5, p. 37, 1995.

[144] F. A. Longstaff, Pricing Options with Extendible Maturities: Analysis and Applications, *Journal of Finance*, 45, p. 935, 1990.

[145] R. E. Maeder, *Programming in Mathematica*, Addison-Wesley, New York, 1991.

[146] A. J. Marcus and D. M. Modest, The Valuation of a Random Number of Put Options: An Application to Agricultural Price Supports, *Journal of Financial and Quantitative Analysis*, 21, p. 73, March 1986.

[147] W. Margrabe, GARCH Forecasting in Practice, *Global Derivatives Conference Proceedings*, Paris, 1996.

[148] W. Margrabe, Triangular Equilibrium and Arbitrage in the Market for Options to Exchange Two Options, *Journal of Derivatives*, 1, p. 60, 1993.

[149] W. Margrabe, The Value of an Option to Exchange One Asset for Another, *Journal of Finance*, 33, p. 177, 1978.

[150] G. Marsaglia and A. Zaman, A New Class of Random Number Generators, *Annals of Applied Probability*, 1(3), p. 462, 1991.

[151] G. Marsaglia and T. A. Bray, A Convenient Method for Generating Normal Variables, *SIAM Review*, 6, p. 260, 1964.

[152] J. J. McConnnell and E. S. Schwartz, LYON Taming, *Journal of Finance*, 41, p. 561, 1986.

[153] R. C. Merton, Theory of Rational Option Pricing, *Bell Journal of Economics and Management Science*, 27, p. 141, 1973.

[154] R. C. Merton, Optimum Consumption and Portfolio Rules in a Continuous Time Model, *Journal of Economic Theory*, 3, pp. 373–413, 1971.

[155] R. Miura, A Note on Lookback Options Based on Order Statistics, *Hitosubashi Journal of Commerce Management*, 29, p. 15, 1992.

[156] I. Nelken (Editor), *The Handbook of Exotic Options, Instruments, Analysis and Applications*, Irwin, New York, 1995.

[157] I. Nelken, Square Deals, *Risk*, 6, p. 56, 1993.

[158] B. Oksendal, *Stochastic Differential Equations*, 4th Edition, Springer, Berlin/ Heidelberg, 1995.

[159] J. Okunev and M. Tippett, A Multifactor Option Pricing Model, *Advances in Futures and Options Research*, 6, p. 67, 1993.

[160] A. Papoulis, *Probability, Random Variables and Stochastic Processes*, McGraw-Hill, New York, 1991, pp. 571–574.

[161] S. Paskov, Applying Low Discrepancy Sequences for the Pricing and Risk Management of Complex Financial Instruments as an Alternative to Using Monte-Carlo Methods, *Global Derivatives Conference Proceedings*, Paris, 1996.

[162] N. D. Pearson, An Efficient Approach to Pricing Spread Options, *Journal of Derivatives*, 3, p. 76, 1995.

[163] A. Pechtl, Classified Information, *Risk*, 8, p. 59, June 1995.

[164] W. H. Press, S. A. Teukolsky, W. T. Vetterling, and B. P. Flannery, *Numerical Recipes in C—The Art of Scientific Computing*, Cambridge University Press, New York, 1992.

[165] R. Price, A Useful Theorem for Nonlinear Devices Having Gaussian Inputs, *IRE, PGIT*, Vol. IT-4, 1958.

[166] K. Ravindran, Option Pricing: An Offspring of the Secretary Problem?, *Mathematica Japonica*, 38, p. 905, 1993.

[167] K. Ravindran, Low-Fat Spreads, *Risk*, 6, p. 66, 1993.

[168] E. Reiner, Quanto Mechanics, *Risk*, 5, p. 59, March 1992.

[169] D. R. Rich, The Mathematical Foundations of Barrier Options, *Advances in Futures and Options Research*, 7, p. 267, 1994.

[170] D. R. Rich and D. M. Chance, An Alternative Approach to the Pricing of Options on Multiple Assets, *Journal of Financial Engineering*, 2, p. 271, Sept. 1993.

[171] P. Ritchken and L. Sanakarasubramanian, Averaging and Deferred Payment Yield Agreements, *Journal of Futures Markets*, 13, p. 23, 1991.

[172] P. Ritchken, L. Sanakarasubramanian, and A. M. Vijh, The Valuation of Path Dependent Options on the Average, *Management Science*, 39, p. 1202, 1993.

[173] P. Ritchken, On Pricing Barrier Options, *Journal of Derivatives*, 3, p. 19, Winter 1995.

[174] P. Ritchken and L. Sankarasubramanian, A Multifactor Model of the Quality Option in Treasury Futures Contracts, *Journal of Financial Research*, 18, p. 261, Fall 1995.

[175] P. Ritchken and L. Sankarasubramanian, Near Nirvana, *Risk*, 8, p. 109, Sept. 1995.

[176] L. C. G. Rogers and Z. Shi, The Value of an Asian Option, *Journal of Applied Probability*, 32, p. 1077, 1995.

[177] S. Ross, Options and Efficiency, *Quarterly Journal of Economics*, 90, pp. 75–89, 1976.

[178] M. Rubinstein, Return to Oz, *Risk*, 7(11), p. 67, 1994.

[179] M. Rubinstein and E. Reiner, *Exotic Options*, University of California, Berkeley, Working Papers, 1991–1994.

[180] M. Rubinstein and E. Reiner, Unscrambling the Binary Code, *Risk*, 4, p. 575, 1991.

[181] M. Rubinstein, Options for the Undecided, *Risk*, 4, p. 43, 1991.

[182] M. Rubinstein, Double Trouble, *Risk*, 5, p. 73, 1991.

[183] M. Rubinstein, One for Another, *Risk*, 4, p. 30, 1991.

[184] M. Rubinstein, Pay Now, Choose Later, *Risk*, 4, p. 13, Feb. 1991.

[185] M. Rubinstein, Somewhere Over the Rainbow, *Risk*, 4, p. 63, Nov. 1991.

[186] M. Rubinstein, Two Into One, *Risk*, 4, p. 49, May 1991.

[187] M. Rubinstein and E. Reiner, Breaking Down the Barriers, *Risk*, 4, p. 28, 1991.

[188] M. E. Rubinstein, Implied Binomial Trees, *Journal of Finance*, 69, p. 771, 1994.

[189] J. Rumsey, Pricing Cross-Currency Options, *Journal of Futures Markets*, 11, p. 89, Feb. 1991.

[190] A. Ruttiens, Classical Replica, *Risk*, 3, p. 33, 1990.

[191] J. A. Schnabel and J. Z. Wei, Valuing Takeover-Contingent Foreign Exchange Call Options, *Advances in Futures and Options Research*, 7, p. 223, 1994.

[192] M. Schroder, A Reduction Method Applicable to Compound Option Formulas, *Management Science*, p. 823, July 1989.

[193] M. Selby and S. D. Hodges, On the Evaluation of Compound Options, *Management Science*, p. 347, March 1987.

[194] T. K. Seng and K. R. Vetzal, Early Exercise Regions for Exotic Options, *Journal of Derivatives*, 3, p. 42, 1995.

[195] S. Sharma, *Applied Multivariate Techniques*, Wiley, New York, 1996.

[196] D. C. Shimko, A Tail of Two Distributions, *Risk*, 7, p. 12, 1994.

[197] D. C. Shimko, Options on Futures Spreads: Hedging, Speculation and Valuation, *Journal of Futures Markets*, 14, p. 183, 1994.

[198] J. Sikorav, Installment Plan, *Risk*, 6, p. 36, 1993.

[199] C. W. Smithson and C. W. Smith, *Managing Financial Risk: A Guide to Derivative Products, Financial Engineering and Value Maximization*, Irwin, New York, 1995.

[200] R. C. Stapleton and M. G. Subrahmanyam, The Valuation of Multivariate Contingent Claims in Discrete Time Models, *Journal of Finance*, 39, p. 207, March 1984.

[201] R. Stulz, Options on the Minimum or Maximum of Two Risky Assets, *Journal of Financial Economics*, 10, p. 161, July 1982.

[202] G. Sullivan, Correlation Counts, *Risk*, 8(8), p. 36, 1995.

[203] N. Taleb, *Dynamic Hedging*, Wiley, New York, 1997.

[204] A. C. Thompson, Valuation of Path-Dependent Contingent Claims with Multiple Exercise Decisions Over Time: The Case of Take or Pay, *Journal of Financial and Quantitative Analysis*, 38, p. 271, 1995.

[205] J. A. Tilley, Valuing American Options in a Path Simulation Model, *Transactions of the Society of Actuaries*, 45, p. 83, 1993.

[206] R. R. Trippi and D. M. Chance, Quick Valuation of the 'Bermuda' Capped Option, *Journal of Portfolio Management*, 20, p. 93, 1993.

[207] S. Turnbull and L. M. Wakeman, A Quick Algorithm for Pricing European Average Options, *Journal of Financial and Quantitative Analysis*, 26, p. 377, 1991.

[208] S. M. Turnbull, Interest Rate Digital Options and Range Notes, *Journal of Derivatives*, 3, p. 92, 1995.

[209] S. Turnbull, The Price is Right, *Risk*, 5, p. 56, 1992.

[210] T. Vorst, *Analytic Boundaries and Approximations of the Price and Hedge Ratios of Average Rate Options*, Econometric Institute, Erasmus University, Rotterdam, 1990.

[211] T. Vorst, Prices and Hedge Ratios of Average Exchange Rate Options, *International Review of Financial Analysis*, 1(3), p. 179, 1992.

[212] J. Wei, Pricing of Nikkei Put Warrants, *Journal of Multinational Financial Management*, 2, p. 45, Nov. 1992.

[213] J. Wei, Pricing Options on Foreign Assets when Interest Rates are Stochastic, *Advances in International Banking and Finance*, 1, p. 65, 1995.

[214] A. E. Whalley and P. Wilmott, *Optimal Hedging of Options with Small but Arbitrary Transaction Cost Structure*, Mathematical Institute Working Paper, Oxford, U.K., 1993.

[215] P. Wilmott, J. Dewynne, and S. Howison, *Option Pricing*, Oxford Financial Press, Oxford, 1993.

[216] P. Wilmott, S. Howison, and J. Dewynne, *The Mathematics of Financial Derivatives: A Student Introduction*, Cambridge University Press, Cambridge, U.K., 1995.

[217] S. Wolfram, Random Sequence Generation by Cellular Automata, *Advances in Applied Mathematics*, 7, pp. 123–169, 1986.

[218] S. Wolfram, *The Mathematica Book*, Cambridge University Press, New York, 1992.

[219] M. Yor, From Planar Brownian Wingdings to Asian Options, *Insurance: Mathematics and Economics*, 13, p. 23, 1993.

[220] P. G. Zhang, Flexible Arithmetic Asian Options, *Journal of Derivatives*, 2, p. 53, 1995.

[221] P. G. Zhang, A Unified Formula for Outside Barrier Options, *Journal of Financial Engineering*, 4, p. 335, 1995.

[222] P. G. Zhang, Correlation Digital Options, *Journal of Financial Engineering*, p. 75, 1995.

[223] W. Cheung and I. Nelken, Costing the Converts, *Risk*, 7, p. 47, July 1994.

[224] J. Wei, Streams of Consequence, *Risk*, 7(1), p. 42, 1994.

[225] E. Whalley and P. Wilmott, Counting the Costs, *Risk*, 6(10), p. 59, 1993.

[226] K. Leong, Estimates, Guesstimates and Rules of Thumb, *Risk*, 4(2), p. 15, 1991.

[227] M. Garman, Charm School, *Risk*, 5(7), p. 53, 1992.

[228] K. Dehnad, Harmony in Hedging, *AsiaRisk*, p. 3, Nov. 1996.

[229] A. Papageorgiou and J. Traub, Beating Monte Carlo, *Risk*, 9(6), p. 63, 1996.

[230] C. Smithson, Hybrid Securities, *Risk*, 9(4), p. 48, 1996.

[231] O. Grabbe, Copper-Bottom Pricing, *Risk*, 8(5), p. 63, 1995.

[232] E. Jacquier and R. Jarrow, Vital Statistics, *Risk*, 8(4), p. 62, 1995.

[233] S. Das, Differential Strip-Down, *Risk*, 5(6), p. 65, 1992.

[234] D. C. Shimko, Bounds of Probability, *Risk*, 6(4), p. 33, 1993.

[235] B. Dupire, Model Art, *Risk*, 6(9), p. 118, 1993.

[236] T. Wilson, Debunking the Myths, *Risk*, 7(4), p. 67, 1994.

[237] E. Whalley and P. Wilmott, Hedge with an Edge, *Risk*, 7(10), p. 82, 1994.

[238] C. O. Alexander, History Debunked, *Risk*, 7(12), p. 59, 1994.

[239] C. Lawrence and G. Robinson, How Safe is Risk-Metrics?, *Risk*, 8(1), p. 26, 1995.

[240] J. Longerstaey and P. Zangari, A Transparent Tool, *Risk*, 8(1), p. 30, 1995.

Techniques for Normal Integrals

COMMON INTEGRALS

The basic integral for deriving closed-form solutions or expansions is

$$\int_{\infty}^{\infty} e^{-ax^2}\, dx = \sqrt{\frac{\pi}{a}} \tag{A.1}$$

which, by successive differentiations with respect to an auxiliary variable, gives

$$\int_{-\infty}^{\infty} x^n e^{-ax^2}\, dx = \tfrac{1}{2}(1 + (-1)^n)\, a^{-\frac{1}{2}(n+1)}\Gamma\left(\frac{n+1}{2}\right) \tag{A.2}$$

and

$$\int_{-\infty}^{\infty} e^{bx} e^{-ax^2}\, dx = e^{\frac{b^2}{4a}}\sqrt{\frac{\pi}{a}} \tag{A.3}$$

We will use the definitions

$$\Gamma(z) = \int_0^\infty t^{z-1} e^{-t} \, dt \qquad (A.4)$$

$$\Gamma(a, z) = \int_z^\infty t^{a-1} e^{-t} \, dt \qquad (A.5)$$

$$\Gamma(a, z_0, z_1) = \int_{z_0}^{z_1} t^{a-1} e^{-t} \, dt \qquad (A.6)$$

For positive integers n, $\Gamma(n) = (n-1)!$ So the Γ function is the "analytic continuation" of the factorial function for complex numbers.

In terms of the generalized incomplete gamma function $\Gamma(a, z_0, z_1) = \Gamma(a, z_0) - \Gamma(a, z_1)$,

$$\int_a^b x e^{-\frac{1}{2}x^2} \, dx = e^{-a^2/2} - e^{-b^2/2} \qquad (A.7)$$

$$\int_a^b x^n e^{-x^2} \, dx = \frac{1}{2} \left[\Gamma\left(\frac{1+n}{2}, a^2\right) - \Gamma\left(\frac{1+n}{2}, b^2\right) \right] \qquad (A.8)$$

With the following definition for the error function Erf(x),

$$\text{Erf}(x) \equiv \frac{2}{\sqrt{\pi}} \int_0^x e^{-t^2} \, dt \qquad (A.9)$$

we have the useful integral

$$\int_\alpha^\beta e^{ax - bx^2} \, dx = \frac{1}{2} \sqrt{\frac{\pi}{b}} e^{\frac{a^2}{4b}} \left[\text{Erf}\left(\frac{1}{2}\sqrt{\frac{(a-2b\beta)^2}{b}}\right) - \text{Erf}\left(\frac{1}{2}\sqrt{\frac{(a-2b\alpha)^2}{b}}\right) \right] \qquad (A.10)$$

Option pricing formulas are written in terms of the cumulative normal density, which is related to the error function as follows:

$$N(a) = \frac{1}{2}\left[1 + \text{Erf}\left(\frac{a}{\sqrt{2}}\right)\right] \qquad (A.11)$$

It is instructive to show the use of some equivalences. Note,

$$\text{Erf}(-a) = \text{Erf}(a) \qquad (A.12)$$

so

$$\frac{1}{\sqrt{2\pi}} \int_a^\infty e^{-\frac{1}{2}x^2}\, dx = \frac{1}{2}\left(1 - \text{Erf}\left(\frac{a}{\sqrt{2}}\right)\right)$$

$$= \frac{1}{2}\left(1 + \text{Erf}\left(\frac{-a}{\sqrt{2}}\right)\right)$$

$$= N(-a)$$

$$= 1 - N(a) \tag{A.13}$$

In terms of the full normal density, we can write down the useful results

$$\frac{1}{\sqrt{2\pi}\sigma} \int_{-\infty}^\infty x e^{-bx} e^{-\frac{1}{2}\frac{(x-\mu)^2}{\sigma^2}}\, dx = (\mu - b\sigma^2) e^{-b\mu + \frac{1}{2}b^2\sigma^2} \tag{A.14}$$

$$\frac{1}{\sqrt{2\pi}\sigma} \int_{-\infty}^\infty e^{-bx} e^{-\frac{1}{2}\frac{(x-\mu)^2}{\sigma^2}}\, dx = e^{-b\mu + \frac{1}{2}b^2\sigma^2} \tag{A.15}$$

Note the following property of the cumulative normal distribution:

$$N[t, \mu, \sigma] = N\left[\frac{t-b}{a}, \frac{1}{a}(\mu - b), \frac{\sigma}{a}\right] \tag{A.16}$$

which can be obtained by making the linear transformation $x \to ax + b$. Thus, after a linear transformation of the normal variate, the cumulative distribution function of a normal distribution with mean equal to $(\mu - b)/a$ and standard deviation σ/a equals the original cdf at the new point $(t - b)/a$.

CHOLESKY DECOMPOSITION

To perform integrals of the type

$$\int_{-\infty}^\infty \int_{-\infty}^\infty \cdots \int_{-\infty}^\infty e^{-\mathbf{x}^T \mathbf{C} \mathbf{x}}\, d\mathbf{x} \tag{A.17}$$

we can use the Cholesky decomposition of the matrix $\mathbf{C}$. For a symmetric positive definite matrix $\mathbf{C}$, the Cholesky decomposition algorithm returns an upper triangular matrix $\mathbf{U}$ such that $\mathbf{C} = \mathbf{U}^T\mathbf{U}$. Hence, with $\mathbf{y} = \mathbf{U}\mathbf{x}$

$$\mathbf{x}^T\mathbf{C}\mathbf{x} = \mathbf{x}^T\mathbf{U}^T\mathbf{U}\mathbf{x} = (\mathbf{U}\mathbf{x})^T(\mathbf{U}\mathbf{x}) = \mathbf{y}^T\mathbf{y} \tag{A.18}$$

which leads to the Jacobian $|\mathbf{U}|^{-1}$ and the integral

$$\int_{-\infty}^{\infty} \int_{-\infty}^{\infty} \cdots \int_{-\infty}^{\infty} e^{-\mathbf{x}^T \mathbf{C} \mathbf{x}} d\mathbf{x} = \frac{1}{|\mathbf{U}|} \int_{-\infty}^{\infty} \int_{-\infty}^{\infty} \cdots \int_{-\infty}^{\infty} e^{-\mathbf{y}^T \mathbf{y}} d\mathbf{y} = \frac{1}{|\mathbf{U}|} \pi^{n/2}$$

(A.19)

For instance, a common integral that appears in financial applications is the integral of the bivariate normal density

$$e^{-\frac{1}{2(1-\rho^2)}(x_1^2 + x_2^2 - 2\rho x_1 x_2)}$$

(A.20)

This is a special case of the general multivariate normal density

$$\frac{1}{(2\pi)^{n/2} \operatorname{Det} \mathbf{C}} \int_{-\infty}^{\infty} \int_{-\infty}^{\infty} \cdots \int_{-\infty}^{\infty} e^{-\mathbf{x}^T \mathbf{C}^{-1} \mathbf{x}} d\mathbf{x}$$

(A.21)

where $\mathbf{C}$ is the covariance matrix

$$\mathbf{C} = \begin{bmatrix} 1 & \rho \\ \rho & 1 \end{bmatrix}$$

(A.22)

In the two-dimensional case, $\mathbf{C}^{-1} = \mathbf{U}^T \mathbf{U}$ where

$$\mathbf{U} = \begin{bmatrix} \dfrac{1}{\sqrt{1-\rho^2}} & \dfrac{-\rho}{\sqrt{1-\rho^2}} \\ 0 & 1 \end{bmatrix}$$

(A.23)

with

$$\frac{1}{|\mathbf{U}|} = \sqrt{1-\rho^2}$$

(A.24)

and

$$\mathbf{y} = \begin{bmatrix} \dfrac{x_1 - \rho x_2}{\sqrt{1-\rho^2}} \\ x_2 \end{bmatrix}$$

(A.25)

so that Equation (A.20) can be replaced by

$$\sqrt{1-\rho^2} \, e^{y_1^2 + y_2^2}$$

(A.26)

An alternative way to perform this integral, if the eigenvalues and eigenvectors are known, is to write

$$\mathbf{x}^T \mathbf{C} \mathbf{x} = \mathbf{x}^T (\mathbf{P}^T \mathbf{D} \mathbf{P}) \mathbf{x} = (\mathbf{P} \mathbf{x})^T \mathbf{D} (\mathbf{P} \mathbf{x}) = \mathbf{y}^T \mathbf{D} \mathbf{y}$$

(A.27)

where, as before, $\mathbf{y} = \mathbf{Px}$ and $\mathbf{D}$ is the matrix with eigenvalues of $\mathbf{C}$ along the diagonal and zeros elsewhere. Then, using the normalized eigenvectors of $\mathbf{C}$, the integral is just a product of one-dimensional integrals.

These techniques can be used to obtain the set of vectors that generates a three-factor path for Monte-Carlo simulation, if the vector (x, y, z) is transformed to the vector (u, v, w):

$$x = \frac{(\rho_{12} - \rho_{13}\rho_{23})}{\sqrt{1 - \rho_{23}}} v$$

$$+ u\sqrt{\frac{(1 + 2\rho_{12}\rho_{13}\rho_{23} - \rho_{12}^2 - \rho_{13}^2 - \rho_{23}^2)}{1 - \rho_{23}^2}} u + \rho_{13} w$$

$$y = v\sqrt{1 - \rho_{23}^2} + \rho_{23} w$$

$$z = w \tag{A.28}$$

Random Vectors in *n* Dimensions

DENSITY AND DISTRIBUTION

A random vector is a vector

$$X = [x_1, \ldots, x_n] \qquad \text{(B.1)}$$

whose components x_i are each random variables.

$$f(X) = f(x_1, \ldots, x_n) = \frac{\partial^n F(x_1, \ldots, x_n)}{\partial x_1 \ldots \partial x_n} \qquad \text{(B.2)}$$

is the joint multivariate density of x_i and

$$F(X) = F(x_1, \ldots, x_n) = P(x \leq x_1, \ldots, x_n \leq x_n) \qquad \text{(B.3)}$$

is the joint distribution function. If any of the x_i values in $F(x_1, \ldots, x_n)$ are substituted by infinity, we get the joint distribution of the remaining random variables. Integrating the joint density $f(x_1, \ldots, x_n)$ with respect to any x_i over its support gives the joint density of the remaining variables.

TRANSFORMATIONS

Given k functions

$$g_1(X), \ldots, g_k(X) \qquad \text{(B.4)}$$

of the random vector X, we form the random variables

$$y_1 = g_1(X), \ldots, y_k = g_k(X) \tag{B.5}$$

To find the density $f_y(y_1, \ldots, y_n)$, solve the system

$$g_1(X) = y_1, \ldots, g_n(X) = y_n \tag{B.6}$$

If this system has no solutions, then $f_y(y_1, \ldots, y_n) = 0$. If there is one solution, then

$$f_y(y_1, \ldots, y_n) = \frac{f_x(x_1, \ldots, x_n)}{|J(x_1, \ldots, x_n)|} \tag{B.7}$$

where $J(x_1, \ldots, x_n)$ is the Jacobian of the transformation. If there is more than one solution, then replace the right-hand side of the last equation by a sum over all the roots.

INDEPENDENCE

If the events $x \leq x_1, \ldots, x_n \leq x_n$ are independent, then $x_1, \ldots, x_n$ are independent. Then,

$$F(x_1, \ldots, x_n) = F(x_1) \ldots F(x_n)$$
$$f(x_1, \ldots, x_n) = f(x_1) \ldots f(x_n) \tag{B.8}$$

For example, in valuing path-dependent options, such as resettable options or average rate options, we have n terminal random returns

$$y_k = x_1 + \cdots + x_k, \qquad k = 1, \ldots, n \tag{B.9}$$

where the returns for each period are independent of the previous ones. What is the joint density of the cumulative terminal returns for each period, i.e., of the y_k? The system

$$y_1 = x_1$$
$$y_2 = x_1 + x_2$$
$$y_n = x_1 + \cdots + x_n \tag{B.10}$$

has a unique solution:

$$x_k = y_k - y_{k-1} \qquad \text{for } 1 \leq k \leq n \tag{B.11}$$

with the Jacobian equal to unity. So, the joint density of the cumulative returns is

$$f_y(y_1, \ldots, y_n) = f_1(y_1) f_2(y_2 - y_1) \ldots f_n(y_n - y_{n-1}) \tag{B.12}$$

which is very useful in the evaluation of path-dependent option prices.

MEAN AND COVARIANCE

The mean of a function $g(x_1, \ldots, x_n)$ equals

$$\int_{-\infty}^{\infty} \cdots \int_{-\infty}^{\infty} g(x_1, \ldots, x_n) f(x_1, \ldots, x_n) \, dx_1 \ldots dx_n \qquad \text{(B.13)}$$

so that

$$E[a_1 g_1(X) + \cdots + a_m g_m(X)] = a_1 E[g_1(X)] + \cdots + a_m E[g_m(X)] \qquad \text{(B.14)}$$

The covariance C_{ij} of two random variables, x_i and x_j, is

$$C_{ij} = E[(x_i - \eta_i)(x_j - \eta_j)] = E[x_i x_j] - E[x_i]E[x_j] \qquad \text{(B.15)}$$

where η_i is the mean of the ith variable. The variance of x_i is

$$\sigma_i^2 = C_{ii} = E[|x_i - \eta_i|^2] = E[|x_i|^2] - |E[x_i]|^2 \qquad \text{(B.16)}$$

where x_i are called mutually uncorrelated if $c_{ij} = 0$ for all $i \neq j$. Then the variance of a sum of uncorrelated random variables is the sum of their variances. If the random variables $x_1, \ldots, x_n$ are independent, they are also uncorrelated.

If x_i are independent, then

$$E[g_1(x_1) \ldots g_n(x_n)] = E[g_1(x_1)] \ldots E[g_n(x_n)] \qquad \text{(B.17)}$$

The correlation matrix is

$$R_{ij} = E[x_i x_j] = R_{ji} = C_{ij} + \eta_i \eta_j \qquad \text{(B.18)}$$

and is non-negative definite. As mentioned in Chapter 4 on correlation, if we obtain from traded options an implied correlation matrix that is not non-negative definite, a correlation-based arbitrage opportunity presents itself.

For baskets, note that the following result is important. If the random variables x_i are linearly independent, i.e.,

$$E[|a_1 x_1 + \cdots + a_n x_n|^2] > 0 \qquad \text{(B.19)}$$

for arbitrary weights a_i, then their correlation matrix is strictly positive definite, with a positive determinant, as well as positive determinant of all minors.

CONDITIONAL DENSITIES

The conditional density of the random variables $x_n, \ldots, x_{k+1}$, assuming $x_k, \ldots, x_1$ is given by

$$f(x_n, \ldots, x_{k+1} | x_k, \ldots, x_1) = \frac{f(x_1, \ldots, x_k, \ldots, x_n)}{f(x_1, \ldots, x_k)} \qquad \text{(B.20)}$$

with the corresponding distribution function

$$F(x_1, \ldots, x_{k+1} | x_k, \ldots, x_1)$$
$$= \int_{-\infty}^{x_n} \cdots \int_{-\infty}^{x_k+1} f(\alpha_n, \ldots, \alpha_{k+1} | x_k, \ldots, x_1) d\alpha_{k+1} \ldots d\alpha_n \qquad \text{(B.21)}$$

for example

$$f(x_1 | x_2, x_3) = \frac{f(x_1, x_2, x_3)}{f(x_2, x_3)} = \frac{dF(x_1 | x_2, x_3)}{dx_1} \qquad \text{(B.22)}$$

The chain rule is

$$f(x_1, \ldots, x_n) = f(x_n | x_{n-1}, \ldots, x_1) \ldots f(x_2 | x_1) f(x_1) \qquad \text{(B.23)}$$

with the useful special case (Chapman-Kolmogoroff)

$$f(x_1 | x_3) = \int_{-\infty}^{\infty} f(x_1 | x_2, x_3) f(x_2 | x_3) \, dx_2 \qquad \text{(B.24)}$$

CONDITIONAL EXPECTED VALUES

$$E[x_1 | x_2, \ldots, x_n] = \int_{-\infty}^{\infty} x_1 f(x_1 | x_2, \ldots, x_n) \, dx_1 \qquad \text{(B.25)}$$

so that

$$E[E[x_1 | x_2, \ldots, x_n]] = E[x_1] \qquad \text{(B.26)}$$

with the special case

$$E[x_1 | x_2, x_3] = E[E[x_1 | x_2, x_3, x_4]] = \int_{-\infty}^{\infty} E[x_1 | x_2, x_3, x_4] f(x_4 | x_2, x_3) \, dx_4$$
$$\text{(B.27)}$$

so that, as a general rule: To remove any number of variables on the right of the conditional expected value line, multiply by their conditional density with respect to the remaining variables on the right and integrate the product. As an example,

$$E[x_1|x_3] = \int_{-\infty}^{\infty} E[x_1|x_2, x_3] f(x_2|x_3)\, dx_2 \qquad (B.28)$$

CHARACTERISTIC FUNCTIONS AND NORMALITY

The characteristic functions, which are essentially the n dimensional Fourier transforms of the density function, provide a good summarization of everything about the probability distribution. For $X = [x_1, \dots, x_n]$ and $\Omega = [\omega_1, \dots, \omega_n]$:

$$\Phi(\Omega) = E[e^{j\Omega X^T}] = E[e^{j(\omega_1 x_1 + \dots + \omega_n x_n)}] \qquad (B.29)$$

The random variables x_i are jointly normal if, and only if, the sum

$$AX^T = a_1 x_1 + \cdots + a_n x_n \qquad (B.30)$$

is normal for any A. Then, it can be proved that with the covariance matrix C, the joint characteristic function is

$$\Phi(\Omega) = e^{-\frac{1}{2}\Omega C \Omega^T} \qquad (B.31)$$

and the joint density is

$$f(X) = \frac{1}{\sqrt{(2\pi)^n \, \mathrm{Det}(C)}} e^{-\frac{1}{2}XC^{-1}X^T} \qquad (B.32)$$

ORDER-STATISTICS

Given a random variable x distributed according to some distribution with density $f(x)$, with $a < x < b$, we occasionally like to know the density of the maximum or minimum (e.g., in lookback options). Let $X_1, X_2, \dots, X_n$ be a random sample from a distribution having a probability density function $f(x)$. Let Y_1 be the smallest of these, Y_2 be the next smallest, all the way up to Y_n the largest X_i, so that $Y_1 < Y_2 < \cdots < Y_n$. Then the Y_n is called the nth order statistic. The first useful result is that the *joint* density of the Y_i is given by

$$h(y_1, y_2, \dots, y_n) = (n!) f(y_1) f(y_2) \dots f(y_n) \qquad (B.33)$$

as long as $a < y_1 < y_2 < \cdots < y_n$ and 0 elsewhere.

The second useful result is that the marginal probability density function (PDF) of the maximum is given by

$$h_n(y_n) = n[F(y_n)]^{n-1} f(y_n) \qquad (B.34)$$

as long as $a < y_n < b$ and 0 elsewhere, where $F(y_n)$ denotes the cumulative density function with upper limit of integration y_n.

Similarly, the PDF for the minimum is given by

$$h_1(y_1) = n[1 - F(y_1)]^{n-1} f(y_1) \qquad (B.35)$$

as long as $a < y_1 < b$ and 0 elsewhere.

In general, the marginal probability density for the kth order statistic is

$$h_k(y_k) = \frac{n!}{(k-1)!(n-k)!} [F(y_k)]^{k-1} [1 - F(y_k)]^{n-k} f(y_k) \qquad (B.36)$$

as long as $a < y_k < b$ and 0 elsewhere.

Review of Basic Black-Scholes Pricing

In this appendix, readers are reminded in explicit detail how the Black-Scholes formula is computed using the simple probabilistic interpretation: i.e., the price of the option is the discounted present value of the expected future payoff.

Begin with the basic stochastic process

$$dS = a(S, t)\, dt + b(S, t)\, dz \tag{C.1}$$

where $dz \sim \epsilon\sqrt{dt}$ and ϵ is a standard normal variate with mean zero and variance 1.

For a general function $G(S, t)$ of the stock price S and time t, Taylor expansion (Ito) in S and t to second order gives

$$dG(S, t) = \frac{\partial G}{\partial S}\, dS + \frac{\partial G}{\partial t}\, dt + \frac{1}{2}\frac{\partial^2 G}{\partial S^2}\, dS^2 + \frac{1}{2}\frac{\partial^2 G}{\partial t^2}\, dt^2 + \frac{\partial^2 G}{\partial S\partial t}\, dS\, dt + \cdots \tag{C.2}$$

Inserting Equation (C.1) into Equation (C.2) and keeping terms of order dt (use $\epsilon^2\, dt \sim dt$ as $< \epsilon^2 > \sim 1$) gives

$$dG(S, t) = \left(a(S, t)\frac{\partial G}{\partial S} + \frac{\partial G}{\partial t} + \frac{1}{2}b^2(S, t)\frac{\partial^2 G}{\partial S^2} \right) dt + b(S, t)\frac{\partial G}{\partial S}\, dz \tag{C.3}$$

With the usual assumption that returns are normally distributed with a drift, i.e.,

$$a = \mu S \tag{C.4}$$
$$b = \sigma S \tag{C.5}$$
$$G = \ln S \tag{C.6}$$

we obtain the lognormal stochastic process:

$$dG(S, t) = \left(\mu - \frac{\sigma^2}{2}\right) dt + \sigma \, dz \tag{C.7}$$

In terms of distributions,

$$\ln S_t \sim N\left(\left(\mu - \frac{\sigma^2}{2}\right) dt + \ln S_0, \sigma\sqrt{t}\right) \tag{C.8}$$

Now a standard normal probability distribution is given by

$$N(a, \mu, \sigma) = \frac{1}{\sqrt{2\pi}\sigma} \int_{-\infty}^{u} e^{-\frac{1}{2}\left(\frac{x-\mu}{\sigma}\right)^2} dx \tag{C.9}$$

so using Equation (C.8) with

$$x = \ln S_T \tag{C.10}$$

$$\mu = \ln S_0 + \left(\mu - \frac{\sigma^2}{2}\right) \tag{C.11}$$

$$\sigma = \sigma\sqrt{T} \tag{C.12}$$

the probability-weighted price of a simple European call option with expiration time T is

$$\frac{1}{\sigma\sqrt{2\pi T}} \int_{-\infty}^{\infty} \frac{1}{S_T} \max[S_T - K, 0] e^{\left[\frac{\ln S_T - \ln S_0 - \left(\mu - \frac{\sigma^2}{2}\right)T}{\sigma\sqrt{T}}\right]^2} dS_T \tag{C.13}$$

Set

$$z = \frac{\ln(S_T/S_0) - \left(\mu - \frac{\sigma^2}{2}\right)T}{\sigma\sqrt{T}} \tag{C.14}$$

$$\Rightarrow S_T = S_0 \, e^{\left(\mu - \frac{\sigma^2}{2}\right)T + \sigma\sqrt{T}z} \tag{C.15}$$

Then,

$$dz = \frac{1}{\sigma\sqrt{T}} \frac{dS_T}{S_T} \tag{C.16}$$

and the forward expected price of the call option is

$$\frac{1}{\sqrt{2\pi}} \int_{-\infty}^{\infty} \max[S_0 e^{\left(\mu - \frac{\sigma^2}{2}\right)T + \sigma\sqrt{t}z} - K, 0] e^{-\frac{1}{2}z^2} dz \tag{C.17}$$

Now, a numerical integration routine can evaluate this integral without further ado, but to show the analytic evaluation, note that the max function limits the integration region to be nonzero only if

$$S_0 e^{\left(\mu - \frac{\sigma^2}{2}\right)T + \sigma\sqrt{T}z} > K \tag{C.18}$$

so that the z integral has lower limit $z_l = 1/(\sigma\sqrt{T})[\ln(K/S_0) - (\mu - (\sigma^2/2)) T]$. The integral becomes

$$C = \frac{1}{\sqrt{2\pi}} \int_{z_l}^{\infty} \left[\underbrace{S_0 e^{\left(\mu - \frac{\sigma^2}{2}\right)T + \sigma\sqrt{T}z}}_{P_1} - \underbrace{K}_{P_2} \right] e^{-1/2z^2} dz \tag{C.19}$$

Note, now, that the probability of obtaining a number larger than a distributed randomly as a normal variable is given in terms of the standard normal $N(0, 1)$ with zero mean and unit variance as

$$\frac{1}{\sqrt{2\pi}} \int_a^{\infty} e^{-z^2/2} dz = 1 - N(0, 1, a) \tag{C.20}$$

This, along with the risk-neutral assumption that $\mu = r$ with r being the risk-free zero-coupon rate, can be now used to evaluate the two integrals above. The first integral is

$$P_1 = \frac{1}{\sqrt{2\pi}} \int_{z_l}^{\infty} S_0 e^{(r - \frac{1}{2}\sigma^2)T + \sigma\sqrt{T}z} e^{-1/2z^2} dz \tag{C.21}$$

$$= \frac{1}{\sqrt{2\pi}} \int_{z_l}^{\infty} S_0 e^{-\frac{1}{2}(z - \sigma\sqrt{T})^2 + rT} dz \tag{C.22}$$

Shifting $w = z - \sigma\sqrt{T}$, this integral is

$$\frac{1}{\sqrt{2\pi}} e^{rT} \int_{z_l - \sigma\sqrt{T}}^{\infty} S_0 e^{-\frac{1}{2}w^2} dw \tag{C.23}$$

which equals (see Appendix A for formulas)

$$e^{rT} S_0 (1 - N[0, 1, z_l - \sigma\sqrt{T}]) \tag{C.24}$$

The second integral is trivial. Adding the two, and discounting by the continuously compounded discount factor e^{-rT}, the price of the call option is

$$e^{-rT}[S_0 e^{rT}(1 - N[0, 1, z_l - \sigma\sqrt{T}]) - K(1 - N[0, 1, z_l])] \tag{C.25}$$

Now, using the identity

$$1 - N[-x] = N[x] \tag{C.26}$$

the expression for the call option is reduced to the familiar form

$$S_0 N \left[\frac{\ln S_0/K + rT + \sigma^2 T}{\sigma\sqrt{T}} \right] - K e^{-rT} N \left[\frac{\ln S_0/K + rT - \sigma^2 T}{\sigma\sqrt{T}} \right] \tag{C.27}$$

Monte-Carlo Engine in VBA

Here, a simple Excel Visual Basic code for a three-factor Monte-Carlo is given. We will assume that the forward prices and forward volatilities for each asset are given in a column (in the example here, we assume 24 time-step slices). The code can be inserted in a code module with appropriate inputs defined in the calling worksheets. Here, 5000 paths are generated by default—by allocating larger arrays this number can be increased (though see the discussion in Chapter 5 on the problem of repetition for naive generators).

```
Sub generator()

'ALLOCATE ARRAYS AND DEFINE VARIABLES
Dim vol1(24) As Double
Dim vol2(24) As Double
Dim vol3(24) As Double
Dim forward1(24) As Single
Dim forward2(24) As Single
Dim forward3(24) As Single
Dim steps As Integer
Dim paths As Integer
Dim rate1(5000, 24) As Single
Dim rate2(5000, 24) As Single
Dim rate3(5000, 24) As Single
Dim z1(24) As Single
Dim z2(24) As Single
Dim z3(24) As Single
```

```
Dim sumz1 As Single
Dim sumz2 As Single
Dim sumz3 As Single
Dim months As Integer
Dim days As Integer
Dim corr12 As Double
Dim corr13 As Double
Dim corr23 As Double
Dim e1(24) As Single
Dim e2(24) As Single
Dim payoff(5000, 24) As Double
Dim discount(24) As Double
Dim strike1 As Variant
Dim strike2 As Variant
Dim strike3 As Variant
Dim not1 As Variant
Dim not2 As Variant
Dim not3 As Variant
Dim cumpayoff As Double


'USE INPUTS FROM WORKSHEET
'PATHS=NUMBER OF PATHS
'STEPS=NUMBER OF STEPS PER PATH
'MONTHS=TIME IN MONTHS PER STEPSIZE
paths = Range("paths")
steps = Range("steps")
months = Range("months")
days = Range("days")
corr12 = Range("corr12")
corr13 = Range("corr13")
corr23 = Range("corr23")
strike1 = Range("strike1")
strike2 = Range("strike2")
strike3 = Range("strike3")
notional1 = Range("not1")
notional2 = Range("not2")
notional3 = Range("not3")


'ASSIGN FORWARDS AND VOLS TO ARRAY ELEMENTS
For x = 1 To 24
forward1(x) = Cells(7 + x, 4)
vol1(x) = Cells(7 + x, 2)
forward2(x) = Cells(7 + x, 8)
vol2(x) = Cells(7 + x, 6)
forward3(x) = Cells(7 + x, 12)
vol3(x) = Cells(7 + x, 10)
```

```
discount(x) = Cells(7 + x, 14)
Next x

'COMPUTATION ENGINE
cumpayoff = 0
For p = 1 To paths
sumz1 = 0
sumz2 = 0
sumz3 = 0
For s = 1 To steps
z3(s) =
Sqr(-2 * Log(Rnd())) * Sin(2 * Application.Pi * Rnd())
e1(s) =
Sqr(-2 * Log(Rnd())) * Sin(2 * Application.Pi * Rnd())
e2(s) =
Sqr(-2 * Log(Rnd())) * Sin(2 * Application.Pi * Rnd())
z2(s) = (corr23 * z3(s)) + (Sqr(1 - corr23 ^ 2) * e2(s))
z1(s) = e2(s) * ((corr12 - corr13 * corr23) / Sqr(1 - corr23 ^ 3)) _
+ e1(s) * (Sqr(1 + 2 * corr12 * corr13 * corr23 - corr112 ^ 2 - corr13 _
^ 2 - corr23 ^ 2) / (1 - corr23 ^ 3)) + corr13 * z3(s)
'SUMZ REMEMBERS THE PATH DEPENDENCE
sumz3 = sumz3 + Sqr(months / 12) * z3(s)
sumz2 = sumz2 + Sqr(months / 12) * z2(s)
sumz1 = sumz1 + Sqr(months / 12) * z1(s)
rate1(p, s) = forward1(s) * Exp(vol1(s) *
sumz1 - 0.5 * (vol1(s) ^ 2) * s * (months / 12)) _
rate2(p, s) = forward2(s) * Exp(vol2(s) *
sumz2 - 0.5 * (vol2(s) ^ 2) * s * (months / 12)) _
rate3(p, s) = forward3(s) * Exp(vol3(s) *
sumz2 - 0.5 * (vol3(s) ^ 2) * s * (months / 12)) _
'PRINT OUT DIAGNOSTIC PATHS IN WORKSHEET ''PATHS"
Worksheets("paths").Cells(s, 1) = rate1(p, s)
Worksheets("paths").Cells(s, 2) = rate2(p, s)
Worksheets("paths").Cells(s, 3) = rate3(p, s)

'Cells(p + 40, s + 5) = payoff(p, s)
'cumpayoff = payoff(p, s) + cumpayoff
Next s
Next p
'Cells(1, 9) = cumpayoff / (paths)

End Sub
```

Max–Min Algebra

The fundamental pricing formulas for vanilla options are

$$\max(S - K, 0) = \begin{cases} S - K & \text{if } S - K > 0 \\ 0 & \text{if } S - K \leq 0 \end{cases} \tag{E.1}$$

and

$$\min(S - K, 0) = \begin{cases} 0 & \text{if } S - K > 0 \\ S - K & \text{if } S - K \leq 0 \end{cases} \tag{E.2}$$

where, in general, S and K are the expiration price and the strike of the underlying variable, respectively.

Here, an algebra will be constructed of the max and min functions in terms of step functions so that general option portfolios can be constructed in a robust, algorithmic manner (for instance, see the discussions of put–call symmetries and stating hedging in Chapter 5).

Note first that the Heaviside step function is defined as

$$\Theta(x) = \begin{cases} 1 & \text{if } x > 0 \\ 0 & \text{if } x \leq 0 \end{cases} \tag{E.3}$$

so that

$$\max(x, 0) = x\Theta(x) \tag{E.4}$$

and

$$\max(x, y) = x\Theta(x - y) + y\Theta(y - x) = \begin{cases} x & \text{if } x > y \\ y & \text{if } y \leq x \end{cases} \quad \text{(E.5)}$$

Also,

$$\min(x, y) = x\Theta(y - x) + y\Theta(x - y) = x\Omega(x - y) + y\Omega(y - x) \quad \text{(E.6)}$$

Note that

$$\max(x, y) + \min(x, y) = x + y \quad \text{(E.7)}$$

because

$$\begin{aligned}
\max(x, y) + \min(x, y) &= x\Theta(x - y) + y\Theta(y - x) + x\Theta(y - x) \\
&\quad + y\Theta(x - y) \\
&= (x + y)\Theta(y - x) + (x + y)\Theta(x - y) \\
&= (x + y)(\Theta(y - x) + \Theta(x - y)) \\
&= (x + y)(1) \\
&= x + y \quad \text{(E.8)}
\end{aligned}$$

Define a new function $\Omega(x)$:

$$\Omega(x) = \begin{cases} 1 & \text{if } x < 0 \\ 0 & \text{if } x \geq 0 \end{cases} \quad \text{(E.9)}$$

which is a "flip" of the Θ function, so that

$$x\Omega(x) + x\Theta(x) = x \quad \text{(E.10)}$$

and

$$\Omega(x - y) = \Theta(y - x) \quad \text{(E.11)}$$

Also,

$$\Theta(x) = 1 - \Theta(-x) = 1 - \Omega(x) \quad \text{(E.12)}$$

Other properties of $\Theta(x)$ that can be readily derived

$$\Theta^n(x) = \Theta(x) \; \forall \; n > 1$$
$$\Theta(x\Theta(y)) = \Theta(x)\Theta(y) \quad \text{(E.13)}$$

It will now be shown how these manipulations can be used to obtain nontrivial simplifications that prove to be extrememly useful in pricing problems. The essential idea is to massage payoff functions into other functions that we already know how to price. As an example, an option on the maximum of two risky assets can be priced in terms of options that deliver the maximum of two assets or cash. To prove the identity used in Chapter 3 of this book:

$$\max[0, \max(x, y) - K] = \max[x, y, K] - K \qquad (E.14)$$

use simply Θ algebra.

As an exercise, first set $K = 0$. Then,

$$\text{LHS} = \max(x, y, 0)$$
$$= x\Theta(x - y)\Theta(x) + y\Theta(y - x)\Theta(y)$$

and

$$\text{RHS} = \max(0, \max(x, y))$$
$$= \max(0, x\Theta(x - y) + y\Theta(y - x)) \qquad (E.15)$$

Now, using $\Theta(0, x) = x\Theta(x)$ this equals

$$(x\Theta(x - y) + y\Theta(y - x))\Theta(x\Theta(x - y) + y\Theta(y - x)) \qquad (E.16)$$

which, with Equation (E.13), is

$$(x\Theta(x - y) + y\Theta(y - x))(\Theta(x)\Theta(x - y) + \Theta(y)\Theta(y - x)) \qquad (E.17)$$

Now note that, by definition,

$$\Theta(x - y)\Theta(y - x) = 0 \qquad (E.18)$$

so expanding all the terms in our last result we find that the RHS equals the LHS.

Putting a nonzero K term just generates a couple of extra terms which can be massaged to put in terms of the LHS:

$$\max(x, y, K) = x\Theta(x - y)\Theta(x - K) + y\Theta(y - x)\Theta(y - K)$$
$$+ K\Theta(K - x)\Theta(K - y) \qquad (E.19)$$

Volatility and Skews

ESTIMATION

The different meanings of the volatility parameter for use in option pricing models will be summarized here. Due to similar notation used in the literature, there is too much confusion about some of these simple issues, which, if not understood properly, can lead to the application of the wrong estimates to pricing problems. In the relatively illiquid market for multifactor options, the dependence on historical estimates is so important that any errors can be very costly by the time the disagreement with implied parameter values is discovered. Also, the study of volatility leads to a better understanding of correlation. See also Reference [226].

Simply speaking, there are four contexts in which the same short-form "volatility" is used to refer to related measures of dispersion in the world of option pricing.

1. *Instantaneous Volatility* This is the volatility of the instantaneous incremental stochastic process in the model on which the pricing framework is based. In the Black-Scholes case,

$$\frac{dS}{S} = \mu \, dt + \sigma \, dz \tag{F.1}$$

This corresponds to the standard deviation of dS/S, which, in general, can be time and state dependent.

2. *Terminal Volatility*   This is the volatility, or, more precisely, the square root of the variance annualized, of the final state distribution for a specified time in the future. If the returns in the Black-Scholes framework are assumed to be normally distributed, this is the square root of the expected variance (or deviation) of the distribution of the final state returns from the mean return.

3. *Historically Estimated Volatility*   This is the usual estimate of standard deviation of the returns, or of changes, for a given time interval. For instance, in the Black-Scholes framework, one could take daily data, compute the daily returns, calculate the standard deviation of the return time series, and then annualize it by multiplying by the square root of the number of trading days in the year. Assuming that a reasonable time interval is chosen, this can be compared directly with the instantaneous volatility of the returns calculated above from the model.

4. *Implied Volatility from European Options*   The option pricing formula, e.g., Black-Scholes, can be reversed to solve for the volatility that enters it. This volatility corresponds to the standard deviation of the terminal price of the asset returns. Hence, it is compared directly with the calculation of the terminal or "integrated" volatilities of the forwards given above.

First, it has to be understood that the volatility parameter is a model-dependent concept. Depending on what is assumed for the underlying stochastic process, a very specific sampling of historical data leads to the correct quantity that can be interpreted as the volatility.

Assume, for example, that some quantity follows a standard normal process,

$$dS = \mu\, dt + \sigma\, dz \tag{F.2}$$

Discretizing this, we get

$$\Delta S = \mu\, \Delta t = \sigma\sqrt{\Delta t} z \tag{F.3}$$

so that

$$\Delta S \sim N[\mu\, \Delta t, \sigma\sqrt{\Delta t}] \tag{F.4}$$

If we choose now and in what follows to specify our time steps in fractions or multiples of years, then this would mean

$$\Delta S_{\text{One day}} \sim N\left[\mu \times \frac{1}{250}, \sigma \times \sqrt{\frac{1}{250}}\right] \qquad (F.5)$$

Now we estimate the data historically. Assume that the daily data series is given by S_i, and specify the quantity

$$\delta_i = S_i - S_{i-1} \qquad (F.6)$$

for $i = 1, 2, \ldots, n$ and n data points. This is now the daily-differenced series. The usual estimate for the standard deviation of this daily-differenced series is

$$s = \sqrt{\frac{1}{n-1} \sum_{i=1}^{n} (\delta_i - E[\delta_i])^2} \qquad (F.7)$$

where we have denoted by $E[\delta_i]$ the expected values or the sampling average of δ_i.

Now s is an estimate, by construction, of the standard deviation of ΔS given above, so

$$s \sim \sigma \sqrt{t} \qquad (F.8)$$

which implies that

$$\sigma \sim \frac{s}{\sqrt{t}} \sim s\sqrt{250} \qquad (F.9)$$

is the required volatility parameter in annual terms. The standard error of this estimate is $\sigma/\sqrt{2n}$.

This estimate of σ is then used to price options. Note that there is a very subtle leap here. To price an option, we need the terminal variance of the forward price. In the normal model given here, we have

$$S_t = S_0 + \mu t + \sigma W_s \qquad (F.10)$$

where W_s is the terminal stochastic distribution. Then we can calculate

$$\text{Var}(S - S_0) = \sigma^2 \int_0^t dw_s\, dw_s = \sigma^2 \int_0^t ds$$
$$= \sigma^2 t \qquad (F.11)$$

so that the standard deviation equals $\sigma\sqrt{t}$. The upshot is that we can multiply the historically estimated sigma by $\sqrt{t}$ to get the standard deviation of the final price distribution. Now, in option pricing this term $\sigma\sqrt{t}$ appears naturally, which sometimes enables one to skip the intermediate steps in going from the estimated values via the reasoning described here. Also note that the final state terminal standard deviation has to be divided by $\sqrt{t}$ to obtain the σ that is fundamental to the model, and this can be compared to implied option volatilities.

HEDGE READJUSTMENT WITH VOL SKEWS

Using a simple option pricing model to back out the implied volatilities from option prices for different strikes on the same underlying variable, it is observed that the implied volatilities so inferred are not the same. This is commonly referred to as the volatility skew. It expresses, in simplest terms, the sentiment of the market, i.e., the direction which the market is more vulnerable to. In other words, from an option writer's viewpoint, the direction in which the underlying variable becomes more illiquid to hedge short option positions requires a higher relative premium.

It is also observed that as markets trade in a given direction in a given environment, the actual implied volatilities of the at-the-money options change drastically. For instance, in 1994–1995, delta-hedged U.S. interest-rate caps would have lost money, even though rates rose dramatically, because of a change in the volatility, and its effect on pricing and hedging.

The purpose of the current discussion is to tie these two observations, and to point out that a simple delta-hedging scheme, i.e., one based on Black-type models, has to be modified to take into consideration the effect of price–volatility correlation. An important consequence is that out-of-the-money calls(puts) that seem cheaper than out-of-the-money puts(calls) based on implied Black model volatilities might really be more valuable when price–volatility correlation is taken into consideration.

A number of recent studies have shown how to incorporate the traded skews within a numerical option pricing model. These methodologies use the concept of implied trees to fit the general volatility function with respect to changes in strikes as well as time horizons [63,72,188]. Another approach that has been used for a while is to infer the price distribution from empirical data by extracting the statistical moments and reconstructing the density function from which option prices can be computed [196].

We will approach these issues from a somewhat more intuitive direction [22]. If one assumes that prices and volatilities are not independent, but are correlated a posteriori with some correlation coefficient, then a simple simulation model with the underlying price and volatility as two correlated factors can reproduce all the option prices as traded in the market for a given tenor. This approach is similar to the implied tree approach in that the price–volatility correlation is inferred by empirically fitting the traded option prices to the two-factor model. However, it is different in its interpretation—in a given environment a trader can make assumptions about how the at-the-money volatilities will correlate with the level of prices, and he can adjust his delta-hedging scheme to compensate for the effect of the actual price level on the implied volatility level. The delta hedge is normally thought of as the local variation of the option price for small movements of the underlying variable, i.e., the first derivative of the option price with respect to the underlying variable. If a price-dependent volatility is admitted within the option pricing framework, an extra term is needed that is the vega of the option multiplied by the local variation of volatility with respect to price. If underlying price and volatility are uncorrelated, this term vanishes and we are led to the ordinary delta. On the other hand, for positive correlation between price and volatility, this adds to the delta, and for negative correlation between price and volatility, the term reduces the ordinary delta. The magnitude of this term can be inferred from a regression of implied volatilities against underlying price. In symbols,

$$\Delta = \Delta_{\text{Ordinary}} + \text{vega} \frac{\partial(\text{vol})}{\partial(\text{price})} \tag{F.12}$$

where the term $\partial(\text{vol})/\partial(\text{price})$ has all the market-inferred information on price–vol correlation and has explicit dependence on the correlation parameter. Note that since the correction effect is proportional to the vega of the option which is being hedged, at-the-money options are more sensitive to changes in price–volatility correlation.

Looking at a similar equation for the gamma of an option:

$$\gamma = \frac{\partial \Delta}{\partial(\text{price})} + \frac{\partial \Delta}{\partial(\text{vol})}\frac{\partial(\text{vol})}{\partial(\text{price})} \tag{F.13}$$

Since the second term is just the "vanna" (or change of delta with volatility, or, equivalently, change in vega with respect to the price) multiplied by the term inferred from price–volatility correlation data, if it is nonvanishing it can affect the hedge readjustment. For a call option, out-of-the-money options have a higher vanna than at-the-money options, and in-the-money options have negative vanna. Thus, if prices are negatively correlated to vols, the gamma of the option can get reduced as prices rally. So, as the market rallies and the out-of-the-money options become at the money, the effective delta hedge is too large and results in a loss. Conversely, as the market sells off, the delta hedge results in an extra bonus. This is why, during volatile markets, skews are most pronounced for the short-dated options with relatively small initial gammas that can explode rapidly.

Note that the simple methodology outlined so far will only reproduce skews, i.e., monotonic volatility shapes. To reproduce more complex effects, the effect of higher bivariate moments between price and volatility are generally needed. More fancy stochastic volatility models may also be useful [235].

Multivariate Statistical Techniques

OVERVIEW OF MULTIVARIATE METHODS

In the pricing and managing of correlation products, we are required to have in our toolkit an arsenal of methods to extract the statistical relationships between variables of interest. Multivariate statistical methods can be broadly classified as *dependence* methods or *interdependence* methods.

Dependence methods are useful when it is possible to say a priori that a subset of observation variables depends on another subset of observation variables. Interdependence methods are useful when it is impossible to distinguish dependent variables from independent variables.

Univariate methods refer to methods where there is a single dependent and single independent variable. When there is more than one independent and/or dependent variable, the methods are called multivariate. Regression methods are used when the dependent variables and the independent variables are metric. When the independent variables are nominal or nonmetric, the method of choice is called ANOVA (analysis of variance). When the independent variables are metric, but the dependent variables are nonmetric, *discriminant* analysis is used.

Canonical correlation is a generalization of multivariate regression because it allows more than one dependent variable. For nonmetric independent, metric dependent variables, the method used is MANOVA (multivariate ANOVA), and for nonmetric dependent, metric independent variables, MDA (multiple-group discriminant analysis) is used.

Interdependence methods are used when it is not possible to distinguish variables as dependent or independent as, for example, when dealing with different yields in the yield curve, or different assets in a multiasset portfolio. When the variables are metric, principal components analysis, factor analysis, or cluster analysis is used to group data into similar groups. These are known, in general, as data-reduction or aggregation or indexation techniques.

For nonmetric data, the analogue of principal components analysis is called correspondence analysis.

Recently, a number of new statistical methods have appeared for analyzing relationships among a number of variables represented by a system of linear equations. These methods, under the common name of structural models or path models, use parametric equations for observables to estimate the effects of unobservable quantities [195].

COVARIANCE MATRIX EIGENSTRUCTURE

In variable space, for p variables and n observations, we get a scatterplot in p dimensions with n scatterpoints, i.e., n, p-dimensional vectors. In observation space, we have p, n-dimensional vectors.

In observation space, the variance of a time series $\mathbf{x}$ is simply $|\mathbf{x}|^2/(n-1)$ and the covariance between two series $\mathbf{x}_1, \mathbf{x}_2$ is $\mathbf{x}_1 \cdot \mathbf{x}_2/(n-1)$.

Let $\mathbf{X}$ be a p variable, n observation vector, i.e., a p-row, n-column matrix $(p \times n)$ of mean subtracted, variance normalized returns, for instance. The covariance matrix is a $p \times p$ matrix:

$$\Sigma = \mathbf{XX}^T \tag{G.1}$$

With a $1 \times p$ vector of weights,

$$\alpha = (\alpha_1 \alpha_2 \cdots \alpha_p) \tag{G.2}$$

make a new $1 \times n$ variable:

$$\xi = \alpha X \tag{G.3}$$

The variance of this vector is

$$E[\xi\xi^T] = \alpha\Sigma\alpha^T \tag{G.4}$$

with the normalization constraint

$$\alpha\alpha^T = 1 \tag{G.5}$$

Then, to maximize the variance we use a Lagrange multiplier λ as follows. Let

$$Z = \alpha\Sigma\alpha^T - \lambda(\alpha\alpha^T - 1) \tag{G.6}$$

then the p component derivative with respect to the component weight vector has to be zero:

$$\frac{\partial Z}{\partial \alpha} = 2\Sigma\alpha - 2\lambda\alpha = 0 \tag{G.7}$$

i.e.,

$$(\Sigma - \lambda I)\alpha = 0 \tag{G.8}$$

supplemented with

$$\alpha\alpha^T = 1 \tag{G.9}$$

Note that this system only has a solution if $\text{Det}(\Sigma - \lambda I) = 0$, i.e., a polynomial equation of p order, so there are p roots.

Note also that the above equation implies, for the ith eigenvalue,

$$\alpha_i^T(\Sigma - \lambda_i I)\alpha_i = 0 \tag{G.10}$$

$$\alpha_i^T\Sigma\alpha_i = \lambda_i \tag{G.11}$$

since $\alpha_i^T\alpha_i = 1$. So λ_1 corresponds to the variance of the first principal component and is the largest variance in the set of p.

Singular value decomposition expresses any $n \times p$ matrix, where $n \geq p$ as a triple product of three matrices P, D, Q such that

$$X = PDQ^T \tag{G.12}$$

where X is $n \times p$, P is $n \times r$, D is $r \times r$, and Q^T is $r \times p$.

The singular value decomposition of a square symmetric matrix is called its spectral decomposition. Any $p \times p$ square symmetric matrix X can be written as the product of two matrices P, Λ such that

$$X = P\Lambda P^T \tag{G.13}$$

where P is a $p \times p$ square symmetric orthogonal matrix containing the eigenvectors of the X matrix, and the $p \times p$ diagonal matrix Λ contains the eigenvalues of the X matrix. For the covariance matrix Σ,

$$\Sigma = P\Lambda P^T \tag{G.14}$$

so that the trace

$$\begin{aligned} tr(\Sigma) &= tr(P\Lambda P^T) \\ &= tr(P^T P\Lambda) \\ &= tr(\Lambda) \end{aligned} \tag{G.15}$$

so the sum of the eigenvalues of the original covariance matrix equals the sum of the eigenvalues of the new variables (i.e., principal components).

So the results of this section show that principal components decomposition does automatic variance ordering, with overall variance preservation.

APPLIED PRINCIPAL COMPONENTS DECOMPOSITION

Suppose we have p asset prices with $n + 1$ time observations for each asset. We create the $n \times p$ matrix of returns Y. Now we construct the orthogonal principal components $P_1, \ldots, P_m$, where $m \leq p$, by the standard principal components algorithm (see also the codelet in Figure 6–2). First, normalize the data by subtracting the mean for each column of Y and by dividing by the sample standard deviation. This yields the normalized return matrix X. Now suppose W is the matrix of eigenvectors of the normalized, mean subtracted covariance matrix $X^T X$. Then,

$$X^T X W = \lambda W \tag{G.16}$$

where λ is the diagonal matrix of eigenvalues. The full matrix of principal components is

$$\mathbf{P} = \mathbf{XW} \tag{G.17}$$

and due to orthogonality,

$$\mathbf{P}^T\mathbf{P} = \mathbf{W}^T\mathbf{X}^T\mathbf{XW} = \mathbf{W}^T\mathbf{W}\lambda = \lambda \tag{G.18}$$

so

$$\mathbf{X} = \mathbf{PW}^T \tag{G.19}$$

i.e.,

$$X_i = \sum_{j=1}^{p} w_{ij}P_j \tag{G.20}$$

where w_{ij} are factor weights for $\mathbf{X}_i$. In most applications, only a subset of the factors is retained, using a rule such as the "eigenvalue greater than 1 rule," to reduce the dimensionality of the problem.

Distributions

The general algorithm for fitting model parameters to data requires that some assumption be made about the distribution from which the data could have been generated. This contains, but is not restricted to, the specification of the *location*, *dispersion*, *association*, and *shape*. The simplest way of proceeding is first to *bin* the data into intervals, and then to guess a cumulative density function. Then, either by comparing percentile probabilities ("quantile plots") or by matching moments, the value of the parameters can be obtained. To refine this, in general, techniques such as maximum likelihood estimation are utilized. When working with multivariate data, the same procedure can be used, by fitting first the marginal densities for each variable, and then the conditional densities for the remaining variables. Once the marginal and the conditional density estimates are known, the joint density can be created by convolution. This Appendix lists some important univariate and multivariate distributions and their properties, and also describes the moment-matching procedure.

PROPERTIES OF THE LOGNORMAL DISTRIBUTION

If $Z = \log X$ is normally distributed, then X is said to be lognormally distributed. Note that for Δ, a small price change in the asset S,

$$\frac{dS}{S} = d\log S$$

$$= \log(S + \Delta) - \log(S)$$

$$= \log S + \frac{\Delta}{S} - \frac{\Delta^2}{2S^2} + \mathcal{O}(\Delta^3) - \log(S)$$

$$\approx \frac{\Delta}{S}$$

so that log changes are the same as percentage returns. Thus, the distribution of log changes gives the distribution of returns.

The lognormal density is defined as

$$\frac{1}{\sqrt{2\pi}\sigma x} e^{-\frac{1}{2}\left(\frac{\ln x - \mu}{\sigma^2}\right)^2} \tag{H.1}$$

with the cumulative density

$$\frac{1 + \mathrm{Erf}\left(\dfrac{-\mu + \log(x)}{\sqrt{2}\sigma}\right)}{2} \tag{H.2}$$

$$\mathrm{Mean} = e^{\mu + \frac{\sigma^2}{2}} \tag{H.3}$$

$$\mathrm{Variance} = e^{2\mu + \sigma^2}\left(e^{\sigma^2} - 1\right) \tag{H.4}$$

$$\mathrm{Skewness} = \sqrt{-1 + e^{\sigma^2}}\left(2 + e^{\sigma^2}\right) \tag{H.5}$$

$$\mathrm{Kurtosis} = 3\,e^{2\sigma^2} + 2\,e^{3\sigma^2} + e^{4\sigma^2} \tag{H.6}$$

The rth moment of X about zero is

$$\mu_r = E[X^r] = e^{\mu r + \frac{1}{2}\sigma^2 r^2} \tag{H.7}$$

The value x_α such that $P[X \le x_\alpha] = \alpha$ is related to the corresponding percentile u_α of the unit normal distribution by

$$x_\alpha = e^{\mu + \alpha u_\alpha} \tag{H.8}$$

so that, in particular,

$$\mathrm{Median}(X) = e^{\mu} \tag{H.9}$$

Also,

$$E[X] > \text{Median}(X) > \text{Mode}(X) \tag{H.10}$$

and

$$\frac{\text{Mode}(X)}{E[X]} = \frac{1}{\sigma^3} = \left(\frac{\text{Median}(X)}{E[X]}\right)^3 \tag{H.11}$$

The product of n lognormals is, again, a lognormal, i.e., if $X_1, \ldots, X_j$ are mutually independent, then $\prod_{j=1}^{k} a_j X_j$ is distributed lognormally with mean $\sum_{j=1}^{k} \mu_j + \log a_j$ and variance σ_j^2. The sums are harder, as we have seen in the section on baskets. For $S = \sum_{i=1}^{N} X_i$ of N i.i.d. X_j values distributed lognormally, with mean μ and variance σ^2, we can write the characteristic function as

$$\Phi_X(t) = \frac{e^{i\sigma t}}{\sigma\sqrt{2\pi}} \int_{-\infty}^{\infty} e^{-\frac{1}{2}\frac{y^2}{\sigma^2}} e^{i\sigma t(e^y - y - 1)} e^{ity} \, dy \tag{H.12}$$

and then, by Taylor expanding

$$e^{i\sigma t(e^y - y - 1)} = \sum_{n=0}^{\infty} a_n (i\sigma t) \frac{y^n}{n!} \tag{H.13}$$

we get

$$\Phi_X(t) = e^{i\sigma t - \frac{1}{2}\sigma^2 t^2} \sum_{n=0}^{\infty} \frac{i^n \sigma^n}{n!} a_n(i\sigma t) h_n(i\sigma t) \tag{H.14}$$

where a_n are coefficients and h_n are quasi-Hermite polynomials, which are tabulated [10].

The Normal–Lognormal Convolution

An issue that frequently arises is how to combine random variables from different distributions. For example, if interest rates are taken to follow a normal process, and another asset, such as stock prices, are taken to follow lognormal processes, then what is the process followed by the sum of the two random variables?

Suppose Z is a variable with $\log(Z + \alpha)$ distributed as $N(\mu, \sigma^2)$, and Y is a normal variable with zero drift and variance τ, i.e., $Y \sim N(0, \tau^2)$. Then the density of X can be computed using convolutions:

$$f_X = \frac{1}{2\pi\sigma\tau} \int_0^\infty \frac{1}{z} \, e^{-\frac{1}{2}\left[(\frac{\log z - \mu}{\sigma})^2 + (\frac{x-z+\alpha}{\tau})^2\right]} \, dz$$

$$= \frac{1}{2\pi\sigma\tau} \int_{-\infty}^\infty e^{-\frac{1}{2}\left[(\frac{t-\mu}{\sigma})^2 + (\frac{x-e^t+\alpha}{\tau})^2\right]} \, dt \qquad \text{(H.15)}$$

where the transformation $t = \log z$ is used in the second step. Now suppose $\alpha = 0$ and $\tau = 1$, so we have the standard normal and the unshifted lognormal. Then,

$$f_X = \frac{1}{2\pi\sigma} \int_{-\infty}^\infty e^{-\frac{1}{2}\left[(\frac{t-\mu}{\sigma})^2 + (x-e^t)^2\right]} \, dt \qquad \text{(H.16)}$$

In general, the moments of the convolution are

$$E(X^k) = \sum_{j=0}^k \binom{k}{j} E(Z^j) E(U^{k-j}) \qquad \text{(H.17)}$$

where U is a unit normal. In particular,

$$E[X] = -\alpha + e^{\mu + \frac{1}{2}\sigma^2}$$

$$\text{Var}[X] = \tau^2 + e^{2\mu + \sigma^2}(e^{\sigma^2} - 1)$$

MIXED NORMAL DISTRIBUTIONS

Suppose we add k normal densities $f_1(x), f_2(x), \ldots, f_k(x)$ with arbitrary weights to make a new density $f(x)$. Assume the weights are $p_1, p_2, \ldots, p_k$ with means $\mu_1, \mu_2, \ldots, \mu_k$ and variances $\sigma_1, \sigma_2, \ldots, \sigma_k$. Then,

$$f(x) = p_1 f_1(x) + p_2 f_2(x) + \ldots + p_k f_k(x) = \sum_i^k p_i f_i(x) \qquad \text{(H.18)}$$

The mixed density has mean

$$E(X) = \sum_i^k p_i \int_{-\infty}^\infty x f_i(x) \, dx = \sum_i^k p_i \mu_i = \overline{\mu} \qquad \text{(H.19)}$$

which is simply a weighted average of the μ_i.

The variance is

$$\text{var}(X) = \sum_i^k p_i \int_{-\infty}^{\infty} (x - \overline{\mu})^2 f_i(x)\, dx$$

$$= \sum_i^k p_i \int_{-\infty}^{\infty} [(x - \mu_i) + (\mu_i - \overline{\mu})]^2 f_i(x)\, dx$$

$$= \sum_i^k p_i \int_{-\infty}^{\infty} (x - \mu_i)^2 f_i(x)\, dx + \sum_i^k p_i (\mu_i - \overline{\mu})^2 \int_{-\infty}^{\infty} f_i(x)\, dx$$

$$= \sum_i^k p_i \sigma_i^2 + \sum_i^k p_i (\mu_i - \overline{\mu})^2 \tag{H.20}$$

which has an extra term in comparison to the case where random variates are added.

For instance, take a combination

$$wN[\mu_1, \sigma_1] + (1 - w)N[\mu_2, \sigma_2] \tag{H.21}$$

which has mean

$$\mu = w\mu_1 + (1 - w)\mu_2 \tag{H.22}$$

and variance

$$\text{Var} = w\sigma_1^2 + (1 - w)\sigma_2^2 + w(1 - w)(\mu_1 - \mu_2)^2 \tag{H.23}$$

Fat Tails and Mixed Distributions

If we calculate the kurtosis and skewness from a mixed distribution, it might turn out to be very different from the kurtosis and skewness of any of the component distributions. The kurtosis, which is given by $E[(x - \mu)^4]/\sigma^4$, is an index of the fatness of tails in a given distribution. For the normal distribution, this is equal to 3.

Suppose we assume that the true density of returns for a given market is not normal, but is the sum of two normals (this is distinct from adding normal variables!). Let us assume that this true distribution is given by

$$D = \tfrac{9}{10} N(0, 1) + \tfrac{1}{10} N(0, 3) \tag{H.24}$$

so that most of the time, the return distribution is normal, but some of the time, three-sigma events can happen (albeit with one one-ninth of the total probability). For this combination, a simple computation shows that

$$\mu_D = 0$$
$$\sigma_D = 1.34$$
$$\text{Skewness}_D = 0$$
$$\text{Kurtosis}_D = 8.34$$

so that in comparison with the standard normal distribution, this distribution has "fat tails." This kind of *compound* distribution is sometimes used to model options where strike-dependent skews are very pronounced (see Appendix F on volatility skews).

As an extreme case of this, consider the infinite sum of exponentially weighted normal densities

$$f(x) = \int_0^\infty e^{-\sigma} e^{-\frac{1}{2}\frac{x^2}{\sigma^2}} \, d\sigma \qquad \text{(H.25)}$$

which has the high-variance densities weighed much less than the low-variance densities. This integral can be performed to yield results in terms of the MeijerG function, which is a good density for general fitting of tails.

MOMENT GENERATING FUNCTIONS

For any random variable X, the moment generating function is defined as

$$M(t) = E(e^{tX}) \qquad \text{(H.26)}$$

from which all the moments can be extracted by power series expansion. The moment generating function of an $N(\mu, \sigma^2)$ distribution is $e^{\mu t + \frac{1}{2}\sigma^2 t^2}$. Note that the DeMoivre theorem that we used in Chapter 5 for discretizing continuous densities to binomial densities can be motivated with this. Suppose

$$Y = \frac{X - np}{\sqrt{np(1 - p)}} \qquad \text{(H.27)}$$

so that the moment generating function of Y is, in the limit $n \to \infty$,

$$M_Y(t) = E\left[e^{t\frac{X-np}{\sqrt{np(1-p)}}}\right]$$

$$= e^{-\frac{tnp}{\sqrt{np(1-p)}}}\left(1 - p + pe^{\frac{t}{\sqrt{np(1-p)}}}\right)^n$$

$$\rightarrow e^{t^2/2}$$

MULTIVARIATE DISTRIBUTIONS

If $f(x, y)$ is the joint density of two variables, then the marginal densities are

$$f_x(x) = \int_y f(x, y)\, dy$$

$$f_y(y) = \int_x f(x, y)\, dx \tag{H.28}$$

from which the marginal mean μ_X, μ_Y and variances σ_X, σ_Y might easily be computed. Note that the covariance is

$$\text{Cov}(X, Y) = E[(X - \mu_X)(Y - \mu_Y)] = E(XY) - \mu_X \mu_Y \tag{H.29}$$

where

$$E[XY] = \int_x \int_y xy f(x, y)\, dx\, dy \tag{H.30}$$

and the correlation coefficient is

$$\rho = \frac{\text{Cov}(X, Y)}{\sigma_X \sigma_Y} \tag{H.31}$$

The conditional densities are

$$f(y|x) = \frac{f(x, y)}{f_x(x)}$$

$$f(x|y) = \frac{f(x, y)}{f_y(y)} \tag{H.32}$$

Then the conditional means are

$$\mu_{Y|x} = E(Y|x) = \int_y y f(y|x) \, dy$$

$$\mu_{X|y} = E(X|y) = \int_x x f(x|y) \, dx \qquad \text{(H.33)}$$

If $f(x, y) = f_x(x) f_y(y)$, then $f_x(x) = f(x|y)$, and $f_y(y) = f(y|x)$, so that X and Y are *independent*, and this implies (note that converse is not true) that $\rho = 0$.

For bivariate normal distributions, it is true that

- The marginal distributions of X and Y are $N(\mu_X, \sigma_X^2)$ and $N(\mu_Y, \sigma_Y^2)$, respectively.
- The conditional distributions of Y, for given $X = x$, and for X, given Y, are, respectively,

$$N\left[\mu_Y + \rho \frac{\sigma_Y}{\sigma_X}(x - \mu_X), \sigma_Y^2(1 - \rho^2)\right]$$

$$N\left[\mu_X + \rho \frac{\sigma_X}{\sigma_Y}(y - \mu_Y), \sigma_X^2(1 - \rho^2)\right] \qquad \text{(H.34)}$$

METHOD OF MOMENTS

The characteristic function for two jointly distributed variables x and y in terms of the parameters w_1, w_2 is

$$\Phi(w_1, w_2) = \int_{-\infty}^{\infty} \int_{-\infty}^{\infty} f(x, y) \, e^{i(w_1 x + w_2 y)} \, dx \, dy \qquad \text{(H.35)}$$

where $f(x, y)$ is the joint density of x and y.

Note that to describe baskets in the text, we had the choice of assuming distributional forms for the component variables, or a form for the combination. Suppose now that a simple basket is described by

$$z = ax + by \qquad \text{(H.36)}$$

Then the characteristic function is

$$\Phi_z(w) = E[e^{i(ax + by)w}] = \Phi(aw, bw) \qquad \text{(H.37)}$$

so that

$$\Phi_z(1) = \Phi(a, b) \tag{H.38}$$

According to the Cramer-Wold theorem, if $\Phi_z(w)$ is known for every a and b in the above equation, then $\Phi(w_1, w_2)$ is uniquely determined. In other words, if the density of the basket is known for each choice of basket combinations, then the joint density of the component variables is also known. This is an important result for pricing applications, because, in many cases, enough is known about the prices of combinations of assets for different weightings, and one can then try locally to approximate the joint density.

Univariate Case

Now recall how one can reconstruct a single-variable distribution in terms of its moment generating function. Suppose the density is normal, so that

$$f(x) = \frac{1}{\sigma\sqrt{2\pi}} e^{-\frac{1}{2}(\frac{x-\mu}{\sigma})^2} \tag{H.39}$$

and the moment generating function is

$$\int_{-\infty}^{\infty} e^{sx} f(x)\, dx = e^{\mu s + \frac{1}{2}s^2\sigma^2} \tag{H.40}$$

Expanding in a Taylor series,

$$1 + \left(\mu s + \frac{1}{2}\sigma^2 s^2\right) + \frac{1}{2}\left(\mu s + \frac{1}{2}s^2\sigma^2\right)^2 + \cdots \tag{H.41}$$

and comparing with

$$\int_{-\infty}^{\infty} \sum_{n=0}^{\infty} \frac{(sx)^n}{n!} f(x)\, dx = \sum_{n=0}^{\infty} m_n \frac{s^n}{n!} \tag{H.42}$$

we can identify

$$m_1 = \mu$$
$$m_2 = \mu^2 + \sigma^2 \tag{H.43}$$

In general,

$$m_n = \Phi^{(n)}(0) \tag{H.44}$$

i.e., first compute the moment generating function, and, to evaluate the nth moment, calculate the nth derivative of the moment generating function evaluated at zero.

It is frequently simpler to compute moments in terms of the logarithm of the moment generating function (called the cumulant generating function). The cumulants are the appropriate order derivatives calculated at zero:

$$\Psi(s) = \log \Phi(s) = \mu s + \tfrac{1}{2}\sigma^2 s^2 \tag{H.45}$$

with

$$\kappa_1 = \mu$$
$$\kappa_2 = \sigma^2 \tag{H.46}$$

and all other higher cumulants vanishing. Cumulants of convolved densities can be added directly, which proves to be useful. Knowing the cumulant generating function is equivalent to knowing the full distribution. Since only two cumulants of the normal distribution are nonvanishing, knowledge of these two cumulants completely specifies the normal distribution. In practice, this fact is useful because only two parameters need to be used to fit the empirical data to a chosen normal distribution.

Multivariate Case

How does this generalize when we have a multivariate distribution? For the two-variable case, we can write the moment generating function as

$$
\begin{aligned}
\Phi(s_1, s_2) &= \int_{-\infty}^{\infty} \int_{-\infty}^{\infty} e^{s_1 x + s_1 y} f(x, y)\, dx\, dy \\
&= \int_{-\infty}^{\infty} \int_{-\infty}^{\infty} \sum_{n=0}^{\infty} \frac{(s_1 x + s_2 y)^n}{n!} f(x, y)\, dx\, dx \\
&= \int_{-\infty}^{\infty} \int_{-\infty}^{\infty} \sum_{n=0}^{\infty} C_k^n (s_1 x)^k (s_2 y)^{n-k} f(x, y)\, dx\, dy \\
&= \sum_{n=0}^{\infty} \frac{1}{n!} \sum_{k=0}^{n} C_k^n E[x^k y^{n-k}] s_1^k s_2^{n-k}
\end{aligned}
\tag{H.47}
$$

Assuming that $f(x, y)$ is the joint bivariate density, we can evaluate the integral in the first line of Equation (H.47) directly:

$$\frac{1}{2\pi\sigma_1\sigma_2\sqrt{1-\rho^2}} \int_{-\infty}^{\infty} \int_{-\infty}^{\infty} dx\, dy\, e^{s_1 x + s_2 y} e^{-\frac{1}{2(1-\rho^2)}(...)} \tag{H.48}$$

equals

$$e^{\mu_1 s_1 + \mu_2 s_2 + \frac{1}{2}(\sigma_1^2 s_1^2 + \sigma_2^2 s_2^2 + 2\rho\sigma_1\sigma_2 s_1 s_2)} \tag{H.49}$$

which is the moment generating function. Taking logarithms, we can write the cumulant generating function as

$$\Psi(s_1, s_2) = \mu_1 s_1 + \mu_2 s_2 + \tfrac{1}{2}(\sigma_1^2 s_1^2 + \sigma_2^2 s_2^2 + 2\rho\sigma_1\sigma_2 s_1 s_2) \tag{H.50}$$

Evaluating the nonvanishing partial derivatives $\partial^{p,q}\Psi(s_1, s_2)/\partial^p s_1 \partial^q s_2$ at $(0, 0)$, we get all the cumulants:

$$\kappa_{1,0} = \mu_1$$
$$\kappa_{0,1} = \mu_2$$
$$\kappa_{2,0} = \sigma_1$$
$$\kappa_{0,2} = \sigma_2$$
$$\kappa_{1,1} = \rho\sigma_1\sigma_2 \tag{H.51}$$

which are sufficient to describe completely everything about the joint normal distribution of two variables. In general, the method of moments for a general empirical distribution requires that we compute these cumulants from the data series and *reconstruct* the form of the analytic density from the increasing terms in the Taylor expansion using Equation (H.47).

USEFUL NUMERICAL APPROXIMATIONS

The numerical value of the normal CDF can be obtained from

$$R = \frac{1}{\sqrt{2\pi}} e^{-x^2/2}(b_1 y + b_2 y^2 + b_3 y^3 + b_4 y^4 + b_5 y^5) \tag{H.52}$$

where

$$y = \frac{1}{1 + 0.2316419|x|} \tag{H.53}$$

and

$$b_1 = 0.319381530$$
$$b_2 = -0.356563782$$
$$b_3 = 1.781477937$$
$$b_4 = -1.821255978$$
$$b_5 = 1.330274429 \tag{H.54}$$

and

$$N(x) = \begin{cases} R & \text{for } x \leq 0 \\ 1 - R & \text{for } x > 0 \end{cases} \tag{H.55}$$

When the value $N(x)$ is given, this can be inverted to get x by the following recipe. Calculate

$$t = \begin{cases} \sqrt{-2 \log N} & \text{for } 0 < N \leq 0.5 \\ \sqrt{-2 \log(1-N)} & \text{for } 0.5 < N < 1 \end{cases} \tag{H.56}$$

and

$$z = t - \frac{c_0 + c_1 t + c_2 t^2}{1 + d_1 t + d_2 t^2 + d_3 t^3} \tag{H.57}$$

with

$$c_0 = 2.515517$$
$$c_1 = 0.802853$$
$$c_2 = 0.010328$$
$$d_1 = 1.432788$$
$$d_2 = 0.189269$$
$$d_3 = 0.00108 \tag{H.58}$$

then

$$x = \begin{cases} -z & \text{for } 0 < N \leq 0.5 \\ z & \text{for } 0.5 < N < 1 \end{cases} \tag{H.59}$$

with the absolute error $< 4.5 \times 10^{-4}$ in the last approximation.

For the standard bivariate normal distribution, we can use Drezner's approximation [69]:

$$M(a, b; \rho) = \frac{\sqrt{1 - \rho^2}}{\pi} \sum_{i,j=1}^{4} A_i A_j f(B_i, B_j) \qquad \text{(H.60)}$$

with

$$f(x, y) = e^{a'(2x-a')+b'(2y-b')+2\rho(x-a')(y-a')} \qquad \text{(H.61)}$$

with

$$a' = \frac{a}{\sqrt{2(1 - \rho^2)}}$$

$$b' = \frac{b}{\sqrt{2(1 - \rho^2)}}$$

$$A_1 = 0.325030$$
$$A_2 = 0.4211071$$
$$A_3 = 0.1334425$$
$$A_4 = 0.006374323$$
$$B_1 = 0.1337764$$
$$B_2 = 0.6243247$$
$$B_3 = 1.3425378$$
$$B_4 = 2.2626645$$

along with the identities, when the product of a, b, and ρ is negative or zero:

$$M(a, b; \rho) = N(a) - M(a, -b; -\rho)$$
$$M(a, b; \rho) = N(b) - M(-a, b; \rho)$$
$$M(a, b; \rho) = N(a) + N(b) - 1 + M(-a, -b; \rho)$$

When the product of a, b, and ρ is positive, use

$$M(a, b; \rho) = M(a, 0; \rho_1) + M(b, 0; \rho_2) - \delta \qquad \text{(H.62)}$$

where

$$\rho_1 = \frac{(\rho a - b)\text{sign}(a)}{\sqrt{a^2 - 2\rho ab + b^2}}$$

$$\rho_2 = \frac{(\rho b - a)\text{sign}(b)}{\sqrt{a^2 - 2\rho ab + b^2}}$$

$$\delta = \frac{1 - \text{sign}(a)\text{sign}(b)}{4} \tag{H.63}$$

and, as usual,

$$\text{sign}(x) = \begin{cases} +1 & \text{when } x \geq 0 \\ -1 & \text{when } x < 0 \end{cases} \tag{H.64}$$

Stochastic Processes

This appendix contains some useful results and computational techniques from stochastic calculus. A pedagogical approach may be found in References [128] and [158].

A stochastic process is a map $X(t, \omega)$ from the product space of time and a probability space $T \times \Omega$ to R^n. Pick ω in the abstract space Ω, and pick t in (usually) $(0, \infty)$, and calculate the map $X(t, \omega)$ to get a real number in $(-\infty, \infty)^n$.

USEFUL PROPERTIES

Expectations of Brownian Motion

For a Brownian motion starting at x, the expectations with respect to the measure P^x, with $P^x(B_0 = x) = 1$, are defined in the notation of Reference [158] as

$$E^x[B_t] = x \ \forall t \geq 0$$
$$E^x[(B_t - x)^2] = nt$$
$$E^x[(B_t - x)(B_s - x)] = n \min(s, t)$$
$$E^x[(B_t - B_s)^2] = n(t - s) \iff t \geq s$$
$$E^x[(B_{t(i)} - B_{t(i-1)})(B_{t(j)} - B_{t(j-1)})] = 0 \text{ when } t(i) < t(j)$$
$$E^0[B_t^{2k}] = \frac{(2k)!}{2^k k!} t^k \qquad (I.1)$$

The one-dimensional Brownian motion B_t at time t with $B_0 = 0$ has the density

$$p(x) = \frac{1}{\sqrt{2\pi t}} e^{-x^2/2t} \tag{I.2}$$

with the generalization in terms of the n-dimensional joint normal density.

1. If B_t is a Brownian motion and $t_0 \geq 0$, then $B_{t0+t} - B_{t0}$ is also a Brownian motion.
2. If B_t is an n-dimensional Brownian motion starting at 0, and $U \in R^{n \times n}$ is a constant orthogonal matrix, i.e., $UU^T = 1$, then UB_t is also a Brownian motion.
3. $(dB_t)^2 = dt$.

Integrals

We can define the stochastic integral as a formal limit of a sum. For example,

$$\int_0^t B_s \, dB_s = \lim_{\Delta t_j \to 0} \sum_j B_j \, \Delta B_j$$

$$\Delta(B_j^2) - (\Delta B_j)^2 = B_{j+1}^2 - B_j^2 - (\Delta B_j)^2$$

$$= (B_{j+1} - B_j)^2 + 2B_j(B_{j+1} - B_j) - (\Delta B_j)^2$$

$$= 2B_j \, \Delta B_j$$

$$\Rightarrow \sum_j B_j \, \Delta B_j = \frac{1}{2} B_t^2 - \frac{1}{2} \sum_j (\Delta B_j)^2 \tag{I.3}$$

This is a generalization of

$$\int_0^t x \, dx = t^2/2 \tag{I.4}$$

to

$$\int_0^t B \, dB = B_t^2/2 - \frac{1}{2} t \tag{I.5}$$

i.e., for the stochastic integral there is an end-point contribution that is nonstochastic.

In general,

$$E\left[\left(\int_S^T \phi(t, \omega)\, dB_t(\omega)\right)^2\right] = E\left[\int_S^T \phi(t, \omega)^2\, dt\right] \qquad (I.6)$$

and the following integral table can be computed:

$$\int_0^t dB_s = B_t$$

$$\int_0^t s\, dB_s = tB_t - \int_0^t B_s\, ds$$

$$\int_0^t B_s\, dB_s = \tfrac{1}{2}(B_t^2 - t)$$

$$\int_0^t B_s^2\, dB_s = \tfrac{1}{3}B_t^3 - \int_0^t B_s\, ds$$

$$\int_0^t f(s)\, dB_s = f(t)B_t - \int_0^t B_s\, df_s$$

$$\int_0^t X_s\, dY_s = X_tY_t - X_0Y_0 - \int_0^t Y_s\, dX_s - \int_0^t dX_s\, dY_s$$

Also, the iterated integral formula is:

$$\int_{0 \le u_1 \le u_2 \ldots u_n \le t} \cdots \left(\int\left(\int dB_{u1}\right) dB_{u2}\right) \ldots dB_{un} = t^{n/2} h_n\left(\frac{B_t}{\sqrt{t}}\right) \qquad (I.7)$$

where

$$h_0(x) = 1$$
$$h_1(x) = x$$
$$h_2(x) = x^2 - 1$$
$$h_3(x) = x^3 - 3x$$

$$h_n(x) = (-1)^n e^{x^2/2} \frac{d^n}{dx^n}(e^{-x^2/2}), \qquad n = 0, 1, 2, \ldots (I.8)$$

Ito Formula

For k Ito processes that are functions of k Brownian motions,

$$Y(t, \omega) = g(t, X(t))$$

$$dY_k = \frac{\partial g_k}{t} dt + \sum_i \frac{\partial g_k}{\partial x_i} dX_i + \frac{1}{2} \sum_{i,j} \frac{\partial^2 g_k}{\partial x_i \, \partial x_j} \, dX_i \, dX_j \qquad (I.9)$$

where

$$dB_i \, dB_j = \delta_{ij} \, dt$$
$$dB_i \, dt = dt \, dB_i = 0$$
$$d(X_t Y_t) = X_t \, dY_t + Y_t \, dX_t + dX_t \, dY_t \qquad (I.10)$$

With $\Delta = \sum_{i=1}^n (\partial^2/\partial x_i^2)$, the Laplacian, for n-dimensional Brownian motion,

$$f(B_t) = f(B_0) + \int_0^t \nabla f(B_s) \, dB_s + \frac{1}{2} \int_0^t \Delta f(B_s) \, ds \qquad (I.11)$$

In one dimension,

$$g(B_t) = g(B_0) + \int_0^t g'(B_s) \, dB_s + \frac{1}{2} \int_0^t g''(B_s) \, ds \qquad (I.12)$$

Exponentials
Application of the formula to the exponential of a Brownian motion:

$$X_t = e^{ct + \alpha B_t}$$
$$\Rightarrow dX_t = (c + \tfrac{1}{2}\alpha^2)X_t \, dt + \alpha X_t \, dB_t \qquad (I.13)$$

and also to the exponential of the sum of many Brownian motions:

$$X_t = e^{ct + \sum_j^n \alpha_j B_j(t)}$$

$$\Rightarrow dX_t = \left(c + \frac{1}{2} \sum_{j=1}^n \alpha_j^2 \right) X_t \, dt + X_t \sum_{j=1}^n \alpha_j \, dB_j(t) \qquad (I.14)$$

In other words, the exponential of a Brownian motion is lognormal with drift equal to the drift of the Brownian motion plus terms that are related to the variance of the Brownian motion.

GIRSANOV THEOREM AND CHANGE OF DRIFT

This section gives an informal motivation to the theorem, which states that if we change the drift of an Ito process, then the law of the process does not change drastically. A formal statement and proof can be obtained in References [128] or [158].

Suppose B_t is a Brownian motion. Thus, by definition, it has expectation zero for any t (we use z as the symbol for the normal variate):

$$\frac{1}{\sqrt{2\pi t}} \int_{-\infty}^{\infty} z e^{-\frac{1}{2}\frac{z^2}{t}} \, dz = 0 \tag{I.15}$$

under the original measure with mean zero and variance t. Now we want another process,

$$\tilde{B}_t = \theta t + B_t \tag{I.16}$$

for $0 \leq t \leq T$, to be a Brownian motion as well. But note that under the original measure this has expected value θt. Thus, this motion has a "drift." To make this motion with drift into a driftless Brownian motion, we need to change the measure so that the expectation is zero. Note that

$$0 = \frac{1}{\sqrt{2\pi t}} \int_{-\infty}^{\infty} (\theta t + z) e^{-\frac{1}{2}\frac{(\theta t + z)^2}{t}} \, dz$$

$$= \frac{1}{\sqrt{2\pi t}} e^{-\theta z - \frac{1}{2}\theta^2 t} (\theta t + z) e^{\frac{-z^2}{2t}} \, dz \tag{I.17}$$

with which we can make the identification that the change in drift is exactly equivalent to a specific modification of the probability weighting. If θ is positive, the Brownian motion with drift will drift upwards, so the extra term

$$e^{-\theta z - \frac{1}{2}\theta^2 t} \tag{I.18}$$

in Equation (I.17) reduces the probability weight by "pulling it back." Note also that as the time to maturity increases, the correction term dominates the probability more and more to keep the expectation near zero. This extra correction term in the density is the Girsanov correction term and lets one prove results for non-drifting Brownian motions that can be generalized easily to drifting Brownian motions.

Note that this is crucial to the "risk-neutral pricing" methodology. If the market price of risk is

$$\theta = \frac{\mu - r}{\sigma} \qquad (I.19)$$

then valuing a derivative under drift μ and the Brownian motion $-\theta t + B_t$ is the same as valuing it under drift r and Brownian motion B_t:

$$S_t = S_0\, e^{(\mu - \frac{1}{2}\sigma^2)t + \sigma(-\theta t + B_t)}$$
$$= S_0\, e^{(r - \frac{1}{2}\sigma^2)t + \sigma B_t} \qquad (I.20)$$

Thus, one can use any measure that is convenient: in particular, the measure in which discounting is done at the risk-free rate—the risk-neutral measure.

Reflection Principle and One-Touch Probability

Assuming a normal random walk environment for the returns, we ask the following questions:

1. What is $P(\max(B_s) \leq h | B_t = b, B_0 = 0)$ for $0 \leq t$ and $b < h, h \geq 0$?
2. What is $P(\min(B_s) \geq l | B_t = b, B_0 = 0)$ for $0 \leq t$ and $b > l, l \leq 0$?
3. What is $P(h \leq \max(B_s) \geq \min(B_s) \geq l | B_t = b, B_0 = 0)$ for $0 \leq t$ and $b > l, l \leq 0$?

For Brownian motions without drift, these questions are easy to answer, since the reflection principle holds true without modification. In the case given, there is one assumption (from the Girsanov principle) that allows for the reflection principle to be used.

Step 1   The conditional probability $P(A|B) = P(A \cap B)/P(B)$, so the probability that we end at b given that h was hit equals the intersection of all the paths which hit h and all the paths that end up at b divided by the probability that we end at b.

Step 2   We know that $P(b) = e^{\frac{-b^2}{2\sigma^2 t}}$.

Step 3   Since we know that we are ending up at b, the fact that there was drift in the initial random walk is irrelevant, so the reflection principle can be used. Then, the probability that we end up at b and we touch h is the same as the simple probability that we end up at $h + (h - b) = 2h - b$ because then we have to have touched h.

Step 4   So, the required conditional probability is

$$\text{Prob. of breaching barrier} = e^{\frac{(2h-b)^2}{2\sigma^2 t}} / e^{\frac{-b^2}{2\sigma^2 t}}$$

$$= e^{-2h\max(h-b,0)/\sigma^2 t}$$

$$\text{Prob. of not breaching barrier} = 1 - e^{\frac{(2h-b)^2}{2\sigma^2 t}} / e^{\frac{-b^2}{2\sigma^2 t}}$$

$$= 1 - e^{-2h\max(h-b,0)/\sigma^2 t} \qquad (I.21)$$

Similarly, the answer to the second question is

$$\text{Prob. of not breaching lower barrier} = 1 - e^{-2l\min(l-b,0)/\sigma^2 t} \qquad (I.22)$$

Finally, the double-touch probability that either the upper or lower barrier is not hit can be calculated in the same way, and by using $P(A \cap B) = P(A) + P(B) - P(A \cup B)$.

In terms of lognormal variables $h, l,$ and b, where h is the upper barrier and l is the lower barrier, with $d \equiv h - l$, the probability that neither barrier will be hit at any time s before expiration at time t is

$$P(l < \min B_s < \max B_s < h | B_t = b)$$

$$= \sum_{n=-\infty}^{n=\infty} \left[e^{\frac{2nd(b-nd)}{\sigma^2 t}} - e^{\frac{2(h-nd)(b-h-nd)}{\sigma^2 t}} \right] \qquad (I.23)$$

In most cases, no more than four or five terms in the expansion of the infinite sum converge rather rapidly to the full result.

The reader is also referred to the method of images derivation in Chapter 3 and a PDE derivation in Appendix J on PDE methods.

SOLUTION OF STOCHASTIC DIFFERENTIAL EQUATIONS

This section consists of a few examples and an exposition of tricks that are useful in solving stochastic differential equations.

The Mean-Reverting Ornstein-Uhlenbeck Equation

Suppose we want to solve

$$dX_t = (m - X_t)\,dt + \sigma\,dB_t \qquad (I.24)$$

with

$$
\begin{aligned}
E[dX_t] &= m\,dt - E[X_t]\,dt = m\,dt - m\,dt + (X_0 - m)\,e^{-t}\,dt \\
&= (X_0 - m)\,e^{-t}\,dt \\
V[dX_t] &= E[(dX_t - E[dX_t])^2]
\end{aligned}
\qquad (I.25)
$$

Set

$$
\begin{aligned}
X_t &= Q_t\,e^{-t} + m \\
Q_t &= (X_t - m)\,e^{t} \\
dX_t &\stackrel{\text{Ito}}{=} -Q_t\,e^{-t}\,dt + e^{-t}\,dQ_t \\
&= (m - X_t)\,dt + e^{-t}\,dQ_t
\end{aligned}
\qquad (I.26)
$$

Since the drift terms match, we can compare to the σ term of Equation (I.24) and compute away

$$\sigma \, dB_t = e^{-t} \, dQ_t$$

$$\Rightarrow dQ_t = \sigma \, e^t \, dB_t$$

$$\Rightarrow \int_0^T dQ_t = \sigma \int_0^T e^t \, dB_t$$

$$\Rightarrow Q_T - Q_0 = \sigma \int_0^T e^t \, dB_t$$

$$\Rightarrow Q_T = Q_0 + \sigma \int_0^T e^t \, dB_t$$

$$\Rightarrow Q_T = (X_0 - m) + \sigma \int_0^T e^t \, dB_t$$

$$\Rightarrow X_T = Q_T \, e^{-T} + m$$

$$\Rightarrow X_T = m + (X_0 - m) e^{-T} + \sigma \int_0^T e^{(t-T)} \, dB_t$$

which is the final solution.

Also, we can compute the expected value and variance

$$E[X_t] = m + (X_0 - m) e^{-T}$$

$$V[X_t] = E[(X_T - E[X_T])^2]$$

$$= E\left[\sigma \int_0^T e^{t-T} dB_t \right]^2$$

$$= \sigma^2 e^{-2T} \int_0^T e^{2t} \, dt$$

$$= \sigma^2 e^{-2T} \frac{1}{2} (e^{2t} - 1)$$

$$= \frac{\sigma^2}{2} (1 - e^{-2t}) \tag{I.27}$$

A Multivariate SDE

If $(B_1, \ldots, B_n)$ are Brownian motions in n dimensions, and $\sigma_1, \ldots, \sigma_n$ are constants, then the solution of the SDE

$$dX_t = rX_t \, dt + X_t \left(\sum_{k=1}^n \sigma_k \, dB_k(t) \right) \tag{I.28}$$

for $X_0 > 0$ is

$$X_t = X_0 e^{\left(r - \frac{1}{2}\sum_{k=1}^{n} \sigma_k^2\right)t + \sum_{k=1}^{n} \sigma_k B_k(t)} \tag{I.29}$$

which is used for pricing based on principal component indices (see Chapter 6).

LEVEL-CROSSING

Given a random process $x(t)$ and a constant a, let τ_i denote the time instances when $x(t)$ crosses the line L_a parallel to the time axis. Let $n_a(T)$ denote the number of points τ_i in an interval of length T. Then, the expected number of times the level is crossed can be expressed in terms of the first-order density $f_x(x)$ of $x(t)$ and the conditional mean of its derivative:

$$E[n_1(T)] = T f_x(a) E[|x'(t)| \, | \, x(t) = a] \tag{I.30}$$

and the level-crossing density equals

$$\lambda_a = f_x(a) E[|x'(t)| \, | \, x(t) = a] \tag{I.31}$$

The density of extrema can be derived by noting that they correspond to the zero crossings of the process $y(t) = x'(t)$. Using the previous equation with $a = 0$ and $x(t) \to x'(t)$ gives

$$\lambda_{\text{extrema}} = f_{x'}(0) E[|x''(t)| \, | \, x'(t) = 0] \tag{I.32}$$

FIRST-PASSAGE TIME

The first-passage time problem is the determination of the distribution function $F_\tau(\tau, a)$ of the random variable τ_1.

The reflection principle states: For any x value less than or greater than a,

$$P[x(t) \le x | \tau_1 \le t] = P[x(t) \ge 2a - x | \tau_1 \le \tau] \tag{I.33}$$

and, if $x \le a$, then

$$P[x(t) \le x, \tau_1 \le t] = 1 - F_x(2a - x, t)$$
$$P[x(t) \le x, \tau_1 > t] = F_x(x, t) + F_x(2a - x, t) - 1 \tag{I.34}$$

where $F_x(x, t)$ is the first-order distribution of the Weiner process $x(t)$. Since

$$P[\tau_1 \leq t] = P[\tau_1 \leq t, x(t) \leq a] + P[\tau_1 \leq t, x(t) > a] \quad (I.35)$$

we obtain

$$P[\tau_1 \leq t] = F_\tau(t, a) = 2P[x(t) > a] = 2(1 - F_x(a, t)) \quad (I.36)$$

When the barrier is absorbing, the resultant process $y(t)$ equals a for every $t > \tau_1$. Then,

$$F_y(y, t) = F_x(y, t) + F_x(2a - y) - 1, \ y < a$$
$$F_y(y, t) = 1 \, y \geq a \quad (I.37)$$

When the barrier is reflecting, the resultant process $z(t)$ equals $x(t)$ if $x(t) < a$ and equals $2a - x(t)$ if $x(t) > a$. Then,

$$F_z(z, t) = F_x(z, t) + 1 - F_x(2a - z, t) \ \forall z < a$$
$$F_z(z, t) = 1 \ \forall z > a \quad (I.38)$$

PDE Methods

CLASSIFICATION

Based on the characteristics, or curves of information propagation, partial differential equations can be classified as hyberbolic, parabolic, or elliptical.

The prototypical hyberbolic equation is the one-dimensional wave equation

$$\frac{\partial^2 u}{\partial t^2} = v^2 \frac{\partial^2 u}{\partial x^2} \tag{J.1}$$

The prototypical parabolic equation is the one-dimensional diffusion equation

$$\frac{\partial u}{\partial t} = \frac{\partial}{\partial x}\left(D \frac{\partial u}{\partial x}\right) \tag{J.2}$$

with D the possibly space- and time-dependent diffusion coefficient.

The prototypical elliptic equation is the Poisson equation

$$\frac{\partial^2 u}{\partial x^2} + \frac{\partial^2 u}{\partial y^2} = \rho(x, y) \tag{J.3}$$

where $\rho(x, y)$ is the source term.

Note that the first two equations are *initial value* equations or *Cauchy* problems, i.e., once the value of the function is given for some initial time for all values of the space variable, the solution propagates itself for all future values of time. This is the correct context for vanilla European option valuation—once the value of the option is given for zero time to expiration, i.e., the terminal value, the value of the option is, in principle, known for all other times. In contrast, the last equation is a boundary value problem and has a static solution. For initial value problems, if the value of the boundary points in price space (e.g., the payoff function for very large or very small price of the underlying assets) is specified as a function of time, we are working with Dirichlet conditions; if the normal gradients are specified on the asset boundaries, we have Neumann conditions.

NUMERICAL SOLUTION OF THE DIFFUSION EQUATION

Consider the simple diffusion equation

$$\frac{\partial u}{\partial t} = D \frac{\partial^2 u}{\partial x^2} \tag{J.4}$$

and divide the t and x region into a grid with

$$x_j = x_0 + j\delta x \qquad \text{for } j = 0, 1, \dots, J \tag{J.5}$$

for the x direction and

$$t_n = t_0 + n\,\delta t \qquad \text{for } n = 0, 1, \dots, N \tag{J.6}$$

for the time axis. Then, denoting by u_j^n the value of the solution $u(t_n, x_j)$ at the discretized point t_n, x_j, we have derivatives like

$$\left.\frac{\partial u}{\partial t}\right|_{j,n} = \frac{u_j^{n+1} - u_j^n}{\Delta t} + O(\Delta t) \tag{J.7}$$

and

$$\left.\frac{\partial u}{\partial x}\right|_{j,n} = \frac{u_{j+1}^n - u_{j-1}^n}{2\,\Delta x} + O(\Delta x^2) \tag{J.8}$$

Here, we have used the forward-time difference, and, for the first x derivative, a centered time difference. This scheme is thus called the FTCS (forward-time centered-space) scheme.

For the diffusion equation, we get

$$\frac{u_j^{n+1} - u_j^n}{\Delta t} = D \left[\frac{u_{j+1}^n - 2u_j^n + u_{j-1}^n}{(\Delta x)^2} \right] \tag{J.9}$$

To test this equation for stability under the differencing scheme, we can substitute

$$u_n^j = \xi^n \, e^{ikj\Delta x} \tag{J.10}$$

where k is a wave number and $\xi = \xi(k)$ is a complex number. Since n corresponds to the time variable, if $\xi > 1$, then the "amplitude" of the solution grows with time, i.e., the solution will become unstable. To solve for ξ, substitute Equation (J.10) into the differencing scheme of Equation (J.9) to get

$$\xi = 1 - \frac{4D\Delta t}{(\Delta x)^2} \sin^2 \left(\frac{k\,\Delta x}{2} \right) \tag{J.11}$$

which, with the requirement $|\xi| \leq 1$, leads to

$$\frac{2D\,\Delta t}{(\Delta x)^2} \leq 1 \tag{J.12}$$

However, if we evaluate the spatial derivatives at time step $n + 1$ in the above differencing, we get

$$\frac{u_j^{n+1} - u_j^n}{\Delta t} = D \left[\frac{u_{j+1}^{n+1} - 2u_j^{n+1} + u_{j-1}^{n+1}}{(\Delta x)^2} \right] \tag{J.13}$$

which has the amplification factor

$$\xi = \frac{1}{1 + 4\alpha \sin^2 \left(\dfrac{k\,\Delta x}{2} \right)} \tag{J.14}$$

which has $|\xi| < 1$ for all step sizes Δt. This scheme is called the fully implicit or backward time scheme because to get the solution for time n, all spatial derivatives at the next time instant have to be known—so that one rolls backward in time on the grid.

The Crank-Nicholson scheme is simply an average of the explicit (i.e., FTCS) and implicit methods, with

$$\frac{u_j^{n+1} - u_j^n}{\Delta t} = \frac{D}{2}\left[\frac{(u_{j+1}^{n+1} - 2u_j^{n+1} + u_{j-1}^{n+1}) + (u_{j+1}^n - 2u_j^n + u_{j-1}^n)}{(\Delta x)^2}\right] \quad \text{(J.15)}$$

with amplification factor

$$\xi = \frac{1 - 2\alpha \sin^2\left(\frac{k\,\Delta x}{2}\right)}{1 - 2\alpha \sin^2\left(\frac{k\,\Delta x}{2}\right)} \quad \text{(J.16)}$$

so that stability is guaranteed for any size time step Δt.

In more general models where the volatility can be dependent on the level of the underlying asset (as in volatility skew models), we have to allow for general diffusion coefficients $D(x)$. Then, we can also difference the diffusion coefficient, i.e., the difference equation form of

$$\frac{\partial u}{\partial t} = \frac{\partial}{\partial x}D(x)\frac{\partial u}{\partial x} \quad \text{(J.17)}$$

is

$$\frac{u_j^{n+1} - u_j^n}{\Delta t} = \frac{D_{j+\frac{1}{2}}(u_{j+1}^n - u_j^n) - D_{j-\frac{1}{2}}(u_j^n - u_{j-1}^n)}{(\Delta x)^2} \quad \text{(J.18)}$$

ANALYTIC SOLUTIONS OF THE DIFFUSION EQUATION

We want to illustrate the solution of the equation

$$\frac{\partial^2 T}{\partial x^2} = \frac{1}{\kappa}\frac{\partial T}{\partial t} \quad \text{(J.19)}$$

with the initial condition $T(x, 0) = 0$. We can think of this as the temperature distribution in an infinite solid where at some initial time the temperature is zero.

FOURIER TRANSFORM METHOD

We will first solve this equation by Fourier transforms. For this, note the following properties:

$$u(x, t) = \int_{-\infty}^{\infty} \frac{dk}{2\pi} F(k, t) e^{ikx} dx$$

$$F(k, t) = \int_{-\infty}^{\infty} T(x, t) e^{-ikx} dx \qquad (J.20)$$

and also the properties of the Fourier transform ($\mathcal{F}$ denotes the Fourier transform):

$$\mathcal{F}[f'(x)] = ik\mathcal{F}[f(x)] \qquad (J.21)$$

and, similarly, for the second derivative we pick a factor proportional to $-k^2$. Then, transforming Equation (J.19) in the x variable, we get

$$-k^2 F(k, t) = \frac{1}{\kappa} \frac{\partial F(k, t)}{\partial t} \qquad (J.22)$$

which is a simple differential equation with solution

$$F(k, t) = \phi(k) e^{-k^2 \kappa t} \qquad (J.23)$$

Using this at $t = 0$ for the initial condition

$$F(k, 0) = \int_{-\infty}^{\infty} T(x, 0) e^{-ikx} dx = \int_{-\infty}^{\infty} f(x) e^{-ikx} dx \qquad (J.24)$$

we obtain

$$\phi(k) = \int_{-\infty}^{\infty} f(x) e^{-ikx} dx \qquad (J.25)$$

so that, overall,

$$F(k, t) = \int_{-\infty}^{\infty} f(x) dx \, e^{-ikx} e^{-k^2 \kappa t} \qquad (J.26)$$

Now, to get back the solution in x space we invert the Fourier transform:

$$T(x, t) = \int_{-\infty}^{\infty} \frac{dk}{2\pi} e^{ikx} \int_{-\infty}^{\infty} dy f(y) e^{-iky} e^{-k^2 \kappa t}$$

$$= \int_{-\infty}^{\infty} dy f(y) \int_{-\infty}^{\infty} \frac{dk}{2\pi} e^{ik(x-y)} e^{-k^2 \kappa t} \qquad (J.27)$$

The k integral is simple and just gives back the characteristic function of the Gaussian, so

$$T(x, t) = \int_{-\infty}^{\infty} dy f(y) \frac{1}{\sqrt{4\pi \kappa t}} e^{\frac{-(x-y)^2}{4\kappa t}} \qquad (J.28)$$

The function

$$G(x, t; y) = \frac{1}{\sqrt{4\pi \kappa t}} e^{\frac{-(x-y)^2}{4\kappa t}} \qquad (J.29)$$

goes by the name of the *Green function* or the density function for this problem. In option pricing problems, we have seen that the price at any time is given by an equation similar to Equation (J.28) that is derived as a simple probability weight over terminal payoffs. The fact that these two results are the same is a consequence of the Feynman-Kac theorem.

Now the analogue of a digital option which pays off 1 dollar if the stock price is exactly S at expiration (an "Arrow-Debreu" security) is a point source where

$$f(x) = \delta(x) \qquad (J.30)$$

Inserting this into Equation (J.28), we get

$$T(x, t) = \frac{1}{\sqrt{4\pi \kappa t}} e^{\frac{-(x)^2}{4\kappa t}} \qquad (J.31)$$

which has a Gaussian dependence in x, and whose width (volatility) increases as $\sqrt{t}$.

LAPLACE TRANSFORM METHODS

It will now be shown how the Laplace transformation in time can be used to find explicit Green function solutions (or densities) for the Black-Scholes equation:

Density of the Black-Scholes Equation

Begin with the basic equation

$$\frac{\partial C}{\partial t} = rC - (r - d)S \frac{\partial C}{\partial S} - \frac{1}{2} \sigma^2 S^2 \frac{\partial^2 C}{\partial S^2} \qquad (J.32)$$

Make the change of variables

$$R = \frac{S}{K}$$

$$G = KC$$

$$\tau = \sigma^2 (T - t)$$

$$\rho = \frac{r}{\sigma^2}$$

$$\mu = \frac{r - d}{\sigma^2} \qquad (J.33)$$

to obtain

$$\frac{\partial G}{\partial \tau} = \frac{1}{2} R^2 \frac{\partial^2 G}{\partial R^2} + \mu R \frac{\partial G}{\partial R} - \rho G \qquad (J.34)$$

with the delta function initial condition

$$G(R, \tau = 0) = K\delta(S, K) = \delta(R, 1) \qquad (J.35)$$

Applying a Laplace transformation in time with parameter ξ, i.e.,

$$H[\xi] = \int_0^\infty d\tau \, e^{-\xi \tau} G(\tau) \qquad (J.36)$$

we get

$$\xi H - \delta(R, 1) - \frac{1}{2} R^2 \frac{\partial^2 H}{\partial R^2} - \mu R \frac{\partial H}{\partial R} + \rho H = 0 \qquad (J.37)$$

which for $R \neq 1$ is a homogeneous equation with power law solution, i.e.,

$$\frac{1}{2} R^2 \frac{\partial^2 H}{\partial R^2} + \mu R \frac{\partial H}{\partial R} - (\rho + \xi)H = 0 \qquad (J.38)$$

This is an ODE with solution R^λ, and with $\alpha \equiv \mu - \frac{1}{2}$:

$$\lambda_\pm = \alpha \pm \sqrt{\alpha^2 + 2(\rho + \xi)} \tag{J.39}$$

Now, as $R \to \infty$ and $R \to 0$, we require that the solutions converge. Also, we want the solutions to match at $R = 1$. This gives

$$H_<(R) = \frac{R^{\lambda_+}}{\sqrt{\alpha^2 + 2(\rho + \xi)}}$$

$$H_>(R) = \frac{R^{\lambda_-}}{\sqrt{\alpha^2 + 2(\rho + \xi)}} \tag{J.40}$$

Now we can invert the Laplace transform, using $y \equiv \ln R$:

$$G(\tau) = \frac{1}{2\pi i} \int_{\epsilon - i\infty}^{\epsilon + i\infty} d\xi\, e^{\xi\tau} H(\xi)$$

$$= \frac{e^{-\alpha y}}{2\pi i} \int_{\epsilon - i\infty}^{\epsilon + i\infty} d\xi\, e^{\xi\tau}\, \frac{e^{-|y|\sqrt{\alpha^2 + 2(\rho + \xi)}}}{\sqrt{\alpha^2 + 2(\rho + \xi)}} \tag{J.41}$$

Since the integrand is multivalued, we put a branch cut on the negative x axis and complete the integration contour using a Hankel contour. With the branch point at $\xi' = \alpha^2 + 2(\rho + \xi)$, we have:

$$G(\tau) = \frac{e^{-\alpha y - (\rho + \frac{1}{2}\alpha^2)\tau}}{2\pi i} \int_{\epsilon - i\infty}^{\epsilon + i\infty} d\xi'\, e^{\frac{1}{2}\xi'\tau}\, \frac{e^{-|y|\sqrt{\xi'}}}{\sqrt{\xi'}} \tag{J.42}$$

We can break the integration limit for the full integral into three pieces, then use Cauchy's theorem and a change of variables from $\xi' \to e^{i\pi}\chi^2/\tau$ to get

$$
\begin{aligned}
G(\tau) &= -\frac{e^{-\alpha y - (\rho + \frac{1}{2}\alpha^2)\tau}}{2\pi i}\left[\int_{-\infty + i\epsilon}^{0 + i\epsilon} + \int_{0 + i\epsilon}^{0 - i\epsilon} + \int_{0 - i\epsilon}^{-\infty - i\epsilon}\right] d\xi' e^{\frac{1}{2}\xi'\tau}\frac{e^{-|y|\sqrt{\xi'}}}{\sqrt{\xi'}} \\
&= \frac{e^{-\alpha y - (\rho + \frac{1}{2}\alpha^2)\tau}}{2\pi\sqrt{\tau}}\int_{-\infty}^{\infty} d\chi\, e^{-\frac{1}{2}\chi^2 - \frac{i|y|\chi}{\sqrt{\tau}}} \\
&= \frac{e^{-\frac{1}{2}\frac{y^2}{\tau} + \alpha y + (\rho + \frac{1}{2}\alpha^2)\tau}}{2\pi\sqrt{\tau}}\int_{-\infty + i|y|/\sqrt{\tau}}^{\infty + i|y|/\sqrt{\tau}} d\chi\, e^{-\frac{1}{2}\chi^2} \\
&= \frac{1}{\sqrt{2\pi\tau}}e^{-\left[\frac{1}{2}\frac{y^2}{\tau} + \alpha y + (\rho + \frac{1}{2}\alpha^2)\tau\right]} \\
&= \frac{1}{\sqrt{2\pi\tau}}e^{-\frac{1}{2\tau}(y + \alpha t)^2}
\end{aligned}
\tag{J.43}
$$

which, after replacing with the original definitions, yields the familiar Black-Scholes lognormal density:

$$
C(S_t, t) = \frac{e^{-r(T-t)}}{\sqrt{2\pi(T-t)}\sigma S_T}e^{-\frac{1}{2\sigma^2(T-t)}\left[\ln\frac{S_T}{S_t} - \alpha(T-t)\right]^2}
\tag{J.44}
$$

Single Barrier

Working directly in $y = \ln R$, and following the manipulations of the last section, we obtain

$$
\int_0^\infty d\tau\, e^{-\xi\tau}\frac{\partial G}{\partial\tau} = \int_0^\infty d\tau\, e^{-\xi\tau}\left(\frac{1}{2}\frac{\partial^2 G}{\partial y^2} - \alpha\frac{\partial G}{\partial y}\right)
\tag{J.45}
$$

which gives the transformed density with the transformed initial condition

$$
\xi H - \delta(y, 0) = \frac{1}{2}\frac{\partial^2 H}{\partial y^2} - \alpha\frac{\partial H}{\partial y}
\tag{J.46}
$$

and the barrier boundary conditions

$$
H(y = b) = 0
$$

$$
H\left(y \to -\frac{b}{|b|}\infty\right) \to 0
\tag{J.47}
$$

Suppose we take $b < 0$. Then, we can solve the constant coefficient ODE above and below $y = 0$ and match the solutions at $y = 0$ to obtain:

$$H_> = \frac{1 - e^{2b\sqrt{\alpha^2 + 2\xi}}}{\sqrt{\alpha^2 + 2\xi}} e^{(\alpha - \sqrt{\alpha^2 + 2\xi})y}$$

$$H_< = \frac{-e^{2b\sqrt{\alpha^2 + 2\xi}}}{\sqrt{\alpha^2 + 2\xi}} e^{(\alpha - \sqrt{\alpha^2 + 2\xi})y} + \frac{1}{\sqrt{\alpha^2 + 2\xi}} e^{(\alpha + \sqrt{\alpha^2 + 2\xi})} \qquad (J.48)$$

which can be combined:

$$H = e^{\alpha y} \frac{e^{-|y|\sqrt{\alpha^2 + 2\xi}} - e^{(2b - y)\sqrt{\alpha^2 + 2\xi}}}{\sqrt{\alpha^2 + 2\xi}} \qquad (J.49)$$

The Laplace inversion integral has a branch point at $\xi = -\alpha^2/2$:

$$G(\tau) = \frac{e^{\alpha y}}{2\pi i} \int_{\epsilon - i\infty}^{\epsilon + i\infty} d\xi\, e^{\xi \tau} \frac{e^{-|y|\sqrt{\alpha^2 + 2\xi}} - e^{(2b - y)\sqrt{\alpha^2 + 2\xi}}}{\sqrt{\alpha^2 + 2\xi}} \qquad (J.50)$$

Deforming the contour to the right of the branch point by setting $\xi' = \alpha^2 + 2\xi$, we get

$$G(\tau) = \frac{e^{\alpha y - \frac{1}{2}\alpha^2 \tau}}{2\pi i} \int_{\epsilon - i\infty}^{\epsilon + i\infty} d\xi'\, e^{\frac{1}{2}\xi' \tau} \frac{e^{-|y|\sqrt{\xi'}} - e^{(2b - y)\sqrt{\xi'}}}{\sqrt{\xi'}} \qquad (J.51)$$

which equals

$$G = e^{\alpha y - \frac{1}{2}\alpha^2 \tau} \times \left[\frac{e^{-\frac{1}{2}\frac{y^2}{\tau}}}{\sqrt{2\pi\tau}} - \frac{e^{-\frac{1}{2}\frac{(y - 2b)^2}{\tau}}}{\sqrt{2\pi\tau}} \right] \qquad (J.52)$$

which is the same as the solution obtained in Chapter 3 using the method of images. Also, the first term is recognized as the Girsanov factor and the second part is the difference of the source term and the image term.

Double Barrier

Here, we have the same Laplace transformed equation as in the previous section, with the boundary conditions

$$H(y = u) = 0$$
$$H(y = b) = 0 \qquad \text{(J.53)}$$

with solutions

$$H_> = A_>^+ e^{(\alpha + \sqrt{\alpha^2 + 2\xi})y} + A_>^- e^{(\alpha - \sqrt{\alpha^2 + 2\xi})y}$$
$$H_< = A_<^+ e^{(\alpha + \sqrt{\alpha^2 + 2\xi})y} + A_<^- e^{(\alpha - \sqrt{\alpha^2 + 2\xi})y} \qquad \text{(J.54)}$$

which, with matching at $y = 0$ and using the boundary conditions, gives, in terms of $\xi' = \xi + \frac{1}{2}\alpha^2$:

$$A_>^+ = \frac{1}{\sqrt{2\xi'}} \frac{e^{b\sqrt{8\xi'}} - 1}{(e^{u\sqrt{8\xi'}} - e^{b\sqrt{8\xi'}})}$$

$$A_>^- = \frac{e^{u\sqrt{8\xi'}}}{\sqrt{2\xi'}} \frac{1 - e^{b\sqrt{8\xi'}}}{(e^{u\sqrt{8\xi'}} - e^{b\sqrt{8\xi'}})}$$

$$A_<^+ = \frac{1}{\sqrt{2\xi'}} \frac{e^{u\sqrt{8\xi'}} - 1}{(e^{u\sqrt{8\xi'}} - e^{b\sqrt{8\xi'}})}$$

$$A_<^- = \frac{e^{b\sqrt{8\xi'}}}{\sqrt{2\xi'}} \frac{1 - e^{u\sqrt{8\xi'}}}{(e^{u\sqrt{8\xi'}} - e^{b\sqrt{8\xi'}})} \qquad \text{(J.55)}$$

Then,

$$H_> = \sqrt{\frac{2}{\xi'}} e^{\alpha y} \frac{\sinh[b\sqrt{2\xi'}]\sinh[(y - u)\sqrt{2\xi'}]}{\sinh[(u - b)\sqrt{2\xi'}]}$$

$$H_< = \sqrt{\frac{2}{\xi'}} e^{\alpha y} \frac{\sinh[u\sqrt{2\xi'}]\sinh[(y - b)\sqrt{2\xi'}]}{\sinh[(u - b)\sqrt{2\xi'}]} \qquad \text{(J.56)}$$

Now, finally, we can expand the denominator in a series of exponentials:

$$H_> = \frac{e^{\alpha y}}{\sqrt{2\xi'}} (1 - e^{2b\sqrt{2\xi'}}) \left[e^{-y\sqrt{2\xi'}} - e^{(y - 2u)\sqrt{2\xi'}} \right] \sum_{i=0}^{\infty} e^{2i(b - u)\sqrt{2\xi'}}$$

$$H_< = \frac{e^{\alpha y}}{\sqrt{2\xi'}} (1 - e^{-2u\sqrt{2\xi'}}) \left[e^{y\sqrt{2\xi'}} - e^{(2b - y)\sqrt{2\xi'}} \right] \sum_{i=0}^{\infty} e^{2i(b - u)\sqrt{2\xi'}}$$